# Sexuality and the World's Religions

# Sexuality and the World's Religions

David W. Machacek and
Melissa M. Wilcox, Editors

A B C · C L I O

Santa Barbara, California • Denver, Colorado • Oxford, England

**Library of Congress Cataloging-in-Publication Data**

Sexuality and the world's religions / [edited by] David W. Machacek, Melissa M. Wilcox.
    p.  cm.
  Includes bibliographical references and index.
  ISBN 1-57607-359-9 (alk. paper) — ISBN 1-85109-532-2 (eBook)
  1. Sex—Religious aspects.  I. Machacek, David W.  II. Wilcox, Melissa
M., 1972–

BL65.S4S5   2003
291.1'78357—dc21

                                    2003008056

13 12 11 10    10 9 8 7 6 5 4 3 2

This book is also available on the World Wide Web as an eBook. Visit http://www.abc-clio.com for details.

ABC-CLIO, Inc.
130 Cremona Drive, P.O. Box 1911
Santa Barbara, California 93116–1911

This book is printed on acid-free paper ∞.
Manufactured in the United States of America

*To Jeff and Janet*
*With love*

# Contents

Preface ix

Introduction xiii

About the Contributors xix

## Part 1
## Gender and Sexuality in the World's Religions

1 Sexuality and Gender in African Spiritual Traditions 3
   *Randy P. Conner*

2 Gender, Sexuality, and the Balance of Power in
   Native American Worldviews 31
   *Julianne Cordero and Elizabeth Currans*

3 Harmony of Yin and Yang: Cosmology and Sexuality
   in Daoism 65
   *Xinzhong Yao*

4 A Union of Fire and Water: Sexuality and Spirituality
   in Hinduism 101
   *Jeffrey S. Lidke*

5 Buddhist Views on Gender and Desire 133
   *Liz Wilson*

6 Sex in Jewish Law and Culture 177
   *Rebecca Alpert*

7 The Vatican and the Laity: Diverging Paths in Catholic
   Understanding of Sexuality 203
   *James C. Cavendish*

8 Varieties of Interpretations: Protestantism and Sexuality       231
   *Amy DeRogatis*

9 Islamic Conceptions of Sexuality                               255
   *Aysha Hidayatullah*

# Part 2
# Religion, Gender, and Sexuality in the United States

10 Casting Divinity in My Image: Women, Men, and the
   Embodiment of Sacred Sexuality                                295
   *Nancy Ramsey Tosh and Tanya Keenan*

11 Innovation in Exile: Religion and Spirituality in
   Lesbian, Gay, Bisexual, and Transgender Communities          323
   *Melissa M. Wilcox*

12 Religion and Sexual Liberty: Personal versus Civic
   Morality in the United States                                359
   *David W. Machacek*

*Suggestions for Further Reading*                               385
*Index*                                                         409

# Preface

The experience that inspired this text is one with which most scholars just beginning academic careers are familiar: I was asked to teach a course for which I was almost entirely unprepared. The class was entitled "Religion and Sexuality," and because it was a more desirable subject than most classes that junior scholars are asked to teach, I eagerly accepted.

As a sociologist of religion, I was, of course, familiar with Bronislaw Malinowski's fascinating studies of sexuality and marriage among the Trobriand Islanders. Certainly, I thought, there would be an abundance of texts from which to choose that followed Malinowski's lead.

Indeed, the inviting subject of gender and sexuality in the world's various religious traditions has stimulated a large body of recent manuscripts. However, I was stunned to find that the only text that attempted to treat the subject in a comparative religions perspective was published long before any of this exciting new body of literature was produced. I refer, of course, to Geoffrey Parrinder's *Sexual Morality in the World's Religions*. Although it served the purpose of introducing students to the subject, the text was singularly unhelpful when it came to guiding them through the voluminous recent literature, much of which addresses issues that hardly receive mention in Parrinder's text: the feminist critique of religious traditions; changing gender roles as a result of cross-cultural contact and new patterns of migration; and debates over the place of homosexual, bisexual, and transgender persons in religion.

As I taught the course, familiarizing myself as much as possible with the more recent literature on sexuality in the world's religions, it became apparent that the time was ripe for a new text that dealt with gender and sexuality from a comparative religions perspective. It also became clear that this would be a task much too large for one person to accomplish alone, especially one as new as I was to the material.

These thoughts remained in my mind for about a year, as other, more immediately pressing projects took up most of my time. The idea came rushing to the fore, however, during a conversation with Richard Hecht one day in the spring of 2000. He was serving as an adviser on a set of books that ABC-CLIO was planning to produce on the world's religions. Most of the books would focus exclusively on individual religious traditions, but some would be topical, covering issues of contemporary interest such as religion and economics, religion and politics, and, of course, religion and sexuality. A proposal was on Todd Hallman's desk within the week, and he readily agreed to publish the book.

It remained clear to me that what I had proposed was a large task, especially for someone who could claim only a cursory knowledge of the literature and whose name would be virtually unrecognizable to those specialists in the subject who would be most qualified to write the respective chapters. It was my good fortune, therefore, to know Melissa Wilcox, recently graduated with a Ph.D. in religious studies from the University of California at Santa Barbara. She is a specialist in the topic of sexuality and religion who is recognizable as a promising new scholar to others in this field from her regular presentations at national conferences and from several publications in books and journals. She eagerly agreed to coedit the book and took the leading role in recruiting the outstanding lineup of scholars who contributed, for which I am most grateful.

Being something of a novice to the subject matter turned out to be an unexpected benefit because the contributors were superb educators. They each replied promptly, patiently, and clearly to my numerous requests for explanation, definition, or elaboration. Compiling and editing this book was, therefore, a rich educational experience, and the product is a book that is accessible, interesting, and useful.

Contrary to the popular image of the solitary scholar surrounded by dusty old books, academic writing is a collective undertaking. Thus, certain acknowledgments are in order. Foremost, we owe thanks to James Ciment, who took over as our editor after Todd Hallman left ABC-CLIO for greener pastures. His enthusiasm for the project and patience when some deadlines were pressing are most gratefully acknowledged.

A further debt of gratitude is owed to the faculty in the Department of Religious Studies at the University of California at Santa Barbara. We have had the good fortune of working on this project in the context of one of the most engaging and collegial faculties one could hope for in academia. In particular, we wish to thank Richard Hecht, who, as already mentioned, first presented the opportunity to compile this book. Further thanks is extended to Phillip Hammond, whose influence is recognizable in Chapter 12 but who also endured innumerable lunch conversations about the progress of this text.

Finally, I wish to acknowledge the patience, understanding, and loving support of my life partner, Jeff. This book is dedicated to him.

*David W. Machacek*

The topic of religion and human sexuality is a pressing and important one in the contemporary climate of change and diversity. Numerous religions are currently embroiled in national or international debates over many of the issues touched upon in this book: women's religious roles; the ethics of technology; the rights of lesbian, gay, bisexual, and transgender (LGBT) people; women's bodies and sexuality; and the role of religious sexual ethics in society at large. Also interwoven with all of these issues are overwhelming dynamics of power, which interest me especially strongly given my focus on religion, oppression, and resistance.

Many of the political battles over the human body that rage today turn on religious issues, as David Machacek notes in the final chapter of this book. Religious activists populate both sides of the abortion debate and appear on the front lines of both pro- and anti-gay rights activism. Debates over the visibility of sexuality itself and the ways in which it is treated are especially fierce in religious settings and in areas where some wish to see religion play a central role. Religion is important in debates over what and when public schools should be teaching about sexuality and what resources schools should make available to students. And women's bodies, so often the center of attention in both secular and religious settings, have been fought over all the more voraciously in recent years—with men and women frequently relying on religious arguments to support *both* sides of women's rights issues, feminist theology, ordination debates, the religious significance of women's bodies, proper clothing (usually for women), and many other hotly contested issues. For all these reasons, this book is an important and necessary addition to the current literature on religion as well as that on human sexuality.

Thus, although my main research interests center around feminist, gender, and LGBT studies in religion, working on this book has been a fascinating and rewarding experience—as I hope reading it will be for those who pick it up. Like David, I wish to thank the skilled and knowledgeable authors who generously contributed their time and expertise to the book's production. They have ensured that this volume is a readable, accurate, up-to-date, and informative resource for students, academics, and lay readers alike. Thanks also to Richard Hecht for putting David and myself in touch with Todd Hallman at ABC-CLIO, to Todd for helping us develop the proposal and the initial stages of the book, and to Jim Ciment for taking over the project when Todd left the Santa Barbara area. Finally, I am ever grateful to Janet Mallen for her partnership, caring, and support and for steadfastly believing in the importance of my work during these challenging times.

*Melissa M. Wilcox*

# Introduction

mericans describe the sometimes dreaded task of teaching youngsters about human sexuality as telling them "the facts of life." That characterization is truly ironic because these "facts" usually include many culturally relative assumptions about gender, sex, and reproduction.

There is probably no better illustration of just how much culture influences human understandings of gender and sexuality than Bronislaw Malinowski's studies of marriage and sexuality among the Trobriand Islanders. Malinowski expressed some disbelief when his hosts explained to him that there was no connection between sexual intercourse and reproduction. Just as to Malinowski, it was perfectly evident that sex was very much a part of the process of reproduction, to the Trobriand Islanders, it was perfectly evident that the two had nothing to do with each other, and both were able to cite evidence to support their views.

Ultimately, the Trobriand Islanders took Malinowski into their confidence and explained the facts of life to him. Pregnancy occurs, they taught him, when a spirit comes in the night and sits on the head of a sleeping woman. The spirit is absorbed into the woman's head, which causes her to experience headaches and then descends slowly to her stomach, which causes morning sickness. It then descends further, causing her belly to swell, and finally emerges as a newborn child. To the Trobriand Islanders, then, sexual intercourse between men and women was enjoyable and fun and helped to promote positive feelings between husbands and wives but was of little significance otherwise. Male same-sex intercourse was also well known in this culture; it occurred in the ritual context of boys' initiation into manhood. Because the boys had absorbed so much of their mother's female essence—vaginal fluid and menstrual blood—from having been in her womb and from eating and sleeping with her from infancy, to become men they needed first to be cleansed of any residual femininity and then to ingest, through oral and sometimes anal intercourse with adult males, as much male essence—semen—as they could. It was said that boys who were deprived of this ritual process grew into women or at least failed to develop the physical features of adult males. It is not clear whether the Trobriand Islanders considered ritual intercourse between men and boys to be "sexual" or whether girls had similar same-sex experiences. What is clear, however, is that the category of the "homosexual"—someone with a lifelong preference for same-sex erotic encounters—did not exist for them and would probably have made little sense. Although all young boys were expected to have ritual contact with older men's semen, once having become a man through this ritual, each also was expected to marry a woman.

Malinowski also teaches us a second lesson about cross-cultural studies of religion and sexuality. Though his work was and still is highly respected by many as an example of early anthropology, diaries published after his death reveal a rather grim underbelly to this ostensibly respectable field of study. Like many Europeans of his era who visited cultures vastly different from their own, Malinowski took a dim view of the people with whom he was living. His diaries, at times, show little or no respect for their religious beliefs, intelligence, way of life, integrity, or even human rights. Suffering from what we now would term severe "culture shock," he often privately derides his hosts and their culture. Moreover, it is blatantly clear that he did not place Trobriand women and European women in the same class; his diaries record numerous instances in which he took liberties with the women who were his hosts that would have cost him his reputation and probably his personal freedom had his victims been European women rather than Pacific Islanders.

Clearly, it is impossible to understand a culture's beliefs, values, and practices with regard to sexuality and gender without considering their religious worldview. Moreover, in order truly to understand such worldviews, it is critical to approach each culture on its own terms and with a measure of self-critical awareness. However, as is made clear from the example above, learning about a culture's values, beliefs, and practices of gender and sexuality is also a very instructive way to learn about religion—especially given the central role of such practices in political, cultural, and theological debates across the contemporary world. This argument—stated explicitly here—is made implicitly throughout the chapters of this book.

Indeed, apart from the encounter with death, there is probably no human experience that so closely resembles certain religious experiences as sexuality. As in some religious experiences, sexuality can arouse feelings of both dread and fascination—*mysterium tremendum et fascinans,* as Rudolf Otto describes it—especially in the uninitiated. It is sometimes experienced as an encounter with the "wholly other"—both physical and emotional—particularly in the case of heterosexual intercourse. As in religion, sexuality involves a traversing of boundaries, of the material and spiritual realms in the case of religious experience and of the physical body and emotional self in the case of sexual experience. As in the religious experience, the sexual experience may involve a sense of losing oneself, which can lead to feelings of utter dependence. Few other aspects of human experience can arouse such intense emotional responses as sex and religion. And in fact, there have been instances in the history of many religions in which the similarities between sexuality and ecstatic religious experience have been acknowledged explicitly—religious practice has been likened to sex, contact with the divine has been described in sexual terms, and both homosexual and heterosexual eroticism have served as a source of spiritual enlightenment. In some religions the deities are explicitly sexual with one another, and in some their sexuality is occluded; others hold the divine to be strictly nonsexual. In all these cases, though, sexuality and the body—both human and divine—have been central topics of religious concern.

For these reasons, sexuality, again like matters of the spirit, is sometimes seen as being extremely powerful—both potently productive and potentially dangerous. All sorts of harm may befall the one who misuses it, and if it is not treated with great care, the result is chaos. It is no wonder, then, that most cultures have explicit rules for proper sexual conduct and feature elaborate—often religious—rituals of love, courtship, marriage, and sexual intercourse. This is not because human sexuality is seen as profane, as is often the perception in the West, but because it is deemed sacred.

Moreover, gender is a critical variable around the world in religious teachings about sexuality and the body, in part, simply because women's and men's bodies differ in ways that affect religious concerns: women bring life into the world, for instance, whereas men do not. Since religion frequently is involved in welcoming new life and determining each new person's role in the world, it must take this difference into account. Religions concerned with physiological changes, with bodily boundaries, or with what goes into or comes out of the human body are also likely to differentiate between the female body and the male one, simply because women menstruate but men do not, men produce sperm but women do not, women give birth but men do not, and so on. Finally, the common intertwining of religion with cultural values and practices means that social gender roles and religious ones will be closely interrelated and that religions will have much to say—both positive and negative—about changes in gender roles and sexual practices.

This book functions, therefore, as a topical study in comparative religion. The first and longest section of the book focuses on nine major world religions or families of religions. Although we indicated a special interest in the currently high-profile topics of homosexuality and women's sexuality when we first contacted the contributors to this volume, we have asked each author in Part 1 first and foremost to discuss those aspects of human sexuality that are most relevant to each religion today. To locate the reader in the tradition at hand, the chapters in this section begin with a broad overview of the tradition itself before focusing on its beliefs, values, and practices with regard to gender and sexuality.

In many if not all cases, however, such traditional beliefs, values, and practices have been challenged by contemporary realities. Colonialism disrupted some of these traditions, and it must be kept in mind that much of the information currently available on such traditions may come from the distorted records of the invading colonists or from postcolonial attempts at reconstruction and revitalization. This is particularly true in the case of the African and Native American indigenous traditions covered in the first two chapters, although colonialism has had a heavy impact on Hinduism and Islam as well. Furthermore, new patterns of migration have brought many of these traditions into closer contact than ever before. Although immigrants usually attempt, in varying degrees, to maintain their religious traditions in new social contexts, they also inevitably transform those traditions as they adapt to new cultural and social settings. The chapters of Part 1, therefore, also address issues of sexuality and gender in diaspora religions, particularly as those traditions are understood and practiced in the United States.

Further challenges to traditional religions have come from feminists and from lesbian, gay, bisexual, and transgender people, who have called upon religious leaders and members to rethink inherited assumptions and norms about gender and sexuality. These norms have prevented some people from full participation in their religions and, consequently, from full participation in social life. In some cases, religious norms have prevented the recognition of certain people—based on gender, sexuality, race, religion, class, or other factors—as fully human beings. As Malinowski's experiences with the Trobriand Islanders—and theirs with him—should aptly demonstrate, rethinking traditional beliefs and values about gender and sexuality is no small task. Many of the chapters in Part 1 detail contemporary struggles over religious definitions of gender, sexuality, and personhood.

Those who read through all the chapters in Part 1 will notice that certain themes recur repeatedly, especially in the context of the contemporary United States. Several factors have shaped the current religious complexity in this country, and we have elected to include a final section that covers these issues thematically. Chapter 10 considers some of the changes recently wrought on the U.S. religious scene by feminism and the growth of new religious movements through a close examination of one key example: attempts by neopagans to reconsider gender and sexuality. Chapter 11 addresses the interactions of religious individualism, feminism, and the gay rights and queer movements in the United States as it explores the roles of religion and spirituality in lesbian, gay, bisexual, and transgender communities. Finally, Chapter 12 examines the influence of a constitutionally secular government on issues of gender and sexuality in the context of debates over the proper role of religion in U.S. civil society.

Although we (and here we speak on behalf of all the contributors) have attempted to treat these discourses fairly and objectively, our respective biases probably remain. We ask readers, therefore, to take these chapters in the spirit in which they are intended: as an introduction to gender and sexuality in the world's religions, rather than as the final say. Both primary and secondary resources abound in this fascinating area of study. Our own and our contributing authors' recommendations for further reading appear at the end of the book, and we hope that readers interested in this area will avail themselves of the opportunity to explore further the topics that interest them most.

*Melissa M. Wilcox and David W. Machacek*

# About the Contributors

**Rebecca T. Alpert** is the codirector of the Women's Studies Program and associate professor of religion and women's studies at Temple University. A rabbi and the former dean of students at the Reconstructionist Rabbinical College, she has taught and published extensively in the areas of women in religion, medical ethics, contemporary Judaism, and gay and lesbian studies. She is the coauthor (with Jacob Staub) of *Exploring Judaism: A Reconstructionist Approach* (1986; updated and expanded, 2000), author of *Like Bread on the Seder Plate: Jewish Lesbians and the Transformation of Tradition* (Columbia University Press, 1997), and editor of *Voices of the Religious Left: A Contemporary Sourcebook* (Temple University Press, 2000). Her most recent work is an edited anthology, *Lesbian Rabbis: The First Generation*, with Shirley Idelson and Sue Levi Elwell (Rutgers University Press, 2001).

**James C. Cavendish** is assistant professor of sociology at the University of South Florida. His research on such topics as the influence of Christian base communities on democratization in Latin America, conflicts over women's ordination in the United States, church-based community activism among U.S. Catholic parishes, clergy mobilization strategies in church-sponsored antidrug protests, and the reconciliation of contradictory identities among gay and lesbian Catholics has been published in the *Journal for the Scientific Study of Religion, Social Psychology Quarterly,* and *Social Science Quarterly.* He is currently researching the Catholic Church's inclusion of African Americans in its life and leadership for the U.S. Conference of Catholic Bishops.

**Randy P. Conner** is the author of *Blossom of Bone: Reclaiming the Connections between Homoeroticism and the Sacred* (HarperSan Francisco, 1993); coauthor of the *Encyclopedia of Queer Myth, Symbol, and Spirit* (Cassell, 1996); and author of numerous articles on gender, sexuality, and the sacred. Having taught in the Literature Department at the University of Texas for many years, he is presently attending a doctoral program at the California Institute of Integral Studies (CIIS) and is completing his book *At the Crossroads of Desire: Same-Sex Intimacy and Gender Diversity in Santeria, Candomble, and Vodou.*

**Julianne Cordero** is a member of the Santa Barbara Chumash community and doctoral student in the Department of Religious Studies at the University of California at Santa Barbara. Her article on changing paradigms in the interpretation of Chumash spiritual traditions, identity, culture, and colonial history has been accepted for publication in the upcoming Oxford anthology, *Religious Healing in America,* a joint project between the Harvard Center for the Study of World Religions and Boston Medical University. She also has articles on Native American healing ceremonies and traditions, medicinal plants, and traditional notions of power among the Chumash in *American Indian Religious Traditions: An Encyclopedia* (ABC-CLIO, forthcoming).

**Elizabeth Currans** is a Ph.D. student in the Department of Religious Studies at the University of California at Santa Barbara. She has published encyclopedia articles about Native American culture and spirituality and classical mythology in Fitzroy Dearborn's *Reader's Guide to Lesbian and Gay Studies.*

**Amy DeRogatis** is assistant professor of American religion and culture at Michigan State University. She has written on American Protestant missionaries, gender and American religion, and apocalypticism.

**Aysha Hidayatullah** studies Islam and gender in the Department of Religious Studies at the University of California at Santa Barbara, where she is completing a doctoral degree.

**Tanya Keenan** is completing her doctorate in depth psychology from Pacifica Graduate Institute in Carpinteria, California. She has presented papers at the American Sociological Association annual meeting as well as at the National Women's History Month conference and has been a guest lecturer in courses at the University of South Florida and Ventura College.

**Jeffrey S. Lidke** is visiting assistant professor of religion at the University of Virginia. His doctoral thesis, "The Goddess within and beyond the Three Cities: The Paradox of Power in Nepala-Mandala," is a historical, textual, and ethnographic study of Hindu Tantra and politics in the Kathmandu Valley. He is the author of *Visvarupa Mandir: A Study of Changu Narayan, Nepal's Most Ancient Temple* (Nirala Publications, 1996). Dr. Lidke is a Fulbright fellow and recipient of the Raimundo Pannikar Award for Excellence in the Study of South Asia.

**David W. Machacek** is the director of the Religious Pluralism in Southern California Project and lecturer in religious studies at the University of California at Santa Barbara. His recent publications include *Soka Gakkai in America:*

*Accommodation and Conversion* (with Phillip E. Hammond, Oxford University Press, 1999) and *Global Citizens: The Soka Gakkai Buddhist Movement in the World* (edited with Bryan Wilson, Oxford University Press, 2000).

**Nancy Ramsey Tosh** is an instructor of sociology at the Ventura County Community College District. Her publications include "Mirror Images: Wicca from the Inside Out and Outside In" (in *Toward Reflexive Ethnography*) and "Marginal Realities: Insider Scholarship in a 'Magical World,'" which appeared in *The Chronicle of Higher Education.*

**Liz Wilson** is associate professor in the Department of Comparative Religion and affiliate in the Women's Studies Program at Miami University, where she directs the graduate program in comparative religion. She is the author of *Charming Cadavers: Horrific Figurations of the Feminine in Indian Buddhist Hagiographic Literature* (University of Chicago Press, 1996). Her article, "Seeing through the Gendered 'I': The Self-Scrutiny and Self-Disclosure of Nuns in Post-Ashokan Buddhist Literature," was recognized by the *Journal of Feminist Studies in Religion* with a Young Scholar's Award.

**Melissa M. Wilcox** teaches religious studies and women's studies at the University of California at Santa Barbara. Her research interests center on issues of religion, identity, oppression, and resistance. She is the author of *Coming Out in Christianity: Religion, Identity, and Community* (Indiana University Press, 2003) and is currently working on a study of religion and spirituality among lesbian, bisexual, and transgender women in Los Angeles.

**Dr. Xinzhong Yao** is professor of religion and ethics in the Department of Theology and Religious Studies at the University of Wales, Lampeter, United Kingdom. He has taught Chinese religions and comparative philosophy in Wales since 1991 and has published widely in the areas of religion and ethics, both in English and in Chinese. His recent English publications include *An Introduction to Confucianism* (Cambridge University Press, 2000) and *Confucianism and Christianity* (Sussex Academic Press, 1996; Chinese translation by China Social Science Publishing House, 2002).

Part 1

# Gender and Sexuality in the World's Religions

Chapter 1

# Sexuality and Gender in African Spiritual Traditions

*Randy P. Conner*

*Erotic fertility shrine wood carving. Yoruba people, Nigeria. (Werner Forman/Art Resource, NY)*

Given the variety of indigenous traditions present on the continent of Africa, it is impossible to make general statements about beliefs and practices of African "religions" without doing an injustice to some or even most. Moreover, practitioners of these "religions" frequently do not look upon their faiths as such because they perceive religion as completely interwoven with the entirety of their life experiences rather than as a demarcated arena of life experience. Furthermore, even among practitioners of Christianity and Islam, ancient spiritual practices continue to be carried out, albeit beneath the rubric of the more recently adopted faiths. Thus, in this chapter, I will generally refer to "spiritual traditions" rather than to "religions" to express this complex perspective regarding spiritual experience.

Although it is risky to generalize about African spiritual traditions, we can say that in many of them, a belief in the sacredness of nature is paramount; thus, these traditions are frequently described as "pantheistic." The source of divinity permeates the universe, often in the form of a mystical energy similar to the *élan vital* or what younger readers might envision as "the force," as popularized in *Star Wars;* among the Yoruba of Nigeria, for instance, this force or energy is named *ashé.* An allied belief imparts that the source of divinity may manifest in multiple—perhaps even infinite—ways; these expressions of divinity resemble archetypal forces or energies. Although the notion of a single source of divinity may be associated with monotheism, or the worship of one god, multiple expressions of godhead in many of these traditions—often characterized as "lesser divinities"—may be linked to polytheism, or the reverence of many gods. Thus, many African spiritual traditions may be described as pantheistic, monotheistic, and polytheistic simultaneously.

As in many ancient religions, such as those of Egypt and Greece, deities in African spiritual traditions are associated with natural elements (including earth, air, fire, and water, as well as particular plants, animals, and stones), life experiences (such as birth, loving union, and death), occupations (spiritual leader, warrior, artist, and so on), and other matters, including gender and sexuality. Although many deities are perceived as being male or female, African spiritual traditions also embrace deities who transcend or transgress masculine and feminine gender categories. Moreover, although a majority of deities are associated with heterosexuality, a number of these traditions include deities who are associated with the expression of same-sex intimacy. As in ancient Egypt and Greece, the goddesses and gods of African spiritual traditions are envisioned as having their own life experiences and as playing active roles in the lives of humans. Beyond deities, ancestral spirits also play a central role in African spiritual experience.

Where spiritual practices are concerned, among the most significant is communication with the deity by way of prayer, offering and sacrifice, divination, and embodiment of the god or goddess (often referred to as "possession" in western texts). Spiritual healing and magic involving the aid of a deity also are considered important in African spiritual life, as are rituals marking life passages, such as those into adulthood, marriage, parenthood, and spiritual maturity (including becoming a priest or priestess). Frequently, these practices are linked to concerns with and expressions of gender and sexuality.

Indigenous African traditions generally permit both women and men to serve as spiritual leaders, teachers, or guides. Although one's gender might determine the specific spiritual role one plays, it rarely prevents one from assuming spiritual authority. Moreover, a number of African traditions—especially in the past, prior to the introduction of Christianity and Islam—have included priests and priestesses who might be described as "androgynous" or "transgendered," as well as those whose sexual expression may have included same-sex intimacy.

## MASCULINE AND FEMININE
## IN THE REALM OF THE GODS

In some African spiritual traditions, gender is not a marker of identity, so the terms "masculine" and "feminine" are viewed as meaningless. In others, "masculinity" and "femininity" possess traditional designations resonating rather remarkably with the yin-yang symbolism of Chinese Daoist cosmology. For instance, among some West African peoples, masculinity often corresponds to positive, right, air, fire, light, north, east, shea butter,[1] semen, chalk, and frankness; femininity corresponds to negative, left, earth, water, darkness, south, west, red palm oil, blood, (red) camwood paste,[2] and secrecy. Nevertheless, both masculinity and femininity are more complicated than this dichotomy would indicate. Indeed, these terms are used in this chapter primarily to assist the western reader.

For instance, the gender of Yoruban deities is so fluid that some scholars, such as Oyèrónké Oyěwùmí reject the idea that they have gender at all. One finds that the definition of masculinity changes depending upon which deity, or *òrìsà*, one is considering.[3] For instance, the masculinity of the creator-deity Obàtálá—who is perceived as both male and female—is associated with patience and compassion, whereas the masculinity of the warrior Ògún is linked to aggression and violence. That of the thunderbolt-wielding Sàngó (Shango) is linked to aggression but also to sensuality and elegance, whereas that of the intercessory-trickster Esù (Eshu, Elégbá[ra], Legba, Elleggúa)—who is, like Obàtálá, considered both male and female or beyond gender—is associated with excessive sexuality as well as prank playing, maliciousness, eloquence, and generosity.

Along the same lines, the femininity of Òsun (Oshun), goddess of love and the arts, is linked not only to beauty, grace, elegance, and charm (in the magical sense as well) but also linked to prosperity, independence, warriorhood, and rulership. In a praise song, she is described thus: "She dances, and takes the crown / She dances without asking permission / She keeps her own counsel." Moreover, Òsun's femininity is linked to wisdom and healing: "She is the wisdom of the forest / she is the wisdom of the river. / Where the doctor failed / she cures with fresh water" (Gleason 1994, 177). Likewise, the femininity of Oya, goddess of the tempest, is associated with both warriorhood and motherhood. Although "Oya" means "she tore," she is also known as the "mother of nine."

A host of African religions and traditions speak of a time when a goddess or goddesses—Massassi of the Wahunga of Zimbabwe, Wagadu of the Soninke of the Sahel—held precedence over male deities or else coruled with them and a time when women ruled the earth or ruled equally with men. There followed, however, a period—extending into the present—of male domination and the supremacy of male deities. Such tales are linked to others that speak of women's attempt to regain control through witchcraft and men's consequential attempt to wrest the power of witchcraft from women or to eradicate witches.

Ethnographic research indicates that an ancient center of goddess reverence and a stronghold of women's authority existed at the Igbo town of Nnobi in Nigeria. Here, possibly for millennia, women and men have worshipped the goddess Idemili, naming the nearby river after her. The town Nnobi invokes another of her names, the "mother of Obi," her son. Although her worship was somewhat weakened, together with women's authority, at some as yet undetermined point in Igbo history when the patriarchally minded Nri Igbo began to wield influence over the people of Nnobi, the reverence of Idemili nevertheless continues into the present. Masai (primarily of Kenya and Tanzania) report that long ago, women were thought to be stronger than men and to make better warriors. Jealous of the women, the men accompanying them into battle stabbed them while they slept in order to create vaginas; previously, women warriors had possessed only very small orifices through which to urinate. Following this event, women no longer went to war but stayed at home, rearing children. Dominated by men, they eventually became weaker, whereas Masai men became renowned warriors.

Similarly, among the Dogon of Mali and Burkina Faso, a tale is told of a primordial earth goddess who was considered as having masculine characteristics, because she possessed a clitoris, which was imagined to be phallic. Chief among her possessions was a magical fiber skirt dyed red with blood. A mortal woman (perhaps a priestess of the goddess), by placing it on herself, established rule over men. Ultimately, the men stole it from her, claimed it as a royal garment, prohibited its use by women, and wore it during rituals.

This tale resonates with masked rituals among the Yaka of the Democratic Republic of the Congo that suggest that rites once performed by women were later transformed into occasions for mocking women's sexuality. It also resonates with Yoruba tales of men's wresting magical power from women, which occur in the oracles, or *odùs,* named Ogúndáméjì, Osáméjì, and Ogúndáketè. In the last of these, the warrior *òrìsà* Ògún, infuriated by women's spiritual authority and particularly by their control of ceremonial masquerades invoking the ancestors, takes it upon himself to steal control from the women and offer it to men, who consequently take charge of the masked rites. Somewhat paradoxical is the present-day belief that the Gelede masquerade—which grants Ògún precedence and is chiefly performed by men—pays homage to the very women from whom it may have been appropriated.

Despite a legendary or actual loss of women's spiritual and social authority in African cultures, certain women living in our own time powerfully evoke a vision of a prepatriarchal—or perhaps postpatriarchal—culture. Among these is the South African Zulu rain queen Modjadji V, who is not allowed to marry men but who has more than thirty wives and is believed to possess rainmaking powers. Women's secret societies like Sande of the Mende of Sierra Leone, with its reverence of Sowo and Tingoi (the mermaid), goddesses or spirits of the waters, its complex initiation process, its masked rites, and its elaborate ethical and aesthetic codes, are likewise evocative of such a spiritual tradition and culture.

## SEX ORGANS, BODILY FLUIDS, AND MENSTRUATION

It is not surprising that practitioners of African spiritual traditions have been somewhat reticent to share their views on sex and gender. Perhaps no other spiritual traditions have been—and continue to be—so exoticized, maligned, and demonized by outsiders. Nevertheless, these traditions offer illuminating insights into the intersection of sexuality, gender, and spiritual life.

Nude male and female figures often signify fertility and potency, as well as ancestral power, in African spiritual traditions. Exemplary are the figures molded into the *kargbee* spirit houses of the Senufo of the Côte d'Ivoire; these figures possess exaggerated sexual organs and are decorated with human hair. The Igbo number among those who regard such figures as imbued with spiritual energy or force. Especially in southern African rock art, nonhuman figures such as circles, crocodiles, snakes, and genet cats also signify fertility and potency.

In various African spiritual traditions, female genitalia are signified by or correspond to vegetables (the calabash), animals (the cow), technical objects (the anvil), colors (red and green), and abstract shapes (the circle and the triangle). So sacred and mysterious is the vagina that in numerous cultures, men are not permitted to touch it with their hands. Female breasts, sometimes compared to calabashes (which signify containment of the cosmos on a macrocosmic plane and containment of sacred beverages and foods on a microcosmic plane), profoundly connect women to female divinities, particularly those ruling the waters. Male genitalia are signified by or correspond to millet, the dog and the ram, the spear, yellow and white, and pillars of mud and stone. As with female organs, male genitalia connect men to phallic deities, such as the Yoruba *òrìsàs* Esù and Orìsà Oko.

Unsurprisingly, menstrual blood and semen are regarded as powerful, magical substances. Generally speaking, menstrual blood is greatly feared by males, who often refer to it in negative terms; it can also be dangerous to other women. The Dogon, for example, compare it to the use of vulgar language. For the Dogon, moreover, the origin of menstruation may be traced to either the punishment of a primordial goddess by a male deity disturbed by her possession of a clitoris (which was considered masculine) or to the rape of the goddess by one of her offspring, both acts resulting in a flow of "bad blood." In a majority of African cultures, menstruating women are secluded from their communities and are considered dangerous. The Dogon, Azande (Sudan, Democratic Republic of the Congo, Central African Republic), and other peoples maintain that contact with a menstruating woman can bring about illness, pollution, and even death. It can render magic ineffective and transform order into chaos. Nevertheless, the Dogon, like the Zulu and Yoruba, also hold that menstrual blood can be a source of potent magic.

Although semen occasionally is thought to be a dangerous substance, as among the Suku of the Democratic Republic of the Congo, it is more often than not regarded as beneficial. The Yaka believe that semen contains a vital force called *mooyi* that nourishes the bones of offspring, promotes physical strength, and heals illness. The Koma of Ethiopia, Sudan, and Zambia believe that semen nourishes the child growing in the womb, just as the mother's milk will nourish it upon birth; as a food, semen is referred to as *bayab*, or "porridge." The Tabwa of the Democratic Republic of the Congo associate semen with the revered culture-bringer Mbidi Kiluwe, and the Yoruba, who regard semen as stimulating intellect, associate the substance with the creator-deity Obàtálá.

Among the Giriama (Kenya) and Dogon, architecture and interior design reflect religious and mythological concepts relating to sexuality. For the Giriama, phallic stones are viewed as "penetrating" the feminine hearth. For the Dogon, the vestibule of the house signifies the male partner, ancestor, or deity and the front door his penis; the central room and storerooms signify the female partner, female ancestor, or goddess. The granary is perceived as a woman or female deity awaiting her male partner to engage in sexual intercourse, with the door of the granary signifying her vagina. One of the most unusual architectural constructions employed by the Dogon is referred to as the "Dogon Door," a carved door rich in symbols, sometimes including dancers and breasts, which announces that a woman inside is menstruating.

## INITIATION, CEREMONIAL EROTICISM, MARRIAGE, AND TRANSGRESSIONS

For both males and females, initiation processes frequently commence with training in various fields, reach an apex with ceremonial circumcision or clitoridectomy, and culminate with wedding ceremonies. Although westerners, especially those of European heritage, might have a tendency to look upon these rites as secular, in African cultures, they are profoundly spiritual in nature. They typically involve periods of seclusion with members of the same sex and age group and with elders, often but not always of the same sex, who guide the young initiates through the initiatory process. Young women are trained in the domestic arts, occasionally in hunting, and in women's mysteries; young men are trained in hunting, warriorship, and in men's mysteries. Such initiation rites may be traced to the earliest periods of African prehistory, as is evidenced by southern African rock art. One panel discovered in South Africa, for instance, depicts an elder woman guiding a group of seven young women wearing wigs and jewelry and carrying hunting equipment in what appears to be an initiatory rite speaking to both hunting and menstruation, the latter signified by lines flowing between the women's legs.

As Dogon religion suggests, one of the primary reasons for both male and female circumcision may lie in the belief that infants, mirroring certain deities and ancestral spirits, are neither male nor female. For them to fully participate in a culture that insists upon gender dichotomies and childbearing for the majority of its members, their gender ambiguity must be sacrificed. This sacrifice occurs when the physical correlate of the female's masculine energy—her clitoris—and the physical correlate of the male's feminine energy—his foreskin—are ritually severed. In this way, the children *become* male and female.

Female circumcision is related to the myth mentioned above concerning the forced impregnation of a primordial earth goddess. When the male deity Amma wished to have intercourse with her, her clitoris, symbolized by a termite mound and signifying her gynandrous nature—as opposed to her vagina, represented by an anthill—prevented him from satisfying his urge; thus, he destroyed the termite mound and metaphorically initiated the process of clitoridectomy. Since that time, according to the Dogon, men have dominated women. However, the severed clitoris is transformed into a scorpion, a lethal creature in Dogon spirituality. By comparison, when a male is circumcised, the foreskin or prepuce is transformed into either a feeble shadow or a lizard—a beneficial creature associated with the sun.

In the Yoruba religion, clitoridectomy and circumcision are primarily associated with the warrior *òrìsà* Ògún. Male circumcision is sometimes viewed as a sacrifice to the phallic *òrìsà* Esù. In Yoruba, "to circumcise" is *dako—da,* "to be acceptable as a sacrifice," and *oko,* "penis" or, in this context, "foreskin."

For the Taneka (Tânba) of Benin, the eight-month male initiation process culminates with circumcision. The man's age may vary from late adolescence to the early thirties. During this period, he is trained in men's pursuits and men's mysteries. His training is guided in part by tricksters named *kumpara,* whose antics include simulated same-sex eroticism employing large wooden penises, in which the initiate assumes the traditionally receptive role. Immediately prior to the ceremony of circumcision, a ritual dance is performed, and chickens are sacrificed. When the circumcision takes place, the young man is forbidden from showing signs of pain. His penis is wrapped in a banana leaf bound by a raffia cord and will remain so for three months. During this period, he must abstain from sexual relations.

It should be noted that in recent years many individuals and groups, among them women practitioners of African spiritual traditions, have struggled to end the practice of clitoridectomy, insisting that the physical, psychological, and spiritual suffering inflicted by the ceremony is irreparable. To a somewhat lesser extent, a movement to end the practice of male circumcision in Africa and elsewhere has also emerged. Growing concern about human rights leads to contradictory impulses in this regard: On the one hand, there is a desire to respect religious and cultural differences and to avoid imposing western values on other cultures; on the other, there is concern about the human rights of individuals who must undergo these painful experiences.

During the initiation process, ritual dances emphasizing the wearing of ceremonial masks are common. Among the Yaka, for example, the *kholuka* mask traditionally portrays a man with an enormous phallus. In the past, participants chanted bawdy verses as the male dancer wearing the mask thrust his hips forward, exposing either a large wooden phallus or his own penis to the other participants. Female initiates—such as the Shai and Krobo of Ghana and the Swazi of Swaziland—often engage in sensuous ritual dances, sometimes while in seclusion and at other times in public, dressed in elegant and seductive attire, with the goals of displaying grace and beauty and attracting male partners. Among the Himba of northwestern Namibia, men assume the role of herders and women that of oxen in a courting dance called *ondjongo;* the female dancers end their individual performances by turning their backs to the men and flipping up their skirts to reveal their buttocks. Attracting female partners is one of the primary goals of extremely aggressive stick fights undertaken by Surma men from Ethiopia, as it is among Masai warriors celebrating the *eunoto.*

Despite the fact that in many African cultures marriages are arranged and romantic love is downplayed, erotic attraction plays a key role in establishing intimate relationships. Among the Yoruba, women's *kóló* tattoos, associated with the *òrìsà* Ògún, are designed to arouse men sexually, just as slitted eyes, swanlike necks, and elaborate coiffures, associated with the Mende goddess or spirit Sowo, are thought to attract men. Among the Wodaabe (or Bororo of Niger, Nigeria, Cameroon, Central African Republic, and Chad) at the time of the return of the rains, men who might mistakenly be perceived by many in the West as transvestites or drag queens participate in a ceremonial beauty pageant. Dressed in elegant attire with exquisite facial makeup, they dance the *yaake* together, making quivering gestures to charm female spectators.

The *nomdede,* undertaken by young Zulu women, is an elaborate ritual that speaks at once to initiation, ceremonial eroticism, marriage, and childbearing. This ritual honors Nomkhubulwana, a goddess or ancestral female spirit, described as a beautiful woman dressed in white or in all the colors of the rainbow, who resides in the heavens. Participants pray to her for lovers, spouses, and children. With prayers and singing, the young women dress in men's clothes, drink beer (considered a masculine beverage), dance nude, and simulate sexual intercourse with bananas. Recently, Nomkhubulwana has become syncretized with the Virgin Mary, apparently so that young Christian women may continue to take part in the beneficial *nomdede* rites.

Ancient rock art in modern Algeria suggests that ritual eroticism in Africa emerged at least 8,000 years ago. In what may be a fertility rite, a central male figure is surrounded by a group of women and animals, including an antelope, while a key female figure lies on her back, apparently waiting to be impregnated. Another prehistoric rock painting found in present-day Botswana depicts a group of thirty-five women and men; the men have erect penises and wear antelope masks in what appears to be a fertility rite. One of the most intriguing works of this kind, found in the Akakus Mountains in Libya, shows two males, one wearing a dog or jackal mask, having sexual intercourse with two women. Above the couples, a feline entity with an enormous phallus seems to preside over the ceremony. This work may represent a fertility rite having the goal of bringing rain. In these and other instances, depictions of ritual eroticism seem to conjure a primordial epoch in which human and animal realms were less demarcated. Such depictions resonate with tales like that of the beautiful Adowi, who either was raped by or fell in love with a panther and gave birth to Agassou, a deity of the Vodun pantheon and the ancestor of the kings of Dahomey (Benin).

West African metal art of a much later period that depicts frontal as well as oral and anal intercourse among heterosexual couples—sometimes linked to animal figures such as crocodiles, which may represent deities—suggests that ritual eroticism may have continued throughout millennia and across numerous African cultures. Adding weight to this possibility is a carved wooden block fashioned by a Yoruba artist that portrays orgiastic heterosexual sex accompanied by music. Both female and male participants appear to be wearing feminine "beehive" hairdos and may be priests of a particular cult—possibly that of the phallic, androgynous trickster Esù, as suggested by use of the letter *x* and red paint.

Ritual eroticism does not only occur, it should be noted, within the context of initiation. For example, it also traditionally occurred at the time of the hunt in Rwanda, when the ruler was expected to have public sexual intercourse with one of his wives. The rite was apparently extended to include a wider group of participants during the sorghum ritual. It also occurred during the construction of *mbari* spirit houses by the Owerri Igbo, who otherwise appear to have condemned ceremonial eroticism together with many other forms of sexual activity deemed deviant. During the Yoruba yam harvest festival, priestesses of Orìsà Oko— a phallic deity of agriculture—led carnivalesque processions and erotic ritual dances, possibly including expressions of same-sex intimacy.

If eroticism has been celebrated in African spiritual traditions, however, it has also been subjected to numerous prohibitions. Certain Igbo groups prohibit sexual intercourse during the daylight hours, particularly in the open air. The Beng (Côte d'Ivoire) believe that having sexual intercourse outside the village may bring about difficulties in childbearing, drought, and even death because no kapok tree has been ritually planted beyond the village's boundaries, and it is this ritual planting that sanctifies lovemaking. Moreover, numerous African spiritual traditions hold that individuals must abstain from sexual relations during the hunt and for brief periods of time preceding and following it. In other traditions, such as that of the Mandja (Central African Republic), potters are not permitted to have sexual relations during the lengthy process of making pottery because it is believed that the clash of two equally potent sacred activities might prove disastrous to both potters and their creations.

An exaggerated focus on "arranged" marriages seems to have led scholars of religion, anthropology, and folklore to neglect courtship as a stage in historical African life experience. We know, however, that courtship played an important role in intimate relationships. The Dahomean *amuxoda xogbe,* or "dew-on-hair" chants, describe lovers spending nights in the open and exchanging vows as dew collected on their hair. Mende trysts at the riverside, abode of the female divinity Sowo, also reveal the significance of courtship rituals.

In numerous African cultures, the ritual of marriage follows initiation and courtship and commences with either the families of the partners or a professional go-between—often a spiritual functionary—negotiating a marriage contract. This contract frequently involves a family's exchange of their daughter for prized possessions such as cattle; the exchange is often described as "bride-price" or "bride-wealth." Once negotiations are completed, the male partner pays a highly ritualized visit to the bride's family's home, at which time symbolic gifts are exchanged. Nearer the time of the wedding, the bride is secluded from the community, except for certain family members and (typically) female attendants who prepare her for the wedding ceremony and for marriage.

Among the Himba, a culture profoundly influenced by reverence of female ancestral spirits, the mother adorns her secluded daughter's skin and hair with a ritually prepared unguent of butter fat, ochre, and aromatic herbs and bestows on her a ceremonial *ekori* headdress made of hide, which symbolizes her journey from her childhood home to her new husband's dwelling. In a similar manner, the Ndebele bride (South Africa, Zimbabwe) is secluded in a brightly painted women's compound. She is given a *nguba*—a red ceremonial blanket—and a beaded leather bridal apron to wear, as well as a parasol that functions like the *ekori* headdress, all of which signify her new life. The period of seclusion ends when the bride is called out from hiding by female attendants and guests.

Wedding ceremonies include prayers, chanting and singing, dancing, sacrifices, feasting, and the exchange of gifts. Prayers focus on the couple having a harmonious marriage and on their bearing healthy children. At Yoruba weddings, ancestors are invoked to bless the couple; as the participants taste sacred kola nuts, honey, and sugar cane they chant: "They will ripen, they will eat and not grow hungry, they will grow old. Their union will be sweet." Among the Igbo of Nnobi, the *dibia* priestess requests that the couple interlock fingers as they share a ceremonial meal of fish and palm nuts. Igbo women of another area sing to the bride: "Be you as beautiful as a mermaid; the beauty of a woman is to have a husband." Surrounding the new couple, the women celebrate the *upiti* mud dance, pouring palm wine on the earth, as the bride and groom dance in the center. The songs become increasingly bawdy, with the cry "Biam! Biam!" signifying both the rhythm of sexual intercourse and an infant's first sounds. As in most cultures, nuptial rites tend to culminate in lovemaking.

Once a couple has wed, other rituals help to ensure a harmonious marriage. In some cultures—the Woyo of the Democratic Republic of the Congo and the Dagara of Ghana, Côte d'Ivoire, and Burkina Faso—ritual pots are fashioned for the new couple. These pots may contain talismans, sacred plants, and water and are perceived as imbued with vital forces that promote harmony and childbearing. Dagara couples renew their relationships periodically by creating a sacred circle with ash, invoking spirits and natural forces, having spiritual elders renew the blessing of their pots, and bathing ritually. Disharmony also may be expressed, however, by way of the pots. A Woyo wife who feels that her husband has abused her may embarrass him when their friends dine with them by serving him a bowl of food covered with the lid of a pot bearing symbols speaking of respect within marriage; in a culturally accepted reversal of meaning, this act signifies his disregard for this principle.

Although polygyny (a husband having numerous wives) is accepted in numerous African cultures, its opposite—polyandry—is not. Adultery also meets with great disapproval. Yoruba traditions hold that adultery not only harms a couple but also offends the deities and ancestors who have sanctioned the marriage. When adultery is not punished by worldly authorities, deities or spirits may cause adulterers to fall ill, become infertile, or die. In certain cultures, a wife who so much as cooks a meal for a man other than her husband may be suspected of adultery. Among the Mossi of Burkina Faso and elsewhere in West Africa, the loyalty of the king's wives was ritually monitored by a eunuch who, employing the diviner's tool of a calabash filled with water and sacred leaves, was able to see the wife with her adulterous partner, if one existed. Women who are suspected of adultery, whether guilty or not, often address their prayers to female divinities like the Yoruba Òsun, who was herself accused of committing adultery by her husband Orúnmìlà.[4]

African spiritual traditions strongly disapprove of prostitution. Owerri Igbo associate prostitution with insanity, evil, and foreigners and with Mgbeke, a negative *mbari* spirit. The Yoruba tell of Ere, who was punished for prostitution long ago by being trampled in a bog. The Gelede masquerade viciously mocks prostitutes (*asewò*). The oracular *odù* Obàrà' dí encourages prostitutes to relinquish their profession and reform themselves by making sacrifices, consuming medicinal soups, purifying their genitalia with shea butter, and taking ritual baths with sacred leaves.

Although rape and incest are condemned in most, if not all African traditions, tales of rape and incest by such revered male deities as the Yoruba *òrìsàs* Esù and Ògún abound. Esù, for example, is said to have raped and slain three women because they failed at divination by cowries. Perhaps the most well known Yoruba tale of rape concerns that of Yemoja by her son Aganjù, which resulted in the birth of numerous other *òrìsàs*.

## GENDER DIVERSITY AND SAME-SEX INTIMACY

Many African spiritual traditions acknowledge that at least in isolation, "masculinity" and "femininity" may not account for all divine or human

17

expressions of gender. Among the Yaka, the very essence of life, *mooyi,* is described as both male and female. Abrao, Aku, Awo, and Tano of the Akan (Guinea Coast), Faro of the Bambara (Mali), Mawu-Lisa and Nanan-Bouclou of the Dahomean/Fon, Mwari of the Shona (Zimbabwe), Esù, Loogun-Ede, Nana Burúkú, Obàtálá, Olókun, Òsanyin, and Osumare of the Yoruba, and myriad other African spiritual beings are frequently depicted as transcending, traversing, or transgressing traditional masculine and feminine boundaries. A number of them spend half of each year as a male and the other half as a female. For example, Loogun-Ede (or Logunedé) spends six months as a hunter in the forest, followed by six months as a river nymph. Others, such as Obàtálá, possess various aspects, one or more of which may be described as feminine, masculine, or a mixture of the two. Still others, like Esù, are portrayed as simultaneously possessing masculine and feminine attributes, such as a large phallus and a woman's coiffure.

Somewhat ironically, the union of the Dogon deity Amma and the earth goddess, which destroyed her gynandrous nature when Amma removed her clitoris, produced a pair of hermaphroditic twins called the Nummo. Unlike the earth goddess, the Nummo twins are not viewed negatively. Indeed, they are considered "perfect and complete." The Nummo are described as being half human and half serpent, with green or rainbow-hued skin and smooth, sleek bodies covered with short green hair. They are also said to have reddish eyes and forked tongues like serpents. Associated with the element of water, as well as with the chameleon, copper, and the rainbow, they dwell in the heavens and are enveloped by light. In another ironic twist, it is the Nummo who, together with Amma, determined that although divinities or spirits may be androgynous, transgendered, or hermaphroditic, mortal women and men (other than spiritual leaders, it would seem) may not. For this reason, they established the rites of circumcision and clitoridectomy.

"Supernatural" creatures are sometimes considered androgynous. The red water serpent with one male head and one female head of the Kikongo (Democratic Republic of the Congo, Angola) is associated with the rainbow and with magic. The catfish spirit of the *mbwoolu* healing cult of the Yaka nurtures initiates as they are "born again" from the maternal river bottom (the catfish is thought to be androgynous because the male nurtures the eggs). We have already encountered the Dogon belief that the scorpion is a masculine manifestation of the female clitoris and that the sun lizard is a feminine manifestation of the male foreskin.

Ancient African rock art found in the Drakensberg region of southern Africa indicates that gynandry once was celebrated in female initiation rites, with young women carrying bows and quivers. Among the Dagara, similar rites occur today in which women wearing artificial beards are led by the *pure* (the "female father") to honor their "masculine" energy. Ceremonial fluidity of both gender and sexuality is suggested by a performance of a masked rite among the Chokwe of central Africa, during which a male wearing the female mask of Mwana wa Pwo makes sexual advances to a female spectator.

Numerous African spiritual traditions have included androgynous or gender-diverse practitioners; among these, some also have engaged in same-sex or transgendered intimacy. One may count the *agule* of the Lugbara (Uganda), the priest(ess) of the Baganda deity Mukasa (Uganda), the *isanus* of the Xhosa (South Africa), and possibly the actual or legendary *adandara* ("wild cat") lesbian witches of the Azande as female-to-male transgender or as lesbian or bisexual. Examples of androgynous male, male-to-female transgender, and possibly homosexual or bisexual include the *isangoma* of the Zulu (these spiritual leaders may also be female and heterosexual), *omasenge kimbanda* of the Ambo, *okule* of the Lugbara, *ashtime* of the Maale (Ethiopia), *mugawe* of the Meru (Kenya), *'yan daudu* of the Hausa *bori* cult (Nigeria), *jo apele* of the Lango (Uganda), and *mwaami* of the Ila (Zambia and Zimbabwe).

Unfortunately, a lack of specificity concerning practitioners has made it difficult to determine in many instances whether certain of these figures identify as members of their original anatomical sex or as members of the sex (or gender) into which they have transformed or that they have determined to be correct; in many cases, their sexuality also remains ambiguous. These practitioners frequently have served as diviners, healers, magicians, and ritual artists (especially musicians). Apparently, it is the resemblance between the gender ambiguity of these persons and the transgender or genderless nature of the gods that qualifies them as ritual specialists, who can transgress the boundaries of the mundane world.

The *omasenge kimbanda* is exemplary of this group of specialists. The *omasenge* serves as an intercessor between the Ambo people and the supreme being Kalunga, as well as performing sacrifices, healing with herbs, practicing divination and magic, and playing a sacred stringed instrument—the *omakola*—during rituals. He (or possibly "she," depending upon one's interpretation of his or her gender) is thought to be possessed by a female spirit, wears women's clothes, and may join in marriage with a traditionally masculine male. Similarly, the *buyazi* of the Gisu (Uganda) do not complete rites of circumcision. They dress in women's clothes, adopt women's mannerisms, and perform women's ceremonial roles, such as playing drums at funerals and ritually mocking youths who are undergoing circumcision.

Also described as transgender or genderless are the *hogon* and *binukedine* priests of the Dogon. It appears that although gender fluidity is not permitted among "ordinary" women and men, who undergo clitoridectomy and circumcision to eradicate it, it is revered in spiritual leaders. The *hogon,* who serves as leader of the Lebe serpent cult and embodies the mystery of death and rebirth, is perceived as feminine and represents the maternal earth. The *binukedine,* who serves in a shamanlike capacity as a healer, diviner, sacrificer, and magician, is perceived as androgynous, and his ability to traverse boundaries is echoed in his ambiguous sexuality. These two spiritual leaders engage in a metaphoric sexual union as farmer (*binukedine,* masculine) and earth (*hogon,* feminine) in the *bulu* ritual celebrating the rebirth of the millet grain. Dagara elders Malidoma and Sobonfu Somé have suggested, somewhat controversially, that the "gatekeepers" (typically male) and "witches" (typically female), who play an essential role as facilitators of communication between the human and divine realms in the Dagara spiritual system, might be compared to present-day, spiritually grounded gay men and lesbians.

Although same-sex and transgendered intimacy are shunned in a number of African cultures and spiritual traditions, in others they are reserved for spiritual leaders, and in still others they are generally tolerated or accepted. In the Owerri Igbo *mbari* cult, these practices are associated with nightmares, goats (which are considered evil), insanity, foreigners, and the demonic phallic spirit Okpangu. The Dogon, however, seem to reserve these practices for spiritual leaders. In cultures such as the Azande, Nuer (southern Sudan), Nama(n) (Namibia), Korongo (Sudan), and Mesakin (Sudan), these practices were to some degree tolerated or even accepted, at least in the past. Among the Fanti of Ghana, an individual is thought to be attracted to men or women depending upon whether he or she is born with a "light soul" (attraction to women) or a "heavy soul" (attraction to men); thus, sexuality is almost entirely divorced from gender.

In some cultures, male-male intimacy is believed to carry a sacred energy. Among the Fang peoples (Bene, Bulu, Yaunde, and Ntumu) of Cameroon, Guinea, and Gabon, male-male intimacy is thought to promote prosperity. Among the Azande, male partners celebrate ceremonies of union that include gifts of spears and jewelry, and the partners address each other as *badiare,* "my lover." Nama(n) males, in union ceremonies called *sore' gamsa,* share coffee as a sacred beverage to strengthen their bond.

Similarly, young Buissi (Democratic Republic of the Congo) women believe that premarital lesbian relationships promote harmonious heterosexual marriages as well as fertility. Lovers are described as "those who mix their bloods and intermingle their shadows." When two Azande women wish to enter into a formal relationship, they hold a *bagburu* ceremony. This ceremony centers on a cob of red maize called *kaima,* which symbolizes blood. The women recite a love spell over the cob, after which it is planted. Their lovemaking includes the use of phalluses made of sweet potatoes, manioc root, and bananas (recalling the *nomdede* rite of Zulu women). Henceforth, the women call each other *bagburu.* In the same vein, Dagara women lovers form part of a larger women's circle that bonds them, the circle, and their ancestors for life.

Although mixed and complex attitudes concerning same-sex intimacy exist among the Yoruba, numerous priests and priestesses maintain that "the gods do not discriminate—people do." Recently, one of the most respected leaders of the Ifá tradition, *babalawó* (chief priest-diviner) and Àwise Ni Àgbáyé (spokesperson for Ifá in the world) Wande Abimbola has stated, "A *babalawó* must not impose his life on anyone. Who are we to probe into the personal life of another person?" (Abimbola 1997, 28).

## INTIMACY AND CHILDBEARING IN PRAYER, DIVINATION, SACRIFICE, HEALING, AND MAGIC

Prayer in African spiritual traditions frequently focuses on matters pertaining to intimate relationships and childbearing. Those seeking love address their prayers to amorous deities and spirits, such as the Yoruba *òrìsà* Òsun. Prayers may also be offered to deities and spirits to support harmonious relationships. Yoruba couples might pray to the compassionate aspect of Obàtálá to nurture harmonious relationships. Or they might address such a prayer to Esù, who can bring about harmony or disharmony between intimate companions.

One cannot overemphasize the importance of childbearing in African cultures and spiritual traditions; giving birth to children is revered as a sacred act. Even in those cultures in which women are not respected as equals, they are honored as mothers. Generally, infertility is regarded as a curse, and abortion is met with great disapproval, although the maternal Yoruba *òrìsà* Yemoja, in her porcupine aspect of Ika, may occasionally sanction abortions. Although menstruation is typically described among the Yoruba as a "hot" and "fiery" state of being, pregnancy (which is considered its opposite) is portrayed as "cool" and "calm." This "coolness" results in part from the male's contribution of semen—a "white" as opposed to a "red" body fluid—and in part from a "cooler" diet consisting of "white" foods, including snails. In other instances, white is associated with female divinities and ancestral spirits of water, and it is aquatic feminine energy that ushers in the "cool" state of pregnancy. Among the Dogon, although menstruation has been compared metaphorically to "bad words," pregnancy has been compared to "good words."

Women wishing to bear children habitually pray to divinities and spirits of the waters, such as the Igbo goddesses (or aspects of a "great goddess") Ogbuide, Uhammiri, Ava, and Nne Mmiri; Mami Wata of Togo and Benin; or the Yoruba *òrìsà* Yemoja, the "Mother of the Waters." Women may also offer prayers to divinities of the earth and agriculture, such as the Igbo goddess Ale (or Ala), the Baga goddess Nimba (of Guinea, Guinea-Bissau, and Sierra Leone), and the Yoruba *òrìsàs* Onilé (the "Owner of the Earth") and Odùdúwà. Zulu women pray to the "heavenly princess" Nomkhubulwana to become mothers, asking especially for large breasts to better nourish their infants. These female divinities, it should be noted, not only promote fertility but also frequently hold the power to shape or alter destiny and to take away life.

Males who suffer from impotence may also offer prayers to deities, such as to the Yoruba *òrìsà* Esù, who controls potency. Yorubas also address prayers to Ògún to protect women from having miscarriages. Affirmation chants are linked to such prayers: "See a lot of children behind me, see a lot of children behind me."

Divination is among the most significant elements of African spiritual traditions. The Ifá oracle of the Yoruba—one of the richest African spiritual texts in terms of its insight, poetry, and complexity, comparable in scope to the *I Ching*—is associated with 256 divinatory signs, many of which signify courtship, marital relationships, fertility, and childbearing. *Odùs,* particular oracular signs with accompanying proverbs and tales, typically culminate with a strong suggestion to offer a particular sacrifice

if one wishes to see the negative aspects of one's life experience transformed. The Osémèjì suggests that those wishing to attract a lover or
spouse should make sacrifices to Òsun, the patron of sensuous love.
Occasionally, *odùs* aid in the selection of the best among potential partners, as with the *odù* Ogbèwónrí. *Odùs* such as Otúrá-àikú also warn
against entering into potentially disastrous relationships. Sacrifices need
to be made, OtúráKònràn reveals, to oust rivals. Ogúndá-Bàrà encourages husbands to make sacrifices so that their wives will not become
bored and wish to leave them. Wives may make sacrifices, Ofún-
Otúrúpòn suggests, if they wish to prevent their husbands from behaving violently toward them. Idí' bàrà, Otúrúpòn' Rosù, Otúrá-Irosù,
Owónrín-Egúntán, and Ofún-Túrá recommend sacrifices in order to
prevent arguments and enhance harmony between a couple.

The *odù* Oyèkúmèjì cautions against polygyny, warning that jealousy
among wives may lead to disaster. Ikáméjì cautions against adultery on
the part of the wife, encouraging the husband to sacrifice two cobra
heads and a rope in order to prevent this transgression; it seems that
adultery may be linked to witchcraft in this *odù*. The *odùs* Oyèkú
Wónrín and Owónrín Yèkú indicate that if individuals who have committed adultery do not confess and make sacrifices, they will die. Obàrà'
dí, as mentioned above, encourages prostitutes to give up their profession and reform themselves.

Iká Yèkú, an *odù* addressing fertility and childbearing, lists the sacrifices that a husband must make and a ritual bath he must take in order
to overcome sterility. Idíméjì and Irosùméjì suggest that a woman desperate to become a mother must sacrifice to the *òrìsà* Orúnmìlà, the
deity of divination. Owòrì-Osé suggests that even an older woman who
has ceased menstruating may transform her condition through sacrifice
and medicines and thus bear a child or continue to bear children.
Miscarriages and premature deaths of infants may be avoided, according
to the *odùs* Iwòrì' túrúpòn, Owónrín-Otúrúpòn, and Obàràtúrúpòn, by
way of sacrifices and a special fish and herbal soup.

Sacrifices aimed at finding a lover or spouse, aiding fertility, becoming pregnant, and bearing healthy offspring include cotton, cowries
(sometimes tens of thousands of them), fish, goats (especially female
ones), hens, pieces of cloth (especially knotted or white cloth), pigeons,
rams, rats, shea butter, sheep, snails (it is said that "two snails never
clash"), and yams. Occasionally, *odùs* prescribe medicines to aid fertility
and childbearing, often in the form of beverages, soups, or baths, the

primary ingredients of which are sacred leaves, hen's blood, cloves, eggs, and—for baths—black soap.

Just as it is rather difficult to disentangle divination from sacrifice in African spiritual traditions, it is sometimes difficult to demarcate sharply the boundaries between sacrificial and magical operations in these traditions. Rather than emphasizing the placation of a divine being who might grant one's wishes, African magical practices generally involve an individual or group acting in accordance with or against the wishes of divinities or spirits to transform a situation. Moreover, magical operations are sometimes difficult to distinguish from operations described as medical. And as with divination and sacrifice, magical and medical operations often pertain to sexuality and reproduction.

Generally speaking, medical or magical operations undertaken by males are regarded with less suspicion than those undertaken by women because women practicing traditional medicine or magic are frequently suspected of being witches. Unlike contemporary Wiccans and neopagans and rather more like Laguna Puebloans and other indigenous peoples of the American Southwest, the practitioners of African spiritual traditions tend to view witchcraft primarily in negative terms, opposing it to "medicine." In recent years, however, some practitioners and scholars have suggested that the conception of women's witchcraft as evil may have arisen from the fear of women's spiritual power and from a more generalized awe of elder women. Although individuals do not as a rule admit to being witches, many practitioners of African spiritual traditions feel certain that witches exist. Many, such as the Yoruba, tend to believe that witches (*ajè*) possess supernatural powers, such as the ability to transform themselves into birds and fly about at night performing works of magic, unnoticed and far from their homes. It is thought that witches inherit their powers from certain divinities. Among the Yoruba, these include Esù, Yemoja, and Oya. Witchcraft arose, some believe, as a result of men's abuse of women. Some say that witches work magic with the menstrual blood and pubic hair of other women and that they may borrow a man's penis as he sleeps in order to enjoy sex with it or to use it for sex with another sleeping mortal, presumably another woman.

In many African cultures, in which childbearing is celebrated as one of a woman's greatest accomplishments, a woman's inability to bear children is regarded as a curse. In certain instances, barrenness signals that a woman is being punished by a deity or deities or by powerful ancestral spirits because she committed serious transgressions in a former lifetime. It also may signal that she is being punished by practitioners of traditional medicine for transgressions in this life. In still other cases, barrenness may be attributed to negative witchcraft. (Ironically, infertile women also are frequently suspected of being witches.) Barrenness may be induced, for instance, by placing cursed salt inside a coconut and then placing the coconut in a tree haunted by witches, by placing an image of the woman in a haunted tree, and by casting an image of the woman or a piece of her clothing bound to "medicines" into the bush. Incidentally, pregnant women also are thought to be preyed upon by witches, as well as by the spirits of deceased children who wish to displace the spirit of the child growing in the womb.

In some instances, barrenness brought about by such means may be healed through the sacrifices suggested by divinatory consultations. The *odùs* Okanranmeji and Iwòrì' rosù suggest that rubbing ritually prepared camwood paste on a woman's belly or all over her body may nurture pregnancy and ease parturition. Later, the mother will be encouraged to rub camwood paste on her newborn's body to support his or her growth and health. Similarly, *oloiboni,* the Masai elder women acting as priestesses, prepare honey mead for women desiring children and smear honey on the bodies of pregnant women. To the Masai, honey possesses magical power linked not only to fertility but also to clairvoyance.

Childbearing also may be encouraged through the magical use of sacred dolls. In many African spiritual traditions—including those of the Ambo (Angola and Namibia), Asante (Ghana), Balante (Guinea-Bissau, Guinea, Senegal), Bamana (Republic of Mali), Fali (Cameroon), Gcaleka (South Africa), Igbo, Landuma (Guinea-Bissau), Mossi, Ndebele, Sotho (Kingdom of Lesotho and elsewhere in southern Africa), Swazi, Tabwa, Tsonga (Mozambique, Zimbabwe, Swaziland, South Africa), Turkana (Kenya and Sudan), Xhosa (South Africa), Zaramo (or Wazaramo, Tanzania), and Zulu—young women are given ritually prepared dolls, which they must regard as living entities prefiguring their future children. Called by names like *mwana hiti* (in Zaramo, "wooden child"), *wa udongo* (in Tabwa, "earthen children"), and *di kori* (in Landuma, "son of bone") and believed to possess spiritual force, these dolls are fed, bathed, dressed, given gifts (including money), and often carried on the woman's body until the birth of her child, after which they are kept in an honored place.

Among the Azande, men frequently practice traditional medicine, magic, and what some have described as witchcraft. Their actions often focus on sexuality and include enhancing sexual prowess, healing impotence, and taking vengeance on other males who might engage in intercourse with their wives. To increase sexual drive and especially to achieve long-lasting erections, they tie *gbaga,* the fruit of the palm tree, to their waists and pray, "You are *gbaga.* May I be very potent sexually." To cure impotence, or *imazigba,* a man may rub his penis with a ritually prepared ointment, which is believed to transform magically into seminal fluid and restore potency. To punish an adulterer, after eating an antidote and surreptitiously having his wife do the same, a man might rub his penis with a substance made of *moti,* a purple-flowered plant believed to produce venereal disease, so that any man having sexual contact with his wife might become infected and perish. Deeply concerned with male beauty, Wodaabe men powder their faces with a mixture containing dried chameleon, which is thought to enhance attractiveness magically. For the same reason, they wear leather pouches around their necks containing seeds, roots, and barks deemed to exert magical influence.

One of the most intriguing tales of erotic attraction and love in African magic is told in the Yoruba *odù* Ofún-Egúntán. King Onibara fell madly in love with a mysterious woman who came from far away. Jealous of her beauty, many warned the king not to marry her because she was a prostitute. He paid no heed to their warnings, however. Shortly after they were married, the king's new wife explained that her diet consisted solely of meat. The king provided her with all the meat in the palace and then all of the meat from neighboring households. When, despite his position, his subjects had begun to call him a thief, he decided to take a potion that would enable him to transform into a tiger. Each night, in the tiger's form, he hunted meat for his beloved wife. One night while hunting, however, he was fatally wounded. The next morning, the king's body was found wrapped in a tiger's skin. The people then slew the queen, terminating this tale of magic, meat, and obsessive love.

## DREAM LOVERS AND SPIRITUAL UNIONS

Erotic dreams of mortal lovers are as common among Africans as others, but their dreams may also include unions with deities and spirits. The Baule of the Côte d'Ivoire share intimate relationships not only with human partners but also with *blolo,* "otherworld" partners. Each person is thought to have either a *blolo bian,* an otherworldly male lover, or a *blolo bla,* an otherworldly female lover. These partners are ranked above one's mortal partners and are encountered primarily in dreams and by way of statuettes called *waka sran*. These statuettes are fashioned in response to dream descriptions and divinatory consultations. Comparable in some respects to fertility dolls, *waka sran* are considered living entities. Once ritually seated in one's home, they must be saluted, fed, and caressed, as *blolo* lovers can bring prosperity or disaster, depending upon the respect and reverence they are given.

Many Africans participate not only in initiatory rites of passage but also in spiritual initiations into religions or cults. Spiritual initiations are frequently described in terms relating to intimacy, loving, and sexual relationships. Both female and male initiates may be called "brides" of the god(s) and the deity referred to as "husband and lord." As brides, initiates wear traditional women's attire. In the Sàngó cult of the Yoruba, prior to the male initiate's first public appearance as a member of the priesthood, he enters a dance in which the gestures and movements of other priests may include allusions to sexual intercourse. When a priest or priestess is possessed by the deity, he or she is described as being "mounted" by the god.

Beyond this type of spiritual union exists another that may bear an even closer resemblance to erotic relationships: that between a worshipper and a god/dess. This type of union—which one finds especially in the Mami Wata cult of Togo and Benin and which has become increasingly central in the African-diasporic religion of Vodou—may even be formalized with an elaborate ceremony, complete with marriage contract. Included in this contract is an agreement that the worshipper must periodically abstain from sexual relations with his or her mortal partner to be ready to receive his divine partner. The worshipper typically creates a shrine in which this divine union may occur. As with Baule *blolo* dream lovers, these relationships must be taken very seriously, since they may engender prosperity or disaster.

Among the Ijo-speaking people of the Niger River Delta, women who experience problems with relationships, fertility, illness, finances, and other matters have traditionally wed one of the deities or spirits of the waters, such as the male spirit Anji. To him, the lover chants:

Pulling riches from the sea, my waterspirit lover
gently, gently drawing nearer to me

Anji, we cannot resist you, you are too handsome
We lust for you, lust for you, lust for you. (Gleason 1994, 184)

## CONCLUSION

African spiritual traditions rely upon a cornucopia of symbols signifying gender and sexuality. Many of them are taken from nature, to celebrate the richness of existence in all its complexity. Expressions of the divine in many African spiritual traditions also reflect this complexity. Rites of passage, including marriage rites and initiations into spiritual life, enhance participants' awareness of the sacred dimensions and purposes of gender and sexuality. Prayer, divination, sacrifice, healing, and magic nurture human-divine interaction. A number of African traditions pay special homage to women—particularly as mothers—and accept diverse expressions of gender and sexuality as divinely sanctioned, in some cases granting special roles to persons we might today call "lesbian," "gay," "bisexual," or "transgender." Of all intimate relationships in indigenous African spiritual life, however, it is perhaps the union with an otherworldly or divine companion that is most cherished.

Although Christianity has been practiced in Africa since the era of Roman occupation and Islam has been a significant presence since the ninth century C.E., African indigenous religions were not threatened with extinction until the eighteenth and nineteenth centuries, which saw massive and tremendously violent efforts to convert Africans to these faiths. Beliefs and practices cherished by many Africans for thousands of years have since been denigrated and demonized. This process is especially evident where beliefs and practices regarding sexuality and gender are concerned. In Christianity and Islam, the divine is envisioned as masculine or—rarely—as a genderless being; feminine or androgynous/transgendered depictions of the divine have no place. Furthermore, gender diversity and same-sex intimacy are rarely tolerated by Muslims and Christians. As a result, the spiritual authority of women in African cultures has decreased dramatically and that of transgendered or same-sex-loving individuals has all but vanished. Divination and magic, which often pertain to matters of sexuality, loving relationships, childbearing, and (in the case of magic) women's mysteries, are condemned.

Despite the broad Christianization and Islamicization of Africa, however, many ancient beliefs and practices persist. Certain African spiritual traditions, such as those rooted in Yoruba and Fon cultures, have continued to thrive and might even be said to be experiencing a renaissance today, not only in West Africa but also in Cuba (Santería, Regla de Ocha, Lucumí, Ifá), Brazil (Candomblé, Macumba, Umbanda), Haiti (Vodou), the United States (all of the aforementioned), and other parts of the world. Notably, these "New World" expressions of African spiritual traditions grant women heightened spiritual authority and frequently embrace lesbian, gay, and bisexual practitioners.

## NOTES

1. A butterlike substance made from the kernels of an indigenous African tree, which is used in cooking, soap, and medicine.
2. A ritual concoction made from the bark of the *Baphia nitida,* also used in dyeing and cabinet making.
3. I should note that many of my examples will derive from the Yoruba, for several reasons. First, many informants speak English, and many texts concerning the Yoruba have been written in English. Additionally, because of slavery, the religion of the Yoruba was carried to the Americas and continues to be practiced today. Much of what is said about African religion in this chapter is based on my own research as a participant-observer in this spiritual tradition.
4. In Yoruba spiritual texts, they are not always considered husband and wife.

## REFERENCES

Abimbola, Wande. 1997. *Ifa Will Mend Our Broken World: Thoughts on Yoruba Religion and Culture in Africa and the Diaspora.* Roxbury, MA: Aim Books.

Amadiume, Ifi. 1987. *Male Daughters, Female Husbands: Gender and Sex in African Society.* London: Zed.

Beckwith, Carol, and Angela Fisher. 1999. *African Ceremonies.* New York: Harry N. Abrams.

Beier, Ulli, ed. 1970. *Yoruba Poetry: An Anthology of Traditional Poems.* Cambridge, MA: Cambridge University Press.

Epega, Afolabi A., and Philip John Neimark. 1995. *The Sacred Ifa Oracle.* San Francisco: HarperSan Francisco.

Gleason, Judith. 1994. *Leaf and Bone: African Praise-Poems.* 2nd ed. New York: Penguin Books.

Griaule, Marcel. 1975. *Conversations with Ogotemmêli: An Introduction to Dogon Religious Ideas.* Ralph Butler, trans. New York: Oxford University Press.

Murray, Stephen O., and Will Roscoe, eds. 1998. *Boy-Wives and Female-Husbands: Studies in African Homosexualities*. New York: St. Martin's Press.

Olupona, Jacob K., ed. 2000. *African Spirituality: Forms, Meanings, and Expressions*. New York: Crossroad.

Oyěwùmí Oyèrónké. 1997. *The Invention of Women: Making an African Sense of Western Gender Discourses*. Minneapolis: University of Minnesota Press.

# Chapter 2

# Gender, Sexuality, and the Balance of Power in Native American Worldviews

*Julianne Cordero and
Elizabeth Currans*

*Claudia Griggs is painted by her godfather, Roland White, during her Sunrise Dance in East Fork, Arizona, 2001. The painting ceremony marks the moment when she officially becomes a woman in the Apache tribe. Today, many Native American women and their families recognize a woman's time of power and practice the ceremonies observed by their nation. (AP/Wide World Photos)*

Imagine living in a world where respect for an individual's contributions to society is built into the society's worldview. Imagine living in a society in which this respect and acceptance is such a natural part of the social fabric that it is not necessary to have a category for "civil rights." Imagine being profoundly surprised to find out that there are societies whose worldviews are built on the domination and subordination of women; people of color; and lesbian, gay, bisexual, transgendered, intersexed, and queer (LGBTIQ) people.

The physical and ideological collision between the indigenous peoples of the North American continent and Christian European colonists was a clash of historic proportions, one that continues to be deeply felt—and constantly reexperienced—in North America today. As indigenous people change and adopt new strategies for dealing with modernity, traditional Native American values and practices of respect for each other and for the natural world remain central parts of their worldviews. Also strongly expressed is the ongoing Native resistance to the colonial superstructures that continue to destroy Native homelands and systematically disrespect and disenfranchise Native people. The lands have been drastically altered; naturally, the people of these lands have also been severely affected, but nevertheless they have had a strong hand in creating change that will ensure indigenous survival in modern times.

Many modern Native Americans express a complex mix of traditional indigenous cultural beliefs and practices; western religions, education, and consumer economics; intertribal cultural sharing; and respect for many of the peoples from around the world who have immigrated here. For most indigenous North American cultures, precontact traditions of respect for men, women, and two-spirit people (people believed to possess aspects of both genders or "spirits") are not the same as they once were, even though those cultures still observe ancestral traditions regarding the powerful roles played by women and two-spirit people in both precontact and contemporary indigenous settings.

This mixture of traditional with western belief systems has been enormously problematic for many indigenous peoples. One system represents, generally speaking, sophisticated understandings of the interconnectedness of all life, in which matter is constantly moving and changing according to a system of reciprocal checks and balances. The other system, speaking generally again, has its roots in the dualist, rationalist worldviews that developed in Europe during the Protestant Reformation, the Scientific Revolution, the Enlightenment, and the Industrial Revolution and have since permeated the world's ideas of reality. It would be tempting to try to categorize the varying degrees to which Native American people have embodied "traditional values" or "western values," but to do so would blind one to the fluidity of contemporary identity—both Native and non-Native—as expressed by women and two-spirit people.

Native American women and two-spirit people often operate under different conceptions of power, agency, and identity than those generally recognized in mainstream North American societies. Many traditionalist Native American women and two-spirit people look to the holistic inclusion of all genders that is instilled by traditional indigenous values. In order to discuss Native American women's power and the gender roles performed by indigenous women and two-spirit men and women, it is therefore necessary to include a discussion of the ways in which many traditional, indigenous male roles reciprocate female roles. Western ideas of sexuality tend to emphasize mainly who is having sex with whom and why, which can obscure the important place of gender in interpersonal relationships in traditional Native American societies. This procreation-based focus on sexuality is also considered an invasion of privacy by many contemporary Native American women and therefore is not discussed in this chapter.

Much of the previous scholarship on indigenous women's sexuality was produced under conditions of exploitation and gross misinterpretation by mostly non-Native scholars. For this reason and for the reasons described above, in this chapter we will shift the focus slightly in order to provide an overview of existing scholarship on Native American conceptions of power, reciprocity, and balance in the roles performed by women and two-spirit people. These views form the basis for ideals of social harmony between the genders in traditional American Indian societies, ideals that are religious or spiritual in nature. In many indigenous traditions, as in Western society, cultural roles are informed by religious or spiritual beliefs. As mentioned above, the Protestant Reformation deeply informed changes in the scientific and economic foundations of the Western world. The dualist ideals that crystallized during this period created a social climate in which women, people of color, and non-heterosexuals were assigned statuses in opposition to the "norm," the white, Protestant, capitalist, heterosexual male. Describing this dualist worldview in 1949, Simone de Beauvoir wrote, "all who inhabit other countries are 'foreigners'; Jews are 'different' for the anti-Semite, Negroes [*sic*] are 'inferior' for American racists, aborigines are 'natives' for colonists, proletarians are the 'lower class' for the privileged" (Beauvoir 1961, xxiii). Women, in this modern European spin on reality, are designated not merely as half of humanity, but as the decidedly inferior half.

In most indigenous American Indian religious worldviews, women were and are seen as representations of the female aspect of the divine: not inferior or superior to but *in balance with* the male aspect. Socially, indigenous nations such as the Delaware of what is now Pennsylvania "*generically* referred to themselves as 'women,' considering the term to be supremely complementary" (Jaimes and Halsey 1992, 317). Although most Native North American nations did not use this particular linguistic designation, instead employing gender-neutral pronouns, the respect accorded women was exemplified in other significant ways:

> While patrilineal/patrilocal cultures did exist, most precontact North American civilizations functioned on the basis of matrilineage and matrilocality. Insofar as family structures centered upon the identities of wives rather than husbands—men joined women's families, not the other way around—and because men were usually expected to relocate to join the women they married, the context of Native social life was radically different from that which prevailed (and prevails) in European and Euro-derived cultures. (Jaimes and Halsey 1992, 138)

In many of these societies, people who possessed traits or "spirits" of both genders, although fairly rare, were seen as a natural part of the world and thus were accorded levels of status and respect in their respective nations.

Since 1492, the year Christopher Columbus first encountered the original peoples and lands of the Americas, European economic expansion fueled and justified by Christianity and the ideals of Manifest Destiny has permeated the social and economic climate of the world. The ability of indigenous nations to accord status and respect to their members has been severely compromised by the genocidal tides of Western colonization. In the wake of this ongoing destruction, Native Americans, who have been profoundly affected by the changes in the land and the murder of millions of indigenous people, not only have survived but continue to improvise new strategies for survival, including the recontextualization of traditional values. Much has been written on the self-conscious renewal and recreation of contemporary cultural practices by American Indian people. However, it has only been in the last decades of the twentieth century that researchers (particularly American Indian scholars) have attempted to present these sophisticated, nondual socioreligious worldviews in their full complexity. In this chapter we will present a brief overview of some of the traditional conceptions of power, respect, and balance in Native American understandings of gender and sexuality, in both precontact cultures and the adaptations of those traditions by modern indigenous peoples. We will also discuss briefly the loss of traditional values of respect and reciprocity in some contemporary Native American communities.

## EXPLANATION OF TERMS

In the course of this chapter, we use a number of specialized terms: worldview(s), gender identity, gender role, gender status, LGBTIQ, American Indian, Native American, indigenous North American, First Nations, and Native North American. A brief definition of each follows.

When discussing the beliefs, practices, and traditions of the numerous cultures that call the continent now known as North America their home, it is useful to use the term *worldview.* This word refers to an individual's or a group's general outlook on the world; it is useful when discussing Native American communities because they do not separate the spheres understood as "religious" and "secular" in contemporary Euro-

American terms. Because all aspects of life were and are understood by traditional Native Americans to be interrelated, it is difficult to identify what is meant when someone discusses Native American "religions." In this chapter, we use the term *worldview* to acknowledge the connection between all aspects of culture.

Three terms are useful in understanding how gender functions within a culture: *gender identity, gender role,* and *gender status.* Throughout this chapter, we use Sabine Lang's definitions of these terms: "gender identity [is] the subjective, felt perception of gender membership on the part of the individual; gender role [is] the outward expression of this perception; and gender status [is] the social position assigned to the individual by that person's culture" (Lang 1998, 50). In the latter part of the chapter, we examine gender-role crossing and gender-role change. Gender-role change refers to giving up the responsibilities and privileges of the gender role associated with one's biological sex in exchange for the responsibilities and privileges of the gender role associated with the other sex. Gender-role crossing, however, refers to the performance of some of the responsibilities and privileges of the gender role associated with the other sex without a complete role and status change.

*LGBTIQ* is an acronym that stands for "lesbian, gay, bisexual, transgender (people who undergo gender-role changes), intersexed (people born with both male and female genitalia), and queer." Because it is an umbrella term, it does obscure very important differences between communities, identities, and political agendas. However, since these differences and the political and cultural dynamics that underlie them are beyond the scope of this chapter, we use the umbrella term for convenience and brevity.

There has been considerable argument in recent years over the correct term to use when discussing the indigenous people of the North American continent. Many Native people, including indigenous scholars (and more than a few non-Native scholars) objected to the use of "American Indian." The latter word of that term has perhaps caused the most confusion because it resulted directly from the ignorance of Christopher Columbus, who, having arrived at the homeland of the Taino people—an area now known as Cuba—thought that he had found the western route to India. This term has become increasingly problematic as more and more American Indians and East Indians have become neighbors, friends, and colleagues—although most treat the confusion with some measure of ironic amusement. The word *America* comes from the Italian explorer Amerigo Vespucci, who explored the South American coast from 1499 to 1504. The issues surrounding the dispute over these terms focus on European explorers' tendency to impose their own names on people and places that already had established names and histories (Grounds 2001, 287). Many indigenous people consider this an act of dominance and control and point to the arrogance and violence of the invaders as they worked to eradicate indigenous names, histories, and presence in the land that the colonists claimed.

In response to this act of dominance, Native people of different regions have taken action to determine for themselves what they would like to be called. In Canada, most indigenous peoples refer to themselves as First Nations people, in recognition of the primacy of their residence in that land. The name also reflects an ongoing struggle for the return of their sovereign territories. In the United States, many refer to the original peoples of this land as Native Americans. The usage of that term is mixed fairly equally with the term *American Indian.* Most Native people in the United States simply call themselves and each other Indians. In Mexico, as in the United States and Canada, indigenous people still battle with severe racial prejudice and persecution. To be called an *Indio* or even a Mestiza (literally "mixed," a term that refers to people of both indigenous and European heritage) is considered by many to be a grave insult. However, many of the first peoples of Mexico are strong nations, despite the harsh racial and economic persecution they suffer at the hands of the Mexican government and private corporations. *Indio* is now, for many indigenous people of Mexico, a term of pride, as is Mestiza. In this chapter, we use all of these terms—Indians, Native Americans, First Nations people, indigenous people, Native North Americans, and Native people—interchangeably, reflecting the practices of the indigenous peoples themselves.

## GENDER AND POWER IN NATIVE NORTH AMERICA

It is important for the reader to consider that the cultures we discuss here and the men and women who embody them are changing even as we speak—many of them rapidly—and therefore generally resist systematic categorization. Native American women have always defied historical attempts to categorize, typify, or otherwise simplify their complex and enormously diverse lifeways. The views reflected here—even when ascribed to a specific indigenous group—do not necessarily reflect the views of all members of that group. Any attempt to learn or write about "the Native American woman" would be tantamount to reducing all the cultures of China, Europe, or Russia to one single female destined forever to represent billions of women from many distinctive cultures. Yet such a reduced image of woman does indeed confront scholars of Native North American cultures in the stereotypes of the "drudge," "squaw," or "digger" on the one hand and Disney's sexually idealized "Pocahontas" character on the other. Most Native women who live in modern Native cultures informed by ancient traditions of respect for women as real human beings live at neither dehumanized extreme.

Tasks associated with female gender roles are typically devalued in Western mainstream culture. Caring for children, staying at home, and manufacturing household items and clothing (which do not, in fact, comprise all facets of women's work in Native North America) are seen as mundane and inferior in the western European worldview. Masculine tasks, such as hunting, fishing, doing battle, and participating in political activity, are glorified by Western cultures, which emphasize domination and control.

Gender roles typically associated with females in Native North America were and are considered powerful within the context of indigenous understandings of power. The ability to work and live sustainably as an integral part of an ecosystem requires rigorous attention to the rules of that system. People who have great skill in listening to, watching, sensing, and remaining open to the mysterious changes in the natural world are more likely to be able to interact productively with it and thereby refine their people's ability to survive and thrive. Because animals, plants, and even minerals exhibit the highest level of innate skill in this regard, they are respected by Native American people. Many indigenous people consider these entities to be nations of *people* (Hallowell 1975, 141–178) who are older, more experienced, and therefore more knowledgeable about how to live in this world than humans. In Native North America, humans who are able to learn from the elder species about how to be productive in a manner that can be sustained indefinitely and can understand these lessons and teach them to others are seen as having special spiritual and intellectual powers and nurturing abilities. These knowledgeable humans are important members of a sustainable biotic community—a community that includes humans but in which humans are not necessary to the survival of other species. Indigenous human power develops through joining forces with nature rather than in overpowering or subduing it, which is seen as counterproductive to human usefulness and survival.

Although the first European settlers thought of women's food-gathering activities as evidence of their cultural backwardness and mental simplicity (Hurtado 1988, 172), Native American women have long maintained intimate and sophisticated relationships with the huge variety of species of plants and animals that live alongside their families in Native homelands. As naturalists trained in traditions thousands of years long, indigenous women use their intellect and skills to provide food, building and tool materials, and a vast, refined array of medicinal plants for the sustenance of their families. As the suppliers of usually more than half the food supply and materials for trade, women played a fundamental role in traditional economies.

From this perspective, gender roles act as means to power, a power that is defined in many indigenous languages differently from the ways in which it is defined and acted upon in English. In Western cultures power is understood in the sense of domination, but in many indigenous American cultures power is understood as power *with,* rather than power *over.* In the Barbareño Chumash language of central California, the word for power is *'atïswïn,* which means both to heal and to poison.[1] *'Atïswïn* is also the word for a power object that has been prayed for and meditated upon by a person seeking spiritual assistance in his or her life. This conception of power can also be seen in the properties of many medicinal plants, such as tobacco and datura, both of which are used to treat arthritis pain, fight infection, and heal wounds but are also highly toxic members of the nightshade family.

When the people are hungry, a Chumash person with strong *'atïswïn,* will skillfully provide and prepare an abundant variety of high-quality plant and animal food. When families are exposed to the elements, a person's *'atïswïn,* is again demonstrated as he or she helps provide sustainably gathered building materials and well-crafted clothing. Those with extraordinarily refined relationships with these natural materials rise to positions of great respect among the people of their area through their artistry, including brilliantly dyed, tightly woven woolen blankets, perfectly symmetrical pottery, complicated bead- and quillwork on buttery soft animal hides, and watertight baskets woven with designs of stunning geometric complexity.

Also held in high esteem are the people whose dreams and knowledge of hundreds of species of plants and understandings of health within a cosmologically balanced life path guide them to heal the sick. Many of these medicine specialists are also feared for their ability to inflict harm and illness, even over long distances (Margolin 1981, 93–99). In northern California, the most powerful doctors are predominantly women, who receive early dreams and visions of their coming gifts. The physical manifestations of a doctor's healing powers are called "pains" among the Yurok (Margolin 1981, 93–99; Kroeber 1953, 117). Many of the women doctors are guided throughout their lives by a voice, which instructs them during their cures. Although there are still many women healers in Native California, less common today are the specialists known as "sucking doctors." Mabel McKay, a much-beloved woman doctor among the Pomo of northern California, told this story of her powerful guide's instructions on how to perform a sucking cure:

> Once, while she was singing over a woman from Colusa, she found herself unable to extract the pain in the woman's chest. Her hand had located the pain, what the spirit described as a tiny spotted fish, but she was unable to pull it up, out of the woman. "Now you have to use your mouth," the spirit said as Mabel sang. "How am I going to use my mouth?" she asked. The spirit said: "Your throat has been fixed for many years. Now it's ready to use. And that basket you completed a while back, that spitting-out-sickness-basket at your side, it's ready too. It's hungry. . . . The song has put the little fish to sleep. Take it out with your mouth. . . ." And Mabel took the fish into her throat and coughed it out into the basket. The Colusa woman was healed that way. (Sarris 1994, 94)

These indigenous women doctors are so powerful that many of their people believe that their passing from this life can alter weather patterns.

However, even women without extraordinary doctoring abilities are considered to have special powers. Feeding, clothing, sheltering, curing with plants, and using one's artistic skill and political and organizational savvy were and are considered healing medicines among indigenous North American people.

A contemporary indigenous woman's knowledge of how to interact with the land as she cultivates and gathers materials—and with the people who rely on these materials through trade relationships—is the central strength around which all her cultural activities revolve. "We take from the earth. We give back to the earth. We say thank you," says Julia Parker of the Yosemite Mewok/Kashaya Lake Pomo people of northern

California (Ortiz 1991, 5). Performed today in nearly all areas of Native North America, this reciprocal give-and-take goes far beyond the traditional practice of leaving an offering of tobacco whenever a plant, animal, or mineral is taken for the people's use. It also means continuing the intimate, interspecies relationships that have been carefully cultivated over thousands of years by previous generations. In more concrete terms, it means using methods of agriculture, wild plant harvest, materials collection, and hunting that not only do not degrade an area but have a nurturing, positive influence on the ecosystem. One of the more striking examples is the use of controlled burns to stimulate the growth of certain plants used for food, medicine, animal forage, and habitat, as well as to keep the ground clear of fuel that can cause a fire to explode into a more devastating burn. Also practiced throughout North America are methods for digging roots, bulbs, corms, and tubers that aerate the soil and dramatically increase the yield of useful plants—a yield that benefits all the animals that use those plants, including humans. Taking nature's cue, the women know when and how to clip, prune, thin, aerate, replant, and burn. When indigenous women conduct their gathering rounds, visiting the places their mothers, grandmothers, and great-grandmothers' great-grandmothers visited and loved, when they do their women's work gathering food and medicine for the people, the land responds with a great, easily gathered bounty of delicious food, strong medicine, and quality crafting materials. A reciprocal relationship with nature—never taking more than one gives—is the key.

The principle of reciprocity also characterizes relationships between sexes and genders, wherein people's contributions to their society are recognized and returned in kind. When one understands some of the philosophies and methods behind indigenous North American gender roles, it is easier to see why feminine tasks were not devalued among Native Americans as the work of a subservient class. Europeans who first encountered indigenous women at their work coined racial slurs such as "squaw drudge" and "digger," the latter term being used by California settlers to denigrate the women's job of digging for bulbs, roots, and tubers with a specially designed digging stick. Quite the contrary, women's relationship to the land expressed a sophisticated, socioreligious model of sustainable economy that was in place for thousands of years.

The health of the homelands of Native Americans is intrinsic to the health of modern Native identity, family, and cultural practices. When the traditional homeland of an Indigenous nation is destroyed by development or the industrial extraction of natural resources, it not only violates the cultural and subsistence rights of that nation but infringes on religious freedom because of its devastating impact on Native women's and men's ability to sustain culturally constructed gender roles that were formed in relation to the spiritual interaction with the natural landscape. Many indigenous peoples draw ideological parallels between the destruction of the land and the domination of women.

Ironically, an increasing number of the descendants of European settlers are now looking to indigenous women to help them learn about the complexities of living in harmony with an ecosystem. Beverly Ortiz, an anthropologist who works closely with California Indian women, respectfully explains that prior to colonization, "California was truly a garden, nurtured and loved for generation after generation—not the wilderness many newcomers were so quick to label it" (1991, 5).

### Native Women Leaders

When Spanish explorer Juan Cabrillo first encountered the Chumash of the South Coast of California, he and his men were greeted warmly and hospitably by scores of swift Chumash canoes, called *tomol*s, loaded with gifts of food, fresh water, and finely made art items. The chief of the large trade village Syuxtun, now called Santa Barbara, climbed aboard Cabrillo's ship and extended formal welcome to the Spanish explorers. The Spanish descriptions of the chief, who, as the leader of a center of trade, held great influence up and down the coast, range from admiration to utter astonishment and outright disgust. Imagine their surprise at being welcomed by the sovereign leader of a powerful nation—a woman, and a mostly naked, brown woman, at that.

The name of that chief—or *wot,* in the Barbareño Chumash language—was not recorded by the Spanish explorers, but much ethnographic and ethnohistoric data suggests that powerful women chiefs among the Chumash were not uncommon. A hereditary post of immense responsibility, the position of chief usually passed from father to son, but daughters of Chumash chiefs who exhibited skill at accounting or trade, a sharp sense of protocol for intervillage relationships, and a well-developed sense of humility and service to their people could be chosen for the responsibilities of leadership by their people and by the chief's cabinet of advisers. One notable Chumash woman chief was Luhui, who was not only a village head but was also the regional *wot* for all four islands of the Santa Barbara Channel, an important network of villages and shipping ports (Hudson and Underhay 1978, 17). Ethnographic accounts collected in the early twentieth century suggest that she was in power at the time of the Spanish conquest and that she was privy to advance council regarding the coming of the Europeans as well as to the devastation that would follow. Against all odds, Luhui is still today a potent role model for Chumash girls and women, who continue—simultaneously in resistance to and in accordance with the mainstream culture—to influence events, public policy and opinion, and cultural continuity in California's south coast.

Luhui was just one of numerous influential women in Native North America. Among many East Coast and southern nations, elderly women have traditionally formed the backbone of their democratic governing processes. So influential were these councils of clan mothers that no important decisions would be made without their deliberation and recommendation. In the event of the death of a head chief of the Choctaw Nation—virtually always a man—a vice chief would take his place until the people could assemble to select a new leader. However, because of the influence of the women, "the vice-chief was not necessarily the one chosen. It is said that if the women wanted a certain chief he was almost certain of election" (Swanton 1995, 101). On certain occasions, women would stand and speak for the people. "If the head chief or captain died suddenly and the vice-chief could not be present at an assembly which had already been summoned, the wife of the deceased took his place and spoke for him, she having been kept informed by him of any business in hand" (101).

Political influence and leadership are not outside the sphere of Native American feminine tasks. In Native America today, indigenous women continue to form the backbone, flesh, and blood of the 500-year resistance against the colonization of indigenous lands and peoples. Big Mountain, the sacred center of the Diné (Navajo) universe in Arizona, would today be a pit coal mine were it not for the grandmothers, the clan matriarchs of the Diné people, standing guard and fighting Peabody Coal, one of the largest and most powerful corporations in the world. In Washington state, women such as Janet McCloud (Tulalip) and Ramona Bennett (Puyallup) assumed leading roles in the battles over fishing and treaty rights in the 1960s, "efforts which, probably more than any other phenomena, set in motion the 'hard-line' Indian liberation movements of the following day" (Jaimes and Halsey 1992, 311). Many of the most important and beloved indigenous women leaders are unknown outside their own communities. They are the aunties, mothers, sisters, partners, and grandmothers of the people. Without them, incalculable bodies of knowledge and huge tracts of unspoiled sacred land would be lost forever.

### *Women's Blood: Power and Responsibility*

Perhaps one of the most misunderstood aspects of indigenous regard for the power of women are customs surrounding female menstrual cycles, which have long been viewed through the Christian lens of Anglo-American ethnographers. Alfred Kroeber, in his famous 1925 work on the indigenous nations of California, *Handbook of the Indians of California,* rarely fails to express his dismay at what he perceives as the backwardness of tribes who ritually show respect for a woman's menstrual cycle: "The Hupa stand one slight grade lower than the Yurok in the scale of civilization by one test that holds through most of California: the attention bestowed on the recurring physiological functions of women" (1953, 135). Casting about for an explanation for the Hupa Nation's supposed degradation, Kroeber posits: "The influence of their hill neighbors may be responsible" (1953, 135). The language Kroeber uses to devalue the respect surrounding a woman's menstrual period reveals ethnocentric and misogynist traits common to academics of the time.

Traditions observed around menstrual periods are still practiced by millions of indigenous women. These observances are meant to honor women by offering them a much-needed bodily and spiritual respite. Among indigenous North American families practicing traditional ways, when a girl has her first menstrual period, it is considered a time for her family to show the girl great honor and respect as she enters into a new phase in her life as a woman. She will now be instructed in her role as an Indian woman and is honored through days-long ceremony, dance, and songs such as this Wintun puberty ritual song:

> Thou art a girl no more,
> Thou art a girl no more;
> The chief, the chief,
> The chief, the chief,
> Honors thee
> In the dance, in the dance
> In the long and double line
> Of the dance

Dance, dance
Dance, dance. (Margolin 1981, 16)

Ancient theories and practices surrounding the mystery of a woman's blood time (often called "moontime" by contemporary women) are still observed, although many women have discontinued these practices as their lives become more assimilated to mainstream Western culture. These practices vary from area to area, but everywhere the cycles of a woman's body and the blood she produces are thought of as powerful, chaotic, and subject to strict rules. Girls are warned about their tremendous, uncontrollable power during their periods. If a girl does not heed the proper restrictions, tradition holds, she can bring ruin not only to herself but to all those close to her. One story, recounted among the Wintun of northern California, tells of a girl who did not observe restrictions against the tasting of flesh or salt during her "moon-sickness" and sucked at a cut on her finger. The blood and fat tasted so sweet that she ate her finger and then uncontrollably ate her whole arm, then her legs, and then her entire body until she was nothing but a rolling head. The girl's head, ever thirstier for the taste of flesh, rolled into nearby villages and "threw the people into her mouth. She did not linger, she turned the village upside down as she devoured them all" (Margolin 1981, 19). Nothing could stop her until a man who was fishing lured the girl's rolling head into the river, where a fish jumped up and swallowed her.

Among the Blackfeet of northern Montana, menstrual blood is considered such a powerful force—both protective and repellent—that men in earlier times would apply a small amount of their wives' menstrual blood to their battle regalia as a warning to enemies that they would be rendered powerless if they were to come into contact with it. According to Gordon Se-buh-ta of Heart Butte, Montana (in the heart of today's Blackfeet reservation), some traditional men still observe this practice in a different form (personal interview, February 19, 1999). It is used to protect men from powerful spiritual forces and to give them good luck while playing stick game. Stick game is an enormously popular Blackfeet game of chance, often with very high stakes. A wife's menstrual blood dabbed on a medicine bag or some other hidden place, according to Se-buh-ta, who is a traditional Blackfeet healer and consummate gambler, will cause the other team to have extraordinary bad luck. Se-buh-ta also notes, however, that many contemporary Blackfeet people are Christians and no longer believe in or observe these practices.

Today, many Native women and their families ritually recognize a woman's time of power and observe whatever practices they can. Each group has different ways of observing traditional restrictions. Some common practices observed during the four days of menstruation are the avoidance of meat, grease, or salt; using a special "scratching stick" to scratch oneself; retiring to a special area for four days; abstaining from basket weaving and other arts; and taking care not to look at or handle the tools and ceremonial objects of others. Among the Mississippi Choctaw, some women spend four or more days sleeping separate from their partners. If there is not a child's bedroom where a woman can set up a second bed, then often her partner will sleep on the living room sofa to give her the space of their bedroom for four days. If possible, she avoids cooking for her family, and one of her children or her partner serves food to her. If she does not have a job from which she can be fired for absenteeism, she stays at home. Any important decisions either will be decided without the menstruating woman's input or more often will be put off until her time is completed (Randall Sevedge, personal interview, May 12, 2001). These restrictions demonstrate honor for the woman in her time of power and protect people from what is believed to be an inherently chaotic sort of power, over which neither the woman nor her family has any control.

Sometimes women observe these traditional restrictions while also practicing Christianity, and many women observe some practices but must forgo others. A trend toward the recovery of certain practices that reflect long-held values regarding a woman's power during her menstrual period is prevalent among many indigenous groups. Among the Chumash of central California, it is rare for women to observe all of the menstrual restrictions discussed above. Because of the very high cost of living in central California, most Native American families are economically compelled to leave aside traditions that require time off from work, even though those traditions are considered by many to be vitally important. Even so, some Chumash women strictly observe practices of avoidance during their menstrual periods by staying away from ceremonies, feasts, or places where people's special tools and ceremonial regalia will be visible. Some women attend these events but sit apart and refrain from touching any powerful or ceremonial object, particularly eagle feathers, canoes, pipes, drums, and the like. At these events, female members of their families will respectfully serve the "moon-sick" women. Some Chumash women avoid cooking for their mates during their periods.

Often they are treated to their partner's respect and care, and he or she does all the cooking and serving.

Strictly avoided by menstruating women throughout Native North America are the Sun Dance, Native American Church meetings (also called the Peyote Church), the various forms of sweat ceremonies, and other tribally specific ceremonial events at which both men and women are present. The belief that the woman could bring harm or serious illness to the ceremonial participants is very strong, despite centuries of forced Christian missionization and assimilation. Although many indigenous women long for the times when they could rest for four whole days in isolation or sit with their female friends and relatives to enjoy their company, many other Native American women have assimilated into Western culture and no longer have the luxury or the desire to practice traditional menstrual observations.

### Ritual Prohibitions

The menstruation prohibitions discussed above are not isolated phenomena; rather they exist within systems of prohibitions that affected both women and men. According to Lillian A. Ackerman's exploration of the ethnographies from the 1930s, among the Plateau tribes on the Colville reservation (including the Sanpoil-Nespelem, Colville, Lakes, Southern Okanogan, Methow, Palus, Chelan, Entiat, Wenatchi, Moses Columbia, and the Chief Joseph band of Nez Perce), a system of ritual precautions existed that included sexual abstinence. It is likely that these practices persist today. According to Ackerman, each "prohibition for one gender was balanced by a similar one for the other" (1995, 96). The prohibitions for men included avoiding the ovens where women prepared roots for consumption, as well as women's tools and engaging in ritual cleansing and sexual abstinence before hunting and in sexual abstinence during hunting. For women, the ritual precautions included menstrual taboos (avoiding the men's fishing weirs and taking water from the streams where traps were set, in addition to precautions similar to those discussed above), avoiding gathering the materials for the weir lashings, avoiding men's tools, and engaging in ritual cleansing and sexual abstinence before gathering roots and probably sexual abstinence during gathering. Victoria D. Patterson notes a similar, although less complex, set of rules among the Pomo. Not only can women not participate in ceremonies during their periods, but husbands of menstruating women are prohibited from "hunting, fishing, ceremonial dancing, gambling, [and] war" (1995, 140).

Indigenous societies were and continue to be complex systems that seek to create and maintain balance in all things. This complementary gender system provides both men and women with rules that seek to create a well-balanced society in which excesses are avoided.

Ironically, some non-Native people who wish to imitate Native American ceremonial ways and who have the leisure time and resources to do so are creating "moon lodges" where non-Indian women retreat during their menstrual cycles for singing and drumming (Rose 1992, 403–421). Usually not lasting the entire four or five days of a woman's period, these "traditional Native American ceremonies" fly in the face of actual indigenous traditions by including drums and other ceremonial items that would be strictly forbidden, because of the power associated with these items, in a traditional context. In addition, the period of seclusion during menstruation practiced by some indigenous women is not considered a ceremonial event per se, but rather a time for women to protect themselves and their communities from the dangerous encounter between their powerful moontime presence and the delicate balance of power in everyday life. Non-Native appropriation of any indigenous ceremonial knowledge is bitterly contested by indigenous people, many of whom equate this action with someone deciding to play-act or appropriate sacred ceremonies from other world traditions, such as a Jewish bar mitzvah or the consecration of bread and wine by a Catholic priest during Mass. These appropriations do not take the ritual systems—which are an intrinsic part of Native American menstruation prohibitions—into consideration and thus do grave injustice to the integrity of the cultures from which they are "borrowed."

It is problematic that classic anthropological texts continue to inform modern students of Native American cultures and continue the long history of misunderstanding and cultural misogyny toward indigenous women. Books like Alfred Kroeber's are valuable, however, not only for their historical information but also for the implicit evidence they present about Euro-American values of that period. Read critically, the writings of scholars in the classical period of anthropology can provide modern students with a rich tableau of Victorian-era colonial values and worldviews. These worldviews shaped racist and sexist stereotypes about indigenous peoples that have been used until the present day to justify the perpetuation of colonization. We may also use them to remind ourselves that our current views, too, might someday be viewed as hopelessly outdated and archaic.

## TWO-SPIRIT PEOPLE

Current political debates about the rights of LGBTIQ people are heirs to conceptions of both sexuality and gender that have developed over the course of American history. These understandings are closely connected with the Christian worldviews held by the people who have colonized this continent.

This chapter began with a discussion of gender roles in the context of indigenous conceptions of power. Understandings of masculinity and femininity developed from the relationships between the people and the land and have been cultivated into much more than tactics for survival. Gender roles exhibit the deep respect and honor accorded to individual women and men and the contributions each make to the continued existence of Native American communities. These traditions have continued in forms that reveal both acceptance of and resistance to Euro-American models of gender and sexuality. Like all cultural relations, gender norms and roles are subject to change because of new circumstances, but changes do not imply "inauthenticity"; rather, they provide examples through which continuities can be traced in order to gain a better understanding of what aspects of gendered relations are privileged by a given community. Understandings of gender identities, roles, and statuses need to be kept in mind when considering two-spirit people.

The term *two-spirit* is a relatively recent label given to the variety of "nontraditional" gender statuses that were present in many precontact nations and that continue to exist in both traditional and innovative forms. Intersexed people—those who have a combination of male and female genitalia—are considered to be two-spirit by many cultures, as are biological males choosing to express feminine gender characteristics and biological females choosing to express masculine gender characteristics. These latter two groups will be discussed here.

Until the 1990s, anthropologists called two-spirit people born with male anatomy *berdaches,* and those born with female anatomy were sometimes called female *berdaches.* The term *berdache* has roots in a Persian word meaning "young captive" or "slave." By the time colonists encountered Native American peoples, *berdache* was used in both England and France to refer to a younger, more passive partner in an age-differentiated male homosexual relationship (Lang 1998, 6–7; Roscoe 1998, 7–8).

This history has brought the application of this term to Native American gender variations into question in recent years.

Many Native and non-Native activists and scholars prefer the term *two-spirit* because it acknowledges the position of people with nonnormative gender identities as existing between masculinity and femininity and therefore having both spirits within them.[2] *Two-spirit* is the English translation of a northern Algonquian term, *niizh manitoag* (Anguksuar 1997, 221). Anguksuar, a Yup'ik scholar from Alaska, explains that "each human is born because a man and a woman have joined in creating each new life; all humans bear imprints of both, although some individuals may manifest both qualities more completely than others" (221).

## A Question of Gender Rather Than Sexuality

In traditional tribal worldviews, people were understood to be two-spirit because of the gender they chose to express rather than their choice of sexual partner. This is not to say that there was no sexual component to the lives of two-spirit people, but the focus within Native communities was upon what tasks such people performed rather than their choice of sexual partner. Some two-spirit people formed partnerships with people of the same biological sex, whereas others had partners of the "opposite" biological sex; this choice varied by both tribe and individual. Both gender-role change and gender-role crossing occurred in precontact Native American nations and continue to occur today.

These phenomena have been mistakenly understood to be defined by sexual desire between people of the same sex. However, the tendency to equate sexual activity with identity in contemporary American culture obscures some of the important nuances of desire, relationships, and spirituality in Native cultures, both past and present. Sexuality is a social phenomenon, and the behaviors that constitute LGBTIQ identities in the contemporary West may not be understood in the same way in other places or times.

Western understandings of the connections between gender and sexual expressions focus on categories such as heterosexuality, homosexuality, and bisexuality, which give primacy to the sexual dimensions of interpersonal relationships. In contrast, Native American understandings of interpersonal relationships focus primarily on gender—specifically, what role a person performs within a given relationship or community. Therefore, contemporary discussions of transgendered people more closely approximate traditional understandings of two-spirit people within tribal communities than western discussion of homosexuality. In *Transgender Warriors,* Leslie Feinberg (1996), a transgendered activist and writer, provides a global history of gender variation. S/he includes the Crow *badé* (sometimes spelled *boté*), the Chumash *joya,* and the Navajo *nádleehí* alongside female warriors from cultures across the world and well-known Western figures, including Joan of Arc, RuPaul, and Brandon Teena. Although Feinberg's text runs the risk of obscuring important cultural differences between the examples cited and erasing the cultural systems within which these examples occur, it does acknowledge that when discussing two-spirit people, the focus needs to be on gender rather than sexuality.

Same-sex erotic behavior did occur within Native American nations, but the focus was on the gender role performed by individuals. The cultural lens with which colonial Western observers viewed the people they encountered on this continent, however, left us with little knowledge of the history of same-sex eroticism in Native cultures. Of particular interest here is the spiritual aspect of two-spirit identities. Gilbert Herdt describes the Mojave as recognizing "a distinctive ontology of two-spirit persons, expressed in heartfelt desires, task preferences, and cultural transformation with respect to the genitals and to personal pronouns. The social role was sanctified by spiritual power—an attribute lacking in the Western conception of these variations of sex/gender" (1997, 279–280).

According to Sabine Lang, two-spirit people existed in 148 precontact nations in North America (1998, 5). Will Roscoe cites 155 nations with two-spirit people (1998, 7), and Gay American Indians, an organization formed to assess and address the needs of gay, lesbian, bisexual, and transgendered Native Americans, lists 133 (1988, 217). These figures are drawn from written sources primarily assembled by outsiders and do not reflect innovations that have occurred within the rapidly shifting contemporary cultural landscape. In some nations, it was possible to occupy two-spirit status for a period of time and then return to masculine or feminine status (Lang 1998, 61). An individual usually made a gender-status decision prior to assuming adult responsibilities (Roscoe 1998, 8–9). Interestingly, the colonial and anthropological sources provide more examples of women-men (males performing feminine roles) than men-women (females performing male roles). Although this discrepancy may be related to the privileging of male informants over female ones by male researchers and the greater visibility of biological males dressing as women and performing feminine tasks, the incongruity is great enough that it can be assumed that women-men were more common.

Prior to contact with Europeans, individual nations accorded different statuses to women-men and allowed for varying degrees of flexibility (Lang 1998). For example, the performance of feminine tasks, including gathering food, preparing meals, weaving baskets, and sewing, was noted among many California tribes, including the Chumash, Pomo, Yuki, and Yurok. Feminine occupations for women-men existed among the Kutenai, Klamath, Quinault, Aleut, Ojibwa, Winnebago, Crow, Cheyenne, Teton Lakota, and Santee Dakota. The Crow *boté,* the Chumash *joya,* the Cocopa *elxa,* and women-men among the Santee Dakota, Oglala Lakota, Navajo, Ute, Papago, and Pomo had an early proclivity for feminine tasks. Other women-men performed a combination of masculine and feminine tasks. In some nations, including the Crow, Apache, Santee Dakota, Klamath, Hopi, Chumash, Navajo, Cheyenne, Papago, Ute, Yuma, Zuni, and Pomo, women-men married or had sex with men; conversely, scholars report sexual relationships between women-men and women among the Zuni, Navajo, Papago, Crow, Klamath, and Osage. In some cultures, women-men remained celibate, but in others, they were sexually available to many tribal members. Among the Cheyenne, Chumash, Natchez, Cree, Kutenai, Crow, Papago, Yuma, and Pima, researchers noted an early preference for female company among women-men. The Lakota *winkte,* Zuni *lha'ma,* and women-men among the Santee Dakota, Osage, Hopi, Cheyenne, Navajo, and the Yuki also spoke in a feminine manner.

Individual life stories provide insight into the complexity of two-spirit existence. Osh-Tisch (which means "Finds Them and Kills Them"), a Crow *boté* discussed by Roscoe (1998), Walter Williams (1992), and Lang (1998), considered herself to be the last *boté.* Osh-Tisch received her name during the Battle of the Rosebud, in which the Crow and Shoshone fought with U.S. forces against the Sioux and the Cheyenne, traditional enemies of the Crow whose encroachment onto Crow territory led to an alliance with the U.S. government. Although a vision at a young age had established her as both a *boté* and a medicine person, Osh-Tisch was compelled to take part in this battle. She wore women's clothing even while fighting (Roscoe 1998, 30).

Osh-Tisch's presence was valuable to the community, and those leading the Crow defended her against attempts by Bureau of Indian Affairs (BIA) officials to force her to wear men's clothing and perform masculine tasks. In the 1890s, one agent was asked to leave the reservation because of his hostile treatment of Osh-Tisch (Williams 1992, 179). The Crow reservation became known for its openness, and in 1879 a two-spirit from the Hidatsa tribe fled oppression from Europeans and found protection with them (Roscoe 1998, 35). Considering the strength of the BIA and other U.S. government forces at the time, these incidents are quite remarkable. The efforts of Baptist minister and schoolteacher William A. Petzoldt to denounce indigenous customs—including the *boté* role and ceremonial dances—did not lead to the rejection of Osh-Tisch or a change in her behavior and attire; however, according to traditional Crow elders, his message did keep young people from taking on the *boté* role (Roscoe 1998, 36). Recently there have been signs of change, and some Crow men again have chosen *boté* status (Lang 1998, 118).

Man-woman status (a biological female performing a masculine role) in nations across the continent also allowed for flexibility in dress, work, and sexual relationships. Among the Achomawi of northern California, men-women dressed in feminine clothing but performed masculine work and married women (Lang 1998, 273). A Klamath man-woman took on masculine responsibilities, including marriage, but continued to wear primarily feminine clothing (275). Mohave, Paiute, and Quinault men-women wore masculine clothing, performed masculine tasks, and often married women (274). Warfare, a task usually associated with men, could be performed by women but did not necessarily coincide with masculine or ambiguous gender identification. Thus, female warriors were not necessarily understood as having changed gender roles and therefore are excellent examples of gender-role crossing without full status change.

Same-sex erotic behavior between women has been largely ignored in anthropological literature, in part because of the inability and unwillingness of predominantly male researchers to access women's lives and the presumption by Westerners of female passivity and heterosexuality (Lang 1998, 22). In the case of men-women, the lack of discussion of sexual behavior between women may also be due to the fact that "gender role crossings were frequently possible for women without involving an ambivalent, nonfeminine gender status. This is above all true for the war/raiding complex and, in isolated cases, also for masculine activities such as hunting or participating in certain ceremonies" (Lang 1998, 261). It may have been easier for women to perform traditionally male tasks without signaling a change of gender role than it was for men to perform traditionally female tasks without signaling a change, which may partially account for the larger number of gender-variant roles available for men than women.

One example of gender-role change among women is Ququnak patke, the Manlike Woman of the Kutenai (Lang 1998, 275; Williams 1992, 236). After marrying a European fur trader, Ququnak patke returned to her tribe and announced that she had been changed into a man. S/he began wearing men's clothing and performing masculine tasks, and s/he married a woman. Although there had been no precedent for women taking on masculine roles among the Kutenai, Ququnak patke was eventually accepted and served as a warrior and a healer. She died a warrior's death in battle with the Blackfeet (Williams 1986, 239).

Women-men and men-women often had specialized roles within precontact nations. Women-men were healers, "gravediggers, conveyers of oral tradition and songs, and nurses during war expeditions; they foretold the future, conferred lucky names on children or adults, wove, made pottery, arranged marriages, and made feather costumes for dance" (Lang 1998, 151). The incidences of women-men healers often occurred within cultures in which female healers were common or prevalent. Because women-men were considered to have both masculine and feminine spirits, they were believed to have extraordinary access to the spirits and special insight into relationships between men and women. For example, the Lakota *winkte* were considered to have special powers and energies that were symbolized by the wearing of women's clothing, much as other powerful people carried symbols of their spirit healers in medicine bags. Feminine clothing represented their connection to spiritual power, a connection so potent that medicine people approached *winktes* for advice (Lang 1998, 157; Williams 1986, 35).

Much of the available literature includes brief references to two-spirit people without providing in-depth examinations of the lives of women-men and men-women. Other life histories in the literature include Hastíín Klah, a Navajo *nádleehí* or "transformed person" (Roscoe 1998, 40; Lang 1998, 68), Woman Chief of the Crow (Roscoe 1998, 78; Williams 1986, 244), and We'wha, a Zuni *lha'ma* (Roscoe 1998, 113; Roscoe 1991).

The connections between these historical figures and contemporary LGBTIQ and two-spirit Native Americans are complex because of the immense changes that have occurred within Native American cultures since contact with European colonists. The process of forced integration of Native Americans into the United States included the suppression of rituals and ceremonies. Religious traditions and understandings of gender that differed from colonial European practices were at the core of Native cultures and therefore were heavily affected by the gradual conquest of indigenous land and the denial of indigenous land claims by the U.S. government. Women's positions of power were undermined by the necessity of naming male heads of households for the new arrangements of families in the modern European nuclear family model. Two-spirit people did not fit into these new arrangements and therefore found themselves without property or access to government funds (Williams 1986, 176).

Missionization was and continues to be especially problematic for two-spirit people. Although both missionization and colonization began hundreds of years ago, their effects are still felt, and neither process can be said to have ended. Native Americans are still denied the rights to practice their religions in some areas, and traditional land is more often than not in the possession of non-Native peoples. Some nations are not even given the basic acknowledgment of federal recognition.

Two-spirit people who were medicine people for their communities at the time of contact faced a threefold oppression—as leaders of religions deemed illegal, as gender-variant people, and as Indians. Missionaries to Native communities understood conversion to be a sacred duty; moreover, the process included Westernization as well as Christianization because European civilization was (and is) viewed as emblematic of Christian ideals. Walter Williams reminds us that in "its most ethnocentric form, everything Western was sanctioned by the will of God, while everything belonging to an indigenous culture was evil" (1986, 181). Missionization became a means of controlling colonial subjects by changing their worldviews. Christian subjects were and are (often rightly) viewed as more likely to accept the changes brought by colonization.

Christian conversion and suppression of indigenous religious expressions have proven to be forceful tools for Western expansion. Many Native American tribes have partially or fully internalized Western Christian values, including a tendency to focus on sexuality rather than gender when categorizing two-spirit people and their intimate relationships. Both homophobia and a distrust of non-Christian beliefs and practices exist in contemporary Native communities. As a result, Native Americans with nonnormative gender and sexual identities often feel ostracized on reservations and therefore either suppress their desires or find their way into mainstream gay communities.

The condemnation of two-spirit people by Westerners and Native Americans is rooted in a conflict of beliefs. In the preface to *Two-Spirit People: American Indian Lesbian Women and Gay Men,* Duane Champagne writes that in many tribal contexts, "Alternative gender roles were respected and honored, and believed to be a part of the sacred web of life and society. If the Great Spirit chose to create alternative sexualities or gender roles, who was bold enough to oppose such power?" (1997, xviii). He continues with the observation that

> [in] many American Indian worldviews, the universe is composed of beings of various power and purpose. All are to be honored and respected as part of the plan of the Great Spirit. Human beings, only a small part of creation, are not privy to the grand plan of the Great Spirit, but honor and respect must be given to the course of events, and humans must play out the role assigned to them as individuals and nations. (xx)

The roles played by individuals within Native communities, as well as people's understandings of themselves and their missions in life, often are based on spiritual experiences. For example, two-spirit status can be established through a spiritual quest. As Champagne notes:

> Dreams or visions gained in ceremony or during fasting can provide information about an individual's sacred life quest or role, or provide knowledge about the future of the community. Because an individual's life quest is gathered from sacred spirits, the revelation is regarded as personal and sacred. . . . Since individuals have sacredly revealed missions, their activities, regardless of how strange they may seem to others, cannot be interfered with without retribution from the beings who are directing the sacred mission. Thus in many Indian nations, individualism is highly regarded, and each person may have a sacred mission in the world to perform as part of the great unknowable plan of the Great Spirit. (xix–xx)

Gender expression is among the choices valued by many Native American peoples. Cultivation of individual skills and strengths is considered to be an asset to the nation, and a strong community consists of individuals whose talents are used for the benefit of both the individual and the collective.

Creation stories are excellent sources for examining cultural self-understandings. The inclusion of two-spirit people in creation myths shows at the very least an acknowledgment of their presence within a given society and often an acceptance of two-spirit people. Two-spirit people are accounted for in Zuni, Arapaho, Pima, Mohave, and Navajo creation stories (Williams 1992, 18–23). In all except the Pima story (in which the presence of two-spirit people is blamed on the neighboring Papago, with whom the Pima historically have been in great tension), two-spirit people are depicted as both natural and positive aspects of tribal culture. In the Navajo tale, *nádleehí* twins Turquoise Boy and White Shell Girl invented baskets, pottery, axes, and grinding stones—essential tools and art forms. *Nádleehí* means "changing one" or "one who is transformed" and refers to intersexed people, women-men, and men-women (Williams 1992, 19). Human existence, according to the Navajo, has benefited greatly from these creative twins whose gender identities fall outside the basic binary.

### Reclaiming Two-Spirit Roles

Some contemporary Native Americans identify with traditional understandings of two-spirit people and their connection to tribal communities and the spiritual realm. Anguksuar, a Yup'ik man, identifies himself as two-spirit. A Lakota-Ojibwa woman told him of a prophecy that "at a time directly preceding a great cleansing in society, the *winkte* and *koshkalaka* would reappear, as out of the grass. Not just a few but in great numbers" (Anguksuar 1997, 220). Despite the homophobia that exists within both mainstream and Native communities, some Indians still view two-spirit people as signs of cultural continuity and symbols of hope for increased tolerance and spiritual and cultural renewal.

Although it is true that Native American cultures have changed and two-spirits do not perform exactly the same functions as in precontact times, that does not make contemporary Native people who identify as two-spirit "inauthentic." Anguksuar states:

An academician may wish to assert that there are no more classic "berdaches," that they are simple remnants of Native cultures, and that Native people, in large part no longer know who they are nor know their traditions. These rather narrow Western parameters and definitions mark a startling contrast to the ways that many Natives regard their lives and origins. Our methods of measuring may not exactly mesh with what aca-

demia regards as acceptable or empirical knowledge, but we do continue
with our dreams, prophesies, and other esoteric knowledge. (1997, 221)

Thus, although there may be few, if any, two-spirit people who completely fit the historical examples in colonial and anthropological literature, contemporary individuals have reinterpreted the role and status of two-spirit people to address contemporary issues. The two-spirit, like all cultural roles, is flexible and adaptable; after all, the two-spirit is known as the changing one.

For these reasons, it is important to listen to the voices of contemporary two-spirit people rather than simply examine historical figures. Beverly Little Thunder, a Standing Rock Lakota woman, asks scholars to focus on the lives of living people: "Instead of focusing on one or two people who lived in the past it is now time to begin to write about those of us who live today. Anthropologists of today have the opportunity to record the contemporary life of our people, not just our history, for future generations" (Little Thunder 1997, 209). Living two-spirit people, like the living cultures in which they exist, are dynamic and adaptable.

### Contemporary LGBTIQ Native Americans

Native American gay men—like all American gay men—have been struck by the acquired immunodeficiency syndrome (AIDS) epidemic, and like all people of color in U.S. society, they have difficulties accessing adequate health care. According to Ron Rowell, the founder of the National Native American AIDS Prevention Center in Oakland, California, and a member of the Choctaw nation, 79 percent of the people with AIDS in Native American populations are gay or bisexual and male. There is also a higher incidence of AIDS among Native American women than among Euro-American women. Moreover, some fear that the total number of cases among Native Americans has been underreported because of the difficulty of recording multiethnic status on surveys; Native Americans with AIDS often are counted as either White or Hispanic (Rowell 1997, 87).

The spread of human immunodeficiency virus (HIV) and AIDS, like all viruses that can be transmitted sexually, is connected with one of the leading health problems among Native Americans: alcoholism. The reduction of inhibitions under the influence of alcohol can lead to increased sexual activity and decreased concern about safe sex. Lisa Tiger, an HIV-positive Cherokee activist, encourages abstinence from drinking in her

AIDS education program. She also stresses spirituality: "I remind my audiences that Native Americans see life as a sacred circle where no one is above or below anyone else. I make the point that our tribes and other minorities must teach each other and learn from each other and support each other's goals" (Tiger 1995, 202). Native people need to take care of one another to survive and thrive.

The devastating reality of AIDS is compounded by the fact that many Native communities, like other communities worldwide, do not know or will not accept that AIDS has entered their population. HIV/AIDS is still seen by many as a disease that only affects gay men. Although this population remains at the highest risk for contracting the disease, AIDS is rapidly moving into all segments of the U.S. population. The denial that AIDS is a part of life on reservations and in urban Native communities, combined with what Tiger identifies as reduced self-esteem among an oppressed group of people, has the potential of allowing the AIDS pandemic to reach epic proportions (Tiger 1995, 203). Both Rowell and Tiger fear that the AIDS crisis might be yet another disease epidemic that decimates entire Native American cultures—a very real fear, given the devastating role played by European diseases in Native American history.

Reactions to AIDS in many Native communities are evidence of the internalization of Western homophobia and gender expectations. According to Melvin Harrison, the director of the Navajo Nation AIDS Network, "the Navajo Nation is generally homophobic, and people have a difficult time coming out of the closet as a result. There are places on the reservation where this is not so, especially among the traditional elders, but among younger people there is a lot of ridicule and intimidation" (Rowell 1997, 89). Traditional honor and respect for individual gender and sexual expression still exist, but the deep impact of the continued processes of colonization and missionization has introduced heterosexism into many Native communities.

The homophobia sometimes encountered in Native communities often leads two-spirit and LGBTIQ Native people to search for understanding in predominantly white communities that are not always sensitive to the needs of Native people. White gays and lesbians sometimes appropriate the two-spirit as an ancestor to contemporary sexual identities—an unfortunate extension of the Euro-American tendency to use aspects of other cultures for their own purposes. The claim that two-spirit identities are ancestors of Euro-American gay identities denies the complexity of the cultures in which two-spirit people exist. As Beverly Little Thunder explains:

In the non-Native community of lesbians and gay people I have been told that being two-spirited means that I am a special being. It seems that they feel that my spirituality was the mystical answer to my sexuality. I do not believe this to be so. My spirituality would have been with me, regardless of my sexuality. This attitude creates a feeling of isolation. I live in a white society that finds me exotic. (1997, 207)

Even in the absence of overt racism, the pressure for people of color to conform within LGBTIQ communities can be overwhelming. Like most other areas of American culture, gay culture historically has been defined by white standards. Michael Red Earth, a Sisseton Dakota, recalls: "I learned to define myself as a gay man by my exposure to white American culture" (1997, 214). These cultural crossovers can create tensions between Native people's ethnic and sexual identities. As Red Earth explains, "even though I knew I was sexually and affectionately attracted to men, I thought I was the only Native gay there was" (213). Historical acceptance of two-spirit people and an increasingly active and vocal Native LGBTIQ movement helped Red Earth to integrate his identities, but he does not identify fully with the role of *winkte*.

In 1975, Gay American Indians was organized in San Francisco. Since then, the organization has worked to address the needs of LGBTIQ Native Americans, which has included examining two-spirit roles and providing a forum for people to express their frustrations with being identified as two-spirit. Some people, like Michael Red Earth, want to identify as gay, lesbian, or bisexual Native Americans rather than as two-spirit people because of the realities of their lives within contemporary U.S. society. Others, like Anguksuar, identify with contemporary adaptations of traditional two-spirit roles. Often two-spirit or LGBTIQ status complicates the prejudice already faced by Native peoples; in some cases it is cause for discrimination within Native communities. However, Anguksuar's choice to express a consciously selected blend of traditional and modern values reflects many Native Americans' adaptations to the modern world.

## CONCLUSION

The connections between Native American worldviews and sexuality are complex and cannot be understood without examining changing conceptions of gender and the deep impact of 500 years of colonial occupation.

Today, Native Americans continue to face racial, sexual, and religious discrimination. However, significant progress has been made since the 1970s toward gaining understanding and tolerance for LGBTIQ people. Native women continue their respected work as leaders alongside male leaders in their communities. Continued activism has yielded some significant gains in the area of Native rights, most notably the 1992 passage of the Native American Graves Protection and Repatriation Act, which mandates the repatriation of certain artifacts and ancestral remains that are currently housed in museum and university archives. Environmental movements have also begun to see the important links between conserving natural resources and Native understandings of the connections between humans and the world in which we live.

In all these movements, calls for systemic change to Western ways of thinking increasingly have been heard and acted upon. Thus, although the colonial process that began 500 years ago has not yet ceased, resistance against that process—by both Native Americans and their non-Native allies—continues unabated.

## NOTES

1. The reader may note a certain reliance on examples from the Chumash community of the Santa Barbara area. Julianne Cordero is a member of the Santa Barbara Chumash community. Raised in Seattle, Washington, she moved home in 1995 and is now recognized in her community as a traditional herbalist, basket weaver, and apprentice canoe builder. Because of the proximity of the Chumash community to the University of California at Santa Barbara campus, much of Elizabeth Currans's research into indigenous religious traditions has involved this community.

2. The terms *women-men* (biological males in feminine roles) and *men-women* (biological females in masculine roles) also have been proposed (Lang 1998). In this discussion, whenever a culturally specific term is unavailable, the terms *women-men, men-women,* and *two-spirit* will be used, especially when the focus is on general descriptions of such gender expressions.

## REFERENCES

Ackerman, Lillian A. 1995. "Complementary but Equal Gender Status in the Plateau." Pp. 75–100 in Laura F. Klein and Lillian A. Ackerman, eds.,

*Women and Power in Native North America.* Norman: University of Oklahoma Press.

Anguksuar [Richard LaFortune]. 1997. "A Postcolonial Colonial Perspective on Western [Mis]Conceptions of the Cosmos and the Restoration of Indigenous Taxonomies." Pp. 217–222 in Sue-Ellen Jacobs, Wesley Thomas, and Sabine Lang, eds., *Two-Spirit People: Native American Gender Identity, Sexuality, and Spirituality.* Urbana: University of Illinois Press.

Beauvoir, Simone de. [1961] 1973. *The Second Sex.* H. M. Parshley, trans. and ed. New York: Bantam Books.

Champagne, Duane. 1997. "Preface: On the Gift of Sacred Being." Pp. xvii–xxiv in Lester B. Brown, ed., *Two-Spirit People: American Indian Lesbian Women and Gay Men.* New York: Haworth Press.

Feinberg, Leslie. 1996. *Transgender Warriors: Making History from Joan of Arc to Dennis Rodman.* Boston: Beacon Press.

Gay American Indians, with Will Roscoe (coordinating editor). 1988. *Living the Spirit: A Gay American Indian Anthology.* New York: St. Martin's Press.

Grounds, Richard A. 2001. "Tallahassee, Osceola, and the Hermeneutics of American Place Names." *Journal of the American Academy of Religion* 55: 287–322.

Hallowell, A. Irving. 1975. "Ojibwa Ontology, Behavior, and World View." Pp. 141–178 in Dennis and Barbara Tedlock, eds., *Teachings from the American Earth: Indian Religion and Philosophy.* New York: Liverwright.

Herdt, Gilbert. 1997. "The Dilemmas of Desire: From 'Berdache' to Two-Spirit." Pp. 276–283 in Sue-Ellen Jacobs, Wesley Thomas, and Sabine Lang, eds., *Two-Spirit People: Native American Gender Identity, Sexuality, and Spirituality.* Urbana: University of Illinois Press.

Hudson, Travis, and Ernest Underhay. 1978. *Crystals in the Sky: An Intellectual Odyssey Involving Chumash Astronomy, Cosmology, and Rock Art.* Santa Barbara, CA: Ballena Press/Santa Barbara Museum of Natural History.

Hurtado, Albert L. 1988. *Indian Survival on the California Frontier.* New Haven: Yale University Press.

Jaimes, M. Annette. 1992. "Federal Indian Identification Policy: A Usurpation of Indigenous Sovereignty in North America." Pp. 123–138 in M. Annette Jaimes, ed., *The State of Native America: Genocide, Colonization, and Resistance.* Boston: South End Press.

Jaimes, M. Annette, and Theresa Halsey. 1992. "American Indian Women: At the Center of Indigenous Resistance in Contemporary North America." Pp. 311–344 in M. Annette Jaimes, ed., *The State of Native America: Genocide, Colonization, and Resistance.* Boston: South End Press.

Kroeber, Alfred L. [1925] 1953. *Handbook of the Indians of California.* Reprint. Berkeley: California Book Company.

Lang, Sabine. 1998. *Men as Women, Women as Men: Changing Gender in Native American Cultures.* Austin: University of Texas Press.

———. 1999. "Lesbians, Men-Women, and Two-Spirits: Homosexuality and Gender in Native American Cultures." Pp. 91–118 in Evelyn Blackwood and Saskia E. Wieringa, eds., *Female Desires: Same-Sex Relations and Transgender Practices across Cultures.* New York: Columbia University Press.

Little Thunder, Beverly. 1997. "I am Lakota Womyn." Pp. 203–209 in Sue-Ellen Jacobs, Wesley Thomas, and Sabine Lang, eds., *Two-Spirit People: Native American Gender Identity, Sexuality, and Spirituality.* Urbana: University of Illinois Press.

Margolin, Malcolm, ed. 1981. *The Way We Lived: California Indian Songs, Stories, and Reminiscences.* Berkeley: Heyday Books.

Ortiz, Beverly. 1991. *It Will Live Forever: Traditional Yosemite Indian Acorn Preparation.* Berkeley: Heyday Press.

Patterson, Victoria D. 1995. "Evolving Gender Roles in Pomo Society." Pp. 126–145 in Laura F. Klein and Lillian A. Ackerman, eds., *Women and Power in Native North America.* Norman: University of Oklahoma Press.

Red Earth, Michael. 1997. "Traditional Influences on a Contemporary Gay-Identified Sisseton Dakota." Pp. 210–216 in Sue-Ellen Jacobs, Wesley Thomas, and Sabine Lang, eds., *Two-Spirit People: Native American Gender Identity, Sexuality, and Spirituality.* Urbana: University of Illinois Press.

Roscoe, Will. 1991. *The Zuni Man-Woman.* Albuquerque: University of New Mexico Press.

———. 1998. *Changing Ones: Third and Fourth Genders in Native North America.* New York: St. Martin's Press.

Rose, Wendy. 1992. "The Great Pretenders: Further Reflections on Whiteshamanism." Pp. 403–421 in M. Annette Jaimes, ed., *The State of Native America: Genocide, Colonization, and Resistance.* Boston: South End Press.

Rowell, Ron. 1997. "Developing AIDS Services for Native Americans: Rural and Urban Contexts." Pp. 85–95 in Lester B. Brown, ed., *Two-Spirit People: American Indian Lesbian Women and Gay Men.* New York: Haworth Press.

Sarris, Greg. 1994. *Mabel McKay: Weaving the Dream.* Berkeley: University of California Press.

Swanton, John R. [1931] 1995. *The Source Material for the Social and Ceremonial Life of the Choctaw Indians.* Reprint. Philadelphia, MS: Choctaw Museum of the Southern Indian.

Tiger, Lisa. 1995. "Woman Who Clears the Way." Pp. 192–204 in Barbara Findlen, ed., *Listen Up: Voices from the Next Feminist Generation.* Seattle: Seal Press.

Williams, Walter L. 1992. *The Spirit and the Flesh: Sexual Diversity in American Indian Cultures.* Boston: Beacon Press.

# Chapter 3

# Harmony of Yin and Yang

## Cosmology and Sexuality in Daoism

*Xinzhong Yao*

*Seventeenth-century Chinese painting showing mixed age group studying the yin-yang symbol. Daoism has made the yin-yang symbol a key part of its cosmic speculations and worldview. The symbol is an essential part of its cosmology and its theory of sexuality. (The Art Archive/British Museum)*

Daoist attitudes toward women, gender, and sexual relations are based on Daoist views of the cosmos, life, and society. Because of the complexities of Daoist traditions and ambiguities with regard to part of Daoist terminology, it is difficult to define clearly what attitudes toward sex are typically Daoist, and it would be even more difficult if we come to evaluate these attitudes in the light of modern (Western) sexuality. This difficulty has also affected the understanding of sexuality among contemporary Daoists and Daoist practitioners and prevented them from engaging in an integrated discourse on sex and sexual relations. Nevertheless, Daoism does have its own conception of sexuality, and it is possible for us to describe its basic principles. Therefore, the aim of this chapter is to explore the meaning and significance of the Daoist perception of sexuality, which is essentially derived from its cosmology of yin-yang harmony and which in turn has a significant effect on Daoist understanding of the cosmos. Daoist sexuality can be fully understood only in its metaphysical view of the universe, and for some Daoist schools, human sexuality plays an enormous part in maintaining or disturbing the harmony of the universe.

## DAOISM AND THE WAY OF HARMONY

Although Daoism has existed more than 2,000 years, there is not yet a definition accepted by all scholars to summarize its essence. Indeed, many are still suspicious of the generic term *Daoism,* insofar as it suggests a single tradition that covers a vast range of theories and practices. The term *Daoism,* as used in contemporary writings, may mean a philosophical system, a religious institution, or a way of life, depending on which aspect of the tradition is emphasized.

Philosophically, Daoist cosmic genealogy says that everything originates from Dao: According to Hao Tzu in the *Daode jing,* "The way begets one; one begets two; two begets three; three begets the myriad creatures" (*Daode jing,* chap. 42, author's translation). In that way, Daoists have attempted to define the relations between universal power and individual virtues, between being and nonbeing, between one and many. Philosophical Daoism emphasizes the limits of human knowledge and of the human ability to grasp the true nature of things. Certain Daoist philosophers therefore distinguish two kinds of knowledge: ordinary knowledge (the knowledge of things) and true knowledge (the knowledge of Dao). For them, ordinary knowledge is not only temporary but also obstructive and harmful for gaining the eternal knowledge of Dao. In their minds, the way to gain eternal knowledge, the knowledge of Dao, is different from the way in which we acquire ordinary knowledge. We accumulate ordinary knowledge through experience, but the knowledge of Dao requires that we empty ourselves and reduce our sensational experiences and desires.

In the West, Daoism is commonly thought of as a religion. Daoism indeed demonstrates a strong spiritual tendency and has developed its own form of religious organization, involving temples, monasteries, a priesthood, and systematic rituals and liturgies. The religious aim of Daoism is to relieve human suffering by leading a natural and meaningful life and by cultivating a religious and spiritual understanding of all beings and things. "Being natural," in this context, means that human efforts are oriented to the source of the universe rather than to the world itself. Furthermore, certain Daoist branches strive for longevity or even immortality, either through cultivating vital energy (*qi*), which is believed to have been endowed in all beings by the interaction of the cosmic powers, or by gaining access to an elixir of immortality. The earliest examples of this tradition were the activities of *fang shi* (medicine practitioners), and Daoist priests of later days incorporated these medical treatments and shamanist practices into a systematic religious system.

It is, however, apparent that as a religion Daoism is complicated and peculiar. Many of its beliefs and practices, sometimes complementary and sometimes contradictory to each other, do not necessarily lead to an overview of what religious Daoism might be. John Blofeld, for example, observes that although to certain scholars Daoism means the philosophy contained in a couple of volumes by the sages Laozi and Zhuangzi, "to most ordinary Chinese people, Taoism meant teachings covering a great range of occult practices alleged to have originated with no less a person than the Yellow Emperor (third millennium B.C.E.) and the three immortal ladies who advised him in skills both mystical and erotic" (1973, 19).

In part because of the increasing popularity of Buddhism in China, with its elaborate iconography and temples, Daoism eventually encompassed a large pantheon of gods and goddesses, immortals and others, together with many myths and legends. Despite the vast pantheon we find in Daoist temples and writings, the fundamental Daoist faith is in the sublime and impersonal Dao. On the one hand, Dao is formless and infinite, and knowledge of it is the ultimate truth. On the other hand, because only a few people are able to grasp the formless and others may only be able to comprehend recognizable forms, Daoism provides the people with visible deities, by which followers can see the truth they otherwise would not have understood. Daoism also exists and functions in a culture in which religion, ethics, and the way of life are integrated to a great extent, and it may be considered the most elevated expression of Chinese popular religion because its doctrine and practice incorporated and refined a complex synthesis of indigenous cultural elements, both religious and secular.

Recognizing that for a long time Daoism did not have any organizations and existed only as a school of thought, some suggest that it is better described as a way of life or ethos for the Chinese. It is true that in its earlier form Daoism was no more than a distinctive way of life practiced by a group of people who withdrew themselves from society and led a natural life by following Dao. They took Dao, not human morality, laws, or divine commands, as their model. As Kristofer Schipper describes, "Daoism is the search for the Dao, the way of Nature, which, if you could become part of it, would take you to the edge of reality and beyond" (1993, 2). As a way of life, Daoism has had a great influence on all aspects of Chinese culture, including the arts (painting, poetry, literature), food, and medicine.

Most of these contradictions might have been caused by the confusion of the two traditions within Daoism. In China, Daoism is divided between philosophical Daoism (*daojia*) and religious Daoism (*daojiao*).

*Daojia* refers to the earlier form of Daoist thinking, which had its first "manifesto" in a book later known as *Daode jing* (*The Way and Its Power*). This short collection contains sayings and aphorisms of a group of thinkers who contemplated Dao, the mysterious and unfathomed source of the universe, and were determined to lead their life in accordance with the fundamental principles of Dao. Although traditionally attributed to Laozi, supposedly an elder contemporary of Confucius (551–479 B.C.E.), the *Daode jing* is now generally believed to have been compiled during the early Warring States period (475–221 B.C.E.). Another representative of early Daoist philosophy is Zhuangzi (369?–286? B.C.E.), who preferred leading a simple life in a natural environment to pursuing the life of wealth and high ranks in the capital and who regarded life and death as nothing more than different stages of the great transformation of Dao. Institutionalized Daoism developed a few centuries later, first in a number of religious-military movements that claimed to base their political ideals and religious principles on the teachings of the *Daode jing.* Under Buddhist influence, it gradually formed different sects emphasizing particular scriptures and rituals and incorporating monastic systems. Since the thirteenth century, religious Daoism has manifested itself in two major traditions, *Quanzhen,* or "Perfect Truth Daoism," and *Tianshi,* or "Celestial Master Daoism." The headquarters of the former is located in Beijing, whereas that of the latter is on the Mount of Dragon and Tiger in the South.

It is not too difficult to detect major differences between *daojia* and *daojiao,* although the latter always claims to be based on the thinking of the former, and Laozi is considered to be the founder of Daoist religion. *Daojia's* main interest lies in exploring the cosmic principle or power by which the ideal way of life can be developed. *Daojiao's* main pursuit is longevity or immortality, enforced by institutionalized rituals and personal practices. *Daojia* normally shows a strong moral and political indifference toward, if not a total ignorance of, politics and ethics. *Daojiao,* appealing more to the layperson, stresses the importance of moral commitment and political engagement. Whereas early Daoist philosophers committed themselves to no spiritual power but only the Dao itself, religious masters made use of ritual and worship, taking spiritual beings as anthropomorphic embodiments of Dao. *Daojia* takes life and death as natural processes and considers social engagement the source of human corruption. *Daojiao* aims to prolong life and to avoid death, and immortality is therefore taken as the highest goal.

It is generally held that Daoism is more a way of life than a sect or an organization and that everybody can claim to be a Daoist, with or without a particular association with Daoist temples or rituals or sects, if he or she lives by the belief that the universe is fundamentally harmonious and centered on the omnipresent Dao, actively balanced by its two cosmic powers, yin and yang, and constantly changed by the vital energy that is called *qi.*

## THE COSMIC FOUNDATIONS OF DAOIST SEXUALITY

Dao, *qi,* and yin-yang constitute the core of Daoist doctrines. They underlie all existence and change in the world, natural as well as human, and activate and maintain cosmic harmony.

### Dao and the Mysterious Female

In Daoist cosmology, Dao represents the primary energy, momentum, source, and principle of the universe. Julia Ching attempts to identify Dao with two Greek words: *logos* (the word) and *hodos* (the way) (1993, 88). The difficulty in determining the nature of Dao is exacerbated by the two uses of the term in the *Daode jing:* the eternal or constant Dao and the temporary Dao. In the first sentence of the first chapter of the book, the *Daode jing* states that the eternal Dao cannot be told or described in human language. Dao is whence "ten thousand things" come, but Dao itself, as the origin of "Heaven and Earth," cannot be described. Since the eternal Dao is beyond the grasp of human intelligence, any attempt to define Dao would distort or limit it, and what is talked about is already not the Dao as the origin of the universe, but the ordinary *dao,* diverse common ways.

In Chapter 4 of *Daode jing,* Dao is said to be "the ancestor of ten thousand things," and it is admitted that nobody knows from whence it comes. The only guess is that it seems to have existed before the Lord (*Di*). In Chapter 25, Dao is called the "Mother of Heaven and Earth," a phrase used by Daoists to refer to the origin of the universe. It is said to be motionless and formless, to stand alone and never change. Dao is like the "spirit of valley" because it embraces all things without rejecting any of them; and it is named after the mysterious female, for it "gives birth to" all creatures and human beings: "The spirit of valley never dies. It is named the Mysterious Female. The Doorway of the Mysterious Female is the root from which Heaven and Earth came into being" (chap. 6).

71

As the mystery of the universe, Dao is hidden from our senses. However, we can contemplate its manifestations: "The highest virtue is like water. Water is beneficent to all things, but does not contend with them. Water stays in places which other things despise. Therefore it comes close to Dao" (chap. 8).

As the source of the universe, Dao also sets guidelines for all beings: "Humans conform to the way of Earth, the Earth conforms to the way of Heaven, Heaven conforms to the way of Dao, and Dao conforms to its own nature" (chap. 25). Dao not only provides the principle or laws for all activities and all things but is also their vitality: "The great Dao flows everywhere. All things depend on Dao for life" (chap. 34).

Through the metaphors of the mother, the female, water, and the valley, Dao is undoubtedly associated with feminine features such as softness and tranquility. However, despite traditional associations of femininity with weakness, the feminine aspect of Dao is the power by which everything else can be overcome: "The female always overcomes the male by tranquility" (chap. 61).

### Yin-Yang Harmony

Daoists define the nature of Dao in terms of harmony. It is believed that harmony is intrinsic to the cosmos and is achieved by the interaction of the two powers of yin and yang: "One yin and one yang, that is the Dao" (*Book of Changes,* Great Commentary I, author's translation).[1] For a Daoist, the ultimate goal is to be one with Dao, which means to return from the phenomena to the origin, from the surface to the core of existence, and from the temporal to the eternal. As the source, Dao initiates the cosmic generating process from the one to the two cosmic powers, and through the "cosmic intercourse" of yin and yang, myriad things are born. Coming from the same Dao, yin and yang require each other for completion, and the one cannot be understood without the other. Yin and yang complement each other, yet at the same time they are opposites, keeping each other in balance while opposing each other. In this way, they reach harmony: "All ten thousand things carry yin and embrace yang. Through the blending of these vital forces, they achieve harmony" (*Daode jing,* chap. 42). Therefore, the relationship between yin and yang is not dualist but polar. The unity of yin and yang is best illustrated by such reciprocal relationships as the self and others, heaven and earth, parents and children, and so on. The yin-yang polarity means that the world is in a process of transformation rather than of creation and destruction.

Although the idea of yin-yang polarity predates what we usually think of as the Daoist tradition and is not exclusively Daoist, Daoism has made it a key part of its cosmic speculations and worldview. It is an essential part of its cosmology and its theory of sexuality. First, the relationship of yin and yang is characterized by interconnectedness, interdependence, and openness, which opens up the potential of mutuality and complementarity in sexuality. From this idea, the majority of Daoists deduce that women and men, as human manifestations of yin and yang, are mutually needed, and the male and the female rely on each other for completion.

Second, yin and yang function in different ways to drive the process of transformation. Yang is associated with heaven, representing day, the sun, fire, light, warm, and the male and masculine qualities; yin is associated with earth, manifested as night, the moon, water, dark, cold, and the female and feminine features. The relation between yin and yang is therefore cosmic (that between earth and heaven), anthropological (that between woman and man), and ethical (that between gender roles in family, community, and society), and their order (yin preceding yang) strengthens the tendency in Daoism to give precedence to the feminine over the masculine.

Third, yin-yang is the Daoist way to depict the productivity of cosmic powers and the model of human regeneration. When yang (heaven) and yin (earth) work together, there is growth and production of plants, fruits, and so on. Heaven is seen as a fertilizing agency, taking the initiative from above and thus generating life. Earth is seen as existing below, receptive and passive, but developing life in its "womb": giving birth to and nourishing its offspring. The cosmic law also applies to the male and the female: "Heaven and Earth mingle their essence to transform and generate the ten thousand things; while the conjoining of the essences of the male and the female leads to the transformation and birth of all creatures" (*Book of Changes,* Great Commentary II, chap. 5).

Fourth, neither yin nor yang exists as an isolated entity. The opposition and complementarity between yin and yang are manifested at the cosmic level (earth and heaven, the moon and sun, tranquillity and activity), in nature (water and fire, lake and mountain), in family (wife and husband, sister and brother, daughter and son), in religion (the soul from earth—*po*—and the spirit from heaven—*hun*), in the moral realm (yielding and aggressive), and in the human body (kidney and liver, emotion and reason). All these are of the same yin and yang powers, and disturbance in one area can disrupt other areas. The cosmic yin-yang harmony can only be maintained if there is harmony in nature, the state, the family, and the human body; damaging any of them can cause disorder in the whole universe.

Fifth, Daoist yin-yang cosmology takes the gender of a human as the result of yin and yang balance. A female is one in which the yin force dominates, whereas a male is where yang overwhelms yin. At the same time, they rely on and penetrate each other. Yin and yang contain each other in themselves, and thus the male is not exclusively yang, nor is the female exclusively yin. In other words, yang qualities such as generating or being aggressive, forceful, or harsh—in one word, masculinity—and yin qualities such as procreation, yieldingness, weakness, softness, or kindness—femininity—are not exclusive properties of the male or the female. Both male and female possess all these qualities, albeit in different degrees or quantities.

## *Qi and the Necessity of Cultivation*

One of the major concerns for Daoists is how to lift human life to the level of Dao so that humans can last as long as heaven and earth. In this sense, "A Taoist is by definition a man or woman who attempts to attain immortality in the present life" (Saso 1990, 3). Seeking immortality in the present life takes various forms in the Daoist tradition, of which the inner cultivation of the vital force—*qi*—is of great importance for Daoist sexual practice.

*Qi* is the manifested form of Dao. As the underlying principle and genealogical origin of the universe, Dao is formless and motionless. However, as the creative power of the cosmos, it is manifested as the flowing and changing *qi*, a kind of "matter-energy." *Qi*—originally referring to vapor, breath, and air—is taken as the unifying power penetrating the whole universe, pervading the whole cosmos, and all living and nonliving things, including human beings: "All that is under Heaven is one breath" (Zhuangzi 1996, 188). Originally, there was only *qi* in the universe. The *qi* of this state is called the original or "primordial breath" (*yuan qi*), which is what activates the "bellows" of the cosmos (*Daode jing*, chap. 5) and which is the "vast breath of the universe" (Zhuangzi 1996, 8). The *qi*, through condensation and combination, forms various beings and things. There are many different species in the world; however, in the last analysis, they are all products of *qi* or various manifestations of the original *qi* that is the source and resource of all energy and power generating and regenerating the universe.

Dao manifests itself in *qi*, and *qi* has genders. When the original *qi* expanded itself, the pure and light component (i.e., the yang *qi*) ascended and formed heaven (the first yang phenomenon), whereas the coarse and heavy element (i.e., the yin *qi*) descended and formed the earth (the first yin phenomenon). The yang *qi* from heaven and the yin *qi* from earth combined to produce myriad things, including human beings. Like all other beings, humans are composed of and animated by *qi*. It is believed that both the human mind and the human body have their origin in bipolar *qi*: the intellect or essence (*jing*) comes from heaven, and the human form or body is endowed from earth. These two combine to constitute a person, as described by Han scholar Wang Chong (27–91 C.E.): "Heaven and Earth conjoin their *qi*, and ten thousand things come into being. This is like the husband and his wife who conjoin their *qi*, hence a child is born" (Huang 1990, 775). As a being, each human lives both on internal power and on external powers, which are of the same nature and from the same source and therefore can be used to strengthen each other. Inhaling external *qi* and circulating it through the body is the same as cultivating the internal *qi* to make it strong and powerful through meditation, physical exercises, and sexual practices.

It is typical of the Daoist understanding that the human body functions in correspondence to the primordial working of the universal principles by which yin and yang operate. The body functions well or poorly, depending on the particular combinations of yin and yang. It is also suggested that the changing balance between yin *qi* and yang *qi* determines the stages of human life. At birth, a human is full of the yang *qi*, and according to Saso (1990, 19), as one grows:

> *Yang* waxes until at maturity it has reached its peak. But *Yin* too is present, in germinal form within man. As life goes on, *Yin* increases, and *Yang* gradually flows away. Finally, at the moment of death, the balance of *Yin* and *Yang* is no longer effective, man's breath, spirit, and seminal essence are dissipated.

Death is therefore not a separation of the body and spirit as it is understood in the West, but is rather the separation of the yin *qi* and the yang *qi* within the human body.

*Qi* exists in and motivates both the cosmos and the human person. Having been formed by the vital forces of heaven and earth, humans are capable of cultivating cosmic powers, refining the *qi* within, and absorbing the *qi* without into their own existence. In Daoist terminology, this process involves working on the vital power, or *qi gong,* a way of refining one's mind and body by controlling one's breath or by taking in the cosmic power. *Qi* can be cultivated because it is believed that *qi* is closely related with life essence (*jing*) and spirit (*shen*).[2] *Qi* is where human vitality lies, but the potential power of *qi* in the human body is mostly neglected, and the clear nature of humans is thus obscured by the desires. It is believed that if one cultivates one's body and concentrates one's mind, the *qi* within the body and the *qi* of the mind can be refined and empowered. When *qi* is powerful, one's essence will be full of vitality, and one's spirit will be in harmony. The necessity of cultivating *qi* also comes from the fact that our daily activities "contaminate" the original *qi.* The original *qi* exists in void, quietness, and simplicity; penetrates into every being; and becomes its life and energy. However, the original *qi* within one's body is confined to a limited area as soon as one has developed consciousness and engaged in daily activities. It is therefore a Daoist conviction that to practice *qi* is to dismantle human-made obstacles and "to return" to one's beginning—infancy— when human vitality is at its peak, "concentrating *qi* on becoming soft and tender like a baby" (*Daode jing,* chap. 10). Believing that the energy in the body is latent, Daoists develop various methods to make it manifest and strong, such as opening *qi* channels and guiding *qi* to flow along the large or macrocosmic circulation (i.e., the circulation of *qi* in the whole body) and the small or microcosmic circulation (i.e., only through the two main meridian lines in the upper part of the body). Besides these methods, some Daoist schools also have developed sexual practices by which the male's yang *qi* can be strengthened by the female's yin *qi* and the female's yin *qi* nourished by the male's yang *qi.*

In this sense, Daoism can be described as the way of harmony, in which all beings and things are conceived of as a continuum of one order of being, differing only as a matter of degree. Humans are regarded as an integrated part of the cosmos and the human body as a microcosm of the universe, which not only is governed by the same laws operating in the universe but also is animated by the same forces that drive cosmic changes. The Daoist perception of life and human gender is closely related to its cosmology.

Daoist cosmology and sexuality are therefore mutually contained: sexuality must be interpreted or explained by cosmology, and cosmology can be illustrated by sexuality. On the surface, Daoist discourses on sexuality seem to be totally concerned with individuals' cultivation of life and closely related to medical practices. At its root, however, Daoism regards woman and man as human manifestations of yin and yang and believes that their relationship simply reflects the cosmic unity and harmony. Just as the harmony of yin and yang is crucial for the whole universe, the relationship between different genders is mutually supplementary and harmonious.

## ETHICS, GENDER, AND FAMILY

The interdependence and mutual supplementation of cosmology and sexuality is the key to understanding Daoist sexuality. Not only did Daoists develop an understanding of sexuality based on their cosmic conception, but also mental and physical practices (including sexual ones) reinforce fundamental values of Daoist cosmology. In this way Daoism generates a unique cosmo-sexual way of dealing with issues and problems arising from gender and sexual relations.

### The Cosmic Ethic of Sexuality

From their efforts to reconstruct the cosmos in human beings and in human life, Daoists derive a particular ethic of sexuality. At least in the early stages, social requirements were not a primary concern for the practitioners of Dao; it is the pursuit of immortality that carries the force of ethical imperative in Daoism. Rules of sexual morality are primarily viewed as an extension of cosmic principles. Man and woman are simply considered the microcosmic embodiments of heaven and earth, and therefore they should observe and follow the way of heaven and earth, as is advised in one of the earliest extant writings, *Shi wen,* or the *Ten Questions:*

> The gentleman who desires long life must follow and observe the tao [*dao*] of heaven and earth. The ch'i [*qi*] of heaven waxes and wanes with the phases of the moon, and therefore it lives forever. The ch'i [*qi*] of earth alternates cold and hot with the seasons of the year; the difficult and the easy supplement each other. In this way, the earth endures without corruption. The gentleman must study the nature of heaven and earth and put this into practice with his own body. (Wile 1992, 12)

Sexuality facilitates the cosmic unity of yin and yang. It is believed that yin-yang harmony not only underlies cosmic evolution and change but also is the fountainhead of life and joy, without which nothing is left for humans but death and destruction. This is confirmed by Su Nü, the Plain Girl, one of the immortal specialists on sex: "Because heaven and earth have attained the *tao* [*dao*] of union, they are eternal; because mankind has lost the *tao* [*dao*] of intercourse, he suffers the onset of early death" (Wile, trans., 1992, 85). Thus, this cosmo-sexual understanding leads some Daoists to regard all human organs, sexual relations, and sensations as cosmic elements. For example, the heart and genitals are likened to fire and water, and sexual arousal is compared to the rising sun. Since heaven revolves to the left and earth spins to the right, men and women should do the same in preparing for coition. Sexual postures are characterized by names derived from different animals and landscapes. In *He yin-yang,* or the *Uniting Yin and Yang,* a work dating to the second century B.C.E. or earlier, the ten basic sexual movements are called "roaming tiger, cicada clinging, measuring worm, roe deer butting, locust spreading, monkey's squat, toad in the moon, rabbit bolts, dragonflies and fishes gobbling" (Wile, trans., 1992, 78–79), and these postures are described in a work of the Sui-Tang era (581–907 C.E.), *The Classic of Su Nü,* in a more detailed way (Wile, trans., 1992, 88–89). Finally, sex is considered one of the important means of physical cultivation, either in the form of nourishing one's vital energy (*qi*) or as part of strengthening one's essence (*jing,* associated with semen in men and blood in women), both necessary for one's spiritual and physical well-being and for warding off potentially harmful physical and mental forces. For Daoist sexologists, it is clear that "nearly all destruction or self-destruction, almost all hatred and sorrow, almost all greed and possessiveness, spring from starvation of love and sex" (Chang 1977, 13).

Applying cosmic principles to human sex, certain Daoist schools developed a code of conduct in relation to human sexuality. This code is elsewhere said to be the *dao* (way) of sex, which we are repeatedly told in various sexual manuals is capable of harmonizing human sexual activities with the cosmic movement. Underlying the Daoist way of sex is the belief that yin and yang, or woman and man, are mutually dependent and that when united they not only produce things and beings but also transform themselves. In practice, the way of sex is observed in one's sexual relationship with one's partner, which although described differently in different texts, requires the sexual partners to strengthen rather than to weaken each other. For example, in *The Classic of Su Nü,* the Yellow Emperor is advised to pay great attention to the following matters before and during sexual practice: how to regulate one's own life energy and harmonize it with that of one's sexual partner(s), how to avoid various damages that may arise from sex, and how to gain maximum benefits from the union of yin and yang (Wile 1992, 86).

It is crucial that sexual partners regulate and harmonize their own life energy (*qi*) within. Sex in Daoism is basically driven by life energy, and without first cultivating and harmonizing that energy, one should not enter the realm of the bedchamber. For these purposes, sexual partners must know each other's desires and the signs of arousal. "When the man desires intercourse but the woman is not pleased, or if the woman desires intercourse but the man is not desirous, their hearts are not in harmony and their *ching-ch'i* [jing-qi] is not aroused" (Wile 1992, 86).

In some branches of the Daoist tradition, sex is believed to hold the key for curing illnesses and for strengthening one's body. Therefore a very important part of the Daoist code of sex focuses on how to benefit from sexual intercourse. One text advises that in sex, man and woman should seek eight benefits, which will guarantee each other a proper unity of yin and yang: "strengthening the life essence (*jing*)," "calming the vital energy (*qi*)," "profiting the internal organs," "strengthening the bones," "regulating the circulation," "nurturing the blood," "increasing the fluids," and "regulating the whole body" (Wile 1992, 90).

### Gender and Gender Equality

Gender and gender equality are complicated issues in the Daoist tradition, not only because of the changes of attitudes toward women from the early texts to the later literature but also because of the interaction between Daoism and Confucianism. Both Confucians and Daoists sought cosmic justification for their views of gender. They observed that there was a fixed order in the universe—of summer following spring, of things being high and low, first and last, strong and weak—and thought that these immutable truths must apply also to human relations. If the earth rose above heaven, woman rose above man, or winter came before autumn, then there could be little doubting that the universe must be out of balance and human communities in chaos.

However, Confucians drew the significance of gender differentiation from a social-political structure that maintained hierarchical relations, such as between the ruling and the ruled, husband and wife, and parents and children; early Daoists took a naturalistic attitude toward gender and gender equality, considering men and women to have been naturally endowed with intrinsic values and to have had particular positions in the cosmic scheme.[3] In this sense, Daoist sexuality can be said to be a revolt against the traditional mentality in which the male was given the position of superiority and dominance over the female, and the relationship between men and women was primarily conceived of as the means to produce offspring for continuing the ancestral tradition in a socially sanctioned way. In an environment in which ethical codes prevailed that required women to accept and know their place in society and family, early Daoists opted for a different type of gender morality, which, as some scholars claim, propagated a kind of gender equality (Kleinjans 1990, 99–127).

The early Daoists indeed tended to endow the female with great cosmic significance, believing that it was she rather than the male who was closest to Dao, the source and primary power of the universe, and that Dao was better described in terms of the female or the mother rather than those of the male or the father. This cosmic conception of femininity enabled Daoists to allow women a more important role in society, family, and sexuality and to give priority to feminine qualities such as tranquillity and flexibility. Some later Daoist schools of sexual practices even claimed that the *dao* of sex must be established on this principle: "Women are superior to men in the same way that water is superior to fire" (*The Classic of Su Nü,* Wile, trans., 1992, 85). Although this characteristic attitude toward femininity was later overshadowed to a great extent by the more patriarchal ethic propagated by Confucianism, Daoism has nevertheless acted as a counterbalance to patriarchy.

On such a theoretical foundation, religious Daoism nurtured an affection toward female deities, such as that which led to the fervent worship of the Queen Mother of the West (Xi Wangmu) during the Qin and former Han dynasties (221 B.C.E.–8 C.E.), and to the prominence of the female religious leaders in Daoism, such as Wei Huacun (251–334 C.E.), a married woman and mother of two, who became the matriarch of the Maoshan school of Daoism and is considered to have been its founder (Schipper 1993, 129). The Daoist understanding of femininity was probably at least partly responsible for the replacement of the male bodhisattva Avalokitesvara by a goddess of compassion (Guan Yin) in Mahayana Buddhism, the widespread faith in the Eternal Mother (Wusheng Laomu) of various messianic movements in the Ming and Qing dynasties (1368–1911), and the popularity of goddesses (*niangni-*

*ang*) in folk religion, where we can see clearly an influence of Daoist views on gender and sexuality.

However, Daoist thinking about the relation between the genders does not accord with modern liberal views of equality. Indeed, modern scholars have argued that the Daoist view of the female, in one way or another, has strengthened the negative, rather than the positive, view of women. In the *Daode jing,* for example, although emphasizing the superiority of the female, the author(s) portray the female virtues as lowness, softness, and weakness and believe that women are more "powerful" than men because they assume a lower and submissive position: "The female always overcomes the male by tranquillity, and by tranquillity she is underneath" (*Daode jing,* chap. 61). It seems that this kind of opinion of women's "strength" does not differ much from the unequal positions traditionally given to men and women, and it is therefore argued that it has helped reinforce, rather than reduce, the inequality between genders in traditional China. In later sexual manuals, men and women are told to follow the way of heaven and earth in the sense that heaven is above and commands, and the earth is below and obeys: "What is above acts and what is below follows" (*Dongxuanzi,* Wile, trans., 1992, 108). Violation of yin and yang, or transgression of above and below, would be harmful to both the man and the woman. It is apparent that this view of the female does not differ much from the Confucian view, which says that women should make their contribution by being content with their own position.[4]

However, even in their similarities, we can identify differences. Both Daoism and Confucianism draw their perception of female virtues from their understandings of the cosmic framework. Both Daoists and Confucians liken husband and wife to heaven and earth. However, while Daoists deduce from this that harmony between a husband and his wife is based upon their natural endowments and should be maintained through the interaction of the cosmic powers, Confucians hold that a woman must take her husband as heaven. From this view emerged a strong emphasis on the loyalty of a wife to her husband and a commandment against the remarriage of widows. Both Daoists and Confucians argue for harmonious sexual relations between man and woman, but certain Daoist schools tend to give more emphasis to the sexual union of yin and yang, whereas most Confucians are more concerned with social consequences such as producing male offspring to carry on the ancestral tradition or maintaining or enhancing the social status of the family through marriage arrangement. Both Daoists and Confucians agree that neglect of one's wife is an offence against the harmony of heaven, earth, and humans, but Daoist practitioners draw from the necessity of yin-yang harmony the techniques of the bedchamber, whereas orthodox Confucians stress that harmony comes only from the strict observance of codes of conduct that starts with the separation of men and women.

The issue of gender equality also can be reviewed from a different point of view: from various manuals on sexual practices that were inspired by the broadly defined Daoist tradition. According to Kristofer Schipper, these "are the only ancient books in the world on this subject that do not present sexuality solely from the male point of view," since they "reflect a rather good knowledge of female anatomy and reflexes" (1993, 126, 238). In these manuals, women's pleasure is defined as one of the preconditions for realizing the sexual energy. And it is noted that in Chinese erotic art, for instance, one often finds the man entreating the woman to have sexual intercourse with him, rather than aggressively pursuing her. Rape is a very rare subject in Chinese erotica (Kronhausen and Kronhausen 1961, 243).

There is a certain limit to the attention paid to women in sexual manuals, for it is apparent that most of the texts on sex were written for men and focused on the male experience. Advice was given to enable a man to gain maximum benefits from intercourse. In extreme cases, men are even warned not to let female partners know the secret of the sexual arts: "Those who would cultivate their yang must not allow women to steal glimpses of this art. . . . If a man wishes to derive the greatest benefit, it is best to find a woman who has no knowledge of this *tao* [*dao*]" (*Secrets of the Jade Chamber*, Wile, trans., 1992, 102).

In late imperial times, especially during the Ming and Qing dynasties (1368–1911), the status of women in sex rapidly deteriorated, which led to the understanding that man and woman are not in harmony but in battle: the battle of the inner chamber, or the battle of yin and yang. The ideas of equality for women and female sexual satisfaction, which had been part of sexual arts in early texts, were largely neglected or totally abandoned. Although the "paired cultivation" tradition in Daoism regards both man and woman as necessary for cultivating Dao, the constant worries of losing one's essence to a woman in intercourse made many a male practitioner treat women with extreme caution and take a woman not as a sexual partner but mainly as a "stove" or "furnace" in which "medicine" could be processed and refined.

However, this does not mean that women do not play a positive role in the Daoist arts of sex. In order to gain benefits from each other, the partners need to arouse each other. Hence lengthy accounts of women's sensibilities and health requirements may be found: "If one proceeds slowly and patiently [in intercourse], the woman will be extremely joyful. She will adore you like a brother and love you like a parent" (*Discourse on the Highest Tao under Heaven,* Wile, trans., 1992, 83). In sexual manuals, women's emotional and physical reactions are studied in detail, and great importance is attached to female satisfaction and the mental and spiritual benefit of both parties. In the conversation between the Yellow Emperor and the Plain Girl, for example, the latter points out that there are five signs, five desires, and ten indications a man must observe and react to:

> First, if there is desire in her mind for union, she will hold her breath. Second, when her private parts desire contact, her nostrils and mouth will widen. Third, when her *ching* [*jing*] desires to be excited, she will quake, quiver, and embrace the man. Fourth, when her heart desires complete satisfaction, perspiration will soak her garments. Fifth, when her desire for orgasm reaches the greatest intensity, her body will go straight and her eyes close. (*The Classic of Su Nü,* Wile, trans., 1992, 87–88)

*The Wondrous Discourse of the Plain Girl* stresses the importance of "respect and love" and "kindness and love" as the basis of conjugal harmony (Wile, trans., 1992, 122–133).

There are also a number of texts that were written solely for women's cultivation, in which women are said to be able to choose between producing male offspring, which enhanced their social position, and seeking the way to eternal youth by exploiting their own yang essence and reverting to girlhood. It is acknowledged that the physical body of women makes it difficult for them to cultivate Dao and that menstruation and childbirth dramatically weaken their "original *qi*" and deplete their "true blood." However, this does not necessarily exclude women from the cultivation of Dao.

There are indeed many female immortals—the Plain Girl, the Mysterious Girl, the Queen Mother of the West, and Immortal Miss He (one of the eight immortals, extremely popular in folk religion)—who are said not only to have entered eternity by using the arts of harmonizing yin and yang, but also to act as instructors for men and women in sexual practices.

### *Celibacy, Marriage, and Family*

Based on the cosmic principle that yin and yang need and complement each other, most Daoists naturally conclude that the male and the female must be interrelated and so benefit each other both physically and spiritually. Historical records show that Laozi had a family and at least one son. Zhuangzi's naturalistic philosophy is also reflected in his relation to his own family members. Zhuangzi is said to have had a wife and children, and when his wife died, Zhuangzi felt sad and mourned but then stopped mourning and sang with joy. Puzzled by this, his friend asked for the reason. Zhuangzi said it was because he understood that she had returned to her cosmic sources, "at peace, lying in her chamber" and "if I were to sob and cry it would certainly appear that I could not comprehend the ways of destiny" (Zhuangzi 1996, chap. 18). The founder of Celestial Master Daoism, Zhang Daoling (active 142–165 C.E.), married, and his movement spread widely and rapidly, particularly under the direction of his son and then his grandson Zhang Lu (active 190–220 C.E.). Ge Hong (283–363? B.C.E.), the author of *Baopuzi,* or the *Master Who Has Embraced Simplicity,* a pioneer of Immortality Daoism and Alchemy Daoism, married, and the couple are said to be the first famous Daoist couple who practiced the "paired cultivation" (discussed below). It was only in the life of Lu Xiujing (406–477 C.E.) that we find a clearly defined instance of a man separating himself from his wife and leaving his family to practice Dao. It seems that Daoist celibacy became a widely accepted practice only after the fifth century C.E., probably driven by the influence of Buddhist celibacy and enforced to a great extent by the pressure from the state and local communities who imposed on Daoists the Buddhist model of celibate monasticism.

From the above-mentioned facts, we can see that most early Daoist individuals approved of or at least did not oppose marriage and family, and some of them chose to abstain from sex, whereas others practiced Dao in their sexual relationships. Taking into account the variety of Daoist practices in relation to asceticism, renunciation, and spiritual cultivation, we may well say that whether Dao is practiced through sex or not is probably more a personal choice than a universal rule. Different Daoist traditions have different regulations concerning the enforcement of celibacy. Although in Celestial Master Daoism, Daoist priests are required to marry and sexual union is part of their initiation (the *Guodu yi* ritual), in the more individual and mystical revelations of the *Shangqing* school, practitioners are enjoined to avoid sex so as to be entirely devoted to divine love partners. Furthermore, it is clear that cultivation of Dao while living in the family (*zai jia*) has been a central practice in Daoism. For quite a long period and in various Daoist schools, there was no necessary contradiction between cultivating Dao at home and cultivating Dao in monasteries. There are Daoist writings dated to the sixth century that advocate *chu jia* (celibacy; literally, "to leave behind the family") and Daoist rites for *chu jia* during the Song era (960–1279), but it was only with *Quanzhen* Daoism that there appeared a real order in which all clerics were celibate. According to Joseph Needham, it "was such a departure from the general tendencies of early Taoism that one can hardly fail to suspect the influence of Buddhist asceticism" (1967, vol. 5, part 3, 205, n. j). Even within the *Quanzhen* tradition, however, there are groups and organizations that defy the celibacy rule (for example, a large lay *Quanzhen* organization was composed of married people during the nineteenth century).

Although it is genuinely believed among Daoist practitioners that Dao can be cultivated anywhere and in daily life, there is always tension between the individual cultivation of Dao and one's commitment to family, and from this tension arises a constant question: can marriage and family life benefit, rather than damage, the personal cultivation of immortality that is the ultimate goal of a Daoist? Reasoning from Daoist cosmology, some have argued that a Daoist does not need to engage in family life for his or her cultivation of Dao. What worries Daoist believers is whether marriage and family life might prevent them from concentrating on Dao and distract them from cultivating vital energy. More detrimentally, by engaging in sexual life within (polygamous) marriage and family, one risks losing one's essence, the fundamental power enabling one to become immortal. This concern can be seen from many conversations recorded in early literature regarding the negative effects of sex on human health, in which Daoist practitioners are constantly reminded that without conscious guard for one's sexual activities, one's life will be in danger. The Daoist solution to this problem is the supreme knowledge of Dao and proper guidance from Daoist specialists, and in many sexual manuals we find an assurance that if a man knows how to nourish his yin and yang through sexual intercourse, he will be like the Yellow Emperor, who is supposed to have slept with 1,200 women and become an immortal. In this kind of literature, communion of man and woman is compared with fire and water, which both kill and give life, as indicated by Ge Hong: "It all depends if one really knows the Way. If knowing the essential way [of sex], then the more women a man makes love with, the better [for his health]. But if he does not know the Way, then just one woman is enough to hasten him to his grave" (Wang 1985, 129).

By the sixth century C.E., more and more Daoists had chosen to be celibate in order to concentrate on cultivating Dao, and Daoist temples (*guan*) emerged, perhaps modeled upon Buddhist monasteries, which provided a sanctuary for those who escaped from family life and embraced celibacy. It gradually became a widespread practice among both male and female Daoists. However, the yin-yang cosmic principle would not totally retreat from the Daoist way of life, and uniting yin and yang was interpreted by some Daoists to mean engaging in sexual practices. Certain manuals therefore advocated a kind of free sex to bring benefits to one's physical and mental health. They suggested that beautiful virgin girls be used to provide the yin essence for a man; women were advised to feed on an energetic man's vital force to become immortals. However, this kind of sex was severely criticized by Confucians and Buddhists as a disgrace to humanity and as criminal behavior. Subsequently, the authorities persecuted all the schools that propagated the "arts of the bedchamber," and orthodox Daoists joined in the condemnation of these arts.

The tension between personal cultivation and sexual practices was only partly overcome by a new approach to the cultivation of Dao: the development of one's vital energy through harmonizing yin and yang within polygamous marriage. Subject to the socially sanctioned mores, the majority of Daoists gradually came to terms with marriage and family in order to minimize social disapproval or criticism, and some of them accepted that sexual practices must be confined to a married couple and sexual relations guided by ethics, not only for the benefit of personal cultivation but also for the benefit of the family. Some Daoists argue that by carefully uniting their yin and yang in accordance with astrological constellations, father and mother not only will give birth to children and be able to determine the sex of the child but also will generate virtue in the family. For example, if one desires to bear offspring who are long-lived, virtuous, intelligent, wealthy, and honored, then one must choose proper times and days to have intercourse. In contrast: "If yin and yang are not united at the proper time, the offspring will be average. If the stars are not united but the time is proper, the offspring will be average to superior. If both stars and time are improper, then the offspring will be common" (*Health Benefits of the Bedchamber*, Wile, trans., 1992, 121).

## DAOIST SEXUAL PRACTICE

It should be clear that Daoist sexuality is not only an attitude toward gender, marriage, and family but also is a type of practice closely associated with the Daoist understanding of the cosmos and life. Three clearly defined purposes are therefore attached to sexual practices: First, sex is a practice to enable one to follow the way of heaven and earth—through the microcosmic intercourse of man and woman, one participates in the macrocosmic harmony of the universe. Second, sex is the way of harmonizing husband and wife and generating descendents to fulfill one's responsibilities to family and society. Third, sex is the way to cultivate one's own *xing* (nature) and *ming* (life or vitality) and to harmonize the mind and the body—that is, through sexual practices, one attains health and long life. In all three aspects, Daoists emphasize complementarity rather than confrontation between sexes.

### *The Arts of the Bedchamber and Paired Cultivation*

There are two kinds of sexual practices traditionally associated with Daoism: the "arts of the bedchamber" (*fangzhong shu*) and the "paired cultivation of yin and yang" (*yin-yang shuangxiu*). For some modern scholars, these two kinds of practice are totally different: the former mainly deals with techniques of sex, including how to manage correctly one's sexual and energetic resources and how to benefit physically and spiritually from sexual orgasm, whereas the latter is a practice of "inner alchemy" (*nei dan*), in which "sexual techniques are used to accomplish alchemical transformations" (Wong 1997, 184).

There was little real connection between Daoist practices and the arts of the bedchamber in the early stages of their development, and the two apparently developed independently for a considerable period of time before they were associated. As far as we know, the arts of the bedchamber appeared earlier than paired cultivation, although "despite their long history, these practices are not well known in China outside Taoist circles" (Beurdeley et al. 1969, 7). In a later stage, the arts were held to be responsible for the corruption of traditional sexual morality and were therefore strongly opposed by orthodox Confucians who, in exercising their powers in administration, had all the literature of this kind branded as evil, degenerate, or at best erotic. This opposition was one of the main reasons why so few texts concerning the so-called arts of the bedchamber survived during the last two imperial dynasties, especially when we compare them to the long lists of the books categorized as the "arts of the bedchamber" or "arts of uniting yin and yang" in earlier dynastic histories. For example, the *Book of the Former Han Dynasty,* compiled during the first century C.E., lists the titles of eight books, each composed of a number of volumes, under the category of the arts of the bedchamber or uniting yin and yang. Apparently, most of these books have been lost.

Although the earliest extant texts already show a special focus on Daoist approaches to physical and mental hygiene and on the Daoist understanding of human sexuality as a way to immortality, the arts of the bedchamber were not explicitly associated with Daoist religion until the end of the Han dynasty (206 B.C.E–220 C.E.), when the religious-military movement called "the Dao of the Five Bushels of Rice" used the arts as ceremonial means to atone for one's sins in order to usher in the "Great Peace" in the human world. By the time of Ge Hong (283–363 C.E.), more than ten schools were active that taught how to use the sexual arts to cure injury or attack illness, to strengthen the yang by absorbing yin, or to achieve longevity or immortality through harmonizing yin and yang.

All these movements had a significant effect on the association of the arts of the bedchamber with the Daoist cultivation of immortality. The exploration of the potential for human immortality laid the foundation for the integration of Daoist cosmology and sexuality. Ge Hong confirmed that human beings must not abstain from the union of yin and yang, for if yin and yang did not interact, disease, sickness, and a shortened life would result. Neither should they overindulge in sex because it would also shorten their lives by draining their vital essence. He therefore recommended the practice of semen retention: "those who desire immortality must conscientiously seek to discover the arts of yin and yang," the essentials of which were "to return the *jing* (essence or semen) to nourish the brain." In this way, one would be able to achieve longevity (Wang 1985, 150).

Strictly speaking, however, paired cultivation of yin and yang as a particularly Daoist practice did not fully develop until after Inner Alchemy Daoism was firmly established in the Song dynasty (960–1279), although its ideas and practices can be traced to a much earlier age. Inner Alchemy Daoism derived its ideas from External Alchemy (*wai dan*), which aimed at producing a "golden elixir" from cinnabar, lead, sulfur, and other elements. External Alchemy became popular in the Han dynasty (206 B.C.E.–220 C.E.) and reached its peak during the Sui and Tang dynasties (581–907 C.E.). However, the toxicity of the "golden elixir" led to the deaths of many Daoists and emperors, and External Alchemy gradually gave way to Inner Alchemy (*nei dan*), which aimed at producing golden elixir within the body by refining *jing* (essence), practicing *qi* (vital energy), and cultivating *shen* (spirit).

Inner Alchemy made use of the terminology of External Alchemy and referred the alchemical terms to elements of the human constitution. For instance, mercury represents the heart, spirit, or the male essence; lead signifies the kidneys, vital force, or the female energy. Although most Inner Alchemy practitioners believed that by harmonizing and refining the essences of yin and yang within each individual (the solo cultivation of Dao), one could achieve longevity, others stressed that the true yin and the true yang exist respectively in males and females and that they must be united through sexual intercourse to achieve immortality. Applying the principles of the Inner Alchemy to sex, they believed that the golden elixir within each of the practitioners could not be made except by a total harmony of yin and yang through properly controlled intercourse, which enabled each of the partners to gather generative energy for transmuting *jing* (life essence, such as semen or "blood") into *qi* (vital energy), and then *qi* to *shen* (spirit).

During the Tang period, paired cultivation was considered significant for human longevity, as is shown in the discussions of "mutual immortality both for men and women" (*Priceless Prescriptions,* Wile, trans., 1992, 117). It was further developed during the Ming dynasty (1368–1644), when a number of Daoists departed from solo cultivation practice, and propagated paired cultivation within marriage. Lu Xixing (1520–1606), an important figure in the paired cultivation of yin and yang sect during this later period, argued, "We must know that the *qi* in man and woman comes from the same *Taiji* or the Great Ultimate, in which the essences of yin and yang are mutually stored in each other's body. Therefore it is impossible to practice single cultivation" (Mou and Zhang 2000, 811).

Clearly different as the arts of the bedchamber and the Daoist way of paired cultivation are, the two were historically associated, not only by the authorities but also by orthodox Confucians and Buddhists, who fiercely attacked Daoism for its alleged "sexual corruption" on moral and spiritual grounds. This undiscriminating attack did not do justice to Daoism because, as a matter of fact, orthodox Daoists always condemned both the arts of the bedchamber and the paired cultivation of yin-yang, regarding their practices and literature as obscene, salacious, and pornographic. When Kou Qianzhi (365–448) reformed the Celestial Master tradition, he attempted to rid Daoist doctrines of all the teachings of sexual arts, and later actions were so extreme as to exclude almost all writings on the arts from the Daoist canon. Many Daoists who practiced paired cultivation were also anxious to disassociate themselves from those who practiced the arts of the bedchamber. To preserve the "pure image" of true Daoists, they criticized the so-called arts of the bedchamber for manipulating sexual techniques for the purpose of mere physical pleasure and for abusing sexual methods in order to violate social ethics.

The paired cultivation of yin and yang is different from the arts of the bedchamber in many respects. The former puts more emphasis on the meditative dimension of intercourse, stressing that sex is only a rationalized and even ritualized stage of the process of transformation; the latter concerns itself with practical methods, contending that sexual practices require both emotional satisfaction and physical orgasm. From the point of view of primary doctrines, however, these two kinds of practice are too close to be completely separated, and any strict distinction between them can be nothing but artificial. As far as the cosmological foundation of sex and the underlying rationale of sexual practices are concerned, no meaningful distinction between them can be made. Both stress that sex is only an extension of the harmony of the feminine and the masculine and that it must strictly follow the cosmic principles. Both maintain that when properly practiced and understood, sex is the means to longevity and immortality, not merely a pursuit of sensual pleasure. For both a vital technique for the cultivation of health and longevity is not to allow vital energy to be carelessly lost. Both consider sexual practices the way to find the harmony of yin and yang and believe that through the interaction of yin and yang, mortal beings can be transformed into immortals.

### Cosmic and Mystic Sex

Either in the form of the arts of the bedchamber or in the tradition of paired cultivation, sexual practices for Daoists are fundamentally cosmic, mystical, and aesthetic. Starting from early Daoist texts, especially the *Laozi* or *Daode jing* and the *Zhuangzi,* Daoist doctrines demonstrate a character of "sexual cosmogony," which is further developed in the commentaries. In *Laozi Xiang'er Zhu,* or *The Xianger Commentary on Daode jing,* accredited to Zhang Daoling or Zhang Lu, the phrase "the gate of the Mysterious Female" is interpreted as the vagina and the "root of Heaven and Earth" as the penis (Harper 1987, 579). Based on their cosmological vision, later Daoist sexual schools took sex as a realization of the mystic union of heaven and earth. Sexual intercourse raises men and women above their lowly places on the earth, and at the moment of harmony (orgasm), they attain an even wider union with the cosmos. In Daoist sexology, human sex is woven into the cosmic web; sexual practice is commanded by the cosmic law and is regarded as an essential part of cosmic harmony. "Heaven and earth have their opening and closing, and yin and yang their activities and transformations. Man must conform to yin and yang and follow the four seasons" (*The Classic of Su Nü,* Wile, trans., 1992, 85). As one who highly valued humans and their function in maintaining cosmic harmony, Li Dongxuan, a Daoist practitioner of the Tang dynasty (618–907), believed that sexual intercourse was an active way to harmonize yin and yang and to fulfill human responsibilities in the cosmos:

> Of all the ten thousand things created by Heaven, man is the most precious. Of all things that make man prosper none can be compared to sexual intercourse. It is modeled after Heaven and takes its pattern by Earth. It regulates Yin and rules Yang. (quoted in van Gulik 1961, 125)

It is a fundamental Daoist tenet that as part of the universe, humans must know when and where they should act, rest, and engage in sexual practice. They must learn how to be in tune with cosmic transformation and how to behave in harmony with natural changes. In terms of seasons, human beings are advised that spring and summer are seasons in which all things are growing and therefore humans must be active, engaging in and making initiatives, whereas in autumn and winter, when everything preserves its energy and the way of heaven is to accumulate its essence, humans should do the same. These principles are also carefully applied to sexual practices, with some Daoist texts giving detailed instructions, such as how many times a man should ejaculate in spring or winter. In order to be in tune with cosmic rhythms, men and women are required to engage in sexual practices not only according to their physical and mental states but also in agreement with the cosmic balance of yin and yang. There are different suggestions with regard to which dates are beneficial for sexual practices. It is sometimes said that the odd-numbered days and particularly the mornings are most beneficial; the even-numbered dates, particularly afternoons, can be harmful. It is also held that that on death days (the fifth, fourteenth, and twenty-third of each month), or during any disturbance of heaven and earth such as thunder or an earthquake, sex would damage one's body and decrease one's essence.

### Medicine, Sex, and Health

Externally, Daoist sexual practices are modeled upon the cosmic union of yin and yang. Internally, sex is taken as the way to the *dao* of life—namely, as the way of leading a healthy and long life. Sex has been considered part of physical health in China, and sexual schools frequently draw their theoretical frameworks from medical practices. According to Douglas Wile, "Sexual practice in its early phases shared a common theoretical foundation with medicine, while developing the special terminology necessary to describe the mutual physiological responses of both sexes during intercourse" (1992, 28). This connection is evident in the earliest extant text on medicine—the *Huangdi Neijing Suwen*, or *Yellow Emperor's Classic of Internal Medicine*, which dates to the late Eastern Zhou dynasty (770–256 B.C.E.)—in which sex is related to medical conditions and is considered to be a remedy for certain physical problems.

Longevity has always been a Chinese obsession. In Daoist literature, long life is not only pursued in terms of quantity but is also measured by quality. Daoists seek a life full of joy, happiness, and health. All these desirable conditions are believed to depend on the quality and vitality of one's *jing* (essence, or man's semen and woman's blood), *qi* (vital energy), and *shen* (spirit). Therefore, sexual practices are intended primarily for preserving, strengthening, and refining these "three treasures." When one's *jing* is plentiful, one's *qi* is strong, and one's *shen* is powerful, one is healthy and free of all illness. It is believed that to be in such a state, one must know how to cultivate *jing, qi,* and *shen* through sexual practices, which are regarded as the key to longevity and happiness: "Those who know the *tao* [*dao*] of yin and yang can fully realize the five pleasures" (*The Classic of Su Nü,* Wile, trans., 1992, 85), which are the states of satisfaction associated with the five senses. On the contrary, if one is ignorant of these practices, one will gradually grow weaker and will die before one's time without ever knowing the joy of life.

To prolong one's life, one must have a calm heart. Therefore in Daoist sexual arts, meditation and cultivation are taken as two important tools for achieving health and longevity, for by these practices one's *qi* will be settled, one's mind calmed, and one's emotions harmonized. The practice of semen retention is also thought to have a positive impact on a man's health; it became popular, in fact, because some had observed that although emission brought a moment of pleasure, it had long-lasting negative effects on the body. As described in the *Classic of Su Nü*:

> After ejaculation a man is tired, his ears are buzzing, his eyes heavy and he longs for sleep. He is thirsty and his limbs inert and stiff. In ejaculation he experiences a brief second of sensation but long hours of weariness as a result. And that is certainly not a true pleasure. On the other hand, if a man reduces and regulates his ejaculation to an absolute minimum, his body will be strengthened, his mind at ease and his vision and hearing improved. (quoted in Chang 1977, 22–3).

Believing that human life is maintained by *jing* and that semen is the most important male life essence, Sun Simao (581–682), a great physician of the Tang dynasty, held that when a man's *jing* (semen) has become scarce, the man becomes sick. Once the *jing* is exhausted, the man will die: "Each time one is able to exercise control it is like adding oil to a flame that is about to go out. If one is unable to control it and wantonly ejaculates, this is like taking oil away from a lamp that is about to burn out" (Wile, trans., 1992, 117).

The authors of sexual manuals also attempted to justify sexual practices on the grounds that yin and yang need to complement each other and that the intercourse of a man and a woman can relieve the anxiety caused by longing for sex: "Man cannot be without woman, and woman cannot be without man. To be solitary but long for intercourse shortens a man's life and allows a hundred ailments to appear" (*The Dangers and Benefits of Intercourse with Women*, Wile, trans., 1992, 120). Unsatisfied desires would cause disturbance in the heart, and the emotional unbalance would damage physical health and spiritual well being: "If he is without a woman, his mind will be agitated. When the mind is agitated, the spirit becomes weary. When the spirit is weary, one's life span suffers," and "ghosts and demons take advantage of this to copulate" with him (Wile, trans., 1992, 120). However, "if one uses the Yang to nurture the Yin, the hundred ailments all dissipate, one's complexion is joyous and lustrous, and one's skin has a thriving appearance" (Harper 1987, 585). It is strongly urged that in order to achieve this state, man and woman must prepare carefully for the union of yin and yang and engage in intercourse by following the principles of yin and yang. Since sex is a means to health and not the end itself, Daoist practitioners require a great deal of preparation and knowledge before entering the union of yin and yang. This knowledge is said to be the *dao* of sex, without which a hundred ailments will appear and life will waste away. For those who have this knowledge, "To know this *tao* [*dao*] is to be joyful and strong. The span of life will be lengthened" (Wile, trans., 1992, 86).

## CONCLUSION

Historically, Daoist sexuality was a matter of controversy and debate. Mainly because of a great number of ambiguities in its theory and practice, there is not yet a clear-cut conception of sexuality among contemporary Daoist believers and practitioners. Traditional Daoist sexuality was shaped by its vision of the cosmic significance of sex. Daoist knowledge of the human body may not be "scientific" in a modern sense, but its understanding of sexual desires and the methods for satisfying these desires has paved the way for a kind of "naturalistic sexuality," which is characterized by the convictions that the natural is the best and that human sex is but a reflection of natural yin-yang harmony. These attitudes about sex might have led a good number of western scholars, after reading Chinese sexual literature, to conclude that sex in China is considered to be perfectly normal and healthy. Having studied Chinese sexual practices in detail, Robert Hans van Gulik maintained that because they were perceived as part of the order of nature, sexual practices in China were never associated with a feeling of sin or moral guilt:

> It was perhaps this mental attitude together with the nearly total lack of repression that caused ancient Chinese sexual life to be, on the whole, a healthy one, remarkably free from the pathological, abnormality and aberrations found in so many other great ancient cultures. (1961, 51)

Although his conclusion is largely true, a thoughtful reflection on Daoist philosophy and practices may prompt us to raise a number of questions and to wonder if Daoist sexuality is really as healthy as it first appears. First, does a sexuality that is based on cosmic principles carry too much mystical value to be "natural"? In the Daoist tradition of paired cultivation, sex is seen as only a part of the process by which one is integrated with the cosmic powers. For this reason, the rituals used before, during, and after sex appear to have overwhelmed sex itself; intercourse became less important than the union with the spiritual and cosmic powers. Second, is Daoist sexual practice an egoistic act? The key to the sexual arts is to nourish one's own essence by making use of the essence or energy of one's sexual partner(s). Although there are many ways to achieve "mutual benefits" in sex and it is always emphasized that sex involves the satisfaction of both parties, the underlying ideas might have opened the path to a kind of sexual exploitation, benefiting oneself at the expense of others. Third, does Daoist sexuality have a sexual bias against women? In our discussion of Daoist cosmology, we have seen that Daoism does have a "feminist" dimension in its cosmic understanding of the universe and that Daoist masters have attempted to elevate the female above the male. When applying this kind of cosmic understanding to human sexual life, many Daoist practitioners of sex attach more value to the female, who is believed to be superior because her yin *qi* is far more lasting than the male's *jing* (semen). However, this so-called feminist position was overshadowed in history by later Inner Alchemy followers' concern about the male's cultivation of Dao, in which the female was taken merely to be a means or "stove" in which the male could process his "inner elixir." Even in those scriptures that focus on women's cultivation of Dao, women are said to be weaker than men and are allowed only a lower position in the ladder of spiritual progression.

Turning our attention from history to the modern era, we can see that Daoism remains to a great extent typical of the Chinese way of life. Daoism continues to be the way of life for the majority of Chinese people in a broad sense, and Daoism as a religion and philosophy is influential in China, Taiwan, Hong Kong, and other overseas Chinese communities. The influence of Daoism is also visible in modern Europe and North America, and certain Daoist values such as "being natural," "harmony," and "the unity of humans with the universe" have been highlighted as possible contributions Daoism can make to world culture and to modern life, although in so doing Daoist philosophy has been considerably transformed in the context of a western understanding (Clarke 2000).

Since the beginning of the twentieth century, Chinese sexuality, in which Daoist ideas play a central part, has caught the attention of western Sinologists—notably Henri Maspero, Robert Hans van Gulik,

Joseph Needham, and more recently Douglas Wile—who study Daoist sexuality by translating and examining extant and newly discovered texts on sexual practices. The translation of Chinese sexual manuals by western Sinologists has led to the publication of a number of "objective" and "historical" studies of sexual life in China.[5]

Largely in their steps, scholars who are from Daoist backgrounds or are Daoist practitioners, such as Jolan Chang and Mantak Chia, have also made attempts to reinterpret traditional theories in a modern context and to introduce the reinterpreted Daoist sexuality to western readers.[6] For them, to engage in the study of Daoist sexuality is to combine theoretical knowledge with personal experience, which has resulted in the publication of a number of "subjective" and "contemporary" sexual manuals in English on the Daoist way of love. These authors enthusiastically argue that the Daoist way of love not only is of historical interest but also continues to be important for modern life. Jolan Chang, for example, himself a practitioner of the Daoist way of sex, believes that "in Taoism was to be found an answer which was both easy and pleasant" to the problems of modern sexual life (1977, 12).

In other introductions to Daoist practices of self-cultivation, sexuality is highlighted as one of the spiritual paths, and occasionally there are reports concerning the ways in which traditional sexual arts are used by contemporary Daoists to promote their physical, mental, and spiritual well-being. However, as far as we know, no substantial studies of contemporary Daoist sexuality are yet available in the West.

In Chinese communities, sexual practices are still largely seen primarily as personal matters within the "bedchamber" and are studied only as part of medical research or psychological counseling. This attitude often precludes unconventional sexual practices from being treated as an important part of modern sexuality. Scrutinizing Daoist texts on women's cultivation, there are some indications that lesbianism is acceptable, and in Daoist monasteries where celibacy is strictly enforced among male clerics, homosexual relations are not unusual. Because there are not yet systematic studies on the contemporary Daoist attitudes toward modern sexualities, we must be content with the general remark that Daoists prefer what are traditionally perceived as "natural" sexual relations over other types of sex, and it seems that in the eyes of those under the heavy influence of Daoist sexuality, homosexuality and other nonnormative sexual relations would be seen as "anti-natural," or "unnatural." Although this designation lacks the moral significance attached to homosexuality in the

West, it suggests that "unnatural" forms of sexuality are detrimental to physical and spiritual health.

## Notes

1.  Although it is generally believed that the *Book of Changes* is a Confucian classic, and the commentaries were traditionally credited to Confucius, the book is also highly revered in Daoism and is taken as a Daoist classic. It is apparent that the final versions of the texts and commentaries were composed under the influence of Daoism and the doctrine of yin-yang and that the ideas contained and explored in this book had a huge influence on the development of Daoism.

2.  *Jing* and *shen* are difficult to define precisely. As far as Daoist inner alchemy is concerned, *jing* can be roughly said to be the refined essence of *qi*. In men, semen is a concrete manifestation of *jing*, and in women, blood is seen as her essence. *Shen* is the ruler of the body, guiding the process of cultivating *qi* and refining *jing*, but at the same time it needs to be nourished and strengthened by *qi* and *jing*, by which the three treasures of *jing*, *qi*, and *shen* can be transformed into golden elixir.

3.  In general, Confucians held a conservative opinion of women, who were to be valued only in the context of the family, as wives or mothers, and confined to a strictly defined role within the home or so-called "inner" realm. The primary virtues of a young woman are described as respect, caution, and obedience, and, more specifically, as filial piety to her parents and parents-in-law, obedience to her husband when married, and education and service to her children. The *Nü Jie*, or *Admonishment on Women*, by Ban Zhao (48–116? C.E.), a female historian and scholar of classics, gives a detailed description of how a woman should behave in the family and toward her husband.

4.  The association of Daoist understanding of women's role with Confucian ethical codes can be seen in the above-mentioned work by Ban Zhao. Although Ban Zhao has been identified with the Confucian tradition and has inspired later female scholars to write more manuals for women, such as *Nü Xiaojing* (the *Classic of Filial Piety for Women*) and *Nü Lunyu* (the *Analects for Women*), what is said in her *Admonishment* demonstrates a mixture of Confucian socio-ethical codes and Daoist cosmo-moral principles. For example, she believed that female virtues were important for a harmonious marriage because these virtues would make a woman an ideal partner in the yin-yang harmony with her husband: the sexual union depends upon yang's ability to dominate and guide and yin's willingness to follow and obey. Man is wonderful for his strength and woman for her

simple submissiveness. Ban Zhao especially emphasized that in the bed-chamber, a woman must discourage excess by her restraint, not by opposing yang but by transforming her own wish for "fire inside the jade pavilion" into transcendental thoughts. Excess sex would induce physical deterioration, which in turn would lead to moral depravity. Apart from the differences of ethical tones, these admonishments could also be accepted by Daoists who practiced sexual restraint to preserve their essential energy.

5.  See, for example, *Sexual Life in Ancient China* by van Gulik and *Art of the Bedchamber* by Wile.

6.  See *The Tao of Love and Sex* by Chang and *Taoist Secrets of Love* by Chia and *Healing Love through the Tao* by Chia and Chia.

## REFERENCES

Beurdeley, Michel, Kristofer Schipper, Chang Fu-Jui, and Jacques Pimpaneau. 1969. *The Clouds and the Rain: The Art of Love in China.* Diana Imber, trans. London: Hammond.

Blofeld, John. 1973. *The Secret and the Sublime: Taoist Mysteries and Magic.* London: George Allen and Unwin.

Chang, Jolan. 1977. *The Tao of Love and Sex: The Ancient Chinese Way to Ecstasy.* London: Wildwood House.

Chia, Mantak. 1984. *Taoist Secrets of Love: Cultivating Male Sexual Energy.* New York: Aurora Press.

Chia, Mantak, and Maneewan Chia. 1986. *Healing Love through the Tao: Cultivating Female Sexual Energy.* Huntington, NY: Healing Tao Books.

Ching, Julia. 1993. *Chinese Religions.* Maryknoll, NY: Orbis Books.

Clarke, J. J. 2000. *The Tao of the West: Western Transformation of Taoist Thought.* London: Routledge.

Harper, Donald. 1987. "The Sexual Arts of Ancient China as Described in a Manuscript of the Second Century BC." *Harvard Journal of Asiatic Studies* 47, no. 2: 539–593.

Huang, Hui. 1990. *Lun Heng Jiaoshi.* Beijing: Zhonghua Shuju.

Kleinjans, Everett. 1990. "The Tao of Women and Men: Chinese Philosophy and the Women's Movement." *Journal of Chinese Philosophy* 17: 99–127.

Kronhausen, Phyllis, and Eberhard Kronhausen. 1961. *Erotic Arts.* New York: Grove Press.

Lau, D. C., trans. 1963. *Lao Tzu Tao Te Ching.* London: Penguin Books.

Mou Zhongjian, and Zhang Jian. 2000. *Zhongguo zongjiao tongshi (A general history of Chinese religions)*, vol. 2. Beijing: Shehui Kexue Wenxian Chubanshe.

Needham, Joseph. 1956, 1967. *Science and Civilisation in China.* Vols. 2, 5 (part 3). Cambridge: Cambridge University Press.

Saso, Michael R. 1990. *Taoism and the Rite of Cosmic Renewal.* 2nd ed. Pullman: Washington State University Press.

Schipper, Kristofer. 1993. *The Taoist Body.* Karen Duval, trans. Berkeley: University of California Press.

van Gulik, Robert Hans. 1961. *Sexual Life in Ancient China.* Leiden: E. J. Brill.

Veith, Ilza, trans. 1966. *The Yellow Emperor's Classic of Internal Medicine.* Berkeley: University of California Press.

Wang Ming. 1985. *Baopuzi Neipian Jiaoshi.* Beijing: Zhonghua Shuju.

Welch, Holmes. 1957. *The Parting of the Way.* Boston: Beacon Press.

Wile, Douglas, ed. and trans. 1992. *Art of the Bedchamber: The Chinese Sexual Yoga Classics, Including Women's Solo Meditation Texts.* New York: State University of New York Press.

Wong, Eva. 1997. *The Shambhala Guide to Taoism.* Boston: Shambhala.

Zhuangzi. 1996. *The Book of Chuang Tzu.* M. Palmer et al., trans. London: Arkana.

## Chapter 4

# A Union of Fire and Water

## Sexuality and Spirituality in Hinduism

*Jeffrey S. Lidke*

*Śiva and Parvati. South Indian dynasties (Dravidian), ca. 800. Together with Parvati, Śiva symbolizes the perfect union and reconciliation of opposites. Parvati is Śiva's creative force and the two are thought to be Divine Lovers. (Giraudon/Art Resource, NY)*

*J*ust as the mighty Ganges River of northern India emerges from a single source high in the Himālayan Mountains and maintains a central current while being fed by and in turn flowing into numerous tributaries, so the Hindu religion has localized origins and core characteristics while being fed by and branching into a multiplicity of interrelated traditions. Hinduism, in one of its many forms, is the living faith of over 1 billion human beings, now spread across the globe. What unites these peoples is a sense of cultural and religious identity that links them to traditions that have developed on the Indian subcontinent (now comprising India, Nepal, Pakistan, Bangladesh, and Sri Lanka) over the last 5,000 years or more.

At first glance, these ideologies and practices appear radically diverse. Some Hindus view this world as an illusion, whereas others see it as the body of divinity. Some believe in the efficacy of rituals, others in the importance of family virtue, and still others in the importance of ascetic discipline. Similarly, attitudes toward sexuality can differ greatly. Some Hindus see sexuality as an expression of one of the four primary aims of human life—pleasure. Hindu ascetics view sexuality as energy to be harnessed. *Tāntrikas,* a special class of yogic practitioners, view sexuality as a potential means to liberation. In short, Hinduism expresses the entire gamut of human attitudes toward sexuality. Like the Ganges with its many tributaries, these diverse attitudes are contained within one greater system, one cultural "river" uniting the diverse lives of Hindus across time and space.

The Ganges is not simply a useful metaphor in our discussion of Hindu sexuality. The great river is revered by Hindus as the earthly embodiment of a divine energy (*śakti*), which is the essence and source of sexual energy. Hindu mythology explains that the waters of the Ganges originally flowed only in heaven. However, one day King Bhāgīratha engaged in intense ascetic practices to cause the Ganges to fall to earth and bring back to life his 60,000 ancestors, who had been reduced to ashes by an angry sage. King Bhāgīratha's practice was so intense that Lord Śiva granted his request that the Ganges fall to earth. Because the river is mighty, the gods feared that it would crush the earth. To buffer the weight of its fall, Lord Śiva agreed to catch the river in his hair. As soon as the goddess Gaṅgā flowed into Śiva's hair she fell in love, and the two deities were married. However, Śiva agreed to let one millionth of the mighty river fall to earth (Dimmitt and van Buitenen 1978, 322). Henceforth, the heavenly river has graced the subcontinent. Every day millions of Hindus bath in and pray to the Ganges, believing that the water is a liquid goddess.

The union of Gaṅgā and Śiva is a union of fluid and fire that serves as a working metaphor for the tradition's understanding of the relationship between sexuality and spirituality. Śiva is a god of fire, who transforms sexual desire (*kāma*) into spiritual heat (*tapas*) through his practice of yoga. Although the inner river of sexual fluid normally flows down and out, Śiva's yogic practice directs the flow of sexuality upward, making it a rising spiritual force. The fourteenth-century *Rudrayāmala-Tantra* explains that the Ganges is in fact the river of Śiva's spiritual power, his *śakti*, which has been enhanced by his meditative practice and control over the fires of passion (*kāma*). Flowing from Śiva's head, the Ganges becomes immortal nectar (*amṛta*) with the power to liberate any Hindu who dies in its purified waters. This is why, each day, hundreds of dead Hindus are carried to burning ghats (cremation grounds) along the earthly Ganges, where fire reduces their bodies to ashes and the water of the Ganges liberates their souls from the endless cycle of death and rebirth. To Hindus, the fire of the ghats and the water of the river are earthly manifestations of divine powers. Indeed, in the Hindu universe, there is a direct correspondence between the body, the world, and the divinity (or divinities) that create all life. In the body is an inner heat, experienced as desire, that corresponds to fire. Fire is, in turn, a spark or manifestation of divine fire. Similarly, sexual fluids within the body correspond to geological substances such as water, which corresponds with a divine fluid that, when combined with fire, produces life.

We mentioned above that a male god, Śiva, is fire, and that a female goddess, Gaṅgā, is water. However, in the intricate universe of Hinduism, fire is also feminine and fluid masculine. As David White has shown (1996, 191) in Hindu traditions of alchemy, the sun is associated with sulfur, which is linked to the sexual fire and fluids of the woman; the moon is associated with mercury and semen. In this complex system of correspondences, the vulva is a fire pit into which the man offers his mercurial fluids during the act of lovemaking, which is understood as a union of fire and fluid, god and goddess. Like the Hindu godhead itself, which, as we will see below, gives rise to the universe by realizing and uniting its male and female aspects, most Hindus believe that all individuals contain within themselves the potency of male and female divinity. This chapter discusses some of the numerous, fascinating implications of this belief.

## THE ORIGINS OF HINDUISM: A MEETING OF FIRE AND WATER

The vast cultural river of contemporary Hinduism flows from at least 5,000 years ago, from religious, cultural, political, and social traditions that began in the Indus Valley (in modern-day Pakistan). The Indus Valley is the site of another important river, called the Sindhu. *Hinduism,* in fact, derives from the Persian word for Sindhu, *hind. Hindu* was initially used by Persians to refer to those communities east of the Indus River. By at least 3,000 B.C.E., these communities were thriving in advanced urban centers. Their religious life appears to have focused on the water-based worship of feminine deities. This equation of water with the feminine derives from a biologic that is fairly universal. The waters of the woman create a nurturing environment in which life develops. Once can surmise that these early communities viewed the Indus and other rivers as feminine deities that made life possible.

However, contemporary Hinduism does not arise from the water-based Indus Valley communities alone. Some time around 3,000 years ago, an Indo-Aryan people entered the subcontinent, migrating southward from the Russian steppes. It was one branch of a greater community that also migrated into Persia, Europe, and the Mediterranean world. These people brought with them a religious ideology and practice rooted in the worship of fire. If we can allow ourselves to roughly characterize the Indus Valley community as "feminine" and "water-based," then the Indo-Aryan community can perhaps similarly be characterized as "masculine" and "fire-based." It is the merging of these two cultures that provides the historical antecedents of contemporary Hinduism.[1]

### The Vedas

Like the Koran for Muslims—of whom there are more than 100 million currently residing in India—the Veda is for Hindus the Word Incarnate. *Veda* literally means "knowledge." However, unlike the Koran, the Veda was not channeled through an intermediary to a single person but was rather received directly by numerous "prophets" (*rishis*). Hindus believe that while meditating, the *rishis* heard the sacred sounds comprising the Veda and later memorized and transmitted them orally. Thus began a process of memorization and preservation that continues unbroken today. As the sound body of the divine, the Veda is for Hindus the eternal source of all creation. Although most historians date the earliest sections of the Veda to at least 2000 B.C.E.—making the Veda the oldest continuous scriptural tradition in the world—most Hindus maintain that the Veda is eternal and ever present.

From the perspective of scholars, the Veda is a composite of four distinct yet interrelated scriptural lineages, known as the Ṛg-Veda, Sāma-Veda, Yajur-Veda, and Atharva-Veda. Each Vedic lineage, preserved by its own school of priests, consists of four textual layers. The oldest section of the Veda is the Saṃhitā, composed of hymns and sacred syllables or mantras. The next oldest section is the Brāhmaṇas, which contain reflections on and instruction for the ritual practice associated with the recitation of the Saṃhitā. Together, the Saṃhitā and Brāhmaṇa portions of the Veda are called the Karma-Kāṇḍa (ritual section), of the Veda. After the Karma-Kāṇḍa came the Āraṇyaka and Upaniṣads, which together form the Jñāna-Kāṇḍa (knowledge section), of the Vedas, comprising philosophical reflections and meditative practices that lead to liberation. Together, the ritual and knowledge sections contain a complete paradigm for religious practice and spiritual liberation.

According to most Hindus, the Veda contains the totality of all knowledge. It is the complete and perfect template of creation. From the Veda arose the paradigm of ritual life for Hindu communities throughout the subcontinent and abroad. At the core of this paradigm is a complex notion of sacrifice.

At the beginning of time, Ṛg-Veda 10.90 explains, the gods made a sacrifice of Puruṣa, the Cosmic Person. The sacrifice began with the con-

struction of a fire altar and the feeding of fluids, mantras, and other offerings into the fire. That was the primordial sexual act that gave rise to
the entire cosmos. Before he was offered to the fire, Puruṣa gave rise to
his feminine self, Virāj, out of his own being, in a manner roughly analogous to the creation of Eve from the rib of Adam. (As we will see below,
this bi-gender thematic will be developed by Hindus in interesting ways.)
After manifesting Virāj, Puruṣa was sacrificed and ritually dismembered.
Through this sacrifice, he became the universe and attained immortality.
In other words, the sacrifice of the Cosmic Person is simultaneously the
birth of all that is ever born. His various ritually dismembered limbs became the sun, moon, stars, animals, plants, and human beings.
Everything in the universe was then assigned its proper place according
to the body part from which it arose. This sense of hierarchical order is
also expressed in the Hindu caste system: the priests, called "Brahmins,"
arose from Puruṣa's head; the warriors, or Kṣatriyas, from his arms; the
merchants, or Vaiśyas, from his legs; and the servile class, or Śudras, from
his feet.

In related passages of the Veda we find that continued sacrifice is
necessary for maintaining truth (*sat*) over untruth (*asat*) and righteousness (*dharma*) over unrighteousness (*adharma*). For this reason, the
Brahmin priests commit themselves to a strict ritual schedule by which
divine order is established and maintained in society. The heart of their
ritual practice is the offering of fluids into fire, a manifestation of the god
Agni, which transmits the ritual offering to the multiple worlds envisioned in the Vedic cosmos. In ancient Hindu society the ability to create and worship this fire was considered the most important social obligation. The fire ritual linked humans to the divine and thereby insured
the continuation of humankind.

It is no accident that fire worship came to be understood as an outer
expression of the inner fire of sexuality, a fire with the capacity to beget
life. Nor is it an accident that the Vedic fire pit was shaped as a downward-facing triangle to resemble a *yoni* (vulva). The fire pit is the primordial womb into which ritual fluids are offered in an act that perpet-
ually regenerates the cosmos. The ritual sacrifice replicates the sacrifice of
Puruṣa in heaven. As Bṛhadāraṅyaka Upaniṣad 6.4.3. explains, it also
replicates the sexual act, in which fluid is offered into the fires of the
womb. "Her lap is a sacrificial altar; her hairs the sacrificial grass; her
skin, the *soma* press. The two lips of the vulva are the fire in the middle.
Verily, indeed, as great as is the world of him who sacrifices with the . . .

[Vedic] sacrifice, so great is the world of him who practices sexual intercourse, knowing this" (quoted in Eliade 1990, 255; ellipses mine).

### Sexuality and the Stages of Life in Classical Hindu Society

Out of the Vedic corpus arose a number of important commentarial scriptures. Like the Vedas, these texts were written in Sanskrit, the "language of the gods." The Vedas are *śruti* (revealed tradition), whereas these commentarial works are called *smṛti* (remembered). *Smṛti* texts include epic narratives; philosophical works; legal treatises; political treatises; treatises on art, architecture, dance, drama, and music; and treatises on love and pleasure. Together, these texts provided the foundations for the Sanskrit-based classical cultures that began to crystallize in India around 2,400 years ago. The core of this classical culture was a system known as the *varṇāśrama-dharma,* which can be translated as the "duties (*dharma*) of the stages (*āśrama*) within the class-system (*varṇa*)." *Varṇāśrama-dharma* needs to be understood in relationship to another concept developed during this time, the "four human aims" (*catur-puruṣārtha*). These four aims are religious duty (dharma), acquisition of wealth (*artha*), fulfillment of sensual pleasures (*kāma*), and spiritual liberation (*mokṣa*). In the classical, Hindu Sanskrit–based vision of the ideal life, each male Hindu of the upper three castes typically goes through four life stages (*āśramas*), during which he systematically attains each of the four human ends.

This journey through the life stages is facilitated by the life-cycle rituals (*saṃskāras*), which link the individual to the greater Hindu community and in turn to the godhead. Naturally, fire and water—or fluid—are the foundation of these rituals. The first life-cycle ritual is conception, which is seen as a sacrificial act in which the male offers his seed into the fire of the woman's womb. The loving relationship of husband and wife replicates the primordial sacrificial act, the sacrifice of Puruṣa. As we shall see below in the discussion of Tantra, sex-as-sacrificial-act is also a potential vehicle for spiritual emancipation. For just as Puruṣa attains transcendence after being sacrificed into the fire pit at the beginning of time, so human beings can attain transcendence through sacrificing themselves to each other in the act of ritualized lovemaking.

At age twelve, a Hindu boy of the upper three classes—*vaiśya, kṣatriya,* and *brahmin*—undergoes a very important life-cycle ritual known as *upanāyana.* In this ceremony, the boy receives a sacred thread that signifies he has entered the first stage of life, known as *brahmācārya,* which literally means "moving in God." After initiation, the boy begins to "move into God" by studying the Vedas and related texts. Toward this end, he maintains celibacy and studies under the guidance of a teacher, or guru, who has mastered the Vedic tradition. During the *upanāyana* ceremony, the boy also receives a threefold sacred fire that he is to maintain and observe for the course of his life. The triadic fire symbolizes at once the burning wisdom of the Vedas and the inner fire, called *tapas,* which he will nurture throughout his life. As a student, he fans this fire through the maintenance of celibacy. During this stage of life, the boy is focused on the acquisition of the knowledge of *dharma,* or religious obligations. This knowledge prepares him to become like Puruṣa, by transforming his life into a sacrificial offering and eventually attain transcendence.

In the second stage of life within the *varṇāśrama* system, the student becomes a householder, called *gṛhasthin,* and shifts his focus toward the acquisition of the next two aims of life: the pursuit of sensual pleasure (*kāma*) and material well-being (*artha*). During this phase, the outer fire received at his initiation is worshipped in his home; the inner fire, cultivated through his prolonged celibacy—classically until the age of twenty-four—bears fruit through the production of progeny and the enjoyment of the senses with his wife, the microcosmic equivalent of Puruṣa's Virāj, or feminine self.

In the third stage of life within the *varṇāśrama* system, the elderly householder, having now witnessed the birth of his children's children, begins to withdraw from societal obligations. This is the stage of the "forest dweller" (*vānaprastha*), in which a Hindu turns his focus toward the final aim of life, called *mokṣa,* defined as the permanent release of the individual self (*ātman*) from all suffering.

The fourth and final stage within the *varṇāśrama* system is renunciation (*saṃnyāsa*). It culminates in *mokṣa.* Just as Puruṣa sacrifices himself to become the universe and thereby attains transcendence, so the Hindu male (although there are paradigms for female ascetics) who reaches the final stage of *saṃnyāsa* seeks transcendence as the fruit of his ongoing sacrifice. Entrance into this stage is marked by the performance of one's own funeral rights. Classically, the funeral rite is the final rite of passage. After death, most Hindus are taken to a funeral pyre, where their bodies are offered to the divine fire. The most famous of all cremation sites is the city of Banaras, which is built along the banks of the Ganges. At Banaras, the ashes of cremated bodies are thrown into the waters of the Ganges. In this way, the body, being the product of fire and water, returns in the end to fire and water, in a final act that reminds one that birth and death contain each other.

For Hindus entering the stage of *saṃnyāsa,* however, the performance of one's own funeral rite marks the death not of the body but of the former, socially determined self. The very same triadic fire that was received from one's teacher and was worshiped in one's house during the householder phase of life is now used to light the funeral pyre in which one symbolically dies. Afterward, the renunciant wears ochre robes representing his immersion in the divine fire that he will generate within until it has completely purified him. Upon his death, he will not be burned. Instead, his body, which has already been burned through the fires of renunciation, will be immersed in the Ganges. Having been burnt by the internal fire of renunciation, his body has become the container for the divine flame of the self, which is now liberated from the cycle of rebirth.

In the *varṇāśrama* system, fire and fluid mark all stages of the male Hindu journey. Life begins with the offering of the male fluid into the fire pit of the womb. The period of study commences with the gift of the Vedic fire during the rite of initiation from the guru. Internal fire, as sexual potency, is generated, and sexual fluids are preserved during this time to create children during the householder stage. And in the end, fire marks the sacrifice of the social self, a sacrificial death by which the Hindu realizes his identity as that very same transcendent, undying person (Puruṣa) who initially gave rise to the universe. It is no accident that those Hindus who have claimed to experience the state of liberation describe it as exponentially more blissful than sex (Muktananda 1976, 164–167). Spiritual liberation is said to be a great bliss (*ānanda*) that is the result of the internalization and transcendence of the very same sexual fire that is experienced in limited amounts through sexual engagement. Ultimately, for Hindus, sexuality is not one thing and spirituality another. They are, rather, two aspects of the very same fire, a fire that both gives rise to life and makes possible its transcendence. Or, one might say that they are but two names for a single internal river, which, as we will see below, has the capacity to flow in two directions.

### The Place of Women in Classical Hinduism

Hindu attitudes toward women and their sexuality are multiple and at times contradictory. In certain passages of the Veda, women are regarded as untruth (*asatya*) and as a danger to be avoided at all costs. Such passages have led scholars to assume that Hindu women are considered a "lesser sex." However, we would be wise to read such passages as telling us more about ambivalent attitudes toward sexuality than women per se (Jamison 1996). What is potentially dangerous to men is the vibrant sexuality embodied by women, not women themselves. For it is the potency of sexuality that entraps one in desire, identified as the root cause of suffering. For this reason, the negative dimensions of sexuality, as it is embodied in Woman, is to be transformed through ritual action. Ritual harnesses the potentially dangerous powers of sexuality and transforms them into benign energies of truth, goodness, and justice.

Although it is true that the *varṇāśrama* system detailed above seems to focus on the interests of Hindu men of the upper three classes, women are also empowered to pursue the four aims of life. Classically, Hindu women find fulfillment of these aims through the duties (*dharma*) and rituals (*saṃskāras*) of serving and loving their parents, husbands, and progeny. Thus do they uphold religious obligation, experience pleasure (*kāma*), and acquire material well-being.

A number of Sanskrit texts are written for the purpose of guiding women toward their social, sexual, and spiritual fulfillment. The fourteenth-century *Strīdharma Paddhati* (*Text on the Responsibilities of the Wife*), for example, details the duties of the Hindu wife. The more famous *Kāma Sūtra* (*Verse on Erotic Love*) of Vatsyāyana (ca. second century C.E.) gives explicit instructions for women on the numerous pleasures and possibilities of love play. Primarily used by the courtesans of kings, the text was also studied by upper-class wives. In it we find a science of pleasure whose purpose is to elevate eroticism to the heights of the mystical. In this text, women are not simply the givers but also the recipients of pleasure. Additionally, the eighty-four sexual postures (*maithunāsana*) described by Vatsyāyana would be learned by both male and female yogins, who would unite with their consorts in imitation of the love play of the gods.

Women are also empowered within the *varṇāśrama* system to attain liberation, the fourth and final aim of life. For many Hindus, there is no sense that men are spiritually superior. In fact, many contemporary Hindu gurus have stated that women are *more* capable of attaining liberation than men. Historically, there have been many famous and powerful female ascetics, gurus, and saints, including Gargi, Lalleśvarī, and Mirabai. Today's Hinduism is enriched by several prominent female teachers, including Gurumayi Chidvilasananda, Amritananda Mayi Ma, and Uma Bharati.

Historically, one of many means for attaining liberation by women is to commit *satī* an act of self-sacrifice in which a woman willingly joins her husband on his funeral pyre. Although banned during the period of British colonialism in the nineteenth century, the practice has continued until the present, although its occurrence is now extremely rare. As Catherine Weinberger-Thomas has shown (1999), the controversial ritual of *satī* has been viewed by many Hindu women themselves as a means of transforming themselves into the goddess.

The myth that relates most specifically to the act of *satī* is found in *Kālikā Purāṇa* 18: 40–50. The context of the myth is a great sacrifice by King Dakṣa, the father of Satī, the bride of Śiva. Because Śiva is not an upper-caste Hindu King Dakṣa attempts to prevent him from entering the sacrificial space. Satī is outraged by this humiliation and enters into a deep state of meditation. In this state, she generates an inner fire that immolates her from within. Seeing that his wife has sacrificed herself on his behalf, Śiva becomes outraged. He places Satī's dead body in his arms and flies throughout the universe in a rage so intense that the gods fear he will destroy everything. In response, the god Viṣṇu uses his discus to systematically sever the various parts of Satī's body. Once her body has been dismembered, Śiva calms down. He realizes that Satī is *śakti,* his own eternal energy from which he is, in truth, never separated. Whenever this energy appears to die, it soon is reborn in another incarnation, and, sure enough, Satī is soon reincarnated as the goddess Parvati, the most famous of Śiva's wives. Meanwhile, Satī's severed body parts—totaling fifty—fell onto India, thereby creating fifty sacred "goddess seats" (*śākta-pīṭhas*) that now mark some of the most holy pilgrimage sites in India. Among these, the most powerful is the site where Satī's vulva fell in the region of Kāmākhya in Assam.

The Satī myth complex reminds us of the continuum between the realm of the gods, the realm of humans, and the inner world of the yogic practice. On an esoteric level, Satī is the inner *śakti,* which must be liberated from the clutches of pride and ignorance, symbolized by her father Dakṣa. By sacrificing herself, Satī attains transcendence. Her dismemberment, subsequent establishment as fifty sacred sites, and eventual reincarnation is interpreted by some Hindus as a reminder that the body must serve the purpose of an undying spirit (*ātman*) that resides within.

The wife who chooses to take *satī* becomes like Satī. That is, she chooses to become a goddess. This act is believed to be the ultimate gesture of faith and love, an act so charged with devotion and purity that it brings liberation the instant the woman leaps into the fire. In fact, it is believed that the Satī, like the renunciant, is burned up even prior to entering into the fire. The external process of entering into the fire is a sort of formality, an external symbol of an internal sacrifice that has already transpired. The intention to commit *sati* transforms the sexual fire into a blazing spiritual fire that consumes the Satī from within. By the time she walks onto the funeral pyre, she is, in effect, already liberated and will not feel the pain of the flames. However, this ideal depiction of *sati* is not always matched by historical realities. Several detailed ethnographic accounts reveal instances when women were forced into the fires, either physically or by the social pressures of a patrilineal system that offered limited options to a widow.

These instances remind us that when one studies religious traditions in their specific social and cultural contexts—"on the ground," so to speak—one finds that gender relations are never as clear-cut as they appear in the textual sources. As Sarah Caldwell has shown in her ethnographic research on southern Indian dance and theater traditions (1999), female sexuality is often treated as a power to be controlled by men. In these contexts, women are at once revered as goddesses but also excluded from privileged access to positions of power. In this way, Caldwell's work, like that of a number of social anthropologists, reminds us that the role and treatment of women in Hinduism remains a matter of considerable debate and critique.

### The Place of the Lower Classes in Relationship to the "Great" Tradition

A second prominent critique of Hinduism regards the status of members of the lower classes, both male and female. The *varṇāśrama* system incorporates only the members of the upper three classes, comprising the priests, warriors, and merchants. However, a great number of Hindus come from the lower classes, respectively termed the Harijan, or children of God, by Mahatma Gandhi. What do we make of their exclusion from the *varṇāśrama* system? How does their expression of sexuality fit into the model of classical Hinduism?

This important question raises the issue of so-called great and little traditions of Hinduism. These terms, applied by scholars, generally refer to Sanskritic and non-Sanskritic traditions, respectively. By and large, Sanskritic traditions comprise Hindus of the upper three classes, whereas non-Sanskritic traditions comprise Hindus of the lower classes. The critique of the use of these terms is that there is an obvious favoring of

Sanskritic traditions as superior, or "greater" than the numerous vernacular traditions that are especially prominent in rural India, the locus of nearly 80 percent of all Hindus. In sheer numbers, the so-called little traditions are considerably greater than the so-called great traditions. For this reason, a number of scholars have argued in recent years that focus needs to be shifted away from a study of Sanskritic traditions to the numerous little traditions found throughout the subcontinent, many of which are not preserved in texts but are transmitted orally. These multiple little traditions vary considerably according to the place in which they arise. Village Hinduism in western Nepal is distinct from village Hinduism in Karnataka, for example. Logically, if one accepts the challenge to take into account the uniqueness of multiple little traditions, then a complete study of Hinduism requires an enormous anthropological project that would put a vast team of scholars in all the village regions of the subcontinent. Given the obvious limitations of such a project—and the limitations of space in this chapter—one can bear in mind that part of what makes the classical Sanskritic tradition "great" is that it reflects the sustained effort of certain Hindus over time to unify the peoples living within the social, political, religious, and cultural boundaries of the tradition. Moreover, Sanskritic Hinduism includes alternative modalities of spiritual practice that in fact arise—at least in part—from the lower classes and as such are consciously crafted to address the interests of those peoples. Two such modalities comprising the so-called little traditions are the Bhakti and Tantric traditions, to which we turn now.

## TWO BODIES, ONE SOUL: THE RITUAL ROOTS OF HINDU SEXUALITY

Our attention now shifts to a concentrated focus on the more esoteric dimensions of Hindu sexuality and a history of ritual practice that culminates with a rite of sexual union that has boldly been proclaimed by some Hindus as a supreme vehicle for spiritual liberation. This history begins with the ritual practices of the Vedas and reaches its apex about one thousand years ago with the traditions of Hindu Tantra, traditions that would be most vibrantly expressed in the realms of art, music, and theater. In Tantra we find an understanding that humanity attains divinity through a cooperation of males and females that results in the realization that all individuals, regardless of their current gender, are, like the godhead, at once bi-gendered and transgendered.

114

Let us turn to the ritual arena itself and examine the strategies by which this abstract philosophy of sexuality and gender is embodied by Hindus. The performance of Vedic rituals is the jurisdiction of a priestly class called Brahmins. As explained above, the brahmin priests belong to the highest level of India's caste system and are male. Yet, no Vedic ritual is possible without the presence of the priest's wife. The priest and his wife are—as one brahmin recently told me—two bodies but one soul. In the sanctified arena of Vedic ritual, their linked actions embody the complete model of Hindu sexuality that over the years would evolve into the elaborate, sexual-yogic technologies of the Hindu Tantra, India's quintessence of spiritualized sexuality.

As mentioned above, the essential feature of a Vedic ritual is the construction of a sacred space identified with the universe, at the heart of which is the fire altar. Fire, as we have seen, is symbolic of *tapas,* the "heat" that is, along with fluid, a key focus of our investigation of Hindu sexuality. Hindu ritual patterns operate according to a tripartite homologizing structure in which the universe (macrocosm) is equated with the body (microcosm) through an intermediary structure (mesocosm), which in the Vedic tradition was the fire altar. At the macrocosmic level, *tapas* is the generative power that gives rise to the cosmos. At the microcosmic level, *tapas* is heat within the body, a heat that is commonly experienced as sexual passion but that can be harnessed as a liberating spiritual power. At the mesocosmic level, heat is the ritual fire, identified with the god Agni (White 1996, 15–19). During the Vedic ritual heat is harnessed and controlled for the purpose of constructing an ideal universe in which well-being is reestablished.

Just as Puruṣa is sacrificed at the beginning of time to give rise to the universe, so the sacrificer and his wife are symbolically sacrificed through a process that is understood to regenerate the universe. The success of the ritual hinges in no small part on their capacity to control their own sexuality through the ascetic practices they adhere to during the course of the ritual. In other words, there is a direct correspondence between the sexual fluid and fire of the sacrificer and his wife, the sacrificial fluids and fire, and the cosmic fire and fluids that exist within the body of god. In the sanctified realm of the ritual, the sacrificer and his wife are that godhead.

### Those Whose Semen Flows Upward

Sometime around the eighth century B.C.E., the development of the Vedas culminated with the writings of the Upaniṣads. These texts were composed by wanderers (*śramaṇas*) who sought the esoteric significance of the Vedic rituals within small communities that lived on the outskirts of the urban centers that were being developed along the Gangetic plains at that time. Whereas the earlier Vedic tradition focused on act (*karman*), the wanderers were interested in the knowledge (*jñāna*) that arose through contemplative practices.

In their writings and practices, we find again the merging of a river with fire. However, the river of their practice was the internal "river" of sexual fluid that normally flows downward and out. The goal of their practice was to reverse the flow of this river. The means to achieving this end was the generation of inner fire through intense meditation practices that culminated with the transformation of desire (*kāma*) into a liberating potency. The ascetics who mastered this practice were called *urdhva-retas,* meaning that their semen (*retas*) flowed upward (*urdhva*). In certain sects, the male ascetics would tie their penis upward as an outward symbol of their internal control.

In essence, these wanderers—usually male, but sometimes female—discovered that one does not need a complex sacrificial system or a partner of the opposite gender to experience spiritual freedom. One's own subtle body and breath contained all that was needed for this highest attainment. In effect, they learned to make love to themselves by creating an internal flow of ecstasy that flowed upward into their own cranial vaults and was there transformed into immortal nectar (*amṛta*) (White 1996, 198–201).

### Sexuality in the Old Stories

While ascetics were conquering their desire, the paradigmatic Vedic model of the sacrificer and his wife continued to develop in a genre of Sanskrit scriptures called the Purāṇas (Old Stories) and Itihāsa (Epics), which began to appear around the fourth century B.C.E. Like the Vedas, these narratives were initially preserved through oral recitation, being passed down for hundreds of years from teacher to disciple, bard to bard, before textual codification. A strong component within these textual traditions is a theological vision that equates divinity with humanity, making the universal godhead indistinct from the individual. The soteriological aim of this kind of nondual theologizing is not to become the divine but to realize that one already is divine. Toward this end, what is needed is a template, a mediating sphere (mesocosm) or practice by which the individual (microcosm) can realize his or her identity with godhead (macrocosm).

One of the prominent deities of the Purāṇas is Śiva, the "erotic asce-tic" (Doniger 1973), whom we have already encountered in conjunction with our discussion of Satī. Śiva is the prototypical yogi: he has matted hair, is naked save for a lion-skin loincloth, is smeared with ashes, and bears a trident and water jug. Appropriately, he meditates for eons atop Mount Kailāsa at the center of the universe, generating within himself the inner heat (*tapas*) that is the fruit of yoga. However, Śiva is not only a paradigm for the way of liberation (*mokṣa-mārga*). He is also a house-holder who fulfills the duty (dharma) of being a husband to his female self, whether incarnated as Satī, Gaṅgā, or Parvatī, the mistress of the mountain. Such duty includes the pursuit of pleasure (*kāma*). Appropriately, his wife, the Goddess, is idyllically beautiful, endowed with curved hips, melonous upward-tilting breasts, and lotus eyes. She can only wait for so long during her husband's period of ascetic practice. When her patience runs thin, she seduces him into lovemaking, and they unite for a period equal to that of Śiva's meditation.

Ultimately, the Purāṇas claim, Śiva and the Goddess are two poles of one being. This unity is reflected in images of the *śiva-liṅga,* which depicts the male *liṅga* arising from or rather entering into a *yoni,* equated with the womb of the goddess. Such images symbolize the di-vine union that begets all creation. Through the uniting of its bipolar self, godhead begets humanity and the universe in which it roams, and through ritualized sexual union, two human beings generate an ener-getic tension that makes possible the cognition of their innate, inter-dependent divinity.

### Tantra and the Secret Rite

With all these elements in place, we now turn to the tradition of Tantra. In Tantra, the riverine and fiery aspects of Hinduism come together in a sophisticated yogic practice that fuses pleasure with liberation. By the sixth century C.E., small spiritual communities had arisen in several re-gions throughout India that celebrated in secrecy the liberating power of the sexual act. These communities called themselves families (*kulas*). Male practitioners were called *kaulas,* and female practitioners were called *yoginīs.* Membership in these communities was not determined by gender or class status. In fact, lower-class women were often seen as the most ideal members of these communities. What was required was the yogic capacity to generate one's inner fire and reverse the flow of sexual fluids. One who had attained this state was eligible for initiation. During

117

initiation, one would unite with an advanced adept and consume a clan-fluid (*kulāmṛta*) containing the by-products of that union. In certain communities, females were dominant and received worship from male adepts. Gathering in open-roofed temples under the secrecy of night, these *yoginīs* were said to unite with male consorts and then enter into an ecstatic state. These practices were the beginning of the infamous left-hand path of Tantra (*vāma-mārga*), which championed sexuality as the vehicle of salvation, uniting pleasure (*bhoga*) with freedom (*mokṣa*) (White 1996).

The culmination of the Tantric path would be masterminded by the brilliant tenth-century exegete, aesthete, musician, and Kashmiri yogin, Abhinavagupta. Abhinavagupta was a *yoginī-bhū,* meaning that his conception occurred during a rite of Tantric lovemaking enacted for the purpose of producing an enlightened child. Born a brahmin, Abhinavagupta would study and master all the major schools of Sanskrit learning, ranging from grammar to ritual to aesthetics to philosophy. The culmination of his study, however, would not come until his meeting with the great Kaula mystic, Śāmbhūnātha. From Śāmbhūnātha he would receive the initiatory descent of power (*śaktipāta-dīkṣā*) that would set him free even while living (*jīvanmukti*). After that meeting, Abhinavagupta would go on to produce numerous writings in which he constructed the Trika-Kaula, a grand theological synthesis that interwove Veda with Tantra, yoga with aesthetics, and spiritual liberation with sexual union. According to Abhinavagupta, the Tantric path begins with initiation from a liberated teacher. At that point, one receives the descent of power that awakens one's dormant spiritual energy, called *kuṇḍalinī-śakti,* which resides at the base of the spine in a fiery energy wheel called the *mūlādhāra-cakra.* When awakened by the teacher, it rises through a column of light in the area of the spinal column, running from the base of the spine to the crown of the head. As the *kuṇḍalinī* rises upward, it purifies all impurities within the body, including even the root impurity, ignorance, which is the root cause of rebirth. To assist the process of raising the *kuṇḍalinī,* the teacher instructs the initiate in yogic and ritual practices that purify the mind and body, preparing him or her for the radical release of liberating power that is *kuṇḍalinī's* ultimate purpose.

Toward this end, the control and cultivation of sexual energy is key. Through the practice of yoga, the initiate learns to refine and channel his or her sexual energy upward, thereby propelling the *kuṇḍalinī.* As the initiate's dispassion grows, the teacher guides him or her into more advanced stages of yoga, until finally he or she is ready for the secret rite (*rahasya-vidhi*), described in detail in the twenty-ninth chapter of Abhinavagupta's masterwork, *Tantrāloka*. In this ritual, advanced practitioners transform themselves into the gods and goddesses. At the culmination of the ritual, yogins unite with female adepts who carry within their vulvas the lineage-knowledge that is transmitted to them from the Tantric teacher. In the context of ritual union, an upward force (*udyama-śakti*) is generated that propels *kuṇḍalinī* to its final abode in the crown center and beyond (Flood 1996).

One of the many paradoxes of the Tantric path is found in the nuances of the word *brahmācārya,* a term most frequently applied to celibates. In his *Tantrāloka*, Abhinavagupta offers three meanings of the term. At the primary level, *brahmācārya* means celibacy in the sense of refraining from sexual activity. At a secondary level, *brahmācārya* refers to the practice of channeling the sexual fluids upward, even in the act of ritual union. Finally, *brahmācārya* refers to the movement into (*ācārya*) consciousness (*brahman*) that happens at the moment of orgasm when the male initiate is united with the female *yoginī*. At this point, orgasm is equated with Śiva's power of bliss (*ānanda-śakti*); it vibrates with the perfect I-awareness that reveals the nondistinction between self and world in a radical shattering of all dualities. In other words, for a Tāntrika, the fulfillment of celibacy is an orgasm that is spiritually liberating. The final testimony to this state is found in the mixing of semen and blood in a cup that is then offered to the guru. All that is impure and taboo in normative Hindu society is transformed into a radical vehicle of empowerment within the ritual environment of Tantric practice.

It is not insignificant that the female consort in these contexts, called *dūtī,* is always someone other than one's own wife (*parākīyā*), as it reveals a Hindu tendency to spiritualize the erotic impulse. The relationship with an illicit partner is charged with the energy of danger that intensifies the erotic encounter such that the ethical transgression becomes the cause of liberation. Abhinavagupta's Trika-Kaula (Tantric theology) is not unique in expounding the importance of sexual union with an illicit partner. In the traditions of Vaiṣṇava Tantra, which focus on the worship of God as Kṛṣṇa, this practice is justified with references to Purāṇic accounts of Kṛṣṇa's relationship to the *gopīs*, or cowmaidens. Kṛṣṇa is the Lord, incarnated for the purpose of reestablishing righteousness (dharma) and revealing his divine nature. In this function, he engages in a variety of relationships that enable people to express their love for him.

The four primary relationships are parent/child, friend, master/slave, and finally, lover. As a lover, Kṛṣṇa reveals both an exclusive and inclusive love. As an exclusive lover, he appears to choose one *gopī* above all others and love her in a special way. As an inclusive lover, he loves all the *gopīs* simultaneously. In each case, the love expressed is understood as a metaphor for God's relationship to the soul. Exclusive love reveals God's unique love for each soul; inclusive love reveals his capacity to love all souls. Vaiṣṇava mystics like Caitanya (ca. fourteenth century) would declare that Kṛṣṇa loves all souls uniquely and equally. That is the esoteric meaning of the great *rasa-līla,* the ecstatic dancing circle of *gopīs*, each of which is joined with Kṛṣṇa, who answers all of their longings in a way that transforms erotic impulse into mystical fulfillment (Dimock 1966).

### Maṇḍalas, Kingship, and the Arts

In both the *rahasya-vidhi* of Abhinavagupta and the *rasa-līla* traditions of the Vaiṣṇavas, Tantric practice is linked to a sexualized aesthetics. Both these traditions drew heavily from aesthetic theory and formulated their respective ritual traditions according to the principles of art and drama. Gerald Larson (1976) has shown that the merging of the aesthetic and mystical was so thorough that the fourteenth-century aesthete and yogin Viśvanāth would proclaim religious experience (*brahāmsvāda*) and aesthetic experience (*rasāsvāda*) to be "twin brothers." Classically, there are nine distinct aesthetic flavors or sentiments, called *rasas*: the erotic, humorous, horrific, disgusting, pathetic, infuriating, wondrous, tragic, and quiescent. In Tantric practice, the last *rasa* is visualized at the heart of an eight-petaled lotus-wheel (*padma-cakra*) within the heart, containing each of the *rasas* on its respective petals. Ultimately, *rasa* is one. It is the essence of consciousness expressed in eight flavors. For this reason, any one *rasa,* if tasted with awareness, can lead one to the experience of *śānta-rasa,* the state of quiescence that is the goal of mystical practice. In Tantric ritual, the erotic sentiment *(śṛṇgara-rasa)* is directed toward the experience of divine consciousness.

Bearing this in mind, we now turn to the loci of the regional kings, called *rājas,* who by the tenth century had established a sociocultural and political vision of kingship based in part, if not primarily, on Tantric ideology and practice in multiple regions within the subcontinent. The key to this vision was the *maṇḍala,* a Tantric cosmogram replete with meaning (Lidke 2000). The origin of the *maṇḍala* is the Vedic fire altar, constructed in its basic form as a square representing the four directions and containing a triangular, open pit representing the fiery womb. In Tantric traditions, this pattern of interlocking squares and triangles was used as a guide or for meditative practice, tools (*yantra*) enabling the initiate to construct a meditative awareness of the nondistinction between the body of divinity and one's own body. In this way, the *mandala* functioned as a mediating sphere (mesocosm) that linked the individual (microcosm) to the totality (macrocosm).

The symbolism of the *mandala* is richly sexual. The Śrī Cakra *mandala,* for example, contains five downward-facing triangles and four upward-facing triangles interweaving at multiple junctures to create a total of forty-three triangles. Among its many meanings, this interweaving is interpreted by Tāntrikas as the union of the goddess Śakti with her eternal beloved, the god Śiva. On the microlevel, the downward-facing triangles are female sexual organs, and the upward facing triangles are phalluses. The very center of the Śrī Cakra is a dot, symbolizing Śiva's semen, the *bindu,* or creative drop, arisen from the union of god and goddess, which gives rise to all of creation. This drop is also the fluid point within a fiery pit, symbolic of the offerings made by priests into the Vedic fire altar. It is symbolic, also, of the offering of sexual fluid into the womb of the female. All these processes are understood as part of a continuum of a divine interplay between fire and water at the heart of a universe that arises from the union of the divine dyad.

Medieval Indian kings used the *mandala* as a template for establishing their kingdoms. One literal meaning of *mandala* is "territory," and in the case of many kings—whether Hindu, Buddhist, or Jain—*mandala* was the word and conceptual category used to delineate their political domains. In certain kingdoms, such as Ānandadeva's (ca. 1233–1287 C.E.) Nepalese kingdom of Bhaktapur, the adaptation of *mandala* ideology played itself out in very concrete terms. Ānandadeva was an initiate of Śākta or Goddess Tantra. Accordingly, he constructed his city as a Navadurgā Yantra, the same image that was the focus of his own meditative practice. He also employed Tāntrikas as his political advisers to help him craft a political ideology rooted in *mandala*-logic. Such logic explained the universe in a way that modern physicists might call "holographic." Like the laser-generated hologram built upon self-replications of its smallest unit, the *mandala* was replicated on multiple levels throughout the king's territory. *Mandala*-logic informed the building of his palace, his city, the multiple temples within his territory, and ultimately his understanding of his own body. Herein sex is certainly power.

The inner heat (*tapas*) harnessed by the Upaniṣadic yogin is cultivated by the king as the power to transform his territory into the orgasmic body of consciousness. In no uncertain terms, this meant that the king's domain was erotically charged.

The link between *maṇḍala,* kingship, and sexuality is perhaps most concretely illustrated in the case of temple architecture. By the tenth century, classical, king-sponsored temples were being constructed according to the guidelines of architectural treatises (*Śilpa-Śāstras*) based on Tantric practice and ideology. Such temples were constructed as three-dimensional Tantric *maṇḍala*s and were thoroughly encoded with Tantric symbolism. The architects of temples like Kaṇḍariyā Mahādeva at Khajaraho (ca. 1000 C.E.) were Tantric initiates who constructed architectural edifices that expressed the ideology of sex-as-power that was the bedrock of medieval kingship. Kaṇḍariyā Mahādeva is well-known for the erotic images adorning its outer walls, images that depict all varieties of sexual interplay. On a surface level, these images suggest the intersection of erotic pleasure (*kāma*) and liberation (*mokṣa*). On an esoteric level, they veil Tantric *yantra*s, the meaning of which is revealed only through initiation. In fact, in the eye of the initiate, each section of the temple is inscribed with a mystico-erotic script (Rabe 1996).

Why would kings invest in three-dimensional testimonies to mystical eroticism? By this time, the paradigm was squarely in place: a bi-gendered divinity had given rise to the universe through a divine sexual act that was the outward expression of its infinite power. All reality is a *maṇḍala* that comes into being as a result of the divinity's self-emission orgasm. The microcosmic orgasm of the individual was then a means to tap this power. The construction of *maṇḍala*-temples created mesocosmic templates that channeled macrocosmic sexuality into the microcosmic bodies.

The presence of mystico-eroticism was not just encoded into the temple's structures and sculptures. It also informed the cultural world that spiraled around and from the king. The king's territory was to be a heaven on earth in which the king's delight was a god's delight. No wealthy king was without his vast assembly of concubines trained in the arts of love. In some cases, these concubines were also trained in the arts of dance and music. Such was the case of the infamous Devadāsīs, the "slaves of God," unjustly branded as harlots by colonialists who misinterpreted their complex practice. Devadāsīs were female initiates of Tantra who lived in temple complexes in Orissa and other regions of the subcontinent. Their art combined Tantric body gestures (*mudrās*) with mystical poetry and classical music in creating dances for God. The dances were in fact rituals, a way of worshiping the deity enshrined at the temple (Margolin 1985). At the culmination of the dance, the Devadāsī would often unite with a wealthy patron, who through the ritual would be transfigured into the god the dancer was worshiping. In this way, the macrocosmic sexuality of the godhead was realized through the microcosmic bodies of the dancer and patron within the context of the temple.

Expressed on the temple walls in complex sculptural forms, sexual imagery pointed to a transcendent state of union with God. At the same time, these images attested to a highly refined culture of pleasure in which sex served its own end as the fulfillment of human desire, enjoyed primarily by elite males endowed with the economic power and social status to explore the possibilities of sexual gratification. Not everyone within the kingdom had such attitudes or opportunities. For many, sexual practice was strictly governed by rules of purity and social status, which decreed that sexual intercourse should stay within the confines of caste boundaries. The ideal wife would sleep only with her husband and then only during certain phases of the moon and certainly not when she was menstruating. Normative Hindu sexual practice was rooted in an ideology of caste purity that demanded monogamy and regulated sexual practice. Across the millennia, the majority of Hindus experienced sex only with their husbands or wives. However, this normative tradition of sexuality has been richly nuanced by religious and cultural practices rooted in a mystical vision of transcendence within and by means of the body.

### Alternative Sexualities and the Transcendence of Gender

In their excellent recent study of same-sex love in India, Ruth Vanita and Saleem Kidwai offer a masterful excavation of references to homoerotic inclinations in classical Sanskritic sources. As they point out, the Śāstra tradition (ca. second century B.C.E. to fourth century C.E.) contain explicit descriptions of homoerotic inclinations. Vatsyāyana's *Kāma Sūtra* uses the term "third nature" to describe a man who desires other men. Citing Michael Sweet and Leonard Zwilling (1996), Vanita and Kidwai point out that a "third nature" or "third sex" can be found in a wide array of textual sources, ranging from medical to grammatical and from Hindu to Jain. Not only is the notion widespread across Indian traditions, it is also ancient, dating back nearly 3,000 years. According to Sweet and Zwilling (1996), the notion of a third gender developed as early as the Veda and went on to influence Jain debates on the question of whether women could attain liberation. The conclusion of these debates was that the homoerotic inclination was the most intense form of desire and could be experienced by either gender.

Vanita and Kidwai point out that attitudes toward the physical fulfillment of such desires are mixed. Clearly, the *Kāma Sūtra* is replete with references to the pursuit of same-sex pleasures. Toward this end, Vatsyāyana and his commentators discuss the "third-natured" person in some detail, including descriptions of those with hermaphroditic bodies who tend toward such professions as hairstyling and massage. Moreover, same-sex desire is not limited to the third-gendered man. Vatsyāyana also describes the young male servants who perform oral sex on men. Additionally, he describes a special kind of friendship in which two men or two women who trust each other deeply engage in oral sex. The overall tone of these descriptions is nonjudgmental. Vatsyāyana in fact notes that there are a multiplicity of sexual inclinations and types. His aim is not to judge them but to describe and categorize them for an educated, mostly city-dwelling audience.

However, in other contemporaneous texts, such as Kauṭilya's *Arthaśāstra* and the *Manusmṛti,* we find descriptions of punishment for same-sex activity. Although the punishment for such acts is not severe, it is clear that the authors of these texts see heterosexual relations as the norm. Nonetheless, a study of classical sources clearly reveals that the category of homoeroticism is well known in Indian textual sources. Important historical documents such as the *Rājataraṇgaṇi,* a chronicle of the kings of Kashmir, suggest that male prostitution was part of regal life prior to the Islamic invasion. Although not seen as "normative," same-sex love was clearly incorporated in the classical Hindu sociopolitical structure.

We must remember that in the Hindu tradition, gender categories are highly osmotic, allowing for a fluid exchange as souls migrate along a vast and complex chain of being, exploring and expressing desires in many complex ways. The fundamental theme is that the essence of the human being transcends gender. Sexual orientation, therefore, has to be understood in terms of a complex array of metaphysical circumstances. Logically, same-sex orientations would be among the numerous possibilities for negotiating the karmic resonances of pleasure.

The Hindu doctrine of rebirth gives rise to an intriguing and fluid understanding of sexuality and gender. The Upaniṣads state that there are 8,400,000,000 forms of life into which the soul incarnates before finally becoming human. Even after entering a human body, the soul's journey is far from complete, incarnating again and again according to the laws of karma. In the course of this potentially infinite chain of rebirth, the soul inevitably assumes both male and female forms. "[R]ebirth," writes Ruth Vanita, "makes fluid categories and boundaries, even those that appear most biologically fixed, such as species and gender categories. Further, the basic Hindu idea, variously expressed, that the universal spirit pervades all things means that in the ultimate analysis nothing is abnormal or unnatural" (Vanita and Kidwai 2000, 29).

The picture of human gender that emerges in the classical age of Hinduism (ca. 300 C.E.) is one in which a bi-gendered soul reincarnates into both female and male bodies, which are themselves bi-gendered in the sense that all bodies always contains both a female principle, called *śakti,* and a male principle, called *Īśvara*. In a theological sense, all beings are spiritual androgynes. Human beings are sexually inclined because sexuality is God's creative energy, and a function of Its inclination to reunite the two poles of Its bipolar being. This thematic is worked out in numerous ways in the Hindu scriptures in such a way that a serious student of Hinduism can find a paradigm for nearly all possible sexual relationships.

Classically, Indian textual and cultural sources express a multiplicity of attitudes toward alternative sexualities. In the Purāṇic literature, we find several important accounts of male divinities engaged in what can be interpreted as homoerotic behavior. One is the account of Agni swallowing Śiva's semen, which is found in the tenth century *Śiva Purāṇa*. In this tale, we encounter again the important union of fire and fluid. However, in this case both the fire and the fluid are generated by a male actor. The tale situates normative sexuality—Śiva's relationship with his wife, Parvatī—against an alternative sexuality in the form of the fire god Agni, who consumes Śiva's semen. The account begins with Śiva making love to Parvatī. The purpose of their union is to produce a son who will lead an army of gods against the demons. Unfortunately for the gods, Śiva is a great yogin who, instead of releasing his seed, channels it upward even as he makes love to his intoxicatingly beautiful wife. Deeply concerned, the gods elect to interrupt the divine couple. Śiva quits his lovemaking to hear the lament of the gods, who simply want Śiva to ejaculate. After listening to their requests for the production of a son, Śiva agrees to discharge his semen to the ground. As Śiva's fiery seed falls to the ground, Agni, the fire god, assumes the form of a dove and captures and swallows the semen.

At this point, Parvatī, disturbed by the absence of her husband, has ventured out from the place of their lovemaking and discovers that her husband has just discharged his semen into the mouth of a male god. Enraged that the seed meant for her womb has gone to another, she curses the gods and particularly Agni. However, Agni offsets her curses by seeking the protection of Śiva himself, who instructs Agni to deposit the seed in the womb of a "good woman." Agni heeds this command by transmitting the seed into the wombs of several brahmin women. However, their husbands then suspect them of infidelity, and so they discharge the seed onto the Himālayas. But the heat of Śiva's seed sets the Himālayas ablaze. Therefore, they caste it into the river Ganges, who then hurls it into a forest, where at last Kartikkeya, the god of war, is born.

Although the consumption of Śiva's seed by a male god is clearly condemned in this account, it is also seen as an act that helps facilitate procreation and is thus a "positive" act. In another, more famous myth from the ninth-century *Bhāgavata Mahā Purāna,* Śiva asks the male god Visnu to assume the female form of the temptress Mohinī, whose captivating beauty conquered the demons at the beginning of creation. In response to this request, Visnu laughs and then assumes a female form of such enchanting beauty that Śiva loses himself in his desire for her. Śiva embraces the scantily clad Mohinī, but she slips away and thus begins an erotic chase, during which the aroused Śiva slowly but steadily loses his seed "like a prize bull chasing a fertile cow." Once all of the seed has been spilt, Śiva remembers that Mohinī is really Visnu, and he awakens from his desire (Vanita and Kidwai 2000, 70–71).

The fascinating, fluidic transgender elements of this story have numerous counterparts in other myths. Among the more famous of such variants is the tale of Śikhandhin in the *Mahābhārata.* The tale begins with Ambā and her two sisters being captured by the warrior Bhisma as wives-to-be for his younger brother. However, Ambā is already in love and so convinces Bhisma to set her free to be with her beloved. Tragically, her beloved rejects her on the grounds that she has been soiled by her abduction. When the rejected Ambā returns to Bhisma, she is doubly rejected, first by his brother who has learned of her love for another and then by Bhisma, who cannot marry her because of a lifelong vow of celibacy that he has made. Spurned on all fronts, Ambā retreats to the forest, where she commits to the practice of austerities and obtains a boon from Śiva to be reborn as a man so that she can kill Bhisma.

At this point, the gender implications of tale become more complex. Instead of being reborn as a man, Ambā is reborn as the daughter of the sonless King Drupada, who for his own reasons also desires the death of

Bhiṣma and toward this end does penance to Lord Śiva, asking for a son to commit the deed. At the culmination of the king's austerities, Śiva informs him that he will have a female-male. Some time later, Ambā is reborn as Śikhaṇḍinī, a girl who is proclaimed and raised as a boy. The truth of her gender is not discovered until after her marriage to the princess of an important and powerful king. The news of her true gender infuriates her wife's father and causes great grief to her own parents. Forlorn, Śikhaṇḍinī enters the forest, determined to fast unto death. However, several days into her fast, she is approached by a compassionate *yakṣa,* or forest deity, who grants her a boon. Śikhaṇḍinī tells her tale of woe, and the *yakṣa* offers her his gender on the condition that she eventually return it. Eventually, Śikhaṇḍinī kills the great Bhiṣma in battle.

Regardless of tropes of alternative sexualities found in classical texts and cultures, attitudes toward sexual orientation would be given a rigid codification by British imperialists, who implemented a legal code that outlawed sodomy and other "unnatural acts." In 1860 the Indian Law Commission incorporated the antisodomy statute, Section 377, into the Indian Penal Code. The law states: "Whoever voluntarily has carnal intercourse against the order of nature with any man, woman or animal, shall be punished with imprisonment for life, or with imprisonment of either description for a term which may extend to ten years, and shall also be liable to fine" (Ranchhoddas and Thakoree 1992). Suparna Bhaskaran (2002, 15–29) argues that Section 377 caused an institutional reaction against same-sex love previously unknown on the subcontinent. The institutionalization of the antisodomy act instilled in Hindu India a homophobic reaction that has yet to be purged or understood. Hindu apologetics were quick to claim that homosexuality and its variants were foreign to Hinduism, that they entered the subcontinent with the Muslims and later with the British, thus ignoring the multiple themes and descriptions of same-sex love in their classical textual and cultural traditions (Vanita 2002, 15–76).

The scene in contemporary India is beginning to change. Although many same-sex lovers speak of facing fear and social intimidation—sometimes resulting in death—a number of voices have spoken out in public forums and with public support. Magazines like *Trikona* are published internationally, placing Hindu gay sexual cultures within a global context. This ambivalent, changing stance toward alternative sexuality was highlighted by international reaction to the recent film, *Fire,* which portrays lesbian love. Reaction to the film was, appropriately, fiery. In Bombay, fundamentalist political groups burned theaters at which the film was shown. Elsewhere, gays and lesbians alike celebrated the fact that a cinematic *Fire* had taken them a step further toward liberation in their current incarnations.

Another "fire" to be noted is the recent uproar over a book titled *Kālī's Child*, written by Rice University scholar of Hinduism Jeffrey Kripal. His thesis—more thoroughly developed in his recent publications—is that spirituality and sexuality are often, if not always, intertwined. His "test case" for *Kālī's Child* was the nineteenth-century saint, Śrī Rāmakṛṣṇa, recognized by his disciples as an incarnation of God. Rāmakṛṣṇa was an ecstatic soul who accepted many teachers and worshiped divinity in many ways. In states of divine intoxication, he sometimes dressed as a *gopī* to love God as Kṛṣṇa. He mastered yogic practice and appeared to live as a monk, claiming never to engage in sexual union with his wife. However, his most beloved deity was the Tantric goddess Kālī. Kripal's highly contested thesis is that Rāmakṛṣṇa had not transcended his sexual impulses. Moreover, Kripal claimed, his impulses were not heterosexual. He was, rather, a highly advanced mystic who nonetheless exhibited sexual impulses which manifested in homoerotic ways. The Rāmakṛṣṇa Order, an institution founded at the beginning of the twentieth century by Rāmakṛṣṇa's most famous and powerful disciple, Swami Vivekānanda, was among many voices that condemned Kripal's thesis. What has resulted is an ongoing international debate that has sparked the concerns of Hindus and non-Hindus alike. Within the realm of academia, a heated debate arose over the right and role of non-Hindu scholars to interpret Hindu saints.[2] Meanwhile, Kripal has written several responses to his critics, and the book has seen a third edition. The intensity of the international debate exposes growing tensions in the politics of interpretation and reminds us that the wounds of colonialism are far from healed.[3]

## CONCLUSION: THE CLASH OF MODERNITY AND TRADITIONAL CULTURE

In Hinduism, sexuality is regarded as a powerful inner fire whose ultimate source is the very same creative fire that gives rise to the universe itself. For this reason, sexuality is regarded with deep reverence. When the heat from this inner fire is channeled outward, it has the capacity to produce life. When channeled upward, it has the capacity to produce spiritual gnosis. In either case, there is a need for awareness and care. If misused, sexuality can destroy. For this reason, Hindu canonical texts contain strict purity regulations regarding proper sexual practices and relations. At the same time, sexual pleasure (*kāma*), is regarded as one of the four aims of human life, and Hinduism certainly allows for the experience of pleasure outside the aims of producing a child. Moreover, traditions of Tantra see pleasure as a vehicle for liberation. In such contexts, the outward and inward flows of sexual energy are merged in such a way that sexuality transforms into spirituality.

Sanskrit literature abounds with descriptions of human and divine persons engaged in a variety of sexual and gender positionalities. What emerges from these traditions is a fluid notion of the human being rooted in a doctrine of reincarnation and a spiritual biology that understands all humans to contain both male and female powers and potentialities.

Hindus today—who now live in nearly all countries of the world—find themselves living in a world in which alternative worldviews are accessed through music, at movies, online, and through dialogue with one's neighbors or with strangers at Starbucks. As a result, the current generation of Hindus has in many ways adopted attitudes toward sexuality that are quite different from those of their parents, let alone their grandparents. Certainly, most teenage Hindus would not recognize much of the above discussion of sexuality and spirituality. For them, sexuality is likely embodied most palpably by their favorite Hollywood film star or international rock musician. For this reason, traditional Hinduism, which for thousands of years has been transmitted from parent to child, guru to student, is now threatened by the alternative lifestyles that Hindus choose to adopt on a daily basis.

For traditional Hindus, this situation is a serious call for alarm. During a conversation in 1996 with my friend and colleague, Mukunda Raj Aryal, professor of history, art, and culture at Tribhuvan University in Kathmandu, he made the alarming comment that he believes traditional Hindu culture in Nepal will be extinct within three generations. His justification for this claim is that very few Nepalese youth are interested in learning the traditional arts, skills, and ideologies that have been passed on for millennia from parent to child. Why learn traditional customs when one can watch Jennifer Lopez's latest video on MTV?

Nonetheless, it is certainly too early to predict the demise of Hinduism. The core of the Hindu tradition has survived over four millennia and despite invasions and cultural exchange with Muslims, Huns, Greeks, and European colonialists. From a certain perspective, modernity appears as just another foreign element that Hinduism is currently in the process of assimilating and incorporating. Certainly, traditional Hinduism is still vibrant. At Banaras, Brahmins still recite the Vedas every morning. Temples throughout the subcontinent and now across the world daily resound with the ringing of bells and singing of mantras in honor of the gods they house. And the Ganges River continues to flow through the matted locks of Śiva, down the snowy slopes of the Himālayas and across the ancient plains of northern India, carrying in her currents a fluid potency that nourishes and bathes millions of Hindus.

## NOTES

1. Recently, some scholars have argued against this invasion theory and have posited instead that Indo-Aryan culture was contained within the Indus Valley civilization as part of a complex urban, multicultural, multiethnic community. According to these scholars, the cause of the collapse of the Indus Valley communities was not invasion by Indo-Aryans but rather a number of natural forces, including the drying up of a major riverbed, the Saraswatī. Whichever of these theories one accepts, the key point is that Hinduism from its origins begins as the result of a cultural exchange between diverse peoples living in a single region in the subcontinent, which now comprises Pakistan, India, Nepal, Bangladesh, and Sri Lanka. One of the brilliant aspects of Hinduism is that over the millennia, it has continually been shaped by and has adapted to the diverse ethnic communities that have entered the subcontinent, including Greeks, Muslims, Huns, British, and the multinational tourists who now come to the subcontinent every year.
2. Much of this debate can be found on the list-serv RISA-L.
3. Rajiva Malhotra highlights these tensions in a recent article, "Wendy's Child Syndrome," *Sulekha Columns,* available at http://sulekha.com/column.asp?cid=239156.

## REFERENCES

### Primary Sources

Arthaśāstra of Kauttilya. 1960. *The Kauttilya of Arthaśāstra.* 2 vols. R. P. Kangle, ed. Bombay: University of Bombay Press.

Bhāgavata Purāṇa. 1971. *Śrimadbhāgavata Purāṇa.* 2 vols. C. L. Goswami and M. A. Shastri, eds. and trans. Gorakhpur: Gita Press.

*Bṛhadāraṇyaka Upaniṣad.* 1934. E. Sénart, ed. and trans into French. Paris: Les Belles Lettres.

*Kālikā Purāṇa.* 1972. B. Nshastri, ed. and trans. 2 vols. Delhi: Chowkhambha Sanskrit Series.

*Kāma Sūtra of Vatsyāyana.* 1994. Translated by Alain Daniélou as *The Complete Kāma Sūtra.* Rochester, VT: Park Street Press.

*Mahābhārata.* 1933–1960. V. S. Sukthankar, et al., eds. 21 vols. Poona: Bhandarkar Oriental Research Institute.

*Manusmṛti.* 1970. Gopala Sastri Nene, ed. Kashi Sanskrit Series, no. 114. Benares: Chowkhamba Sanskrit Series Office.

Rājataraṅgaṇi of Kalhana. [1900] 1979. *Kalhana's Rājataraṅgaṇī, Chronicle of the Kings of Kashmir,* M. A. Stein, ed. 2 vols. Delhi: Motilal Banarsidass.

*Rāmāyana of Vālmīki.* 1960–1975. G. H. Bhatt et al., eds. 7 vols. Barod: Oriental Institute.

*Ṛg Veda.* [1890–1892] 1966. F. Max Müler, ed. Varanasi: Chowkhamba Sanskrit Series Office.

*Rudrayāmala Tantra.* 1980. Yogatantra Department, ed. Yoga Tantra Granthamala no. 7. Benares: Sampuranand Sanskrit Vishvavidyalaya Press.

*Tantrāloka of Abhinavagupta.* [1918–1938] 1987. Mukund Ram Shastri, ed. 12 vols. Delhi: Motilal Banarsidass.

### Secondary Sources

Bhaskaran, Suparna. 2002. "The Politics of Penetration: Section 377 of the Indian Penal Code." Pp. 15–29 in R. Vanita, ed., *Queering India: Same-Sex Love and Eroticism in Indian Culture and Society.* New York: Routledge.

Caldwell, Sarah. 1999. *Oh Terrifying Mother: Sexuality, Violence, and Worship of the Goddess Kāli.* New Dehli: Oxford University Press.

Dimmitt, Cornelia, and J. A. van Buitenen. 1978. *Classical Hindu Mythology: A Reader in the Sanskrit Purāṇas.* Philadelphia: Temple University Press.

Dimock, Edward, Jr. 1966. *The Place of the Hidden Moon: Erotic Mysticism in the Vaiṣṇava Sahajīya Cult of Bengal.* Chicago: University of Chicago Press.

Doniger, Wendy. 1973. *Asceticism and Eroticism in the Mythology of Śiva.* New York: Oxford University Press.

Eliade, Mircea. 1990. *Yoga: Immortality and Freedom.* New York: Bollinger Foundation.

Flood, Gavin. 1993. *Body and Cosmology in Kashmir Śaivism.* San Francisco: Mellen Research University Press.

Jamison, Stephanie. 1996. *Sacrificed Wife, Sacrificer's Wife: Women, Ritual, and Hospitality in Ancient India.* New York: Oxford University Press.

Kripal, Jeffrey J. 1995. *Kālī's Child: The Mystical and the Erotic in the Life and Teaching of Ramakrishna.* 2nd ed. Chicago: University of Chicago Press.

Larson, Gerald James. 1976. "The Aesthetic (Rasāsvāda) and the Religious (Brahmsvāda) in Abhinavajupta's Kashmir Shaivism." *Philosophy East and West: A Quarterly of Asian Comparative Thought* 26, no. 4: 371–388.

Lidke, Jeffrey S. 2000. *The Goddess beyond Yet Within the Three Cities: Śākta Tantra and the Paradox of Power in Nepāla-Maṇḍala.* Ph.D. diss., University of California at Santa Barbara.

Margolin, Frédérique A. 1985. *Wives of the God-King: The Rituals of the Devadasis of Puri.* Delhi: Oxford University Press.

Muktananda, Swami. 1976. *Satsang with Baba: Questions and Answers with Swami Muktananda.* Vol. 2. Oakland, CA: SYDA Foundation.

Rabe, Michael. 1996. "Sexual Imagery on the 'Phantasmagorical Castle' at Khajuraho." *International Journal of Tantric Studies* 2, no. 2: 1–26.

Ranchhoddas, Ratanlal, and Dhirajlal Keshavlal Thakoree. 1992. *The Indian Penal Code.* 27th ed. Nagpur: Wadhwa.

Sweet, Michael J., and Leonard Zwilling. 1996. "'Like a City Ablaze': The Third Sex and the Creation of Sexuality in Jain Religious Literature." *Journal of the History of Sexuality* 6, no. 3: 359–384.

Vanita, Ruth, ed. 2002. *Queering India: Same Sex Love and Eroticism in Indian Culture and Society.* New York: Routledge.

Vanita, Ruth, and Saleem Kidwai. 2000. *Same-Sex Love in India: Readings from Literature and History.* New York: St. Martin's Press.

Weinberger-Thomas, Catherine. 1999. *Ashes of Immortality: Widow-Burning in India.* Translated by Jeffrey Mehlman and David Gordon White. Chicago: University of Chicago Press.

White, David Gordon. 1996. *The Alchemical Body: Siddha Traditions in Medieval India.* Chicago: University of Chicago Press.

Chapter 5

# Buddhist Views on Gender and Desire

*Liz Wilson*

*A Buddhist nun praying. For monks and nuns in most Buddhist Asian countries, keeping the precept on appropriate sexual conduct entails refraining from all sexual activity. (Horace Bristol/Corbis)*

To present the range of Buddhist attitudes toward sexuality is a formidable task. Buddhism is a complex religion without a centralized ecclesiastic authority (such as the Pope in Roman Catholicism). There are numerous varieties or denominations of Buddhism as it exists in Asia and is now increasingly being institutionalized in the West. Although scripture is authoritative for Buddhists, there is no single, agreed-upon body of scripture preserved in a single language that is authoritative for all Buddhists. Each denomination has its own canonical scripture. And even within a single denomination, in which Buddhists share a definition of what is canonical, what is prescribed and proscribed depends to a certain extent on whether one is a lay or monastic practitioner. In *The Red Thread: Buddhist Approaches to Sexuality,* Bernard Faure suggests that one can only assume the existence of a generic Buddhism and a generalized Buddhist attitude toward sexuality for heuristic purposes (1998, 11). Not only do the Asian cultures in which Buddhism found a home differ greatly in their sexual customs, but the major forms of Buddhism in Asia offer such complexity in their various attitudes about sexuality that the task of generalization is fraught with difficulties. Nevertheless, an appreciation of basic Buddhist teachings provides a foundation for understanding some of the various attitudes toward sexuality expressed in Buddhist texts and practices.

## BASIC BUDDHIST BELIEFS

The central problem that Buddhist teachings address is the problem of suffering or dissatisfaction. In his first sermon, delivered soon after he experienced enlightenment, the Buddha is said to have set forth four propositions known as the Four Noble Truths. These propositions affirm that (1) life is dissatisfying, (2) life is dissatisfying because of craving or "thirst," (3) life does not *have to be* dissatisfying—dissatisfaction can end, and (4) there is a path that leads to the end of dissatisfaction.

This fundamental teaching is often compared to a medical diagnosis, in which the Buddha as the great physician identifies the malady at the heart of the human condition and prescribes a cure. In the scriptural languages, the term used to characterize the ills of life is *dukkha*—a Pāli word that means suffering, discomfort, or dissatisfaction. Linguistically, *dukkha* is the opposite of *sukha,* a term meaning ease, satisfaction, or pleasure. Hence *dukkha* can be translated literally as "dis-ease." *Dukkha* plagues all sentient beings and is the ailment or syndrome that Buddhism cures. According to the second noble truth, the source of this state of dissatisfaction or dis-ease is *tanhā* (Pāli), meaning "craving" or, more literally, "thirst." Although often translated as "desire," *tanhā* is narrower in meaning than the English "desire," referring more specifically to desire that is in some sense distorted, excessive, or misdirected. Sometimes *tanhā* is translated as "egoistic grasping" because it refers to an ego-driven feeling—"I want it!"—that wells up inside a person and makes that person see the entire world from the distorted point of view of what permits or prevents fulfillment his or her craving. Craving or "thirst" appears in three forms: first, craving for sensual pleasure, or pleasure derived from taste, touch, and other sense experiences; second, craving for renewed existence; and, finally, craving for the nonexistence of those things and people that disturb us or for our own nonexistence when feeling unhappy.

All three forms of craving lead to rebirth—even a person who craves nonexistence and commits suicide will be born again—and rebirth is considered by Buddhists to be a source of pain. To those with little background in Buddhist teachings, rebirth or transmigration may sound quite pleasant. Since it entails the experience of life in some other form after death, rebirth thus seems to promise novelty and excitement as well as extended life. But none of the various forms of rebirth that Buddhists envision, including extremely pleasant forms of life as a deity, offers the possibility of endless life. Those who take birth in various hells (or who are born as insects or other sentient beings with limited faculties) because of lack of virtue in their present lives will experience tremendous discomfort. Even those who, because of meritorious deeds in their present lives, enjoy tremendous ease and ready satisfaction of physical needs by taking rebirth as gods and goddesses, will eventually die. Rebirth is inherently dissatisfying because life must end, and at the end of each life, one endures not only the breakdown of one's body and the pain of saying good-bye to life but also separation from loved ones. This dissatisfying cycle of rebirth is known as samsara.

Craving, according to the teaching of the Four Noble Truths, keeps one bound to repeated sufferings and dissatisfactions in the cycle of samsara. Craving or thirst is said to be like a fire—the more you feed it, the more powerful it becomes. Once one's cravings are gratified, one begins to crave more. Because one can never satisfy craving once and for all, it is a source of pain. It is especially difficult to satisfy craving when, according to Buddhist teaching, everything that exists is impermanent. Everything changes, and what satisfies our cravings today will not be there tomorrow. We are always hankering after things that do not last. Whenever we get comfortable with a situation, it changes, constant change being the only thing that stays the same in this world of transient phenomena.

To sum up the second noble truth, craving or thirst leads to dissatisfaction or dis-ease. However, the third noble truth asserts that there is an optimistic prognosis for this condition. The malady caused by craving is curable. If the craving ceases, then dissatisfaction ends. Nirvana is the state one experiences when the fire of craving, which feeds on the fuel of ignorance, is put out. The fourth noble truth summarizes the path by which one experiences nirvana. Or, in terms of the medical model, the fourth noble truth lays down a treatment plan.

The path has eight elements, each described as "correct" or "proper," and hence is known as the Noble Eightfold Path. The first is proper understanding, a frame of mind that comes from experientially or existentially understanding the Four Noble Truths. The second element is proper intention, which entails cultivating thoughts free from sensuality, malice, and cruelty. Proper speech—most importantly avoiding dishonesty and harmful speech, such as gossip or slander—is the third element of the path. The fourth element is proper action, which will be discussed further below. The fifth element of the path is proper livelihood, or avoiding occupations that would violate the precepts, such as slaughtering animals or battlefield military duty. The sixth element is proper effort—being energetic and vigilant in monitoring one's thoughts, trying to cultivate pure and compassionate thoughts. The seventh element of the path is proper mindfulness, which refers to the practice of *vipassanā,* or insight meditation. The point of this kind of meditation is to cultivate mindful awareness (sometimes called bare awareness). It can be done while sitting, while walking, or while one is engaged in any number of mundane activities. Proper concentration is the eighth element of the path. It refers to a special form of consciousness known as *samādhi.* In this objectless state of awareness—often described as "going into a trance"—one has no awareness of self or other, no sense of such mundane details as the passage of time. Thus when one goes into *samādhi,* there is nothing to apprehend and no one there doing the apprehending. Practicing proper concentration and reaching the state of *samādhi* is thus an excellent way to realize experientially the central Buddhist doctrine that an eternal soul or abiding self does not exist—a doctrine that will be discussed more fully below.

The fourth element of the path—proper action—is of special interest here. The key aspects of Buddhist morality that guide proper action are encoded in the five precepts that laypeople undertake to follow at all times. The five precepts require that one refrain from killing, stealing, inappropriate sexual conduct, lying, and the use of intoxicants. In addition to the five precepts, monks and nuns cultivate proper action by following a code of conduct contained in the monastic rule (*vinaya*) of their order.

Since sexual expression (as opposed to sexual fantasies or merely thinking about sex) falls under the category of proper or improper action, it is in reference to this fourth element of the path that questions arise as to the appropriateness of different forms of sexual conduct. Lay Buddhists keep the precept on inappropriate sexual conduct by avoiding harmful forms of sexual expression, such as adultery or rape. In some Buddhist cultures, as we shall see below, homosexual acts would also be considered forms of inappropriate sexual conduct, but in others, homosexual activity by laypersons would not be considered inappropriate, unless the act in question were judged to be nonconsensual or otherwise harmful. For monks and nuns in most Buddhist countries in Asia, keeping the precept on inappropriate sexual conduct entails refraining from all sexual activity, including masturbation.[1]

## BUDDHIST ATTITUDES ABOUT SEX AND GENDER

What can we infer about sex from this basic outline of the reasons why the Buddha declared life to be unsatisfactory? Sexual desire is problematic from several viewpoints. Sexual urges belong to the realm of the senses, and their gratification can reinforce one's thirst or craving for pleasures of the senses. But the potential social consequences of heterosexual activity are just as problematic as the psychic consequences of feeding the fire of craving for pleasure. The progeny that result from regular sexual intercourse without modern forms of contraception create a host of obligations, obligations that can seriously hamper progress on the path for someone desperate to escape the cycle of birth and death. One must earn money, engaging in systems of production or other forms of labor, to support one's family. In the extended family system prevalent in India at the time of the Buddha (and still prevalent in much of Asia today), raising a family means caring not only for a spouse and children but also for more distant relatives. How does one find the time to cultivate proper mindfulness and proper concentration while raising children and supporting one's extended family? Such contemplative practices are difficult to master, even when one has few demands on one's time. Distractions of any form are a challenge to meditators, who need large blocks of time in which to train their minds, just as dancers and athletes need extended periods of time in which to train their bodies. Family life can make the cultivation of such rarefied mental states as *samādhi* even more difficult. The ordinary situations that arise in family life—sickness, temper tantrums, family crises—are all potential distractions to uninterrupted meditation. It can also be hard to cultivate the moral virtues that are the foundation for meditation and for the cultivation of wisdom when supporting a family. As the family breadwinner, it may not be easy to avoid unwholesome occupations when work is scarce. And if stealing were the only way to put food on the table for hungry children, how many parents could say that they would not give serious thought to taking what belongs to others?

Legend has it that Gotama Siddhartha, the Buddha or "awakened one" of this present era, left his family behind at the age of twenty-nine, embarking on a search for a path leading beyond birth and death. He had been married by the arrangement of his parents, as was customary, and had, according to the majority of biographical accounts, one child, a baby son.[2] The name that the Buddha is said to have given his son gives some indication of how the early Buddhists who redacted accounts of the Buddha's life viewed domesticity. According to most biographies, Gautama Siddhartha called his young son Rāhula, usually glossed as "impediment." Rāhula would later follow his father and become a monk, thus bringing an end to Gotama Siddhartha's paternal line, at least in the biological sense. Buddhists regard monastic ordination as entry into the spiritual lineage of the sons and daughters of the Buddha, and so in this sense Rāhula joined Gotama Siddhartha's true family by becoming a monk.

The name given to the process of ordination into the monastic lifestyle of the early followers of the Buddha is also telling: it is called "going forth from home to homelessness"—hence, by definition, a homeless or nondomestic life. Not all early followers of the Buddha in India took this homeless path. Many lay followers became supporters of the early monastic community through their gifts of food and clothing and other resources. Lay Buddhists receive prominent mention in early Buddhist texts and were decisive in shaping the course of Buddhism in India and elsewhere in Asia. It is the elite monastic core of celibate monks and nuns, however, who generally served as the standard-bearers and intellectual arbiters of early Buddhist life in India. In the next section, we shall see why that was so.

### Marriage and Family Life

Characterizations of married life as a source of *dukkha* (dissatisfaction) are common in the earliest layers of Buddhist scripture, especially in discourses directed at monastics. Buddhism arose at a time in Indian history when the idea of the autonomous individual was newly emerging. Traditionally, salvation was understood to be a family affair; family members would enjoy (or suffer) afterlife destinies achieved by the ritual activities of the head of the household. Buddhists articulated a religious ideal of individualism, whereby a person stands apart from his or her family and determines an individual destiny for him- or herself as an independent religious actor (by performing meritorious deeds or failing to act meritoriously). In the criticism of family life and the praise heaped upon the untethered existence of the religious wanderer in early scriptural texts, one can see a valorization of the individual who, apart from his or her family, shapes his or her own fate. Celebrations of the holy wanderer equate the homeless life of the religious nomad with the exercise of religious autonomy.

Celibacy is essential to the religious autonomy praised by the Buddha and his early followers. The early Buddhist renunciant was the antithesis of the householder tied down by family obligations. Like the largely celibate cowboy heroes of American Westerns who delight in making their home on the range, early Buddhist renouncers are represented as free agents enjoying a blessed release from domestic entanglements.[3] Similes that contrast the free wandering life of the celibate renouncer with the householder's lack of autonomy are found repeatedly in the *Sutta Nipāta,* a collection of verses that contains some of the earliest poetry composed by Buddhists in India. For example, the "Discourse on the Rhinoceros Horn" in the *Sutta Nipāta* is a poem that warns against the filial and social obligations that entrap the householder. The state of being single that celibate renouncers enjoy is compared to the strong, durable horn of a rhinoceros and the freedom of a deer wandering in the forest:

> Affection for children and wives is like an entangled, overgrown bamboo grove; being unentangled like the new bamboo tip, wander single as a rhinoceros horn. Untrapped like a deer in the forest who grazes here and there at will, the wise man is intent on autonomy: wander single as a rhinoceros horn. (Anderson and Smith 1913, 10–12)

From the perspective of Buddhist mendicants who renounced their land, property, and familial life, the householder who bore children to carry on the family lineage was caught in a web of social obligations that permitted little freedom. The homeless, penniless, but autonomous renouncer stood in stark contrast to those whose lives were devoted to the acquisition and maintenance of wealth, power, and family dynasties. With no obligations save those taken on out of compassion and no constraints on movement, the renouncer wandered through the world freely, unencumbered by mundane concerns. Monks ordained by the Buddha in the fifth century B.C.E. led a seminomadic existence in which the celibate homeless life was equated with a salutary escape from the suffocating closeness of the social world, with its endless web of family and friendship obligations. Wandering the countryside for at least eight months of the year (the monsoon season being a time of retreat in which renouncers avoided the muddy, impassable roads out of compassion for the worms and other creatures likely to be trampled underfoot), the celibate renouncer was said to enjoy freedoms that those bound by the duties of childbearing and breadwinning can hardly imagine: the freedom of propertylessness and of having nothing to take care

141

of beyond the minimal care of the body that is necessary for the pursuit of the deathless state of nirvana; the leisure to spend days in meditation and study; and the ability to travel at will in search of wholesome environments and accomplished teachers. Householders can never know such freedoms.

If celibacy is championed and antimarriage sentiments are frequently expressed in early Buddhist scripture, early sources nevertheless contain some instances of praise for the ways in which good marriages can benefit the laity. For example, in the *Aṅguttara Nikāya,* the Buddha holds up the marriage of Nakula's parents as an example of lay discipleship (Morris and Hardy 1976, 295ff; Hare 1973, 210ff). When Nakula's father is desperately ill and eaten up with anxiety, his wife counsels him about the dangers of dying with a fretful mind and reassures him that she will be able to support the children with her handiwork after his death. She goes on to further reassure her dying husband that she will remain faithful not only to him but also to the Buddhist dharma (a word with so many levels of meaning it is best left untranslated, but which may, for the sake of brevity, be rendered as "teachings" or "truth"). "As long as the Buddha will have white-robed women lay-disciples, householders who keep the virtues in full," she proclaims repeatedly to her husband, "I shall be among them" (Morris and Hardy 1976, 296; Hare 1973, 213). The wife's confidence in her own ability not only to support the family but also to achieve the religious goals of freedom from doubt and self-reliance as a lay disciple allays the husband's anxieties, and he recovers from his illness. Later the husband visits the Buddha and is congratulated for having such an excellent wife as his counselor and teacher.

Buddhist literature also offers models of dharmic lay life in the form of celibate marriages. Biographical narratives about Kaśyapa the Great and his wife Bhadrā, both of whom eventually took ordination and became prominent disciples of the Buddha, show a man and woman living a celibate wedded life together. Although both were inclined from an early age toward the renunciant life and attempted to avoid marriage, the stratagems they devised to prevent getting married failed. Kaśyapa declared to his parents his intention not to marry. Instead, he promised to take care of his parents for as long as they lived; after their deaths, he would renounce the world and take ordination. But to appease his mother, who wished to see her son married, Kaśyapa devised the following strategy: he had a statue of a beautiful woman made and promised that if his parents found a woman as lovely as the statue, he would marry her. The young woman Bhadrā, who had been Kaśyapa's wife in former lives, was found to be the living counterpart of the statue. When the young people learned that a marriage was being arranged for them, they wrote each other letters explaining that they were bound for the monastery and could not consent to marriage. But the letters were intercepted and the marriage arranged as if both parties were in full agreement. Kaśyapa and Bhadrā, however, decided not to consummate their marriage and spent their wedding night separated by a chain of flowers.

This flower-barrier and other mutually agreed-upon disciplines that the young couple used to preserve chastity within the marriage suggest an interesting form of mutuality within the marriage. Together the young couple conspired to keep each other unencumbered by the bonds of domestic cohabitation. These collaborations show Kaśyapa and Bhadrā deciding to outwardly adhere to the wishes of their parents and the expectations of the larger society while secretly subverting the purpose of marriage as an institution for the production of legitimate heirs. Like the story of Nakula's parents, such narratives can be read as supporting the institution of marriage as a salutary arrangement for those dedicated to the pursuit of awakening. But they can also be read as exceptions that prove the rule that marriage and domestic life constitute a form of entrapment, limiting the autonomy of those who seek nirvana. In the *Mahākaśyapa Avadāna,* a poetic rendering of the story of Kaśyapa and Bhadrā preserved in Sanskrit, the couple enumerates many reasons why marriage is incompatible with the religious path they have chosen. Explaining to his father why he prefers not to marry, Kaśyapa equates the marriage bond with bondage to samsara:

> In marriage first there is the shedding of tears which incessantly flow when the smoke of the sacrificial fire irritates the eye; the first joining-together of the hands of the new couple is the veritable knot signifying joint pursuits in the path of vice; the garland is placed round the neck to signify that the ways and orders of the world should not be violated; therefore those alone are delighted in marriage whose minds are shrouded with illusions. (Vidyabhusan 1898, 18–19)

Kaśyapa's next statement to his father vividly describes women's grief at the loss of children. One can well imagine the suffering of Buddhist parents living in times and places in which child mortality rates were extremely high and many children died before reaching adulthood. In this statement, Kaśyapa says that men who become monks may miss out on such sensual delights as hearing music and seeing dancing women, but they also avoid hearing the grief-stricken cries of wives upon the early death of their children:

> Those whose ears have never feasted on the sweet music of harps and lutes attending upon the quick dance of young maidens who appear like tender creepers wafted by the breeze, have not to hear the loud bewailing of their wives uttered at the time of their children passing away from the world. (Vidyabhusan 1898, 19)

This depiction of the grief of women seeing their children die before reaching adulthood sheds light on the negative appraisal of marriage and reproduction in Buddhist texts. Where infant mortality rates are high, grief and mourning over dead children are the cost of reproductive success. One can hardly sustain family lineages without some life being sacrificed—sometimes the life of the mother as well as the life of the child. One can readily see from this connection between reproduction and death why Māra, the Buddhist god of desire, is also the bringer of death. Or to use more western mythological terms, Cupid, with his flower-tipped arrows, turns out to be the Grim Reaper whose visit calls for funerary flower arrangements.

### Female Renouncers

Given the high cost to women of bearing children, it is not surprising that women sought to join the Buddha's spiritual "family" as nuns. Women did join this alternative, renunciant family of monks and nuns, sons and daughters of the Buddha, and in doing so they challenged conventions about how women should behave that prevailed at the time of the Buddha in India. As someone who established the homeless, non-domestic life of the Buddhist renouncer as a countercultural alternative to mainstream society, the Buddha cannot legitimately be characterized as a feminist reformer bent on overturning patriarchal institutions and reforming mainstream society. Some scholars regard the Buddha as a social reformer, depicting him, for example, as a champion of the rights of outcasts and other groups at the bottom of the socioreligious hierarchy prevalent in India at the time. In Buddhist assertions that caste or class is not inherited from one's parents but acquired by moral virtue, we can see some basis for this view. The early Buddhist monastic counterculture, however, did not regard Buddhist monastic institutions as replacing the

social systems of mainstream society but rather as providing an alternative for those who sought release from dissatisfaction in life. Early
monastic communities established themselves as refuges from the social
world, alternative societies in which prevailing social customs had no authority. For those seeking release from the cycle of samsara, reforming the
world outside the walls of the monastery was not a primary concern.

Thus we can no more characterize the Buddha as a champion of
women's rights than we can characterize him as a champion of the rights
of other disenfranchised groups. Having said this, however, there is no
denying that by taking up the homeless life as Buddhist nuns, Indian
women were able to exercise rights and enjoy forms of agency virtually
unknown to the women of mainstream Indian society in the Buddha's
day. Women who renounced domesticity as Buddhist nuns contributed
to the development of new conceptions about women's sexuality and new
forms of female agency.

To understand these new conceptions, one must know something of
the customary gender roles prevailing in India prior to the rise of
Buddhism. Evidence indicates that in ancient times, some Indian women
may have enjoyed a high degree of autonomy. Women who lived in the
era in which the Vedic hymns—the most ancient layers of what is now
regarded as Hindu scripture—were being composed were expected to
participate in religious life. In fact, women were not only encouraged to
participate in ritual; their participation was mandatory. A wife had to be
standing by her husband's side for the ritual to be successful. Women
were given the scriptural training necessary to participate in sacrifices
(ritual offerings to the Vedic gods and goddesses) with their husbands. If
a man's wife died, he would make a clay image of her and place it next to
him whenever he performed sacrifices. In this way, the deities would be
satisfied that the man was acting not alone but in accord with his spouse.
On the basis of such evidence, historians such as Anant Sadashiv Altekar
(1978) and Katherine Young (1987) conclude that in their role as wives
and mothers, women of the Vedic era enjoyed about as much equality
with men as is possible, given the fact that ancient Indian society was
male-dominated.

By about 900 B.C.E., however, with the evolution of a body of texts
called *Brāhmaṇas*—commentaries on the ancient Vedic hymns—women
became disenfranchised as religious actors. Brahmanical authorities sanctified motherhood. As mothers of sons to carry on the paternal lineage,
Indian women of the Buddha's day contributed to the perpetuation of

male lineages that were extremely important to Brahmanical religious life. The idea that women should lead autonomous lives and be entrusted with making independent choices was so far from the norm as to be virtually unthinkable in a society that increasingly emphasized women's role in maintaining distinct social classes through endogamous marriages. The highest virtue for women, Brahmanical texts declare, is obedience to male authority. Women exercising independent agency threatened the purity of the paternal line. Daughters who chose their own sexual or marital partners, rather than allowing parents to find their mates, ran the risk of falling in love with an inappropriate mate and disrupting the purity of the paternal line by bearing children to men of lower social classes.

For these reasons, *The Laws of Manu* and other Brahmanical treatises on religious law dictate that women's lives and sexual activities should be closely regulated by kinsmen. Manu says that a woman should always be under male control: by her father when she is young; by her husband in midlife; and by her son in old age, after her husband has died. Brahmanical authorities suggested that girls should be married by the time they start to menstruate. Fathers who did not arrange the marriages of their daughters by the onset of menstruation were at risk of violating religious law and causing harm to their ancestors. Women who gave birth to many sons were highly valued. Although special time was set aside for boys of the upper classes to study with a guru and receive a religious education, no such time was set aside for girls to be educated. If women were to bear many children, their youthful fertility was not to be wasted on years spent acquiring a religious education. As a result of their lack of education and concomitant exclusion from liturgical life, women came to be seen as unlearned, uncultured, and less adept at spiritual pursuits (except for those religious rituals practiced in the domestic sphere).

Idealizations of women as dutiful daughters compliant with parental marital arrangements and faithful wives bearing many sons had the effect of marginalizing those women who valued autonomy, did not desire to marry, and did not wish to remain under lifelong guardianship of their male kin. Idealizations of women as perpetuators of the paternal line also marginalized women who desired marriage but who failed to give birth to male offspring. By taking up the homeless life as followers of the Buddha, women opted out of confining systems of control over women prevalent in India in the early centuries before the Common Era.

We cannot say precisely at what point in the early history of Buddhism the order of nuns was established. Scriptural accounts place the event during the lifetime of the Buddha, at a point when the Buddha's father had died and his foster-mother, Mahāprajāpatī, came to seek ordination as a nun, along with a group of kinswomen. Mahāprajāpatī asked to be able to go forth into the homeless life just as many of her male relatives had done. The story survives in several forms, preserved both in Pāli and Sanskrit sources.[4] What is most striking about many of the accounts of this scene—and what has received much scholarly attention—is the seeming disparity between two attitudes attributed to the Buddha. In some versions of the story, the Buddha is reluctant to admit the women and relents only after predicting the eventual decline of the Buddhist religion as a result of establishing the order of nuns. Presumably to forestall the predicted decline, the Buddha also institutes eight special rules to be followed only by the nuns; rules that, in effect, made nuns second-class citizens in the monastic sphere by placing them under the control and protection of the monks. However, in the more developed Pāli version of the incident, the Buddha concedes that women are as capable as men of breaking free from the cycle of samsara. All levels of path attainment are possible for women, including the goal that Pāli texts regard as supreme—becoming an arhat (worthy one) who is liberated from craving and no longer bound to rebirth in samsara.

Alan Sponberg (1992) suggests that we read these contradictory accounts as indications that early Buddhists struggled for social acceptability as Buddhism achieved some level of success and enfranchisement in the larger society. Although Buddhist teachings went against many pre-Buddhist social conventions and institutions, Buddhists nonetheless lived among and competed for patronage from those who upheld such social structures. To totally disregard norms regarding women would have undermined respect for Buddhism and threatened the ability of the Buddhist community to thrive. During the life of the Buddha, the Buddha's own charisma tended to forestall issues of social acceptability. But in the centuries after the death of the Buddha, as Buddhists garnered elite patrons from the royal and merchant classes of India, Buddhist teachings gained a much wider currency. Once a relatively marginalized group, Buddhists now faced criticism on account of their "wild," undomestic, "unwomanly" women. Women living as homeless renunciants were far beyond the pale of what Brahmanical authorities regarded as proper. Female renouncers were not unknown in pre-Buddhist India, but institutionalized orders of renunciant women did

147

not exist until the rise of Buddhism and Jainism (a religion established by the Buddha's near-contemporary, Mahāvīra, that like Buddhism rejected the authority of the Vedas and the Brahmanical commentaries on these foundational texts). Sponberg suggests that Buddhists and Jains initially took bold steps in admitting women as renouncers. Both groups—or at least factions within the Buddhist and Jain folds—eventually buckled under social pressure when the status of their nuns became a point of contention. Since Brahmanical authorities regarded the idea of women leading autonomous lives without male guardians as socially and religiously suspect, some Buddhist and Jain factions responded by minimizing opportunities for women to exercise independent decision making. The result of this backpedaling is that editors responsible for redacting the story of how the nuns' order was established—men born long after the death of the Buddha and after the establishment of the nun's order—created documents that make the Buddha look more like a stern Brahmanical authority fretting over the possibility of some impropriety women might commit than like the countercultural critic he probably was.

The special rules imposed upon the order of nuns—whenever they were imposed—meant that women could escape lives of domesticity by becoming nuns but had to accept male dominance as the price of admission into the homeless life. As detrimental as the loss of the nuns' autonomy was the message conveyed to the larger society about the capacities of Buddhist women renouncers. The imposition of special rules meant that lay supporters received the tacit message that Buddhist nuns could not be fully trusted on their own, without constant supervision by their male counterparts, to live perfectly virtuous and upright religious lives. Diminished prestige and financial support for the nuns were the likely consequences of this judgment. Buddhist laity work toward their own eventual awakening by accumulating merit through donations to monastics in the form of food, clothing, and other requisites for living. The more virtuous the recipient of such a donation, the more merit is believed to accrue from the gift. Naturally, a layperson practicing generosity toward monastics would seek out the most virtuous, most accomplished recipient before making a donation. The suspicion that nuns need male supervision because they are more prone than monks to commit improprieties could have devastating results for the financial well-being of Buddhist convents. As Nancy Falk (1989) suggests, the decline and eventual disappearance of the Buddhist order of nuns in many parts of

Asia may be linked to the later Buddhist establishment's imposition of second-class status on its nuns.

## *Buddhist Laywomen*

Given the unfortunate institutional history of Buddhist nuns, it is perhaps no surprise that some of the greatest heroines of Buddhist literature are not nuns but laywomen. Just as women figure prominently in gospel accounts of the ministry of Jesus, even though they were excluded from the ranks of his immediate disciples, so too Buddhist laywomen were crucial to the ministry of the Buddha, even if they did not belong to his band of wandering disciples. It is clear from both scriptural and archaeological evidence that many powerful laywomen supported the Buddha with donations of land and other generous endowments. Among them were a number of wealthy courtesans who supported themselves by the fruits of their own labor and who relied on no male guardians to determine how they would spend their wealth. Courtesans in ancient India— like the *hetairai* (companions to men) of ancient Greece—were educated, cultured women, many of whom could not only read and write but also compose music and poetry in accordance with the most fashionable canons of musical and literary theory. Men were drawn to courtesans not only by their physical beauty but also by their accomplishments in intellectual and artistic pursuits. These attributes made courtesans more entertaining companions for men than their legitimate wives, who often had little education by which to appreciate arcane literary and artistic matters. The courtesans of ancient India were thus "thought-leaders" or "culture-brokers," as the current idiom has it. But they were also power brokers who entertained and received lavish gifts from kings, princes, wealthy merchants, and other well-placed men. Such women, when persuaded that the Buddha's teachings were worthy of their attention, were capable of constituting quite a significant power base for the promulgation of the Buddha's dharma.

One such courtesan was a woman named Sirimā, who lived in Rājagaha. Capable of commanding 1,000 copper coins per day in exchange for her company, Sirimā was a woman of considerable fame and wealth. She became a generous lay patron who made it her habit to feed Buddhist monks each day in her home, serving them with the very best food money could buy. Although by the end of her life, she had gained a reputation for her unstinting generosity and devotion to the Buddhist dharma, Sirimā was not born a Buddhist. She was converted by an amazing event that occurred when Sirimā tried to harm a woman who made her jealous (for a translation of the story, see Burlingame 1990, 3: 103ff.).

The woman who converted Sirimā was named Uttarā, and she was married to a non-Buddhist husband who thought that Uttarā's devotion to Buddhist monastics, with their otherworldly attitudes and shaved heads, was ridiculous. Uttarā's husband claimed that he needed her around the house and forbade her from feeding her "bald little monks." Luckily, Uttarā's parents were very wealthy.[5] Her father gave Uttarā 15,000 copper coins to buy the services of Sirimā for a fortnight. As soon as he saw how beautiful Sirimā was, Uttarā's husband agreed to the arrangement, allowing Uttarā a full fortnight in which to show devotion and generosity to the Buddha and his monks during an important festival. Sirimā, however, did not realize that she was only a temporary concubine, thinking that she was now mistress of the house. When the courtesan found out that Uttarā was this man's wife and the true mistress of the house, she grew angry and threw boiling oil on Uttarā's head. But Uttarā used her mind to counteract the effect of the hot oil. Uttarā thought of all the reasons she should be grateful to Sirimā. Without Sirimā, she would not have been able to earn any merit or hear the dharma being taught. As the boiling oil touched the top of her head, she said to herself, "if it is true that I have no ill-will or anger toward this courtesan, may the oil not burn me." And filling her mind with loving kindness, she found that the hot oil felt like cool water. Sirimā realized that Uttarā was no ordinary woman and begged for forgiveness. Uttarā told the courtesan that it was not in her power to forgive Sirimā. Since her father was still living, Sirimā should go to him and ask him for forgiveness. Sirimā, understanding the patriarchal convention that dictates dealing with other women through male intermediaries, indicated that she would visit Uttarā's father. But it was not her biological father that Uttarā meant. Uttarā sent Sirimā to the Buddha, Uttarā's spiritual father, whom she distinguished from her samsaric father. The story concludes with the Buddha praising Uttarā and converting Sirimā.

What claiming the Buddha as a spiritual father might have meant for female followers of the Buddha is a matter of speculation. It could be yet another indication that Indian society was leery of unguarded women and felt the need to assign them spiritual father figures in addition to their biological fathers. But it could also entail women using the Buddha's spiritual guardianship to justify doing as they pleased in defiance of what their families wanted them to do. Invoking the Buddha as a father could mean that women thereby freed themselves from more concrete familial forms of control.

In the case of a princess named Sumedhā, whose parents had chosen a husband for her despite her wish to become a nun, Buddhist practice clearly gave her the wherewithal to defy her parents and achieve the goals that the young woman had set for herself (Müller 1893, 272–300; Rhys Davids 1948, 221ff). Sumedhā had been taking instruction from the nuns as a lay disciple for several years and had decided not to marry. When she learned that her parents had promised her in marriage to King Anikaratta, Sumedhā retired to her room and defiantly cut off all her hair in imitation of the tonsure ceremony that heralds entry into the monastic life. While getting their heads shaved, novice nuns and monks are given a lock of tonsured hair as an aid to meditation on impermanence; Sumedhā, recreating the ordination ritual in her own home, likewise focused her mind on impermanence while contemplating her shorn hair. In doing this meditation, she entered a trance state and was absorbed in contemplation when her parents entered her room to prepare her for marriage. Emerging from her meditation, Sumedhā gave a very long and passionate lecture on impermanence and how pointless it would be to give her body to a husband when that body was destined for worms in the end. Sumedhā was no mean orator, and in the end she not only convinced her parents to let her become a nun, but she made Buddhists out of her family and household staff as well as her bridegroom and his retinue.

### The Compulsion Is the Cure: *Mahāyāna and Vajrayāna Revalorizations of Sexuality*

If creating a family means feeding the grave over and over again, why bring new life into the world? The Buddhist community in India could have set itself up as a closed community of celibate "singles" in the manner of Shaker communities in the United States, augmenting their membership by taking in orphans. The community could have required that all its members follow the celibate path of the monks and nuns, but it did not. In some ways, it is remarkable that laypeople with families to care for would have found the Buddha's message so attractive. But one of the most important facets of that message was the conviction that it may take many lifetimes before one is in a position to see things as they really are. Before one can hear the wailing of women in mourning echoed within all songs of seduction, one must feed a lot of graves.

Before he won the title of Buddha (Awakened One), the bodhisattva (aspirant to Buddhahood) fed plenty of graves as a family man before escaping the clutches of death in his final lifetime. Biographical traditions about the Buddha's past, preserved in the form of independent collections of *jātakas* (birth stories) and in explanatory narratives within other types of literature, tell of the many past lives the bodhisattva lived as a family man. These narratives became increasingly central as the young religion grew and expanded in India.

It is easy to see that, for laypeople of all denominations, past-life tales of the bodhisattva as family man and breadwinner could serve as examples of how to live virtuously, even while perpetuating oneself within samsara. But for exponents of the Mahāyāna (Great Vehicle), the goal of emulating the bodhisattva as a samsaric but awakening being came to be regarded as more laudable and more true to the spirit of the Buddha's message than the goal of passing away from the cycle of birth and death. Advocates of the Mahāyāna aspired to the full and complete awakening of the Buddha, a larger goal than that of passing away from samsara, in that it includes bringing all sentient beings to awakening.

Calling those who rejected their understanding of the Buddha's message "followers of an inferior way" (Hīnayāna), Mahāyāna texts problematize the goal of becoming an arhat from moral and philosophical viewpoints. To focus on eliminating one's own craving and hence alleviating one's own dissatisfaction is to ignore the needs of others, which is morally questionable. The idea of a self on whom one focuses one's practice is also questionable. It shows flawed thinking from a philosophical point of view, for no such entity exists.

According to the doctrine of emptiness, a philosophical orientation that is systematically expressed by Mahāyāna philosophers such as Nāgārjuna but is also articulated in other Mahāyāna texts, each form that one takes in the cycle of samsara is empty of enduring essence. In the Heart Sūtra, the bodhisattva Avalokiteshvara surveys the world from the perspective of perfect wisdom and finds no suffering, no cause of suffering, no extinction of suffering, and no path that leads to the extinction of suffering. All components of the human being, Avalokiteshvara declares, are empty. The eye, the ear, the nose, and the tongue, as well as the sights, sounds, smells, and tastes that these organs apprehend, are empty of essence. When seen from the perspective of perfect wisdom, eyes, ears, noses, mouths, sights, sounds, smells, and tastes do not arise and do not cease. Each of the component parts that together comprise the human being—including the physical organs of the body as well as sensations, perceptions, volition, and consciousness itself—is a transient phenomenon that arises and ceases through a combination of various factors. Neither these parts nor the human being they comprise can be said to have any enduring reality. Humans and other sentient beings are combinations of component parts, and there is no empirical evidence accepted by Buddhists for a soul or self that dwells within. If the self, independent of others, is an illusion, then one cannot alleviate one's own suffering without also alleviating the suffering of others.

The Mahāyāna ideal of the bodhisattva, or the aspirant to Buddhahood who remains within samsara, derives from earlier usages of the term *bodhisattva,* which refer to the former lives of the Buddha when he aspired to the future state of Buddhahood. But the term takes on new meaning in Mahāyāna contexts as the primary expression of what it means to focus on the needs of all sentient beings. Part of the grandness of this Mahāyāna vision of salvation is that to aspire to become a bodhisattva requires both the courage to suffer within samsara and the wisdom to see that nirvana is already achieved.

Apart from form, there is no emptiness and no alleviation of suffering. Because of the emptiness of form, there is no form. Emptiness means Avalokiteshvara sees no enduring form. Apart from samsara, there is no nirvana. Given this nondifference between samsara and nirvana, the unsatisfactoriness of life is ultimately nothing to fear. By virtue of the nature of samsara (when properly understood with the eyes of perfect wisdom), nirvana is already attained. Hence one need not renounce domestic life and seek to eradicate craving. Craving, when properly understood, is nirvana itself. Advocates of Mahāyāna questioned the sharp division between laity and monastics that characterized those rival sects that the Mahāyānists called "Hīnayāna" (of which the only denomination surviving today is the Theravāda, or "Way of the Elders," that is predominant in Southeast Asia and in Sri Lanka). The Great Way, or Mahāyāna, presents itself in its scriptures as an inclusive path open to all, rather than an exclusive or narrow path in which one can only enter nirvana through the gateway of the monastery.

Given this self-proclaimed inclusiveness and eschewal of monastic primacy and privilege, it may come as a surprise to learn that the Mahāyāna probably originated as a movement by and for monastics and not a "popular" movement, as previously thought (Snellgrove 1987). The creators of the Mahāyāna were for the most part celibate monks and nuns. Nevertheless, although still commending the celibate monastic life as the recommended method for experiencing nirvana, Mahāyāna texts do not exclude the possibility that laity can also know nirvana within the world of production and reproduction. The *Vimalakīrtinirdesha Sūtra,* an important Mahāyāna text greatly appreciated in China, depicts an advanced bodhisattva named Vimalakīrti living outwardly as a married man while secretly observing the discipline of *brahmācārya* (sexual continence).

As this example suggests, celibacy is by no means rendered obsolete in Mahāyāna texts. But in the *Vimalakīrtinirdesha Sūtra,* as in other texts flavored by the doctrine of emptiness, the cloistered life of a monastic and the monastic precepts forbidding sexual activity, intoxication, handling money, and the like are shown to be only provisionally binding. For an advanced bodhisattva set on the goal of universal awakening like Vimalakīrti, all manner of seeming transgressions are permissible if committed strictly for the sake of bringing other beings to awakening. Thus Vimalakīrti frequents bars, houses of prostitution, and gambling halls to bring the dharma to those who patronize such places. Like other aspects of the path rendered irrelevant by the doctrine of emptiness, precepts forbidding sex are no longer binding for those who seek full and complete awakening. Some Mahāyāna texts even condone murder when committed out of compassionate motives (such as killing a serial murderer who is about to take more life in order to save the lives of potential victims and to prevent the murderer from accruing further bad karma). Providing that one is acting out of the right motives, one may kill, steal, and have sex. In East Asia, this antinomian strain of Mahāyāna thought came to constitute a distinctive motif in hagiographical writings detailing the lives of holy Buddhist "madmen." These holy madmen violate all the precepts freely, showing their perfect understanding of the emptiness of all things.

Just as the prohibitions that outlaw sexual contact between the genders are made relative by the doctrine of emptiness, gender itself can dissolve under close scrutiny. Mahāyāna texts contain a number of intriguing and rhetorically powerful narratives in which women prove their level of attainment by changing their gender, sometimes in response to challenges from male interlocutors. As Miriam Levering (1982) has shown, such narratives were used on occasion to challenge women's authority. They can leave the unsettling impression that sooner or later a woman must become male in order to satisfy those prerequisites for higher path attainment that entail bearing male sexual characteristics (such as mani-festing the thirty-two marks of a *cakravartin,* or great emperor, one of which is the possession of a sheathed penis). Rita Gross (1993, 71) sug-gests that some feminist interpreters have taken these sex-change narra-tives out of context, reading them as a confirmation of the superiority of the male gender. The fact that the female protagonists of these narratives become male might appear to be a concession to the arguments of more conservative Buddhists that women can only progress to higher levels of the path by taking birth as men. However, such an interpretation over-looks the metaphysical point driven home again and again in many of these narratives: gender is irrelevant from the perspective of perfect wis-dom because neither male nor female characteristics have any enduring essence.

One of the most well known narratives on the irrelevance of gender from the perspective of perfect wisdom is a dialogue in the *Vim-alakīrtinirdesha Sūtra* between the conservative elder Shāriputra and a goddess who has been practicing the dharma for twelve years in the bodhisattva Vimalakīrti's palace. In the dialogue, Elder Shāriputra as-sumes that a woman of such attainment would naturally seek to change her gender:

> Elder Shāriputra: Goddess, what prevents you from transforming your-self out of your female state?
> Goddess: Although I have sought my "female state" for these twelve years, I have not yet found it. Reverend Shāriputra, if a magician were to incarnate a woman by magic, would you ask her, "What prevents you from transforming yourself out of your female state?"
> Elder Shāriputra: No! Such a woman would not really exist, so what would there be to transform?
> Goddess: Just so, reverend Shāriputra, all things do not really exist. (Thurman 1976, 61).

Mahāyāna texts, which argue that the dharma is neither male nor fe-male, articulate a sex-neutral answer to the presupposition that Buddhahood and higher path attainments are open only to males. (Similarly, Mahāyāna literature also suggests that no obstacles stand in the way of dedicated laypeople who seek higher attainments.)

Did the Buddhists who redacted and preserved Mahāyāna scripture put the female-friendly insights of these texts into institutional practice? It is difficult to know whether the gender-neutral rhetoric of these

Mahāyāna texts reflects a social reality because social history is not easily derived from Mahāyāna literature. The cast of characters in many of these texts numbers in the hundreds of thousands, including not only various celestial Buddhas presiding in other worlds but also numerous bodhisattvas associated with these cosmic Buddhas. The teachings preserved in these texts are often said to have been given in other worlds than our own, by Buddhas surrounded by huge assemblies of celestial figures, visible only to advanced bodhisattvas. Probably the most that can be said is that these remarkable Mahāyāna narratives articulate a gender-neutral point of view that is available to contemporary Buddhist practitioners seeking to establish and institutionalize the equality of women in the dharma.

With the rise of Vajrayāna Buddhism (the Way of the Thunderbolt) in India and South Asia from around the seventh century of the Common Era, Mahāyāna insights into the indistinguishability of samsara and nirvana were operationalized in a thunderbolt-fast path promising the experience of nirvana in this very lifetime. Also known as Tantric Buddhism, the Vajrayāna shares many of the presuppositions of Hindu Tantric texts, including the importance of ritual as a means of breaking down false distinctions that make salvation nearly impossible in this present degenerate age. The Vajrayāna offers esoteric methods, taught only to initiates, for transforming the three poisons of attraction, revulsion, and ignorance into positive forces and requisites for the experience of nirvana. The poisons can thus become nectars of immortality when properly handled in ritually controlled environments. Some male Vajrayāna saints practiced ritualized forms of sexual union with their wives and spiritual consorts and did not cleave to the celibate path of monastic Buddhism. For example, Padmasambhava, who established Buddhism in eighth-century Tibet, had two principal wives. The eleventh-century translator Marpa was married and had eight other spiritual consorts.

As might be expected in a tradition that teaches men that they have nothing to fear and much to gain from the presence of women, Vajrayāna Buddhism offers women many opportunities for path advancement. Filled with feminine images and symbols, such as female bodhisattvas and goddesses committed to the advancement of Buddhism, Vajrayāna texts seem quite favorable to women's full participation. Rita Gross, herself a Vajrayāna practitioner, regards the Vajrayāna's doctrinal stance toward women as "among the most favorable attitudes found in any major religion in any period of its development" (1993, 80). But Gross goes on to say that the institutional culture of Vajrayāna Buddhism as it developed in South and Central Asia shows a discrepancy between rhetoric and reality, just as seems to have been the case with many Mahāyāna Buddhist institutions. Although in principle women are equally competent to teach the dharma and receive accolades for their achievements, in reality few women are accorded such honors. Although there is often lavish support for communities of monks, support for communities of nuns tend to be relegated to an afterthought in the minds of many lay supporters. Consequently, the nun's life is less prestigious, and convents tend to serve as refuges for widows and other women who have few options.

It is possible, as Miranda Shaw (1994) argues, that Vajrayāna women have been written out of the historical record even though they once played central roles in the formation of Tantric Buddhist practice, theory, and iconography. According to Shaw, women shaped the tradition by instructing pupils, introducing new meditation practices, and creating new rituals. Moreover, women were worshipped as divine beings and protectors of sacred knowledge. Even though in many cases women's teachings were preserved only through the agency of their more famous male pupils, Shaw regards the development of male-dominated lineage histories within Vajrayāna Buddhist circles as an androcentric flowering of a gynocentric root. Shaw gives special attention to the role of women as teachers imparting secret oral instructions on ritualized sexual union as a means of liberation. She suggests that it is the sexual nature of these advanced practices that has led many uninitiated Western scholars to overlook the role of women as active shapers of the Tantric tradition. Unable to appreciate the spiritual depth of these practices, such scholars attribute to women practitioners (*yoginīs*) only the qualification of sexual availability. These *yoginīs* are often assumed to be mere ritual objects used by male practitioners (*yogins*) and then cast aside—disposable spiritual batteries for male empowerment, if you will. Shaw takes great pains to show that educated and highly respected *yoginīs* were some of the earliest teachers of sexual yoga. Imparting instructions to male disciples, they spoke with the authority accorded to teachers in medieval Indian society and helped to create an ethos in which reciprocity between male and female practitioners was normative.

Whatever the historical reality, there is no denying that Vajrayāna Buddhist texts show the social reality that shaped many women's lives to be one dominated by parental control over women's sexuality. In

157

Vajrayāna texts, we see women given in marriage without their knowledge or permission, women married while still very young to men considerably older than themselves, and women married to men who already had many wives. Historical studies, such as that of Bimala Churn Law (1927), show that Buddhist women of earlier times were also subject to patriarchal control over their sexuality. Although Buddhism does not regard marriage as a sacrament in the way that other religions such as Hinduism do and therefore places less religious value than some other religions on ensuring that women marry, a perusal of Buddhist literature nevertheless shows women joined to men in marriages designed to serve the needs of their families and the larger society, without full consideration of what may be best for women.[6] Law also notes instances in Buddhist literature in which elite Buddhist women are represented as leading cloistered, sex-segregated lives. As in the practice known as purdah observed by some elite northern Indian women today, these early Buddhist women served as standard-bearers, displaying their family wealth and status by staying home, whereas women of less affluent families had to work outside the home. When these Buddhist women did need to go outside the home, they traveled by chariot and avoided being seen by using parasols or other means of concealment.

### Alternatives to Patriarchal Marriage

Buddhist literature of all varieties suggests the possibility that, women could find a refuge from conventional patriarchal marriage arrangements in Buddhist practice. As we have seen, Indian women who became daughters of the Buddha as nuns ran the risk of exchanging one male authority figure for another. However, records of the early community of nuns in India provide some evidence that women who became nuns could experience unique forms of freedom from domestic life. The *Therīgāthā* is a collection of verses attributed to the first Buddhist nuns in India. The nuns are said to have spoken these verses after achieving the status of arhats, the highest religious goal prior to the rise of the Mahāyāna tradition and still the religious goal of Theravāda Buddhists today. Recorded in the *Therīgāthā* are poetic records of the relief of women set free from the cycle of samsara; their freedom as arhats is depicted in many of their verses as freedom from the dangers of childbirth, the conflicts of polygamy, and the drudgery of domestic labor. For instance, Muttā, who prior to her ordination as a nun was married to an impoverished, hunchbacked priest, declared:

I'm free. Ecstatically free
I'm free from three crooked things:
the mortar
the pestle
and my hunchbacked husband
All that drags me back is cut—cut! (Schelling and Waldman 1996, 50)

*Therīgāthā* 21 records the elation of the wife of a weaver of straw hats after she had become a nun and attained arhatship:

I'm free
Free from kitchen drudgery
No longer a slave among my cooking pots
(My pot smelled like an old water snake)
And I'm through with my brutal husband
And his tiresome sunshades
I purge lust with a sizzling sound—*pop*
"Oh happiness," meditate upon
this as happiness. (Schelling and Waldman 1996, 51)

Many verses in the *Therīgāthā* shed light on the difficult lives of women in early Buddhist India. One can see clearly the suffering of women in childbirth in the days before contraception, family planning, anesthesia, and advanced obstetrical practices. Kisā-Gotamī, who was maddened by grief at the death of her baby son, became a nun after the Buddha cured her grief by sending her on a vain but enlightening search to obtain a mustard seed from a home where no one had died. Her verses refer to the woes of women in polygamous marriages and the abject suffering of women in childbirth:

Being a woman is painful
Miserable sharing a home with hostile wives
Some cut their own throats
More squeamish women take poison. (Schelling and Waldman 1996, 69)

Women in Theravāda countries where the nun's order has lapsed have in effect created a mendicant but uncloistered role for themselves that offers an alternative to conventional marriage.[7] In *Women under the Bo Tree,* Tessa Bartholomeusz (1994) describes how modern Sri Lankan women have adopted various strategies for pursuing a renunciant vocation within a culture largely uncomfortable with women who renounce their families and filial ties. Bartholomeusz interviewed many "Mothers of the Ten Precepts," as these lay nuns are called. Unlike ordinary laywomen, the lay nuns of modern Sri Lanka live apart from their families. Some live in lay convents; others live alone or in groups of two or three, following the early Buddhist monastic pattern of making a hut or other rustic dwelling at the foot of a tree. Their lives are governed by monastic practices such as chastity and restraint in diet. For many Mothers of the Ten Precepts, it would be not only impossible but also undesirable to reestablish the order of nuns in Sri Lanka. If the order were to be established again on the island, it would be under male ecclesiastic control in accordance with the special rules for nuns; therefore, those who took ordination as nuns would lose the autonomy that Bartholomeusz's research suggests is the main appeal of the renunciant lifestyle. As Mothers of the Ten Precepts, lay nuns can engage in the social reproduction of Buddhism, free from the obligations pursuant upon women whose primary task is biological reproduction and free from the ecclesiastical supervision of monks.

### Homosexuality

Generalizing about Buddhist views of homosexuality runs the risk of both anachronism and cultural imperialism. Premodern, non-European historical documents and artifacts can easily be distorted when read through modern, Western lenses. Thus, one risks projecting modern categories of thought into cultural contexts to which they do not apply. These categories can obscure the meaning of the sexual acts and actors in question. This warning, often sounded by historians of sexuality who take a social constructionist approach, needs to be issued here for reasons that will be clear as we begin to examine the extremely rich sexual vocabulary of Buddhist texts.

Social constructionist historians, such as Michel Foucault (1988–1990) and David Halperin (1990) see the label "homosexual" as a modern construct that fails to capture the variety of premodern cultural understandings of same-sex lovemaking. Ancient Greeks and Romans, for example, classified men who engaged in anal intercourse with other men on the basis of whether the man in question took the active sexual role as penetrator or the passive role of allowing penetration. Thus the identity assigned to a male engaging in same-sex acts was both more specific and role-oriented than the modern label "homosexual" allows and more fluid, in that a man's sexual role might change in the course of his lifetime from being the passive partner during youth to being the active partner as a mature man. Conceptual difficulties with the modern category of the homosexual (indicating a distinct personality type thought to be equally expressed by lesbian women and gay men) are compounded by the fact that some premodern cultures view female and male homosexual activities as completely unrelated, separate forms of sexuality. Others conceive of woman-to-woman lovemaking in terms derived from the male model of anal intercourse, as a form of "female sodomy" that entails a woman using her clitoris to penetrate another woman. Clearly, there are many ways in which homoerotic sexual acts can be classified, and much depends on what a culture holds to be socially normative and anatomically possible.

Homoerotic sexual acts—like any erotic act in which a person takes pleasure—can clearly never be seen as inconsequential, given the dangers that pleasures of the body pose for one who seeks the elimination of all craving, as in Buddhism. However, those like Leonard Zwilling, who have studied monastic codes of moral conduct in Pāli and Sanskrit along with commentary and other supplementary literature, have observed that homoeroticism "is not entirely incompatible with the monastic life, in that it presents no temptation for the parties involved to forsake the order to which they are committed, nor does it lead to the family encumbrances many must have joined the sangha [monastic order] to escape" (1992, 29). For monastic actors, such homoerotic acts fall into a hierarchy of potential sexual offenses, and their gravity may be understood by noting where they fall in the hierarchy.

For Theravāda laypersons, the moral code is fairly open-ended in regard to what is often translated as "the avoidance of sexual misconduct." As was discussed above, the lay moral code known as the five precepts is a set of resolutions made by an individual who wishes to show compassion for the suffering of living beings. It is largely up to the individual to determine what constitutes the third precept: the resolution to avoid *kāmesu micchacāra* (transgression in the sphere of sensuality or misuse of the senses). Commentaries specify such harmful sexual activities as rape, adultery, and taking sexual advantage of those over whom one has power and authority. Randy Conner and Stephen Donaldson point out that "what is not included even in the supplementary [Pāli] canonical texts is any condemnation of pre-marital sex or homosexuality as such. . . . the unmarried Buddhist layperson is free to engage in consensual homosexual acts" (1990, 169). Conner and Donaldson assert that Buddhists in

Theravāda cultures have often been tolerant of same-sex relations among unmarried and mutually consenting lay partners, arguing that the Theravāda lay moral code does not have the "absolute prohibitive nature of Western religious codes but is a practical guide toward improving one's karma" (169). As a transitional or experimental form of sexuality, same-sex lovemaking among adolescents is tolerated in some South Asian contexts.[8] However, more social stigma is likely to attach to an adult who continues to engage in same-sex relations after adolescence and who does not conform to the gender roles expected of him or her.[9]

Indian Buddhist literature evinces considerable interest in and concern about men who assume atypical gender roles in their sexual activities. Leonard Zwilling (1992) found a variety of terms in Indian Buddhist terminology to designate sexually nonconforming men who share the common trait of "lacking maleness." The term found most often in Indian Buddhist literature is *paṇḍaka,* a word that Zwilling translates as being metaphorically "without balls," as we say in English. Some scholars have equated *paṇḍakas* with eunuchs, but from the various subtypes of *paṇḍakas* mentioned—the chronically impotent, the voyeur, the temporarily impotent, the "stone butch" (someone who derives sexual satisfaction from performing oral sex on another), and the toy-dependent (someone who uses artificial means to achieve sexual satisfaction)—and from historical evidence suggesting that eunuchs were unknown in India in pre-Muslim times, Zwilling regards this identification as incorrect. The variety of *paṇḍakas* mentioned in Indian Buddhist texts should perhaps in itself give Western scholars pause. Accustomed as we are to the nineteenth-century category of the homosexual that renders the landscape of sexual possibilities manageable by fixing sexual predilections in a stable schema, we may find the extremely rich sexual vocabularies of ancient Indian and other premodern cultures hard to digest.

With the exception of the chronically impotent type of *paṇḍaka,* the *paṇḍakas* of Buddhist Indian literature were evidently capable of erection, ejaculation, and the experience of sexual pleasure but did not meet normative sex role expectations for adult males. The *paṇḍaka's* failure to play a typically male sexual role aligned him (or perhaps her, for gender lines are considerably blurred here) with women thought to be sexually voracious. Buddhaghosa's commentary on the Pāli monastic code of conduct goes into considerable detail on the physiology and psychology of the *paṇḍaka,* asserting that such people are unquenchable in lust, just like coarse young girls and street-walking prostitutes.

As males who failed to play socially normative gender roles, *paṇḍakas* were denied ordination as monks. Gender-atypical women were also denied ordination as nuns. As with all the regulations presented in Buddhist monastic law (*vinaya*) codes, the rule against ordaining *paṇḍakas* is said to have been given by the Buddha in response to a specific problem situation that arose in monastic communal life during his life. As is the case with many such explanatory frame stories found in *vinaya* collections, the problem situation here is one of "bad press" or negative public perceptions of the monastic order. A *paṇḍaka* was ordained, the frame story explains, and went among the young monks, looking for someone to "defile" him (the text says that he approached the monks collectively, saying: "Come, Venerable Ones, defile me"). When the monks sent him away, he turned to a group of strapping young novices with the same collective proposition. When they sent him away, he turned to a group of elephant keepers and grooms, again with the same proposition. The elephant keepers and grooms did not turn him away. They "defiled" him and then began to make angry noises about the kind of monks who were affiliating with the Buddha: "These recluses, these followers of the Buddha, are *paṇḍakas* and those who are not *paṇḍakas* defile *paṇḍakas*. Thus do they all lack discipline" (Zwilling 1992, 208). When the Buddha heard reports that these men (who had just "defiled" a *paṇḍaka*) were claiming that his monks were nothing more than a bunch of *paṇḍakas* or males who "defile" *paṇḍakas,* he proclaimed that henceforth no *paṇḍakas* were to be ordained.

It is difficult to say with certainty just what the problem situation was. That this *paṇḍaka* could have besmirched the reputation of the monastic assembly in this way might have had as much to do with the orgiastic, collective nature of his proposition and his seeming unconcern about the identity of his desired sexual partners (he strikes out with one group and then races off to proposition the next) than with any problem posed by his anatomy or an inherent sexual dysfunction, as modern sexual scientists might put it. Clearly, however, the charge that monks were behaving in an undisciplined, dissolute manner was being leveled. And the Buddha evidently dealt with the problem situation with an eye toward preventing further "bad press," just as he did in regard to complaints about the unconventional behavior of his nuns (at least according to Sponberg's account of the imposition of special rules for nuns).

There is some scope for confusion about the degree of sexual intimacy between members of the same gender in cultures in which homosocial expressions of affection are valued and encouraged. Strong homosocial bonding is common in many communities (Hindu and Muslim as well as Buddhist) in India and other parts of South Asia, where gender segregation is common and young people often develop deep friendships with others of their own gender. Homosocial expressions of affection (such as holding hands) raise no eyebrows, but to an outsider such easy intimacy may appear as sexual intimacy. As for Buddhist evaluations of homosocial bonding, Michael Sweet (2000) cites passages from the earliest layers of Buddhist scripture, such as the *Sutta Nipāta,* that praise friendship, suggesting that nonsexual homosocial friendships were highly valued and encouraged. John Garrett Jones (1979, 113ff) has noted the tendency of Buddhist texts to see the Buddha and his cousin and personal attendant, Ānanda, as close companions in many previous lives. Jones also surveys a number of past-life (*jātaka*) stories about Ānanda with what might be considered not only homosocial but also homoerotic content.

The Theravādin monastic code of conduct (*vinaya*) consists of hundreds of precepts in addition to those that the laity undertake. Since the goal of Theravādin monastic life is the complete uprooting of all forms of craving or thirst, including all thirst for sensual pleasures, *vinaya* regulations forbid all intentional sexual pleasure seeking by monks and nuns and lay down a hierarchy of penalties, depending on the nature of the sexual offense. Sexual intercourse with the intent to derive sexual pleasure is differentiated from acts of rape in which monks and nuns do not give their consent. In addition, nocturnal emissions of semen and other unintended instances of sexual gratification are excluded from the category of sexual actions considered grounds for expulsion.[10] Masturbation, although considered a serious offense, does not lead to expulsion from the order. However, for a fully ordained monk or nun to engage in any penetrative sexual act with a partner of any gender or species is grounds for expulsion. Nonpenetrative acts are deemed lesser offenses, for which penance, but not expulsion, is required.

Conner and Donaldson point out that Buddhism "may be the only instance of a world religion treating homosexual acts more favorably than heterosexual ones" (1990, 169). As an example of the relatively minor status of homosexual offenses, as opposed to heterosexual ones, these authors note that the Theravāda monastic code of conduct punishes a novice monk who has sex with a female by expelling him from the order, whereas a novice monk who has sex with a male commits a lesser offense requiring penance but not expulsion (169).[11] There is some ethnographic evidence to suggest that Conner and Donaldson are correct about homoerotic acts being more acceptable than heterosexual ones. Melford Spiro, who conducted fieldwork in Southeast Asia in the 1960s, was told that homoerotic activity was not infrequent among the monks of Sri Lanka (1970, 366ff), but it should be noted that in his primary field sites in Burma, Spiro found remarkably few documented instances of monks breaking the precepts with partners of any gender.

Given its philosophical outlook and its tendency to regard the moral precepts regarding sexuality as only provisionally binding, Mahāyāna Buddhism has the theoretical potential to favor the development of more positive outlooks on sexual expression in general and homoerotic activity in particular. Provided that they lead to some sort of religious insight, homoerotic feelings and expressions are not necessarily problematic. In Japan, and to a certain extent in China, same-sex relations between men and boys became a prominent feature of the Buddhist landscape.[12] Age-governed homosexuality, in which boys and older men engaged in sexual relations, was prevalent among monks and priests in monastic and temple settings. Early modern European travelers and missionaries in East Asia were often unanimous in their condemnation of homosexuality among Buddhist monks, although in many instances they were full of praise for the literary and artistic achievement of the Chinese and Japanese, as well as for East Asian forms of government and other facets of Asian cultures.

Uniquely "clerical" forms of same-sex love are said to have been introduced into Japan in the ninth century by Kūkai (Kōbō Daishi), founder of the Shingon (True Word) sect of esoteric Buddhism. Although Kūkai's legendary connection with priestly homoeroticism seems to have little historical basis, Paul Gordon Schalow (1992) suggests that it shows that same-sex relations between men and boys were an accepted part of the medieval Japanese Buddhist landscape. One of the earliest surviving manuscripts to associate homoerotic arts with Kūkai is a text that is, in part, a sex manual. Dated 1598, Kōbō Daishi's book describes how a layman went into seclusion to seek his teachings on "the mysteries of loving boys" and was presented, as a reward for his austerities, with a one-volume book describing how young novices communicate their feelings to priests with various hand signals, how priests can ascertain the emotional states of novices and act accordingly, and how to perform anal intercourse in various ways. These techniques of homoerotic love are presented as "mysteries" on a par with the esoteric mysteries of Shingon Buddhism. Shingon esoteric mysteries being transmitted orally from master to disciple thus placed master-disciple relationships at the core of the tradition.

Sexual relations between young novices (*chigo*) and senior monks are celebrated in Japanese tales known as *chigo monogatari* (tales of *chigo*), a body of literature produced in Japan between the fourteenth and sixteenth centuries. Margaret Childs captures the essential ambiguity of these *chigo* tales in the subtitle of her article, "Chigo Monogatari: Love Stories or Buddhist Sermons?" (1980). Given that homosexual affairs between religious functionaries were common in medieval Japan, *chigo monogatari* are love stories about young novices involved in relationships with senior males, often in remote mountain temples. But given that most conclude on a religious note, with a religious awakening (*hosshin*) resulting from the loss of the beloved, *chigo monogatari* can be read as Buddhist sermons. The loss of the young novice in these *chigo* stories often leads to a breakthrough to higher levels of Buddhist insight, as the protagonist and others associated with the *chigo* realize the transience of life and undertake serious efforts to attain awakening. That these love stories tend to end tragically does not indicate any cultural disapproval of homoeroticism. Childs argues that there is no indication "in the tales themselves that homosexuality per se met with disapproval" (1980, 127). Another facet of these tales is the element of hierophany, or manifestation of the sacred. Often the *chigo* is revealed to have been a manifestation of a bodhisattva such as Kannon (Avalokiteshvara), who appeared as an alluring youth for the express purpose of bringing insight to all those whose lives the *chigo* touched.

For gays and lesbians accustomed to seeing homoerotic love treated differently from heterosexual love, it is indeed surprising to see *chigo monogatari* compare homoerotic love affairs with culturally revered examples of heterosexual love. In *Aki no Yo Nagamonogatari* (A Long Tale for an Autumn Night), for example, the narrator compares the protagonist's confusion over the disappearance of his beloved with that of the Emperor Wu mourning his dead wife (Childs 1980, 134).

Although *chigo* tales may be of interest to modern readers on account of their frank acceptance of the reality of homosexual activity in monasteries, they also raise some troubling moral questions about the extent to which boys were being sexually exploited and whether the exploitation of minors was legitimized in the name of religion. In contrast to the romantic, highly idealized portraits of *chigo* love in many *chigo monogatari* are more ribald, satirical depictions that unmask the hypocrisy of worldly monks who relentlessly obtain sexual gratification under the guise of offering education to their young charges. It is not easy to use satire as a basis for social history, since the art of satire naturally involves exaggeration for comic effect, but satirical accounts probably do shed light on some of the less romantic aspects of *chigo* love. Bernard Faure describes the potential abuses inherent in these pederastic and pedagogical relationships, seeing them as "relationships of power, reinforced by the ecclesiastical hierarchy and age differences, and sometimes covering situations that amount to institutionalized rape" (1998, 217). Faure offers a model of careful scholarship on this issue, however, in that unlike some of the early European denouncers of age-based clerical homosexuality in East Asia, he does not conflate his concerns about what our legal system would label "sexual abuse" with global condemnations of homosexuality as an indication of depravity or deviance.

Like many Mahāyānists, Vajrayāna Buddhists tend to evaluate sexual expression in terms of the extent to which sexuality can serve as a means of awakening. Jeffrey Hopkins, an openly gay scholar of Vajrayāna Buddhism and professor at the University of Virginia, notes that Vajrayāna sexual practices presuppose heterosexual intercourse (1998). But as a means of access to more subtle mind states, such sexual practices could be used by gay and lesbian practitioners as well.

Given the variety of culturally based attitudes toward homoerotic activity in the various places where Vajrayāna Buddhism found a home in Asia, it is not surprising to find little consensus among Vajrayāna adepts as to the legitimacy of homoerotic activity. Although a number of Vajrayāna Buddhist teachers have declared homosexuality no more problematic than heterosexuality, the Dalai Lama has gone on record on several occasions with statements to the effect that homoerotic activity poses a problem because inappropriate orifices are used (Conkin 1998). He has also admitted that the historical basis for such judgments probably lies in the Indian concern with maximizing chances of reproduction.

Melvyn C. Goldstein has identified a type of monk found throughout Tibet, especially in larger monasteries, who might be identified as homosexual. In "A Study of the Ldab Ldob" (1964), Goldstein describes a monk easily distinguished by physical appearance and behavior, who might be characterized as hypermasculine in comparison to the appearance and behavior of his monastic cohorts. The Ldab Ldob applies a kind of eye shadow that makes him appear ferocious, wears a longer, lower robe, and sports a lock of hair behind each ear. Known primarily for their penchant for fighting, Ldab Ldobs are often called upon to perform monastic police functions and serve as bodyguards. Because monastic moral codes deem penetrative sexual acts more culpable than nonpenetrative ones, the sexual activities of the Ldab Ldobs, who practice nonpenetrative intracrural intercourse (rubbing the penis between a partner's legs), tend to be seen as relatively minor violations. "Among the monks in Tibet, and especially among the Ldab Ldobs, homosexuality has a status similar to premarital sex in our culture: it is sinful, but widespread" (Goldstein 1964, 134).

There are a number of openly gay Western Buddhist teachers in the West. Lesbian, gay, bisexual, and transgendered Buddhists have established separate meditation centers and other institutions catering to the needs of the lesbian, gay, bisexual, and transgendered (LGBT) Buddhist community. For example, the openly gay Sōtō monk and teacher Issan Dorsey Roshi, who died of acquired immunodeficiency syndrome (AIDS) in 1990, founded Maitri Hospice, a Buddhist hospice for people with AIDS. He was also the first abbott of Issanji Temple in the Castro district of San Francisco. David Schneider's biography of Dorsey's life (*Street Zen: The Life and Work of Issan Dorsey,* 2000) has raised a good deal of controversy in U.S. Buddhist circles by highlighting Dorsey's checkered past as a junkie, prostitute, and drag queen. Letters to the editor of *Tricycle,* a widely read Buddhist magazine for Western practitioners, show mixed reactions to the biography. Although some readers argue that the biography lays out details about Dorsey's early life in order to contextualize Dorsey's commitment to working with drug addicts and others at the margins of society, other readers worry that Schneider sensationalized Dorsey's life to gain a larger readership for the book.

## CONCLUSIONS

Questions about sexuality and gender are among the most interesting issues that contemporary Buddhists face as they work to realize the dharma in their lives as modern persons. A number of Buddhist communities in North America and Europe have split into factions over allegations that their leaders and other high-ranking Buddhist teachers committed sexual improprieties or engaged in systematic sexual abuse (see Kornfield 1985; Butler 1990). The controversies raised by these "sex scandals" have led to some very useful dialogue about what is permissible in student-teacher relationships and what kinds of expectations about moral behavior Buddhists bring when they enter the door of a U.S. or European dharma center.

By convening interdenominational Buddhist conferences and meetings with such figures as the Dalai Lama, LGBT Buddhist practitioners in the West have raised the issue of sexual orientation as a topic worthy of exploration at the highest levels of Buddhist ecclesiastical discussion.

Another issue regarding sexuality that has been raised to a high level of visibility in recent years is the provision by Buddhist priests in Japan of mourning services for aborted fetuses. Reliance on abortion as a means of family planning is widespread in contemporary Japan. Mourning services for aborted or stillborn fetuses (known as *mizuko*, or "water babies") did not exist prior to the 1960s and have been the subject of considerable controversy in recent years (see Smith 1992; LaFleur 1992; Hardacre 1997). Media exposés in Japan have focused on the profits Buddhist temples stand to gain by promoting these memorial services. Feminist analysts lament the lack of alternatives that lead so many Japanese women to seek abortions.

As a religion originally centered around a core community of celibate monastics, Buddhism has tended to place religious value on the freedom from those domestic entanglements that follow from heterosexual activity in the absence of modern forms of birth control and abortion (at least for the select group of those who seek to put an end to dissatisfaction in this life). As we have seen, some Mahāyāna and Vajrayāna Buddhists regard sex as a potential means of progress on the Buddhist path. Some regard lay practice as equal to monastic practice, at least in theory. Those Buddhists, like Buddhists in Japan who have abolished the requirement of clerical celibacy, have moved away from the tendency to consider those committed to celibacy as superior to those who are sexually active. Western Buddhists have also placed less emphasis on celibacy than their early Indian coreligionists did by creating monastic or quasi-monastic roles for noncelibate practitioners.

As effective means of contraception and abortion become more widely available to contemporary Buddhists and sex is thereby separated more and more from procreation, it is possible that some Asian Buddhists (such as Theravādins) who have traditionally maintained a clear division between monastic and lay paths will create quasi-monastic roles that enable sexually active people to take ordination and pursue higher levels of path attainment. It is equally possible, though, that Buddhists in Asia will respond to these developments by identifying such innovations as signs of moral decay, especially given scriptural predictions about the inevitable decline of the dharma. Any shift in ecclesiastical stances toward celibacy (for example, the creation of monastic roles for noncelibate persons) might be viewed as a sign of encroachment by or thoughtless imitation of looser Western standards of sexual conduct. Concerns about Western sexual "promiscuity" might be expected, most especially in postcolonial nations of Asia, where Buddhists have sought to recover and articulate what they regard as traditional practices untainted by the cultural influence of former colonial powers.

## NOTES

1. Japanese- and Vajrayāna-influenced cultures in South and Central Asia are exceptions to this generalization about monastic celibacy. In much of Buddhist Asia, the distinction between laity and monastics is very clear, and monastic morality precludes all forms of sexual activity. However, in Japan and some cultures in which Vajrayāna Buddhism is dominant, boundaries between these two groups have become considerably less clear. In Japan, monastic celibacy is no longer required, and monks are free to marry. Certain segments of the Vajrayāna Buddhist world, such as the Newar Buddhist population of Nepal, are also exceptional in this regard. Entering the courtyard of dwellings in the Kathmandu Valley that are called monasteries (*bahal*), one is likely to see diapers drying on clotheslines and an abundance of children because celibacy is not required of the ritual specialists who live there. Functioning similarly to the Brahmin priests of Hinduism, these ritual specialists pass on to their children the hereditary right to function as *purohits* or family priests. See Allen (1973).

2. The Buddha's son, Rāhula, according to the Gilgit manuscrip of the *Mūlasarvāstivāda-vinaya,* was not yet born when his father left the palace to live apart from his wife. Rāhula was concieved on the eve of the great renunciation and gestated during the six years in which his father sought the Middle Way. Thus the Buddha's son, according to this account, was born precisely at the moment his father achieved awakening at the foot of the Bodhi tree. This rather family-friendly account tells us, moreover, that the name Rāhula denotes a rare celestial event (almost as rare as the appearance of Buddhas in this world), not an impediment to his father's achievement of Buddhahood: the name Rāhula is derived from Rāhu, the supernatural being who causes eclipses. Yaśodharā, more-

over, is depicted as a female counterpart to her husband, attmepting to imitate his ascetic actions and to eat what he eats during the time of his experiments with asceticism.

3. For an interesting comparison of cowboys and religious renouncers, see Jane Tompkins (1992). Tompkins describes the drive for total autonomy that, in Westerns, lures men to leave home and find solace in a life of wandering. In a chapter entitled "Landscape," Tompkins explores some of the parallels between the self-disciplined lives of early Christian ascetics of the Egyptian desert and the austere lives of Western heroes—men who thrive on physical ordeal in harsh desert landscapes, who are satisfied with a life of few creature comforts, and who are largely celibate.

4. See Alan Sponberg's comparison of the Pāli and Sanskrit accounts (1992, 13ff.). For an English translation from the Sanskrit *Mūlasarvāstivāda Vinaya,* see Paul (1979, 82ff.).

5. The story of how Uttarā's parents gained their wealth speaks volumes about the benefits of lay generosity. Uttarā's mother gave her father's midday meal to a Buddhist monk as she was on her way to the field to deliver the meal to her husband. Her husband had been plowing the field for hours on a holiday because the family was so poor. Rather than beating her, as she half expected, her husband was delighted with his wife's generosity. As a result of their mutual pleasure in provisioning the monk, the field turned to gold, and Uttarā's parents became quite wealthy. The story precedes that of Uttarā and Sirimā in the Pāli Commentary to the *Dhammapada* (Burlingame 1990, 3:99–103).

6. Where for Hindus, marriage is a sacrament and service to one's husband is seen as an expression of religious piety, Buddhist texts regard marriage as a purely secular affair. Buddhist scripture does not dictate marriage vows or ritual procedures. Various ceremonies are often associated with marriage in contemporary Buddhist cultures of Asia, and monks may be invited to attend these ceremonies and partake in feasting, but such ceremonies are not mandated by religious law and tend to follow the vagaries of local custom.

7. Since the 1990s, attempts to revive the order of nuns in Sri Lanka have been made. Women have been ordained as nuns, although traditionalist monks deny the legitimacy of these ordinations on the grounds that nuns from non-Mahāyāna countries were required to perform the ordinations. Very recently, there have been moves to revive the order of nuns in Thailand. In February 2002, a fifty-six-year-old divorced Thai woman named Varangghana Vanavichayen was ordained as the novice Dhammarakhita by a body of seven nuns, including a Sri Lankan nun and several nuns from non-Theravāda countries. Thai Buddhist religious authorities have not officially recognized the ordination. But the movement

to bring Thai and other Theravāda Buddhist religious women into prominence and give them equal access to the benefits of recognized monastic
status is growing.

8.  Apart from the work of Peter A. Jackson on Thailand (1995, 1998), there
    is not much secondary literature on homoerotic activity—lay or monas-
    tic—in Theravāda Buddhist cultures. My evidence here is strictly anec-
    dotal, based on the observations of colleagues.

9.  Peter A. Jackson argues that popular Western conceptions regarding a
    general acceptance of homosexuality in Thailand are to some extent exag-
    gerated. In his *Dear Uncle Go: Male Homosexuality in Thailand* (1995),
    Jackson identifies the expectation that people with homoerotic desires will
    also engage in unconventional cross-gendered behavior as the source of
    much of the stigma associated with homosexuality in Thailand. In other
    words, to be gay in Thailand is to be "queer" or different from others of
    one's gender in some fundamental ways. And to be atypical in the perfor-
    mance of one's biological gender role (or to be perceived as such) is to be
    stigmatized. In a more recent article, Jackson suggests than in Thailand
    today, homosexuality is emerging as a category that is free of the tradi-
    tionally associated ideas of gender-deviance or atypical gender-role per-
    formance (Jackson 1998).

10. Three other offenses are also grounds for automatic expulsion from the
    order: murder, theft, and false claims to supernormal powers.

11. For the *sāmaṇera,* or novice monk, who may be admitted into a monastery
    as young as seven years of age and who is not expected to take the higher
    ordination until he has reached his twenties, the full set of *vinaya* rules are
    not binding. A Theravāda novice monk may engage in masturbation, for
    example, without committing an offense. Conner and Donaldson suggest
    that "the more intense sexual drive of the male teenager is tacitly allowed
    for" by the *sāmaṇera* rules (1990, 169). It is worth noting, in this regard,
    that in some Theravāda countries such as Thailand, it is common for
    young men to take the lower ordination as *sāmaṇera* and reside in monas-
    teries for a few months as a rite of passage to manhood.

12. For studies of Japanese homoerotic traditions, see Watanabe and Iwata
    (1989, especially 34–46), Childs (1980, 127–151), Schalow (1990, 1992),
    and Faure (1998). On Chinese homoerotic traditions (not exclusively
    Buddhist), see Hinsch (1990, 96ff.).

## References

Allen, Michael. 1973. "Buddhism without Monks: The Vajrayāna Religion of
the Newars of the Kathmandu Valley." *South Asia* 3: 1–14.

Altekar, Anant Sadashiv. [1938] 1978. *The Position of Women in Hindu Civilization.* Reprint. Delhi: Motilal Banarsidass.

Anderson, Dines, and Helmer Smith, eds. 1913. *Sutta Nipāta.* London: Pali Text Society.

Bartholomeusz, Tessa. 1994. *Women under the Bo Tree.* New York: Cambridge University Press.

Burlingame, Eugene Watson, trans. 1990. *Dhammapadāṭṭhakathā: Buddhist Legends.* 3 vol. London: Pali Text Society.

Butler, Katie. 1990. "Encountering the Shadow in Buddhist America." *Common Boundary* (May–June): 14–22.

Chalmers, Lord, ed. 1932. *Sutta-Nipāta, or Discourse Collection.* Cambridge, MA: Harvard University Press.

Childs, Margaret. 1980. "Chigo Monogatari: Love Stories or Buddhist Sermons?" *Monumenta Nipponica* 35, no. 2 (Summer): 127–151.

Conkin, Dennis. 1998. "The Dalai Lama and Gay Love." Pp. 351–356 in Winston Leyland, ed., *Queer Dharma: Voices of Gay Buddhists.* Vol. 1. San Francisco: Gay Sunshine Press.

Conner, Randy, and Stephen Donaldson. 1990. "Buddhism." Pp. 168–171 in Wayne Dynes, ed., *Encyclopedia of Homosexuality.* Vol. 1. New York: Garland Press.

Falk, Nancy Auer. 1989. "The Case of the Vanishing Nuns: The Fruits of Ambivalence in Ancient Indian Buddhism." Pp. 190–222 in Nancy Auer Falk and Rita M. Gross, eds., *Unspoken Worlds: Women's Religious Lives.* Belmont, CA: Wadsworth.

Faure, Bernard. 1998. *The Red Thread: Buddhist Approaches to Sexuality.* Princeton, NJ: Princeton University Press.

Findly, Ellison Banks, ed. 2000. *Women's Buddhism, Buddhism's Women: Tradition, Revision, Renewal.* Boston: Wisdom Publications.

Foucault, Michel. 1988–1990. *The History of Sexuality.* Robert Hurley, trans. New York: Vintage Books.

Goldstein, Melvyn C. 1964. "A Study of the Ldab Ldob." *Central Asiatic Journal* 9: 123–141.

Gombrich, Richard. 1988. *Theravāda Buddhism: A Social History from Ancient Benares to Modern Columbo.* London: Routledge and Kegan Paul.

Gross, Rita M. 1993. *Buddhism after Patriarchy: A Feminist History, Analysis, and Reconstruction of Buddhism.* Albany: State University of New York Press.

Halperin, David. 1990. *One Hundred Years of Homosexuality and Other Essays on Greek Love.* New York: Routledge.

Hardacre, Helen. 1997. *Marketing the Menacing Fetus in Japan.* Berkeley: University of California Press.

Hare, E. M., trans. [1933–1936] 1973–1979. *The Book of Gradual Sayings (Anguttara Nikaya).* 5 vols. Reprint. Oxford: Pali Text Society.

Hinsch, Bret. 1990. *Passions of the Cut Sleeve: The Male Homosexual Tradition in China.* Berkeley: University of California Press.

Hopkins, Jeffrey. 1998. "The Compatibility of Reason and Orgasm in Tibetan Buddhism." Pp. 335–347 in Winston Leyland, ed., *Queer Dharma: Voices of Gay Buddhists.* Vol. 1. San Francisco: Gay Sunshine Press.

Horner, I. B. 1930. *Women under Primitive Buddhism: Lay Women and Alms Women.* New York: E. P. Dutton.

Jackson, Peter A. 1995. *Dear Uncle Go: Male Homosexuality in Thailand.* Bangkok: Bua Luang Books.

———. 1998. "Male Homosexuality and Transgenderism in the Thai Buddhist Tradition." Pp. 55–89 in Winston Leyland, ed., *Queer Dharma: Voices of Gay Buddhists.* Vol. 1. San Francisco: Gay Sunshine Press.

Jones, John Garrett. 1979. *Tales and Teachings of the Buddha: The Jātaka Stories in Relation to the Pāli Canon.* London: George Allen and Unwin.

Kornfield, Jack. 1985. "Sex Lives of the Gurus." *Yoga Journal:* 26–66.

LaFleur, William. 1992. *Liquid Life: Abortion and Buddhism in Japan.* Princeton, NJ: Princeton University Press.

Law, Bimala Churn. 1927. *Women in Buddhist Literature.* Varanasi, India: Indological Book House.

Levering, Miriam. 1982. "The Dragon-Girl and the Abbess of Mo-Shan: Gender and Status in the Ch'an Buddhist Tradition." *Journal of the International Association of Buddhist Studies* 5, no. 1: 19–30.

Morris, R., and E. Hardy, eds. [1885–1900] 1961–1979. *Aṅguttara Nikāya.* 5 vols. Reprint. London: Pali Text Society.

Müller, E., ed. 1893. *Paramatthadīpanī: Dhammapāla's Commentary on the Therīgāthā.* Vol. 30. London: Pali Text Society.

Paul, Diana. 1979. *Women in Buddhism: Images of the Feminine in Mahāyāna Tradition.* Berkeley: Asian Humanities Press.

Piyadassi (Thera). 1980. *The Virgin's Eye: Women in Buddhist Literature.* Colombo: Buddhist Publication Society.

Ray, Reginald. 1994. *Buddhist Saints in India: A Study in Buddhist Values and Orientations.* New York: Oxford University Press.

Reed, Barbara E. 1992. "The Gender Symbolism of Kuan-Yin Bodhisattva." Pp. 159–180 in José Ignacio Cabezón, ed., *Buddhism, Sexuality, and Gender.* Albany: State University of New York Press.

Rhys Davids, Caroline A. F. 1948. *Psalms of the Early Buddhists 1: Psalms of the Sisters.* London: Pali Text Society.

Schalow, Paul Gordon. 1992. "Kūkai and the Tradition of Male Love in Japanese Buddhism." Pp. 215–230 in José Ignacio Cabezón, ed., *Buddhism, Sexuality, and Gender.* Albany: State University of New York Press.

Schalow, Paul Gordon, trans. 1990. *The Great Mirror of Male Love.* Stanford: University of California Press.

Schelling, Andrew, and Anne Waldman, trans. 1996. *Songs of the Sons and Daughters of Buddha.* Boston: Shambala Publications.

Schneider, David. 2000. *Street Zen: The Life and Work of Issan Dorsey.* New York: Marlowe.

Shaw, Miranda. 1994. *Passionate Enlightenment: Women in Tantric Buddhism.* Princeton, NJ: Princeton University Press.

Smith, Bardwell. 1992. "Buddhism and Abortion in Contemporary Japan." Pp. 185–214 in José Ignacio Cabezón, ed., *Buddhism, Sexuality, and Gender.* Albany: State University of New York Press.

Snellgrove, David. 1987. *Indo-Tibetan Buddhism.* 2 vols. Boston: Shambala.

Spiro, Melford. 1970. *Buddhism and Society: A Great Tradition and Its Burmese Vicissitudes.* New York: Harper and Row.

Sponberg, Alan. 1992. "Attitudes toward Women and the Feminine in Early Buddhism." Pp. 3–36 in José Ignacio Cabezón, ed., *Buddhism, Sexuality, and Gender.* Albany: State University of New York Press.

Sweet, Michael. 2000. "Pining Away for the Sight of the Handsome Cobra King: Ānanda as Gay Ancestor and Role Model." Pp. 13–22 in Winston Leyland, ed., *Queer Dharma: Voices of Gay Buddhists.* Vol. 2. San Francisco: Gay Sunshine Press.

Thurman, Robert, trans. 1976. *The Holy Teachings of Vimalakīrti.* University Park: Pennsylvania State University Press.

Tompkins, Jane. 1992. *West of Everything: The Inner Life of Westerns.* New York: Oxford University Press.

Vidyabhusan, S. C. A., trans. 1898. "The Story of Mahākaśyapa." *Journal of the Buddhist Text and Anthropological Society* 6: 18–19.

Watanabe, Tsuneo, and Jun'ichi Iwata. 1989. *The Love of Samurai: A Thousand Years of Japanese Homosexuality.* D. R. Roberts, trans. London: GMP Publishers.

Williams, Paul. 1989. *Mahāyāna Buddhism: The Doctrinal Foundations.* New York: Routledge.

Young, Katherine. 1987. "Hinduism." Pp. 59–103 in Arvind Sharma, ed., *Women in World Religions.* Albany: State University of New York Press.

Zwilling, Leonard. 1992. "Homosexuality as Seen in Indian Buddhist Texts." Pp. 203–214 in José Ignacio Cabezón, ed., *Buddhism, Sexuality, and Gender.* Albany: State University of New York Press.

Chapter 6

# Sex in Jewish Law and Culture

*Rebecca Alpert*

*Nineteenth-century* ketubah *(a Jewish marriage contract). (Archivo Iconografico, S.A./Corbis)*

$\mathcal{J}$udaism is commonly understood as the system of beliefs and practices of a people known today as the Jews. The Jewish people believe themselves to be the inheritors of traditions of the Hebrews or Israelites in the ancient Near East more than 1,000 years before the beginning of the Common Era. The history, legends, and laws of this period are collected in the Hebrew Bible, also known as the written Torah (literally, "teaching"; the term *Torah* is used to refer to the first five books of the Bible as well). After the Romans destroyed the Second Temple in Jerusalem—the cultic center of Jewish life—in the year 70 of the Common Era, the Jews reconstituted their religious life through the teachings of a group of men known as the rabbis. Their discussions and debates, or the oral Torah, were compiled in a text called the Talmud around 500 C.E. Written over several centuries, the Talmud's laws and lore formed the basis for diverse Jewish societies around the world until the time of the Enlightenment in Europe (and for Orthodox Jews until the present day).

Although the Judaism of the rabbis is based on the teachings in the Hebrew Bible, it also reflects significant innovation and the growth of Jewish civilization over time. The Talmud was interpreted and expanded upon by commentators, philosophers, mystics, and intellectuals during the Middle Ages as Jewish communities spread throughout Europe, North Africa, Asia, and later to the Western Hemisphere. Despite their canonical status, the Hebrew Bible, the Talmud, and these later commentaries reflect only a partial perspective on Jewish life, representing the ideas of the (male) cultural elites of their times. Since the dawn of the modern era, liberal versions of Jewish religion have reinterpreted many of the traditions and added women's voices. But even with the addition of these perspectives, we still cannot begin to know the rich variety of Jewish belief and practice in different communities around the world during the past 3,000 years.

It should not be surprising, then, that it is impossible to describe a single definitive view of sexuality in Judaism. We can examine certain cultural ideals and norms that have been the basis of the textual tradition of the Jews from the time of the Bible until the present day. However, many of these ideals and norms are so contradictory and ambiguous that it would be impossible to create a simple picture of Judaism's approach to sexuality, even if it was based on these texts. For example, Judaism has been described as a tradition with a healthy and positive view toward sex, because unlike Christianity or Buddhism, Judaism lacks an ideal of sexual renunciation. Yet it is overly simplistic to suggest that the absence of a tradition of celibacy indicates only positive attitudes toward sexuality. There are Jewish texts that support ascetic practices as well. Embedded in the Jewish textual tradition are positive views of sexual pleasure alongside efforts to control desire and to limit the variety of sexual expression for both men and women.

## Sexuality in Sacred Law

The Hebrew Bible contains many complicated attitudes toward sexuality. The Israelite tradition is marked by a monotheistic belief system, in which the deity lacks sexual attributes. This God, although described in predominantly masculine terminology (as king, shepherd, and warrior), always referred to by masculine pronouns (he, his, him) and therefore gendered, has neither sexual organs nor a female counterpart with whom to use them, as was common in ancient Near Eastern traditions. This lack of sexuality creates a problem, since the relationship between God and Israel often is described by the metaphor of marriage, although it is desexualized. The prophetic tradition understood marriage and adultery as the primary metaphors upon which the relationship between God and the people of Israel was based. In that relationship, Israel is most often depicted as the (sexually) unfaithful wife and God as the long-suffering and forgiving husband. This juxtaposition places Jewish males in the awkward position of God's spouse and makes women almost invisible in Jewish theology.

The Torah is replete with laws that prohibit and curtail human sexual practices. For example, when the commandments were to be given to Moses on Mt. Sinai, Israelite men were ordered not to engage in sexual relations with women for three days in preparation. It is clear from this and other legal prohibitions that semen and menstrual blood pollute and that to approach holy things, one must be clear of such pollution. Masturbation, homosexual sex, sex with animals, or sex with women who are menstruating, related by blood, or considered to be the property (through marriage) of another man are strictly forbidden. However, men may take multiple wives, and prostitution is not legally prohibited. Furthermore, biblical narratives like the stories of Tamar, Ruth, and David accept the violation of sexual boundaries as commonplace and sometimes even value those violations, as when Ruth initiates sexual relations with Boaz in order to ensure the genealogical line of her mother-in-law. The Song of Songs—a canonical text—is a series of passionate poems of love and desire between a man and a woman who are not presumed to be married. It is therefore impossible to characterize the attitudes toward sexuality in the Hebrew Bible as either totally restrictive or entirely positive about sex.

The traditions of the rabbis who taught and wrote after the destruction of the Second Temple (based on traditions of an earlier period as well) also reflect complex attitudes toward sexuality. The rabbis were deeply concerned with how to control sexual passion, which they viewed as necessary for procreation but potentially dangerous, even though the risk of ritual pollution, which only concerned entrance to holy places in the Temple, was no longer an issue.

The rabbinic tradition sees procreation as a positive value and accepts sexual pleasure as a necessary dimension of marriage. The legal tradition permits any sexual activity for married heterosexual couples and explicitly considers oral and anal sex, as well as vaginal sex with the woman on top (which they call "turning the table"), as acceptable forms of activity. It permits sexual pleasure within marriage, even in cases in which procreation is not possible (such as infertility and old age). Yet other passages in the Talmud include debates over whether sexual activity is permissible naked or in daylight, which casts a different light on the question of sexual pleasure. The rabbis restrict marital sex to approximately half of the woman's menstrual cycle through the laws of *niddah* (seclusion), which also came to be known as the laws of "family purity." They are derived from the biblical prohibitions about pollution in regard to approaching the Temple but were continued after the destruction of the Temple only in the case of menstruating women. The length of time of separation was extended to seven "clean" days beyond the original Biblical prohibition of sex during menstruation. The rabbis also delineate a marital obligation of *onah,* understood as the requirement that a man provide sexual pleasure for his wife, on the assumption that women are not themselves capable of asking for sex and possibly also to ensure procreation and keep men from vows of abstinence. Men are not expected to derive pleasure from their sexual duty and are strictly enjoined from masturbation, even to the extent of being prohibited from holding their penises during urination for fear that such touching might lead to temptation. The rabbis follow the biblical notion that semen is a holy substance, so that it ought only be deposited inside a woman and not spilled. Men should be able to conquer (or in modern terms, sublimate) their sexual desires through study and prayer—two activities that are valued more highly than sex in the rabbinic worldview. The relationship of teachers and students often is said to surpass that of fathers and sons and certainly that of husbands and wives. In the rabbis' world, women are regarded as instrumental to procreation but are not respected in their own right.

The rabbis' recognition of women's sexual needs assumes not only that women have sexual desire but also that they lack the discipline and intelligence to control it. The rabbinic tradition sees women as the source of temptation and sexual anxiety for men. For that reason, severe restrictions are placed on women's learning, dress, public comportment, and participation in ritual life to ensure that men will not be tempted by a woman's presence. Even the sight of a woman's finger or the sound of her voice are understood to have the capacity to lead a man to sexual thoughts. Women are not to be trusted, and the Talmud is replete with injunctions against unnecessary contact with women. A woman who is suspected of adultery (the *sotah*) is described in degrading terms in a rabbinic elaboration on the ritual prescribed for such a woman in the Torah, even when there is no evidence of her guilt. Although the ritual—a trial by ordeal—was not practiced, negative rabbinic attitudes toward women are elucidated in the elaborate commentaries about how to treat an adulterous woman. The man accused with her is not subject to such vile approbation or punishment.

According to the rabbinic texts, study is men's main antidote to desire, and a relationship with God (and with other teachers and students) helps men to master the *yetzer ha ra* (literally, "evil inclination," but better translated as sexual temptation). Although the rabbis see sex as necessary for procreation and procreation as necessary for Jewish continuity, they do not value these activities highly. In the rabbinic era, the heterosexual love poems in the Song of Songs were reinterpreted as a metaphor for the love between God and Israel. The erotic connections between men and women were not holy; that passion was transferred to the relationship between Jewish men and their God.

Medieval commentators elaborated on the sexual restrictions placed on men and women. They were concerned primarily with heterosexual temptation, and although they prohibited homosexual encounters, they did not focus on them or take them seriously. During the Middle Ages, however, sexuality became more highly valued as a part of Jewish religious life. Several medieval poets (who were also commentators on the law) wrote same-sex erotic poetry. Famous examples include Moses Ibn Ezra, Judah haLevi, and Solomon Ibn Gabirol. In medieval mystical tradition, kabbalists reinterpreted the heterosexual sex act as a mirror of divine connection between what came to be understood as the male and female emanations of God. They valorized heterosexual sex (within the controlled circumstances outlined by law) as a dimension of the divine and gave it special status. The Sabbath was seen as a particularly appropriate time for sexual relations between husband and wife, suggesting the way in which sexual activity was channeled into religious fervor. In a well-known medieval hymn, *L'cha Dodi,* which is still incorporated in the Friday evening liturgy, the imagery of the Sabbath as queen, bride, and beloved also reveals the connection of the sexual and spiritual. Taking kabbalistic ideas about sexuality as a mirror of the divine realm to a logical conclusion, messianic movements of Sabbati Zvi and Jacob Frank used sexual imagery and language as part of their efforts to bring about a more perfect world. As in previous periods, we have little sense of how these cultural productions affected everyday life, but they do give us some sense of how sexuality was incorporated in the belief system of Jewish thinkers and writers.

Although medieval rabbis emphasized sexual pleasure in marriage, images of woman as temptress still abounded. The legend of Lilith is a prime example. To explain why the Bible incorporates two creation stories (in the first, male and female are created together; in the second, the female is created from the "rib" or side of the sleeping male), one ancient text suggested that the stories were actually about two different women. Eve was the second wife, created from Adam's rib; Lilith was the first, created along with Adam and then exiled. According to medieval legend, her banishment took place because she demanded equality and wanted to be on top during sex. Lilith became popularized during the medieval period as a demon who killed children out of her rage at being banished from the Garden of Eden; Jewish mothers tied red ribbons on cradles to keep her away from their babies.

## CONTEMPORARY ISSUES IN JEWISH SEXUALITY

In the modern era, many complicated issues developed with regard to Jewish sexuality. Hasidism, a revivalist movement that began in Poland in the seventeenth century, followed the medieval mystical and messianic tendencies to make sexual imagery part of the understanding of the connection between this world and the divine and incorporated a sexual dimension into its spiritual observance. Hasidism was a movement that challenged the very strict traditionalism of its time and place. Men were drawn to study with Hasidic masters and left home for long periods of time, often disrupting their family lives and displacing their relationships with women with an eroticized world of male companionship through study and prayer. The swaying movements of men at prayer simulated movement during sexual intercourse, and the intense fervor of their praying and dancing created an erotically charged same-sex environment, which may have been a dimension of the life in the study house in the rabbinic era as well.

In Western Europe and later in the Americas, the values of the Enlightenment made it possible for Jews to assimilate into Christian cultures and the developing secular national cultures. The religious movements that developed into Reform, Conservative, and Orthodox Judaism each found different ways of incorporating traditional sexual laws and mores. The Orthodox provided rational justifications for traditional laws, whereas non-Orthodox movements liberalized regulations regarding family purity. These movements did not seek to relax laws concerning forbidden sexual relationships outside marriage, although the medieval tradition of marriage at puberty was supplanted by marriage in later adolescence, which often resulted in problems in controlling the sexuality of the young and unmarried. The nineteenth-century shift from arranged marriage to companionate marriage in Eastern and Western Europe also affected Jewish life. As depicted by Yiddish writers in works like the *Dybbuk, Yentl the Yeshiva Boy,* and the stories that became *Fiddler on the Roof,* a marriage based on romantic love and attraction rather than one determined by parents through the institution of the matchmaker (*shadchan*) challenged the authority of the Jewish family. Modernization also created the opportunity for European Jews to consider marriage to Christians, raising the specter of assimilation and the dissolution of the Jewish community.

The incorporation of Jews into Christian society was accompanied by anti-Semitic images that were often sexual in nature. Anti-Semitic literature portrayed the Jewish male as lacking virility, depicting Jewish men as menstruating and having breasts and other female characteristics. Zionism provided an antidote to these images, portraying the "new Hebrew man" as highly masculine and sexualized, and paralleled the growing anti-Semitic images of the hypersexualized Jew that became part of the propaganda of Nazism. (Emphasis on the Jewish nose, for example, was used to suggest the animal nature of the Jews, whose sexuality was understood to be connected to the primitive sense of smell.) At the same time, the writings of Sigmund Freud contributed to a new openness about the meaning of sexuality and its relationship to human psychological and physical health that had a great impact on making these discussions of sexuality public in the Jewish community.

Issues facing the contemporary Jewish community in the United States combine many of these historical concerns with some new ones. The sexual landscape in the United States is complex. U.S. consumer culture espouses open attitudes toward sexuality, but at the same time, conservative forces in society seek to limit sexual freedom outside marriage and procreative freedom within it. The current threat of new sexually transmitted diseases has had a profound effect on the sexual attitudes and behaviors of young people. Sexuality and reproduction, once inextricably linked, now can be considered independent of one another because of the sexual revolution and medical advances. The gay, lesbian, bisexual, and transgender movement has created new understandings of same-sex erotic attractions, and the feminist movement has brought women's perspectives on sexuality into public view. The resulting questions for Jewish tradition are focused on four areas: rethinking the question of forbidden sexual relationships, connecting the sexual with the spiritual through feminist perspectives, reexamining the relationship between sexuality and reproduction, and combating stereotypes of Jewish sexuality.

### Forbidden Sexual Relationships

The textual tradition inherited by the Jews forbids many sexual behaviors and relationships that are common and acceptable in today's society. Although ancient Jews practiced polygamy, accepted sexual encounters between men and women who were not married, and tolerated oral and anal sex within marital relationships, many other sexual practices were forbidden. Contemporary Jews have had to struggle with the conflicts between the social norms of secular society and traditional religious laws and customs. In most instances, they have made an effort to honor the past while at the same time recognizing that new developments in thought and behavior need to be accommodated if a tradition is to remain responsive to the needs of its adherents and to its own values. Still, behaviors that are commonly accepted today—such as masturbation, homosexual relations, sex before (and outside) marriage, romantic love, and sexual relationships with non-Jews—are still troubling issues in traditional Jewish communities (Biale 1992).

In some Orthodox and all Hasidic communities, arranged marriages are the norm and are welcomed by young people who join these communities. In some instances, women join to remove themselves from pressure to be sexual before marriage. More liberal Orthodox communities, however, have come to terms with sex before marriage, and the "tefillin date" is a common experience. Traditionally, young men must say morning prayers wearing tefillin. If they stay overnight with their dates, they need to be prepared to pray in the morning. The decision to carry tefillin along on a date acknowledges this possibility. There is still tension in Orthodox communities on this issue, however, and it appears to exist along gender lines. In these communities, stories abound of women who feel safe because Jewish law protects them from pressure to have sex before marriage and of men who struggle to control their sexual desire until marriage (Goldman 1992). This division conforms to the assumptions made in the Talmud that men's sexual passion needs to be controlled and that women are modest and do not express sexual desire.

Liberal Judaism has come to terms more readily with the expansion of acceptable sexual relationships. Although remaining committed to marriage as the best option, liberal Jews have abandoned other prohibitions around sexuality (Borowitz 1969). Divorce was always an acceptable practice in Jewish law, so it was not difficult to accept serial monogamy as a norm. Single adults having sex outside marriage is considered appropriate and even desirable from the standpoint of mental health. Masturbation is assumed to be a normal part of sexual experimentation. Teens are taught about and encouraged to participate in safe sexual activities, provided they treat the partners they choose with respect. The laws of family purity are no longer practiced, and so sex within marriage is not governed by rules of abstinence. Although there is still some discomfort about marrying outside the Jewish community, marriages with Christians have been welcomed and couples encouraged to live a Jewish life, with or without the conversion of the non-Jewish partner. Gays and lesbians also are respected, although liberal Jews have been slow to accept bisexuals and those who question or change their gender identities. All these issues have required much thought and some anguish, but dealing with the issue of gay liberation has been the greatest challenge to Jewish liberals and traditionalists alike, although prohibitions against homosexuality are less severe than those against other sexual practices.

Homosexuality is mentioned only rarely in the canonical texts of Jewish tradition. The Hebrew Bible does not mention female same-sex relationships at all, although later commentaries suggest that the reference in Leviticus to forbidden "practices of Egypt" is about female-female marriage. The book of Leviticus forbids male same-sex acts and describes them as an "abomination" (although the Hebrew word *toevah* is difficult to translate, that is how most English versions render it). This prohibition occurs twice, and the second time it carries the penalty of death, although even contemporary Orthodox scholars reject the death penalty for this infraction. Recently, scholars have debated the meaning of this interdiction, although it received scant attention prior to the advent of gay liberation. Clearly, the prohibition does not refer to gay relationships as they exist today since such relationships were unknown in ancient times. It is more likely a reference to a particular sexual act—probably anal intercourse—that was prohibited along with other practices, either to distinguish Israelite practices from those of their neighbors or to indicate an abhorrence of mixing together things that were perceived not to belong together—in this case, bodily fluids; in others, fabrics, animals, or foods (Olyan 1994). In any case, it was one prohibition among many concerning sexual behaviors and was not singled out in any particular way. The story of Sodom in the book of Genesis, which describes a group of men who demand homosexual sex from guests and strangers to the town, is the only other instance in which a male homosexual act is mentioned in the Hebrew Bible. Here, it is not the homosexual nature of the act that is condemned but rather the rude and inhospitable nature of the request itself. Christian commentators take this event as a condemnation of homosexuality (hence the term "sodomite"), but Jewish interpretive tradition does not consider the story in that light. Although contemporary commentators have seen love between men in the relationship of David and Jonathan and love between women in that of Ruth and Naomi, there is no evidence to indicate that the authors of the stories intended such readings of the texts.

Following biblical law, the Talmud prohibits two men from sleeping under the same blanket. However, a minority opinion permits this, expressing the idea that Jewish men would not engage in homosexual acts, even if given the opportunity. The Talmud permits women who are known to engage in female homoerotic acts to marry priests (who could only marry virgins) because these acts are not considered sex (which requires penile penetration)—thus they are still virgins. It also assumes that these women, despite having relations with other women, are going to marry men. Similarly, medieval commentaries instruct husbands to punish their wives if they discover them to be engaging in homoerotic acts with other women, but they are considered minor transgressions and are not taken seriously. The medieval period also produced male homoerotic poetry, but we do not know the extent to which its publication indicates widespread behavior or simply an interest in copying Arabic poetic conventions of the times. These written sources tell us that homosexual behavior was clearly known in Jewish societies throughout ancient times but was not considered a matter of concern or a disruption of society.

In the modern period, there are literary sources that mention homosexual relationships. There is a recurring theme in Yiddish literature of cross-dressing women who are thought to carry men's souls in women's bodies (Alpert 1997). But until the gay liberation movement, homosexuality was rarely discussed publicly in the Jewish world, and there was a commonly held notion, not unlike that expressed in the Talmud, that Jews simply were not aroused by same-sex attractions. This idea was shattered in the 1970s and 1980s as many Jews began to identify themselves publicly as gay and lesbian, and the community had to face the reality of openly gay and lesbian people who wanted to join synagogues and serve as teachers and rabbis.

The early reactions were primarily those of hostility and disbelief on the part of communal leaders, resulting in the invisibility of gay and lesbian concerns for quite some time. The newly developing synagogues formed by gay Jews in the 1970s in New York, San Francisco, and Los Angeles were not welcomed by other Jewish organizations in their early years. *Nice Jewish Girls* (Beck 1982), an anthology of coming-out stories of Jewish lesbians, was placed under ban by Orthodox Jews. Schools for training rabbis refused to admit gay men who applied. But by the late 1980s, gay men and lesbians began to find acceptance in the liberal Jewish community. Gay synagogues began to affiliate with religious movements, rabbinical schools began ordaining openly gay clergy, a number of authors published books and articles, and most recently, Jewish organizations have taken the matter of same-sex marriage under advisement. Although the Conservative and Orthodox movements are still unwilling to accept people who identify as gay or lesbian, growing numbers of Jews who want to be involved with these movements are challenging their positions. Given that there are no legal barriers to the acceptance of lesbian sex and only minimal barriers to gay male sex (some have argued that abstinence from anal sex should be the only criterion for Orthodox acceptance of gay men), it is quite possible that this situation may change over time (Greenberg 2002; Lappe 2001).

Bisexuality is another matter. The main factor in many Jews' acceptance of gay men and lesbians is an understanding of same-sex attraction and behavior as not chosen and therefore not amenable to change. As such, it must be accepted as a variation that is part of God's plan for human nature. But there is distinct discomfort with the idea that people are choosing to live lives that do not conform to the heterosexual ideal. According to most of the pronouncements by Jewish organizations, if choice is involved, the individual should choose the path that conforms to the majority's standards—that is, heterosexuality. Bisexuals claim that they are sexually attracted to both men and women and that gender is not a significant factor in selecting a sexual partner. This idea challenges a fundamental assumption in ways that strictly gay and lesbian sexuality does not. That some bisexuals oppose monogamy is also antithetical to the traditional Jewish belief system. Although gay men (and lesbians and heterosexuals for that matter) who form intimate long-term relationships but engage in brief sexual encounters pose the same threat, they generally do not demand public acceptance for this behavior from the community.

Jewish communities also have not publicly supported transgender rights. People who transition from one gender identity to another and those who claim both male and female identities simultaneously are not recognized in Jewish circles despite a history of awareness of women who assume male identities.

Even given these limitations, the liberal Jewish community has been remarkably supportive and welcoming of gay men and lesbians who seek to be involved. Many rabbis will perform commitment ceremonies, welcome gay and lesbian couples, provide a caring educational environment for their children, support families who are dealing with daughters and sons coming out, and allow gay men and lesbians to serve in leadership positions. Gay men and lesbians, in turn, must accept the ideals of the Jewish community and understand that they will be accepted only if they are involved in a monogamous marriage and wish to raise children within a nuclear family model. Other sexual life choices simply are not accepted.

Surprisingly, the state of Israel has been open to the inclusion of gay men and lesbians as well. Although the Orthodox have complete authority in matters of marriage and other issues of personal status, Israel is a secular state and has proven welcoming to gay men and lesbians. They serve openly in the army; are entitled to domestic partnership benefits in some cases; and in recent years have developed a gay and lesbian subculture similar to that which exists in the United States, including publications, media exposure, social and political groups, and public meeting places. Because most non-Orthodox Jews in Israel are not religious, the question of gay rabbis, marriages, and synagogues is not important in this context. Gay synagogues do flourish around the world, however, and the World Congress of Lesbian, Gay, Bisexual, and Transgender Jewish Organizations has representation in Latin America, Canada, Western Europe, and Australia (Walzer 2000).

### Connecting the Sexual and the Spiritual through Feminist Perspectives

Throughout Jewish history, sex has been linked to spirituality. It has been understood as a metaphor for human relationships with God and as a mirror of the divine. Yet sex also has been perceived as an "evil inclination," a powerful force that tempts a person away from spiritual pursuits and that needs either to be sublimated or to be satisfied in a controlled manner. Contemporary Jewish feminist thinkers, from Orthodox to liberal, take a more positive approach to sex, viewing it primarily as an opportunity for spiritual expression and development.

Feminist Judaism is a rethinking of Judaism through the perspectives of women. The ideas and writings that have been preserved throughout Jewish history were those of men, and the world was seen through the perspective of men's concerns. In the mid-twentieth century, an international feminist movement began to question what the world would be like if women had the power to describe it from their own perspectives. Often feminists were critical of Judaism and the other world religions because they were based on traditions that men defined. But other feminists have sought to reclaim religious traditions by imagining how women might have addressed traditional questions and by asking new ones of their own. Jewish feminists have taken an active role in this process. Although many reject the standard denominations of Judaism (Orthodox, Conservative, and Reform), others identify with those groups and seek to engage with them by adding a feminist perspective. They have made innovations by challenging laws on marriage and divorce, creating new prayers and celebrations, demanding leadership positions (except for the Orthodox, all denominations of Judaism now ordain women as rabbis), writing new interpretations of old traditions (known as midrash), and rethinking questions about sexuality. Not surprisingly, feminist Jews have developed a sexual ethos that conforms fairly well to the contemporary understanding that pleasure and intimacy are the main reasons to engage in sexual activities.

Non-Orthodox feminist Jews have rejected the ancient rabbinic model that views sexuality as a powerful and, to some extent, negative force that needs to be controlled. They also have criticized the view that although men can control their sexual desire through study and prayer, women are not capable of controlling their sexual desire, and so men must control it for them. Feminists like the tradition's recognition that women have sexual desire—a fact that is not universally acknowledged by religious traditions—and appreciate the concept of *onah*, the husband's obligation to please his wife sexually. However, they reject the idea that women are primarily sexual beings who must be removed from public spaces so that men are not tempted by their presence (Plaskow 1990).

Instead, non-Orthodox feminists have focused on other dimensions of Jewish traditions about sexuality, particularly those that celebrate sexuality as a link to the realm of the divine. Feminist translations and celebrations of the Song of Songs have been incorporated into feminist Sabbath and holy day liturgy and used to emphasize positive Jewish attitudes toward sexuality. Feminists also have exhibited a strong interest in the Jewish mystical tradition, in which the feminine attains divine status. Some feminists celebrate Shekinah, for example, which in Jewish mysticism represents the feminine aspect of the divine. Prayers to Shekinah written by Jewish feminists and incorporated into worship often allude to the medieval idea that the divine union between God and Shekinah mirrors the sexual union between husband and wife. Feminists have also reinstituted the holiday of Rosh Hodesh, the celebration of the new moon. At one point in ancient times, this holiday was designated as a special day for women. Contemporary feminists link Rosh Hodesh to women's bodily cycle and use it to connect women's sexual and spiritual dimensions through special women-only observances, including song, prayer, and conversation. The goal of many of these rituals and interpretations is for women to claim a more positive relationship to their bodies and to themselves as sexual beings. Through these new prayers and practices, feminist Jews have emphasized the value of sex as a vehicle for intimacy. The idea of making sex an opportunity for emotional connection is a contribution of Jewish feminism to the Jewish textual tradition (Gottlieb 1995).

Although liberal feminists, like liberal Jews in general, have rejected the laws of *niddah* that regulate sexual behavior in marriage, Orthodox feminists have redefined this practice as a means of sexual liberation. They assert that the two weeks when they are forbidden to have sexual relations with their husbands provide a form of sexual freedom. The laws give them the power to have some limited control over when they resume their sexual relations each month, which is particularly useful when the sexual relationship is negative or even abusive. In positive sexual relationships, Orthodox women claim that the period of abstinence increases desire and pleasure by making the sexual connection both holy and special. Other Orthodox feminists have suggested that the ritual immersion that marks the end of their period of separation is itself sexually empowering. An orthodox woman ends *niddah* by going to the *mikveh* (a public ritual bath), where she washes herself completely, removes every extraneous particle from her body (dead skin, hanging cuticles, loose hairs, and so on) and then, completely naked, immerses herself in the ritual bath. This private experience is a prelude to having sexual relations with her husband, which by law takes place immediately after the immersion. Some Orthodox women claim that this ritual calls attention to and enhances the sexual experience (Kaufman 1991).

In all the examples mentioned here, sexuality is understood positively and is linked with the spiritual. In this way, Jewish feminists have claimed a place for women's sexuality and spirituality in Judaism and have emphasized the parts of Jewish tradition in which heterosexual sex is valued and holy. It is not surprising that women who retain a connection to Judaism would look toward the parts of tradition that respect women's sexuality rather than the aspects that denigrate it. By reinterpreting and reclaiming these traditions, Jewish women have made an important place for themselves within Jewish life.

In addition to connecting the sexual and the spiritual, Jewish women have been highly critical of the denigration and profanation of women's sexuality. They have fought, for instance, to improve the situation of the *agunah* (literally, "chained woman"). Since women cannot initiate divorce in Jewish tradition, men can prevent their former wives from marrying again by refusing to grant divorces. Although liberal Jews have either abandoned unilateral divorce or put conditions into the marriage contract to prevent such an occurrence, this situation still affects women in Israel and in traditional communities around the world. Jewish women's groups have worked toward legal solutions on behalf of traditional women who find themselves unable to remarry and have taken political action, such as confronting rabbinic leaders who could create legal solutions to the problem if they so chose (Cwik 1998).

Jewish women's groups also have been involved in working against trafficking in women. Prostitution is legal in Israel and there are a great number of brothels and massage parlors in and around Tel Aviv. Many of the women who do sex work do so willingly. However, others find themselves doing this work because conditions in their home countries (primarily in the former Soviet Union) have compelled them to find avenues of escape. Too often those avenues include organized crime. Young women are helped to emigrate and sold into prostitution. Often deprived of any salary, they labor under terrible working conditions and ill treatment, including rape and abuse (Lerner 1998).

Domestic violence in the Jewish community is another issue about which more Jews have become more aware. For many years, Jewish community leaders believed that violence was not a problem among Jews. However, several groups organized to raise awareness of this problem. In the United States and Israel, Jewish feminist organizations sponsor programs that provide emotional support and legal options for Jewish women and men who experience violence in their homes. These projects also include public programs such as the "Anti–Domestic Violence Sabbath," during which rabbis are urged to give sermons and conduct special study sessions on the topic. These antiviolence groups send out literature and materials to help rabbis understand the seriousness and breadth of this problem. They also make stickers available to place in women's restrooms in synagogues. These stickers give the local domestic violence hotline number so that women can obtain further information in privacy (Graetz 1998; Cohn Spiegel 1999).

### Sexuality and Procreation

Until the last few decades of the twentieth century, sexuality had been linked inextricably with procreation. Today, the use of birth control is widespread, pregnancy can be terminated safely through abortion, and conception may take place in the laboratory and the hospital as well as the bedroom. These developments call into question the simple connection between sex and procreation. Contemporary Jewish thinkers have had to come to terms with what sex means without procreation and what procreation means without sex.

Procreation always has been the main motivation for positive attitudes toward sex in the Jewish tradition. "Be fruitful and multiply" is the first commandment in the text of the Hebrew Bible. Although traditional Judaism accepts sexual pleasure as a separate and positive dimension of the sexual experience, pleasure has been valued only in the context of heterosexual marriage because the ultimate goal of sex in this context is procreation. Relationships that are nonprocreative because of infertility or menopause are permitted, although divorce is also permissible on the grounds of infertility. Nonprocreative sexual acts are allowed in marital relations, but the cycle of *niddah* favors procreation by beginning the sexual cycle on the woman's most fertile days.

Birth control is strictly regulated in Jewish canonical texts. Acts of birth control that block or thwart seminal emission (such as coitus interruptus or condoms) are not permitted. However, the use of condoms is now allowed in order to fight sexually transmitted diseases because the value of *pikuah nefesh,* or "saving a life," supersedes other considerations. The birth control pill, which does not block semen at all, provided a simple solution to the problem of thwarting seminal emission and is considered the most appropriate form of birth control in traditional Jewish circles.

There are extensive discussions in medieval texts about whether certain categories of women, such as those who are prepubescent or nursing, are permitted or required to use a *mokh* (a cloth inserted in the vagina that is similar to a diaphragm). Commentators disagree about whether the text is saying that they *may* do this, in which case it is permissible for others as well, or that they *must* do this, meaning it is required for only these categories of women and that therefore others may not use birth control.

Demographic questions have always been an important factor in determining Jewish attitudes toward birth control. In the Talmud, some authorities suggest that two children are sufficient, whereas a minority opinion holds that a couple must have one child of each sex to fulfill the commandment to "be fruitful and multiply" (although technically, Jewish law obligates only men to fulfill this commandment). During times of plague and destruction, rabbinic leaders encouraged Jews to have more children. In the twentieth century, the Jewish people endured the decimation of one third of their total population as a result of the Holocaust, and living in open societies has led to opportunities for personal freedom, assimilation, intermarriage, and a resultant decrease in the Jewish population. Despite the fact that a new openness to bringing in converts through intermarriage or choice has increased Jewish numbers to some extent, these factors compel Jewish leaders to encourage childbearing. The Orthodox community takes this quite seriously, and large families tend to be the norm. In liberal communities, many people are satisfied with fulfilling the minimal commandment of having two children, whereas others, influenced by contemporary concerns about population growth and personal freedom, choose not to have children at all. This reality has caused a serious demographic crisis for the Jewish community.

Abortion is another issue that is treated differently in orthodox and liberal Jewish circles because Jewish texts about abortion are open to multiple interpretations. To be fair, ancient Jewish texts never dealt with the question of abortion as an issue of choice. All the texts focus on the status of the fetus after a miscarriage caused by an accident or a medical emergency in which the life of the mother is endangered. Nonetheless, contemporary thinkers draw on these texts to render different Jewish views of abortion. It should not be surprising that more traditional communities define the acceptable circumstances for abortion more narrowly than do liberal ones. But all readings of Jewish texts suggest that abortion is neither equivalent to murder, since the fetus is always only a potential life, nor a method of birth control, the use of which is to be determined exclusively by the needs or desires of the woman who is carrying that fetus. The range of Jewish positions lies in between these extremes.

The only mention of abortion in the Hebrew Bible concerns a woman whose fetus is killed because someone strikes her and causes her to abort. The concern of the legal text in which this question arose is whether or not this is a capital crime. The authors conclude that it is not and that the person who struck her owes her husband monetary compensation for the loss of property (potential life) only.

Later texts interpret a line in the story of Cain and Abel as opposing abortion. After Cain slew his brother Abel, God commands, "Do not shed the blood of man by/in man." The interpretation is based on whether the Hebrew character "b" means "in" or "by." Translating the word as "in" (do not shed the blood of man in man), commentators suggest that the "man inside a man" is a fetus and its life should not be taken. If the word is translated as "by," it is understood to be a general reference to killing human beings (do not shed the blood of man by man). Beyond the one reference and this interpretation, biblical texts do not figure into the contemporary discussion about abortion.

The most important Jewish text about abortion is found in the Mishnah (the legal text upon which the Talmud is based), which states that if at the time of birth, the fetus is threatening the life of the woman carrying it, it may be dismembered and killed in order to save the woman's life. Commentators who take a liberal view of abortion in Judaism read this as a warrant for abortion at any point during the pregnancy if the well-being of the mother is threatened in any way. More conservative commentators read this text to mean that abortion is acceptable in Judaism only if the woman's life is in danger. Some suggest that this text should be understood only in reference to the time of birth and not to earlier stages of pregnancy.

The more liberal position is supported by texts, also in the Mishnah, that suggest that if a pregnant woman is convicted of a capital crime, the fetus should be aborted first so that she will not have to wait for her execution for a long time, and so that she will not be embarrassed at being executed while pregnant. Of course, since in the time of the Mishnah, Jews no longer had the authority to perform state acts of killing, it was a hypothetical case, as is much of the text of the Talmud. However, it does give us an idea of the workings of the rabbinic mind on this subject. The pro-abortion position also is supported by a medieval source that suggests that a pregnant woman should be given anything to satisfy her cravings, even if it is known to cause miscarriage. Women's needs are therefore addressed. But it is also clear that the woman's needs determine whether abortion should take place; there is no concern that the fetus it-self might be subject to harm or pain. There is no room in Jewish teach-ing for the idea that abortion could be used to end a pregnancy because the fetus is either carrying a disease or of the wrong sex. No potential life is a wrongful life. A fetus known, as a result of amniocentesis, to have Down's syndrome or Tay-Sachs disease could not be aborted, therefore, according to Jewish teaching unless the mother thought that raising the child would threaten her in some way (Biale 1984).

Jewish leaders have spoken out on both sides of the abortion issue. Because they are inconclusive and interpretations of them are complex, Jewish texts on the subject could be helpful in resolving the polarization on abortion in today's society. Jewish texts both honor the potential life that the fetus represents and at the same time honor the needs, values, and well-being of the woman who carries that fetus in her body. Few of those engaged in the abortion debate are willing to look at the issue from both sides, and Jewish interpretations could be useful in finding a mid-dle ground.

Contraception and abortion have uncoupled sexual relationships from procreation. At the same time, new technologies and techniques have made procreation possible without heterosexual sex. In biblical times, if a woman could not conceive (and the theme of the "barren woman" is common in the Hebrew Bible), her husband would simply se-lect a concubine to bear children who would continue his lineage. In later times, adoption provided the opportunity for infertile people to rear chil-dren. But despite the widespread acceptance of adoption and the fact that children who are adopted from non-Jews are simply converted at birth, there seems to be a preference for children who share the genetic makeup of their parents. To that end, Jews have embraced technologies that en-able couples to have "biological" children.

The simplest of these methods, donor insemination, is also the least acceptable by the standards of traditional Judaism. First, the method requires masturbation, which is problematic if the donor is Jewish since masturbation is still taboo in Orthodox circles. Second, an anonymous donor raises the possibility of incest. Both these problems are best remedied by having a donor who is not Jewish. Since Jewish lineage is passed through the mother, the Jewishness of the child is not in ques-tion with a non-Jewish donor. Contemporary Orthodox thinkers have also raised the problem of adultery, since the woman's body is taking in sperm that is not her husband's. Nonetheless, donor insemination is widely practiced, particularly among Jewish lesbians who are very interested in raising children in contemporary Jewish society.

Traditional Jewish scholars have few objections to other infertility treatments that affect women's bodies, such as in vitro fertilization and embryo transplants, although they, too, require the husband to produce sperm through masturbation. Nonetheless, they are more acceptable because they involve the genetic material of both partners. There is, however, some concern about what to do with the fertilized embryos that are not used in conception. Having a woman act as a surrogate is also controversial, although some scholars have argued it is acceptable in that it is no different from the biblical practice of concubinage (Dorff 1998).

The possibility of separating procreation from sexual relationships increases the necessity of examining other values about sex. Conversations about sex for physical pleasure and emotional intimacy need further development among Jewish thinkers and teachers. Because sex is no longer directly linked to procreation, teaching children about the pleasures and dangers of sexual acts and relationships is important to the Jewish community. Jewish feminists and gay liberationists have been involved in thinking about these issues and bringing the conversation further into the public domain. There are also leaders among the Orthodox who teach about the positive dimensions of sexual pleasure within marriage.

### Stereotypes of Jewish Sexuality

After World War II, Jews became comfortable in U.S. society. Anti-Semitism, which had kept Jews from positions of power in society, became infrequent. Nonetheless, stereotypes of Jews are still common. Those stereotypes express how other Americans feel about Jews having power and assimilating into U.S. society, but they often take the form of commentary on Jewish sexuality. Unlike the stereotypes of overarching hypersexuality produced by the Nazis, sexual stereotypes of Jews in the United States are differentiated by gender. The Jewish man often is seen as effeminate, weak, and unmanly—à la Woody Allen. The Jewish woman is presented as a "Jewish American Princess" or JAP (probably an allusion to the derogatory term used for Japanese Americans during World War II and afterward). The princess is sexually passive, consumed only by the desire to shop and to beautify herself through cosmetics, surgery, and diet. These stereotypes abound in popular cultural novels, music, and films, and most prevalently in humor. Although the stereotypes about Jewish men were common throughout modern history, the princess stereotype is peculiar to the U.S. scene.

Study and prayer are highly valued in Judaism, so it is not surprising that the Jews are known as "the people of the book." Jewish masculinity is defined within the culture as intellectual prowess. In European Jewish societies, women were expected to care for the economic well-being of the family, while men studied. A pious family would take in students so that young men could study without worrying about making money, and a "good match" for a young woman was to marry a scholar. Consequently, U.S. standards of masculinity, defined by physical beauty and strength, were not important in traditional Jewish society.

Although Zionism challenged the scholarly image, and Israeli men even today do not suffer from the "sissy" stereotype, Jewish men in the United States still do. Orthodox men who follow the cultural norms of earlier Jewish societies are expected to be scholars, and women are expected both to care for the home and to have an occupation. Although assimilated men in the United States are no longer expected to be students, they tend to follow more cerebral and less physical career paths, and the stereotype has stuck. The "nebbish" as portrayed by Woody Allen is very interested in sex, but to outward appearances is weak and unattractive. Jokes about effeminate Jewish men (such as the one in the film "Airplane," in which someone is given a blank book entitled *Jews and Sports*) cause Jewish men severe discomfort. Figures like the baseball player Hank Greenberg and the wrestler "Goldberg" are Jewish heroes because they contradict the stereotype and allow Jewish men to take pride in the kind of masculinity respected in U.S. society. Other jokes about Jewish men's lack of sexual endowment (such as the suggestion that Jewish women are bad at math because they are told that this—finger gesture denoting an inch—is 6 inches) make for further discomfort. Unfortunately, this stereotype sometimes compels Jewish men to prove that they are "real men," rather than accepting the idea that a quiet, gentle, and studious demeanor is a good way to be masculine. But there are also Jewish writers who suggest that masculinity can take different cultural forms and urge Jewish men to embrace gentleness as masculine (Brod 1988; Boyarin 1997).

The Jewish American Princess, however, is a stereotype that lacks historical antecedents, having only become prevalent in the United States after World War II. Before that, in keeping with the European stereotypes of the Jewish man as effeminate, Jewish women often were seen as controlling and masculine. This stereotype translated in the U.S. context into the "Jewish mother," who was understood as taking an overpowering interest in the life of her husband and son, rendering them impotent. This scenario is well described in Philip Roth's *Portnoy's Complaint,* where the main character has "sexual hangups" because of his mother. But the Jewish mother stereotype had more to do with the problems of Jewish men than with images of Jewish women. In fact, the Jewish princess is the opposite of the Jewish mother. She has no interest in overpowering her husband or son. She is interested only in herself and in acquiring possessions. She is described as completely desexualized and often as withholding sex from her boyfriend or husband. Orgasmic pleasure is not even in the realm of possibility.

Many feminist scholars have tried to make sense of this stereotype. They suggest that it has to do primarily with anti-Semitic attitudes that are connected to the development of a Jewish upper and upper middle class. As anti-Semitism subsided in U.S. society and Jews began to enter the upper classes, some of the discomfort about their presence and their difference from other Americans was focused on Jewish women. Another possible source of this stereotype is Jewish men's transference to Jewish women of negative stereotypes about their lack of sexual prowess. This theory has much credibility, since it is Jewish men who are most responsible for perpetuating the Jewish princess stereotype (Philip Roth's novella, *Goodbye, Columbus,* is a prime example). Whatever the source of these stereotypes, it is important to be aware that they are stereotypes; they say more about discomfort with Jewish assimilation into U.S. society than about Jewish sexuality (Prell 1999).

## CONCLUSION

Jewish views of sexuality are indeed complex. Celibacy is not part of Jewish tradition, but some have followed ascetic practices. God is masculine yet has no sex. Women's heterosexual needs are recognized, but they often were viewed negatively until the advent of women's liberation in the late twentieth century. Men's sexuality is a source of power but also is in need of control. Jewish views of birth control depend on the perceived need for increasing the Jewish population in any given era. Abortion is neither murder nor completely accepted. Homosexuality is rarely mentioned until the contemporary period, when it is treated generally in a positive light, provided that it is understood as biologically determined and not a matter of choice. Commonly accepted behaviors, such as masturbation, are strictly prohibited, but sexual experimentation between unmarried partners is tacitly encouraged. It is no wonder that outsiders, failing to understand this complexity, are often confused by Jewish sexuality. It clearly does not conform to contemporary secular or Christian norms.

Although it is impossible to create a simple description of Jewish views of and attitudes toward sexuality, it is important to note its vital role in Jewish life. Sexuality has played a part in Jewish history by helping us better understand the role of Jews in the societies in which they live and the relationship between Jewish women and men. It remains a challenge to Jewish legal traditions and figures prominently in Jewish theology and symbolism.

## REFERENCES

Alpert, Rebecca. 1997. *Like Bread on the Seder Plate: Jewish Lesbians and the Transformation of Tradition.* New York: Columbia University Press.

Beck, Evelyn Torton, ed. 1982. *Nice Jewish Girls: A Lesbian Anthology.* Watertown, MA: Persephone Press.

Biale, David. 1992. *Eros and the Jews: From Biblical Israel to Contemporary America.* New York: Basic Books.

Biale, Rachel. 1984. *Women and Jewish Law.* New York: Schocken Books.

Borowitz, Eugene. 1969. *Choosing a Sex Ethic: A Jewish Inquiry.* New York: Schocken Books for B'nai B'rith Hillel Foundations.

Boyarin, Daniel. 1997. *Unheroic Conduct: The Rise of Heterosexuality and the Jewish Man.* Los Angeles: University of California Press.

Brod, Harry, ed. 1988. *A Mensch among Men: Explorations in Jewish Masculinity.* Freedom, CA: Crossing Press.

Cohn Spiegel, Marcia. 1999. "Bibliography of Sources on Sexual and Domestic Violence in the Jewish Community." *Women in Judaism* 2, no. 1. http://www.utoronto.ca/wjudaism/index.html.

Cwik, Marc Steven. 1998. "Bibliography Covering the Agunah Problem, Jewish Marriage, Jewish Divorce, and Related Issues." *Women in Judaism* 1, no. 2. http://www.utoronto.ca/wjudaism/index.html.

Dorff, Elliot. 1998. *Matters of Life and Death: A Jewish Approach to Modern Medical Ethics.* Philadelphia, PA: Jewish Publication Society.

Goldman, Ari. 1992. *The Search for God at Harvard.* New York: Ballantine Books.

Gottlieb, Lynn. 1995. *She Who Dwells Within: A Feminist Vision of a Renewed Judaism.* San Francisco: HarperSan Francisco.

Graetz, Naomi. 1998. *Silence Is Deadly: Judaism Confronts Wifebeating.* Northvale: Jason Aronson Press.

Greenberg, Steven. 2002. "A Gay Orthodox Rabbi." Pp. 36–43 in David Shneer and Caryn Aviv, eds., *Queer Jews.* New York: Routledge Press.

Kaufman, Debra. 1991. *Rachel's Daughters: Newly Orthodox Jewish Women.* New Brunswick, NJ: Rutgers University Press.

Lappe, Benay. 2001. "Saying No in the Name of a Higher Yes." Pp. 197–234 in Rebecca Alpert et al., ed., *Lesbian Rabbis: The First Generation.* New Brunswick, NJ: Rutgers University Press.

Lerner, Michael. 1998. "Prostitution in Israel and the Triumph of the Market Mentality." *Tikkun* 13: 9.

Olyan, Saul. 1994. "And with a Male You Shall Not Lie the Lying Down of a Woman': On the Meaning and Significance of Leviticus 18:22 and 20:13." *Journal of the History of Sexuality* 5, no. 2: 179–206.

Plaskow, Judith. 1990. *Standing Again at Sinai: Judaism from a Feminist Perspective.* San Francisco: Harper and Row.

Prell, Riv-Ellen. 1999. *Fighting to Become Americans: Jews, Gender, and the Anxiety of Assimilation.* Boston, MA: Beacon Press.

Walzer, Lee. 2000. *Between Sodom and Eden: A Gay Journey through Today's Changing Israel.* New York: Columbia University Press.

# Chapter 7

# The Vatican
# and the Laity
### Diverging Paths in Catholic
### Understanding of Sexuality

*James C. Cavendish*

*Detail of* Marriage of Mary *(fresco, 1486–1490) by Domenico Ghirlandaio. The presence of Mary and the image of the Madonna have important influences on Catholics' relationships with God and with their spouses. (Sandro Vannini/Corbis)*

central theme in the recent social scientific literature on Catholicism and sexuality is the growing divergence between the official church teachings on sexuality and the beliefs and practices of the laity, particularly the U.S. Catholic laity (Fox 1995; D'Antonio et al. 1996, 2001; Dinges et al. 1998). If one were to examine official church teachings on various matters of sexuality, one would find a long list of "should nots"; the Church condemns premarital and extra-marital sex, masturbation, homosexual activity, the use of condoms and artificial birth control, sterilization, abortion, and in vitro fertilization. Catholic tradition considers these activities objectively or intrinsically evil, meaning that in each and every context, no matter the participants' intentions or circumstances, these activities are wrong. And the same kind of definitive judgment seems to permeate its teachings with regard to the role of women in the Church and society. Although the Catholic Church has made numerous attempts to affirm the roles of women, it has simultaneously denied women entry into positions of leadership, author-ity, and decision making, claiming in recent years, for instance, that the Church itself does not have the power to grant the sacrament of Holy Orders (ordination to ministry) to women.

At the same time that official church pronouncements appear to be unbending on a host of sexual matters, the Catholic faithful appear to be moving more and more in a direction opposite the official teachings. One need only look at the results of a variety of sociological studies over the past few decades to come to this conclusion. As early as the 1980s, for instance, George Gallup Jr. and Jim Costelli (1987) found U.S. Catholics dissenting from official teachings on a host of sexual issues, particularly birth control and premarital sex. In more recent years, William V. D'Antonio and his colleagues (1996, 2001) revealed that since the 1970s, there has been a clear and consistent consensus among Catholic laity in favor of the use of artificial contraceptives, and there are trends toward increasing acceptance of sexual relations outside marriage, the right to have an abortion under certain circumstances, and the ability of gay and lesbian individuals to make their own decisions about the morality of homosexual relations.

The growing divergence between official Church teachings and the beliefs and practices of the faithful is clearly in need of explanation. What is it that the Catholic Church teaches with respect to sexuality, how did such teachings originate, and why are such teachings losing credibility, particularly among the Catholic laity in the United States? As I will show, throughout much of the Catholic Church's history, beginning with the Patristic period in the second century of the Common Era and continuing until the Second Vatican Council in the 1960s, the Catholic Church's teachings with respect to sexuality have emphasized that the primary purpose of sexuality is the transmission of new life. This way of thinking about sexuality was understandable when the sole bases of the Church's teachings were revelation as found in scripture and a church tradition based on "natural law" (discussed further below). However, in recent decades, Catholic theologians and an educated Catholic laity have begun to supplement this foundation of Catholic moral teaching with the insights of the social and behavioral sciences. Although scripture and church tradition are still seen as valid sources of revelation, modern scholarship has begun to widen its approach to ethics, including sexual ethics. Now, more than ever before, Bible scholars are employing the historical critical method in their interpretation of Scripture, arguing that biblical teachings must be interpreted in light of the historical and cultural context in which they were written. Theologians, likewise, have begun to employ the insights of the modern sciences, particularly the social and behavioral sciences, but also biology, to understand the nature of human sexuality. Moreover, instead of relying solely on deductive logic, in which moral principles are deduced from certain premises about human nature, many contemporary theologians have begun to employ a more inductive logic, in which moral principles are derived through reflection on human experience.

In the sections that follow, I outline the general approach the Catholic Church has used in developing its moral teachings and highlight the key historical developments in the Church's teachings on issues of sexuality. I then attempt to explain the causes of the gap between the Vatican and the Catholic laity, particularly the U.S. Catholic laity, in regard to issues of sexuality. Doing so will entail touching on specific substantive areas of sexuality and gender—artificial birth control, homosexuality, mandatory celibacy, abortion, and the role of women—and showing the extent to which official church teachings have or have not influenced Catholic laity. Before turning to this line of analysis, however, it is first necessary to describe the Catholic understanding of God and the Church's approach to Mary, the Mother of God.

## CATHOLIC IMAGES OF GOD AND THE MADONNA

The Catholic Church, like the rest of Christianity, believes in the same God as does Judaism and hence is monotheistic. However, unlike Judaism, both Catholicism and other forms of Christianity profess that God revealed himself in the person of Jesus Christ, who was born of a virgin in the city of Bethlehem. For Catholics, God comprises three persons in one deity—Father (Creator), Son (Jesus, the Redeemer), and the Holy Spirit—who make up the Holy Trinity. Although both the Father and the Son are described using masculine terminology and are often referred to by masculine pronouns, neither the Father nor the Holy Spirit has a biological sex in the sense that Jesus did during his earthly incarnation. Just as Judaism uses the metaphor of marriage to describe the relationship between God and Israel, Catholicism uses the metaphor of marriage to describe the relationship between Jesus and the Church, but because Jesus was revealed as a man, he is necessarily symbolized by the groom and the Church by the bride.

This image of the divine, along with the accompanying metaphor of Jesus as the bridegroom of the Church, has had profound effects on Catholic understandings of sexuality and the role of women in the Church and society. Perhaps the most profound implication of the metaphor relates to the role of women, as the Church hierarchy uses the metaphor to justify the exclusion of women from the priesthood. If Jesus was a man and if priests act "in the person of Jesus," the Church argues, then it follows that priests must also be men in order to symbolize the Christ figure appropriately.

Although it is fair to say that the image of the divine among Catholics is overwhelmingly masculine, the Catholic Church does have a feminine image with which to relate. That image comes in the person of Mary, the Mother of God. Although Mary is not divine herself, she comes quite close to divinity for many Catholics. Like the saints, Mary is someone to whom Catholics can pray for divine intercession, and she is venerated on a host of feast days throughout the church year. Although there have been attempts in some circles of the contemporary Catholic Church to downplay the doctrines related to Mary and various forms of Marian piety (perhaps out of a desire to promote ecumenical relations), devotion to Mary, or what some have called "Marianismo," remains quite strong among Catholics in general and among women, Hispanic, and Polish Catholics in particular. Andrew Greeley (1990), a prominent Roman Catholic priest and sociologist of religion, suggests that the presence of Mary and the image of the Madonna have important influences on Catholics' relationships with God and with their spouses. The image of Mary, he argues, can increase Catholics' ability to espouse feminine images of God, which can, in turn, promote healthier human relationships. "The Mary Myth's powerful appeal," he states, "is to be found in the marvelous possibility that God loves us the way a mother loves her baby, the way all those Madonnas love all those little *bambini,* the way the Mother loves the Child in the crib scenes" (1990, 252).

## THE FOUNDATIONS OF CATHOLIC MORAL TEACHINGS

What distinguishes Catholicism from many other Christian denominations is that the Catholic Church has never based its teachings solely on the Bible. Instead, believing as it does that the Holy Spirit lives in and guides it, the Catholic Church bases its teachings on both Scripture and tradition—those teachings of the Church passed down through "apostolic succession" from Jesus through the apostles to subsequent generations of bishops and particularly to the bishop of Rome, or the pope. Because the Holy Spirit guides the Church in interpreting Scripture for each generation, the Church reasons that its accumulated teachings must themselves be viewed as a product and source of revelation, or those truths disclosed by God for human salvation. These accumulated teachings, although having their origins in scripture and their inspiration in the Holy Spirit, have been elaborated upon over the ages through an approach known as natural law, in which the Church uses human reason to reflect on human nature. By discerning the laws that govern human nature, the Church believes it can arrive at the will of God for humanity.

What exactly is natural law? Although the idea of a natural law—a set of universally binding moral precepts that can be discerned by human reason—appeared in Asian literature long before the advent of Western philosophy and Christianity, it was Western philosophers who, centuries before Christ's birth, elaborated the concept as a way of explaining the regular recurrence of events in the world. According to the Greek philosophers Plato and Aristotle, the universe had certain predictable patterns of motion, and the only way to explain these patterns was through the existence of some type of ordering principle or universal law that ruled the cosmos independently of human will. They argued further that because human beings were part of the cosmos, they were subject to this same law of nature. Thus, for the Greek philosophers, the morality of human conduct was determined by what was "in harmony with nature." If humans wanted to live a virtuous life, these philosophers believed, they would have to use their reason to discover those "objective principles and ideals" evident in the law of nature and then strive to conform to them (Wassmer 1967, 252).

With this foundation of natural law established by the ancient Greek philosophers, several Fathers of the early Christian Church, including St. Paul, St. John Chrysostom, St. Augustine, and St. Isidore of Seville, sought to wed the ideas of Greek philosophy with the laws revealed in the Christian scriptures. These early Christian writers described the interrelationship between natural and supernatural law by arguing that although natural law is, as the Greek philosophers argued, inscribed in the hearts of all humans, the law itself is derived ultimately from God. In other words, the law's content was to be found principally in the scriptures, particularly in the Ten Commandments, as well as the gospel teaching of the golden rule—do unto others as you would have them do to you.[1] Thus, although the Greek philosophers believed that natural law was discernable by reason, the early Christian Fathers argued that natural law was primarily accepted by faith as revealed in the Christian scriptures.

During the late Middle Ages, natural law reached its most influential and in many ways its final development in the work of St. Thomas Aquinas, who insisted on a new way of reconciling the Aristotelian doctrine of natural law with that of the early church fathers. Instead of rejecting Aristotle's view that natural law was discoverable by human reason, as some church fathers had done in emphasizing the authority of revealed truth in the Bible, Aquinas argued in his *Summa theologiae* that natural law (in the Aristotelian sense) and supernatural law (as revealed in Scripture) emanated from the same source and hence were complementary. Divine law, in other words, was discernable through the employment of both faith and reason. T. A. Wassmer (1967, 253) describes Aquinas's view thus:

> But Aquinas did not destroy the rational basis of the pagan, Aristotelian-Stoic doctrine of natural law by substituting the authority of supernatural law, in the sense of truth revealed in the Bible, in its place. Rather, to use a metaphor, he taught that the single coin of divine law is stamped on one side by the supernatural law of Judeo-Christian theology, accepted on faith, through grace, as the word of God, and on the other side by the natural law of philosophy, perceived by reason. Inasmuch as both laws emanate from a single source, they can never be in conflict.

The Catholic Church has retained much of Aquinas's understanding of natural law and to this day remains its most vigorous proponent. Among the chief features of the Church's natural law ethics are: (1) the law of nature exists apart from human will, has its origin in God, and is discoverable by reason; (2) the law of nature is composed of objective principles and ideals based on what is "in harmony with nature"; (3) that which is "in harmony with nature" is intrinsically morally good and should be pursued; (4) that which is "contrary to nature" is objectively morally evil and should be avoided; and (5) although the conscience of the individual is the source of personal moral responsibility, the individual's conscience cannot be a measure of what is intrinsically or objectively good or evil.

Today, the Catholic hierarchy appeals to this conception of natural law most frequently as a source for evaluating questions of personal morality, including the morality of individual sexual and medical actions. Some contemporary Catholic moral theologians (e.g., Curran 1985), however, have criticized this approach for being too narrow. By evaluating whether particular sexual actions are appropriate to human *biological* nature, they argue, natural law ethics has placed too much emphasis on the physical structure of the act and not enough on its personal, nonbiological components.

This natural law ethic of the Catholic Church, combined with the ethical codes derived from Scripture and from the Church's own tradition, form the basis of Catholic moral theology. The Catholic Church claims that it has the authoritative power to interpret this law and to provide correct guidance in recognizing its moral demands. Through its own tradition and teaching authority, the Catholic Church claims to provide the guidance necessary for an adequate understanding of natural law.

## THE DEVELOPMENT OF
## CATHOLIC MORAL TEACHINGS ON SEXUALITY

The Catholic Church's teachings with respect to sexuality are the product of a 3,000-year development incorporating a variety of religious, cultural, and philosophical influences. These teachings are based on the Bible, but they have also been influenced by the classical Greek philosophies of Plato, Aristotle, and the Stoics, as well as the early church fathers and the Scholastic theologians of the Middle Ages.

It is fair to say that throughout much of this history (at least from the second century onward), the Church has espoused a sexual morality that emphasizes the procreative purpose of human sexuality. Although sexuality could legitimately provide mutual support and serve as a cure for the passions, at least up until the 1960s these functions were regarded by the Church as being secondary to the primary purpose of procreation and the education of children. Where did this teaching originate?

Although neither the Old Testament (the Hebrew Bible) nor the New Testament provides a complete, systematic ethics of sexual conduct (Kosnik et al. 1977), early biblical teaching on sex-related matters emphasized the social importance of reproduction. According to Old Testament teaching, for instance, sexual intercourse is a way to preserve and propagate the chosen people of God, and the power of procreation is a sign of God's blessing. In this view, sexuality is regarded not only as a gift from God but also as the source of responsibility: exercising one's sexual powers for the purpose of procreation is responsible stewardship of the gift God has given to humanity.

New Testament writers, however, and particularly St. Paul, were influenced by philosophical currents other than those found in the Old Testament or in the words of Jesus (at least as they are recorded in the Gospels of Matthew, Mark, Luke, and John). This influence is clear because the Gospels themselves indicate that Jesus was largely indifferent with respect to issues of sexuality, making mention of the topic on only a few occasions and then only for the purpose of making a larger point.[2]

The classical Greek philosophies of Plato, Aristotle, and later the Stoics portrayed the human species as primarily rational. Because these classical philosophers maintained that what distinguished human beings from other animals was reason, it followed that what was essentially human and was most closely identified with the divine was rationality. This attitude led to a dualist philosophy of human nature that saw the body and the soul as two unequal aspects of humanity, with the body being inferior to the soul. Sexual desires, along with other human emotions such as fear and anger, were regarded as irrational aspects of humanity that needed regulation in order to free the mind. Correspondingly, the Stoics believed that sexual powers were to be used only for the rational purpose of procreation.

Although the New Testament continued the Hebrew Bible's emphasis on the procreative intent of sexuality, it conjoined it with the dualist philosophy of the Stoics. The use of sexuality simply to fulfill passions or desires was considered a sin, and consequently passions and desires themselves came to be seen pejoratively as a source of sin. The impact that these philosophical beliefs had on the early Christian community is clear. Not only did Christians adopt the notion that the primary purpose of sexual intercourse was the transmission of life, but in believing that the bodily passions were to be ardently controlled, they elevated the practices of virginity, abstinence, chastity, and celibacy to virtues. Although St. Paul himself rejected the thinking of the zealous ascetics of his time who regarded marriage itself as a sin, Paul did value celibacy above marriage. As Anthony Kosnik and his colleagues (1977, 29) point out:

> Ever since St. Paul, abstinence from sexual pleasure has been seen as an anticipation of that future fulfillment, and passionate desire for pleasure as contrary to holiness. As a result, Christian tradition and spirituality have tended to see a certain incompatibility between sexual pleasure and sanctity. Living a sex life somehow does not seem to fit into living the divine life fully.

Between the second and the fifth centuries C.E., the Fathers of the church, or the "Patristic writers," reaffirmed the teachings of the procreative function of sexuality and gave increasing priority to celibacy and virginity as Christian values. Sexual expression was reserved solely for the married, and even within marriage, it was reserved for those occasions in which new life could be created. In the third century, for instance, Clement of Alexandria recognized the apparent similarities between the Platonic and Pauline concepts of "natural" and began to teach what has become known as the "Alexandrian rule": "to have sex for any purpose other than to produce children is to violate nature" (Boswell 1980, 147). That meant, for example, that intercourse was forbidden among married individuals if the couple was barren or elderly, or if the woman was already pregnant. St. Augustine of Hippo (354–430 C.E.), a prominent philosopher of Roman antiquity who is often credited with fusing early Christianity with Greek philosophy, extended this thinking in arguing that the conjugal act is good insofar as it is directed toward the end to which it is naturally ordered—the procreation of children within marriage. For Augustine, even though sexual intercourse was itself good, any sexual pleasure that resulted from this conjugal act, no matter how unintentional, was a consequence of the original sin of Adam and Eve and therefore contained an element of evil. Sexual pleasure, in this way of thinking, was solely a consequence of the Fall, and neither the pre-Fall state of Adam and Eve nor the afterlife would be characterized by such pleasure. This way of viewing sexual pleasure, as linked to the original sin of Adam and Eve, has had a profound effect on Christian thinking about sexuality. Taken to its extreme, it suggests that it is better to have sex and *not* enjoy it than to have sex and enjoy it.

The teachings of St. Augustine and the early church fathers influenced the Church's beliefs and attitudes regarding sexuality throughout the early Middle Ages. The clearest evidence of the Church's teachings concerning particular acts of sexuality at this time can be found in what are called "penitentials"—handbooks used by priest-confessors to determine penances for various offenses. As in the previous period, procreation was seen as the primary function of sexual activity, and because of this, the penitentials prescribe heavy penances for those who deviated from this norm. As before, married couples were forbidden to engage in sexual relations if they were barren or elderly, or if the husband's wife was already pregnant. Although all forms of sexual expression outside marriage were deemed sinful, the gravest sins were those that, by violating the procreative intent of sexuality, were seen as "unnatural." Such practices included coitus interruptus (or withdrawal of the penis from the vagina before discharge to avoid insemination), other forms of contraception, anal sex, oral sex, and even certain positions during sexual intercourse (see Kosnik et al. 1977, 38–41).

The Scholastic theologians of the high Middle Ages, including St. Thomas Aquinas (1225–74 C.E.), carried on this tradition of the primacy of procreation in evaluating sexual activities. Because of a lack of scientific understanding of biology, reproductive theories of the era held that the male semen contained the active ingredients of human life and that women were mere receptacles of the seed implanted within them. Because these thinkers saw sex as having been designed by the natural order for the implantation of the male semen inside the female's body, they divided sexual sins into those that were "in accordance with nature" and those that were "contrary to nature." Perhaps the most startling aspect of the thinking of the Scholastic theologians found expression in the "moral manuals" used to train priests in the early modern period. These manuals held that sins that preserved the procreative intent of sex (such as fornication, adultery, incest, and rape) were less grievously sinful than sins that violated the procreative intent (e.g., masturbation, sodomy, homosexuality, and bestiality). As a consequence, the Church's moral teachings with respect to sexuality became very "act-centered," in that certain acts were deemed objectively evil solely on the basis of whether they allowed the semen to realize its human potential within a woman's body. Clearly, such an approach did not allow for person-oriented values, such as human intentions or the realization of mutual love, in the evaluation of sexual morality. Instead, the moral manuals simply listed the various practices that were regarded as seriously sinful; and just about any behavior that did not fulfill the procreative purpose was on the list (see Kosnik et al. 1977, 41–43).

In its most extreme form, therefore, Catholic moral theologians defined sexual acts as intrinsically evil if they violated the procreative intent; and in such cases nothing—not even human intentionality or the circumstances of the situation—could diminish the severity of the sin. What was defined as objectively or intrinsically evil was necessarily also subjectively sinful. In the late nineteenth century, Pope Leo XIII enshrined this approach to sexual morality by promoting the theology of St. Thomas Aquinas—one based on natural law theory—as *the* chief Catholic philosophical and theological framework.

With the advent of the modern period and particularly in the twentieth century, the Catholic Church's teachings on sexuality were largely a reaction to advances in modern science and to the positions taken by various
Protestant Christian denominations in response to those advances. In 1930,
the Anglican Church became the first major Christian denomination to
favor publicly the separation of the procreative and unitive ends of marriage
by permitting the use of artificial contraceptives "in those cases where there
is . . . a clearly felt moral obligation to limit or avoid parenthood, and where
there is a morally sound reason for avoiding complete abstinence"
(Proceedings of the 1930 Lambeth Conference, quoted in Kosnik et al.
1977, 45). In a reaction to the Anglican initiative, the Catholic Church,
under the leadership of Pope Pius XI, issued an encyclical on Christian marriage, *Casti Connubii.* In the encyclical, Pope Pius reaffirmed the Church's
historic teaching that sex was intended for procreation: "the conjugal act is
designed by its very nature for the generation of children."

Up until the 1960s, the Catholic Church's teaching on sexuality continued to emphasize the procreative goal of the act of sexual intercourse.
In the 1960s, however, the world's Catholic bishops were summoned to
Rome to embark on the historic Second Vatican Council (Vatican II), the
purpose of which was to enable the Church to speak more prophetically
to the modern world. In Vatican II's *Pastoral Constitution on the Church in
the Modern World,* promulgated in 1965, the church for the first time rejected the hierarchical ordering of the purposes of sexuality in which
"procreation" reigned supreme and insisted instead that the procreative
and unitive ends of sex be regarded as equally important. Because of this
new emphasis on the unitive purpose of sexuality, a new sexual morality
was endorsed, which called for specific sexual practices to be evaluated
not only in terms of whether the act remained open to the transmission
of life but also in terms of whether it served to unify the couple and
thereby integrate the human community.

With Vatican II, therefore, the seeds for a new approach to Catholic
morality—one that showed a new appreciation of the personal dimension
of human sexuality—were sown. Many contemporary Catholic theologians, fueled by the teachings of Vatican II, felt legitimated in adopting
an approach to morality that based judgments of sexual practices on the
context and circumstances of an individual's life, rather than simply on
whether the practice fulfilled its procreative purpose. They judged sexual
expression more broadly in terms of its potential to build relationships
and communities. As Kosnik and colleagues (1977, 63) state:

[In this approach] the sex drive in humans is no longer merely a blind impulse to union of the genders so that the incompleteness of each can be mutually completed as is required biologically for reproduction. Rather it is a drive toward personal encounter, a reaching out from aloneness to "intercoursing" one's life with that of the other. Understood this way, sexuality transcends the male-female differentiation and the notion of complementarity based on gender. In its place is the complementarity of person, the potential of one bodily existence to respond to the yearning of another for escape from isolation and solipsistic existence.

At the same time that Catholic theologians and laity were beginning to adopt this new approach to sexual morality, the Vatican seemed, in some respects, to backpedal on its position. While maintaining that the procreative and unitive ends of sex were equally important, in July 1968 Pope Paul VI issued his encyclical *Humanae Vitae,* which reaffirmed the position of earlier popes. The basis for a divergence in attitudes had been laid.

## EXPLAINING THE DIVERGENCE

Perhaps what best explains the growing divergence between the Vatican and laity on attitudes of human sexuality is the differing bases used by these parties in developing their sexual ethics and moral reasoning. Over the last several centuries, the magisterium (or teaching authority) of the Catholic Church has based its moral reasoning on natural law ethics that began with certain principles about humanity's individual and social nature and then proceeded deductively to arrive at truths with respect to certain sexual behaviors. If, according to natural law, human sexuality had as one of its chief purposes the transmission of new life, then it followed logically that any behaviors that interfered with this function were necessarily objectively evil acts. Notice here that natural law ethics, by beginning with a premise about humanity's nature and deductively arriving at moral principles, does not take into account the actual behavior of people as observed by sociologists and experienced by the laity.

At odds with this particular approach to sexual ethics is the more inductive approach used by some contemporary Catholic theologians and embraced by a wide spectrum of the Catholic laity. This approach begins with human experience as one of the chief sources of normative behavior and revelation. In reflecting on experience, it asks the questions: "Does this or that sexual behavior appear to contribute to, or detract from, the growth of a creative and integrated personality? Does this or that sexual behavior contribute to, or detract from, the love shared by the individuals involved?" Proponents of this approach believe that answers to these questions are essential to developing a truly sound sexual ethics.

Added to these differing bases of moral reasoning are the various cultural and technological forces to which the Catholic laity has been exposed to during the twentieth century. Advances in the behavioral and social sciences led to new understandings of human sexuality; scientific breakthroughs made artificial birth control available to a wider spectrum of the population; the sexual revolution of the 1960s promoted greater acceptance of nontraditional and less restricted expressions of sexuality; and theological developments led to the rejection of act-centered moralities and the adoption of a more person-oriented approach to sexual matters. To the Catholic laity of the late twentieth century, therefore, it mattered less whether sexuality remained open to the transmission of life than whether it served to unify the couple in Christian love and contributed to the growth and development of the person.

These factors clearly help explain the divergence of attitudes on certain issues of sexuality. In respect to some issues, as we shall see, this divergence was first evident in the years following the release of Pope Paul VI's encyclical, *Humanae Vitae.*

### Birth Control

In the years after Pope Paul VI issued *Humanae Vitae,* which upheld the Church's teachings against artificial contraception, it was clear that the attitudes and practices of the Catholic laity had already begun to diverge sharply from official church teaching. By the late 1960s, many Catholic theologians and educated Catholic laity had begun to adopt the call of Vatican II for a more person-centered approach to sexual morality. However, what was found in *Humanae Vitae,* its critics contended, was a specifically act-centered morality that dictated that each and every act of sexuality be open to the transmission of life.

In the years after the encyclical's promulgation, numerous priests, theologians, and laity began to voice their opposition, and survey research showed that the Catholic laity were beginning to withdraw their support from the institutional church. D'Antonio and his colleagues (1996,

49–52), for instance, report that in the years immediately following *Humanae Vitae*, 65 percent of the U.S. Catholic laity said it was possible to practice artificial birth control and still be a good Catholic. By 1993, that number had climbed to 73 percent. The noted priest and sociologist Andrew Greeley also found that both Mass attendance and contributions among the Catholic laity plummeted in the years immediately following *Humanae Vitae* (Greeley 1989). Greeley noted that, beginning in 1969, the year after Pope Paul VI issued the encyclical, "about a third of regular Catholic churchgoers who rejected the birth control teaching (only 15 percent of Catholics accept it) . . . were so offended by the birth control decision that they stopped going to church regularly" (1989, 52). Of the Catholics surveyed in 1999 by D'Antonio and his colleagues (2001, 76), only 10 percent of respondents indicated that Church leaders alone had the authority to judge the morality of contraceptive birth control.

### Homosexuality

According to official church teaching, homosexual orientation, to the degree that it is not freely chosen, is not a sin; homosexual activities, however, are "contrary to nature" and hence "intrinsically evil" because they do not fulfill the procreative purpose of sex. This position is not surprising, given the Catholic Church's history of teachings with respect to judging sin and the morality of sexual practices. According to the Church, in order for something to be sinful, the individual must be aware that it is a sin and fully assent to doing it anyway. Clearly, simply being gay, lesbian, or bisexual does not meet these criteria because there is no choice, no conscious will to do something, involved.

Although this is the Church's current teaching with respect to homosexuality, its approach to this issue has been far from consistent. Historian John Boswell, in his influential book *Christianity, Social Tolerance, and Homosexuality* (1980), presents an account of the history of attitudes toward homosexuality in the Christian West, in which he reveals that the Catholic Church's past relationship with its homosexual members has, at times, been somewhat amicable. Basing his research on the analysis of a variety of legal, literary, theological, and scientific texts spanning the millennium between early Christianity and the late Middle Ages, Boswell finds that the Church's teachings with respect to homosexuality were more a response to—rather than a cause of—the intolerant attitudes toward homosexuals that prevailed during certain periods of the Middle Ages.

According to Boswell, throughout much of the early Christian era and the early Middle Ages (i.e., from 325 C.E. to the eleventh century), when society was fairly tolerant of homosexual activity, the Church had relatively little to say about homosexuality, indicating, in Boswell's estimation, a certain "indifference . . . toward gay people" (1980, 210).[3] Even when Europe experienced a revival of its urban centers in the twelfth century—a revival that sparked an outburst of Christian gay literature celebrating homosexual relations—church authorities repeatedly refused to impose penalties for homosexual behavior. It was not until the Third Lateran Council of 1179 that the Church imposed a sanction for homosexual acts—namely, excommunication. Interestingly, this decision came during a period in which the Crusades had ignited feelings of xenophobia throughout Europe. The council's judgment against homosexual acts, Boswell argues, must therefore be seen in the context of growing intolerance of all forms of noncomformity (1980, 277). After all, the council imposed sanctions not only against those committing homosexual acts but also against moneylenders, heretics, Jews, Muslims, and mercenaries. What some might take as an advance in moral theology was in actuality a response to the more general climate of intolerance that pervaded the Christian West in the wake of the Crusades.

It is unsurprising, therefore, that when the Church began its synthesis of theology and canon law in the middle of the thirteenth century—a synthesis that would define Catholic moral teaching until well into the twentieth century—it defined homosexual behavior, along with masturbation, intercourse with animals, and nonprocreative heterosexual relations, as "vices against nature."

Finally, in the 1970s, when the behavioral sciences expressed virtual agreement that homosexuality was a fixed "orientation" and hence not freely chosen, the Vatican showed its acceptance of this view in the 1975 *Declaration on Certain Questions Concerning Sexual Ethics.* This document acknowledged the distinction between a "transitory" homosexual orientation and a "definitive" homosexual orientation, a distinction that allowed the Church to declare homosexual activity sinful while simultaneously upholding the dignity of the homosexual as a person. Although the document called for respect of homosexuals as persons, it simultaneously argued that "homosexual acts are intrinsically disordered and can in no case be approved of," thereby challenging the argument that homosexual relations could be justified for those whose "tendency is natural" and who desired a "sincere communion of life and love analogous to marriage."

It seemed natural to assume that since the Vatican accepted the position of the behavioral sciences—namely, that homosexuality was an "orientation" and not a choice—it would adopt a position of total neutrality with respect to the condition of homosexuality itself. This, however, did not happen. In 1986, Pope John Paul II issued his first major statement on homosexuality, *Letter to All Catholic Bishops on the Pastoral Care of Homosexual Persons,* in which he stated that because the orientation is a "more or less strong tendency ordered toward an intrinsic moral evil, . . . the inclination itself must be seen as an objective disorder," even though it was not, in itself, sinful. Many gay and lesbian Catholics felt betrayed by this statement; they took offense at being called "objectively disordered."

Here, as with other issues of human sexuality, it appears that the Vatican is losing ground to the behavioral sciences and revisionist Catholic theologians in its influence over the beliefs and practices of the Catholic laity. Although attitudes of the general population regarding homosexuality remain highly negative, there is a trend among Catholics, as in the U.S. population more broadly, toward increased acceptance. Thomas C. Fox (1995, 150) states:

> Shortly after the publication of the 1986 letter, polls conducted by *Time* magazine and the *Los Angeles Times* indicated that 68 and 67 percent of Catholics, respectively, agreed with the teaching that homogenital acts are morally wrong. Two years later, however, after much public discussion generated by the letter, Catholic support of church teaching banning all homosexual behavior had dropped to 58 percent.

Part of the decline may be attributable to the greater visibility of gays and lesbians in society, particularly gays and lesbians who are in committed relationships. In 1992, according to D'Antonio and his colleagues, 45 percent of Catholics said that "sex relations between gay and lesbian persons in a committed relationship can be morally acceptable" (1996, 56). These same researchers find that fewer and fewer Catholics today believe that moral authority regarding homosexual behavior lies with church leaders alone: 32 percent of U.S. Catholics reported in 1987 that church leaders had the authority to judge the morality of homosexual behavior, but that figure dropped to 26 percent in 1993 and 20 percent in 1999 (D'Antonio et al. 2001). A full 80 percent of U.S. Catholics today believe that moral authority on issues of homosexual activity rests, at least in part, with the individuals involved.

Added to this increasing acceptance of homosexual relationships among the Catholic laity has been the emergence of a gay and lesbian Catholic movement, Dignity/USA, which currently has about seventy-five chapters throughout the United States and approximately 2,700 members. Founded in 1969, Dignity/USA is a lay organization that promotes "self acceptance and dignity within individual gay, lesbian, bisexual and transgendered Catholics" (Dignity Mission Statement) and advocates social change in the Church on issues relating to sexual minorities. Ever since the Vatican's release of the 1986 letter reaffirming its traditional teachings on homosexuality, members of Dignity have become more vocal in their belief that gay, lesbian, bisexual, and transgendered Catholics can express their sexuality in a manner consonant with Christ's teachings (Loseke and Cavendish 2001). These changes in lay Catholic attitudes over the last few decades provide clear evidence that Catholics believe, as do many prominent Catholic theologians, that to approach the issue of homosexuality from an act-centered moral framework (that views certain acts as morally evil in and of themselves) overlooks the context of human relationships.

Although surveys of Catholic attitudes and the presence of groups like Dignity/USA suggest growing acceptance of homosexuality and homosexual relationships among U.S. Catholics in general, the recent and recurring scandals over sexual misconduct and child sexual abuse by Catholic priests may cause some groups of Catholics to rethink their position on homosexuality. In January 2002, the notorious cases of Fathers John J. Geoghan's and Paul Shanley's abuse of more than 100 children and teenagers in the Boston Archdiocese focused the media spotlight on the problem of "pedophile priests" throughout the United States. The quantity and depth of media coverage on this issue, which continued unabated for over six months and involved allegations against as many as 250 priests, was unprecedented and pressured the U.S. Catholic bishops to adopt a zero-tolerance policy against church personnel accused of sexual abuse of minors at their June 2002 meeting. As a result of the scandal and the media focus on cases of same-sex abuse by priests, some church officials, including the Vatican's spokesperson, began to interpret the scandal as a "gay menace," suggesting that the problem stems from the high number of gay men in the priesthood (Wills 2002). Many lay Catholic groups, including Dignity/USA, vehemently condemned this scapegoating strategy by church officials, pointing out that homosexuality and pedophilia are not the same thing and are not even empirically linked. They have also questioned the accuracy of media accounts, which tended to focus on the more sensational instances of same-sex abuse, when abuse of female minors has also been alleged. Others have accepted the "gay menace" interpretation, thinking that homosexuality somehow leads to child molestation and calling for a ban of gays from seminaries. To the bishops' credit, the resolution adopted at their June 2002 meeting made no mention of a "problem" of homosexuality in the priesthood and instead framed the issue as one of sexual abuse and violation of trust.

At the same time that some conservatives in the Catholic Church were blaming the "priest pedophilia" scandals on the prevalence of gays in the seminary and priesthood, some liberals were arriving at an entirely different explanation of the problem—mandatory celibacy. It is just one more issue over which many Catholic laity disagree sharply with the church hierarchy.

## Mandatory Celibacy

Celibacy, or abstinence from all sexual contact, has always been valued by the Catholic Church. The New Testament presents clear and consistent teachings that celibacy is the most desirable response to human eroticism, and the Catholic Church continues to teach that celibacy comes as a gift from God and is given to relatively few. For much of the Church's history, though, celibacy was optional for clergy. The earliest Christian communities contained both married and unmarried clergy, and it was not until after the early Christian period that monks began to show their commitment to God by living as celibates in monasteries.

The most strenuous efforts to enforce clerical celibacy did not come until the twelfth century, when Pope Leo IX became the first pope to take decisive action against the marriage of clergy. During the First Lateran Council of 1123, Pope Leo declared all clerical marriages in the Church invalid (Boswell 1980, 216). From that time forward, commitment to celibacy has been required of all Catholic clergy in the Western (Latin rite) tradition and all religious men and women who have committed their lives to the Church by joining religious orders. The Church teaches that the value of celibacy rests in its ability to free men and women from the obligations of family life so they can devote their lives more fully to the service of God and others.

Although celibacy clearly retains some value today, especially when viewed as a countercultural statement in a society that appears sex-crazed, the practice of mandatory celibacy for Catholic priests has come under increasing attack. Not only do the individuals who practice celibacy find it increasingly difficult in today's society, but many Catholics see it as one of the major causes of the current priest shortage in the U.S. Catholic Church. Richard A. Schoenherr and Lawrence A. Young (1993) report that because the number of ordained priests in the United States has been falling steadily since the 1970s—through both resignations and decreasing seminary enrollments—the Church is facing a staggering loss of priests, and there is little chance of reversing the trend in the near future. Furthermore, there is no doubt that this trend is caused by the issue of celibacy. Fox (1995, 169), for instance, reports that of the thousands of Catholic priests who left their ministries in the 1960s, approximately nine out of ten eventually married. In proposing a solution to the priest shortage, Schoenherr and Young state that "the ordination of married men and eventually of women would preserve the priesthood and along with it both the eucharistic tradition and the mechanisms of control over the central belief system and modes of worship" (1993, 354).

It seems that many U.S. Catholics, and particularly those in the younger generations, would agree with this assessment. In a recent study of young adult Catholics, Dean R. Hoge and his colleagues find that only 27 percent of respondents indicated that priestly celibacy was "essential" to their "vision of what the Catholic faith is" (2001, 199, 201). Similar sentiments can be seen in the pronouncements of a group called CORPUS: The National Association for an Inclusive Priesthood, which since its founding in 1974 has drawn together resigned priests and their wives to fight against mandatory celibacy.

Discontent with mandatory celibacy for priests and those who have taken vows of religious life appears to have grown even more widespread in the wake of the 2002 media accounts of sexual abuse of children and teenagers by clergy. Some Catholic liberals have gone so far as to suggest that the requirement of celibacy, which prevents the expression of what society regards as an essential ingredient of human fulfillment, may itself lead to arrested psychosexual development among the clergy, which may, in turn, result in irresponsible sexual behavior. Although numerous commentators have discounted this presumed link between mandatory celibacy and sexual abuse of children and teenagers (see Eberstadt 2002), there is no question that these "priest pedophilia" scandals have heightened U.S. Catholics' reservations about the celibacy requirement and the hierarchical decision-making processes on which it is based. One concrete indicator of growing lay discontent has been the emergence in the Boston Archdiocese of a grassroots church reform advocacy group, the Voice of the Faithful, which is committed to rebuilding the Church from within; its motto is "Keep the Faith, Change the Church." Although the group has not yet taken positions on a married priesthood or women's ordination, it has called for greater lay participation in decision making and an end to the hierarchy's "clericalism" and "unbridled addiction to power," which appeared to be at the root of the sex abuse crisis. Within a short time, the group has grown to include 19,000 members in twenty-two nations (Colbert 2002).

### *Abortion*

Volumes have been written on the Catholic Church's official position on abortion and the influence it has attempted to have on Catholic laity and U.S. society. Ever since the 1973 court ruling in *Roe v. Wade,* which legalized abortion in the United States, the Vatican and U.S. Catholic bishops have fought aggressively for the "rights of the unborn" by taking a stance in favor of a constitutional amendment to prohibit abortion during any stage of pregnancy. The Church's position is that human life is present from the moment of conception, and wherever there is human life, there must also be protection and dignity.

Not so well known, however, is that the Church's teachings have not always been so clear and straightforward. For many centuries, from at least the fourth century to the early modern period, church leaders lacked agreement about when human life began, or when the soul entered the body of the fetus (Callahan 1970, 410–413). Beginning in the fourth century, we have indication that some theologians and philosophers, including St. Augustine, were making a distinction between the "formed" fetus and the "unformed" fetus. The fetus was said to be "formed" when the embryo became a human being (through a process referred to variously as "hominization," "animation," or "ensoulment"). According to Augustine and later Aquinas, because the embryo in its earliest stages was not yet formed, practicing abortion during these stages (within forty days of conception for boys and eighty days for girls) did not constitute the killing of a human life and therefore was not sinful. It was not until the eighteenth century, with the establishment of the Immaculate Conception of Mary as a universal feast day (venerating Mary's sinless soul at the moment of her conception) that acceptance of the distinction between the "formed" and the "unformed" fetus began to break down and attention was focused on the moment of conception. Finally, in 1869, Pope Pius IX declared that abortion at any stage of pregnancy was homicide, a teaching that received indirect support from the 1875 scientific discovery that a fetus was formed from the union of the male's sperm with the female's ovum.

Even though the Catholic Church hierarchy has become, as a consequence, one of the most ardent critics of abortion rights in the twentieth century, survey research shows that the Catholic laity in the United States differ little from other U.S. citizens in their practices and beliefs regarding abortion. Like the rest of the U.S. population, most Catholics are opposed to "abortion on demand," but the majority believes that abortion should be available in cases in which pregnancy resulted from incest or rape or the mother's life is in jeopardy.

Furthermore, the gap between the Catholic hierarchy and laity with respect to attitudes on abortion is widening. Citing Gallup surveys, Fox (1995, 123) shows that in 1987, 45 percent of Catholics said the Church's opposition to abortion had strengthened their faith, but in 1993, only 37 percent gave that response. Using the same survey data, D'Antonio and colleagues (1996, 62) reveal that only 39 percent of Catholics in 1987 said that a person could be "a good Catholic without obeying the Church's teaching regarding abortion," but by 1993, that number had grown to 56 percent. Moreover, 70 percent of Catholics, they find, believe Catholics can in good conscience vote for political candidates who support legal abortion.

## The Role of Women

Perhaps the most significant teaching of the Catholic Church with regard to the role and status of women is that of the "complementarity of the sexes"—that is, different but complementary roles for men and women. Although modern societies have made great strides in recognizing the equality of women, numerous religious institutions, including the Catholic Church, are less likely to think in terms of "equality of the sexes" than "complementarity between the sexes." Indeed, the Catholic Church officially teaches that although women are equal to men, they are different by nature. Much of this, at least for the Catholic Church, is tied up with a symbolic system that centers around a male Christ figure. For centuries, the Catholic Church has used the metaphor of a groom's relationship to his bride to describe Christ's relationship to the Church. If Jesus is the groom, so the reasoning goes, then those who represent Christ to the Church—that is, its priests—must also be male. To believe otherwise, the Vatican argues, is to deny not only this symbolic structure based on complementarity but also Christ's will in selecting only men to be his disciples.

Obviously, the hierarchy's promotion of the idea of complementarity is incompatible with modern feminists' insistence that women's roles not be based on their sexual nature alone. One of the leading problems that the notion of complementarity faces in today's society is that complementary roles, as practiced by the Church, have almost always meant unequal roles. Why, for instance, if ordination to the priesthood is limited to men, must ordination also be a prerequisite for holding positions of power in the Church? Could we not have complementarity—different roles for the sexes—in which positions of power are distributed equally between men and women or distributed in such a way that women have more power? Why not, for example, teach that only men can be priests but that only women can be bishops, cardinals, or the pope? Must all positions of power be restricted to men? The pope's reaction to this line of thinking is to argue that no one should look at the priesthood as an office of power because priests are "called to serve, not to be served." The reality in the Church, however, is that ordination is the only path to positions of decision making in the Catholic Church.

Although the Vatican has recently stated that there should be no more discussion of the ordination of women (Pope John Paul II's 1993 document *Ordinatio Sacerdotalis*), U.S. Catholics in general and Catholic women in particular show signs of increasing opposition to this stance. A 1992 Gallup poll found that two thirds of U.S. Catholics believed women should be ordained, an increase of 20 percentage points over a similar poll conducted in 1985 (Fox 1995, 207). The emergence of numerous groups of laywomen in opposition to the hierarchy suggests growing dissatisfaction among women in particular. Mary Fainsod Katzenstein (1998), for instance, has recently documented the ways in which Catholic feminists are finding support and voice through a variety of organizations, including the Women's Ordination Conference, the Leadership Conference of Women Religious, the National Assembly of Religious Women, Las Hermanas (a Hispanic Catholic women's group), the National Coalition of American Nuns, Call to Action, and many others.

## CONCLUSION

Not only is there a growing divergence of practice and opinion between the Catholic laity and the church hierarchy on issues of sexuality, but it is not at all clear that the paths taken by these parties will come together any time soon. If anything, it appears that the gap between the two will continue to widen in the foreseeable future. As recent survey research has illustrated, "a growing majority of Catholics look to their own conscience, rather than to the magisterium [i.e., the Catholic hierarchy], as the locus of moral authority. . . . [They] distinguish between core features of their religion (the Sacraments, the Resurrection, . . .), about which they look to the magisterium, and sexual issues that are more peripheral, about which they look more to their own conscience" (D'Antonio et al. 2001, 85–86).

Why might the gap between the Catholic laity and the church hierarchy be expected to grow in the future? The answer to this question rests in the fact that neither the Catholic laity nor the church hierarchy shows signs of relinquishing its claim as moral arbiter on issues of sexual morality. At the same time that the laity has accepted Vatican II's call, as expressed in the *Pastoral Constitution on the Church in the Modern World,* for a more person-centered rather than act-centered approach to sexual morality, the Vatican has become more committed than ever to a natural law ethics that judges all sexual practices in terms of their openness to the transmission of life. Because the Vatican has opted for the act-centered morality of its own natural law tradition, for it to give way to the laity or revisionist theologians on any one of the sexual issues outlined above would be tantamount to giving up its own moral tradition.

What might this divergence in practice and opinion and the seemingly growing intransigence of the Catholic hierarchy mean for the long-term sustainability of the U.S. Catholic Church? The answer to this question has yet to be revealed. However, we do know, based on the scholarship of Andrew Greeley (1990), that many Catholics—even those who believe they have received shabby treatment by the hierarchy—opt to remain Catholic and to participate actively in their churches despite the official church's stance on the central issues of sexuality.

## NOTES

1.  It is important to note, however, that "natural law" itself does not have a basis in scripture. The word "nature" does not appear in the Gospels, suggesting that it was not a concern of Jesus, and it appears only twice in the Pauline writings, where it is used with an entirely different meaning (see Boswell 1980, 145–146).

2.  For instance, Jesus never condemned the use of sexuality among the unmarried, said nothing whatsoever about homosexual activity, and never

talked about the procreative intent of marriage. Moreover, although Jesus does emphasize the importance of fidelity and permanence in marriage, it is interesting to note that when he was confronted with adulterers, he recommended no punishment (Boswell 1980, 114).

3. According to Boswell, the only early Christian writer to comment at length on homosexuality was Saint John Chrysostom, whose objections to homosexuality, Boswell persuasively argues, have more to do with gender roles than with the activity itself. What was deplorable about homosexual activity to Chrysostom was the fact that, in the act, one of the male partners allows his body to be used "as that of a woman" (Boswell 1980, 157). By concentrating so exclusively on male homosexual activity (and not at all on female homosexuality) and suggesting that the true obscenity is committed by the passive party, Chrysostom was demonstrating his "mysogynistic revulsion from males doing anything 'feminine,'" rather than articulating a well thought out approach to sexual morality (Boswell 1980, 157–158). Even St. Augustine, who is most credited for developing a system of sexual morality in the early Christian period, addresses his treatises only to heterosexual intercourse (Boswell 1980, 161).

## REFERENCES

Boswell, John. 1980. *Christianity, Social Tolerance, and Homosexuality: Gay People in Western Europe from the Beginning of the Christian Era to the Fourteenth Century.* Chicago: University of Chicago Press.

Callahan, Daniel. 1970. *Abortion: Law, Choice, and Morality.* New York: Macmillan.

Colbert, Chuck. 2002. "4,000 Meet to Give Laity a Voice." *National Catholic Reporter,* August 2, pp. 3–4.

Curran, Charles E. 1985. *Directions in Fundamental Moral Theology.* Notre Dame, IN: University of Notre Dame Press.

D'Antonio, William V., James D. Davidson, Dean R. Hoge, and Katherine Meyer. 2001. *American Catholics: Gender, Generation, and Commitment.* Walnut Creek, CA: Altamira Press.

D'Antonio, William V., James D. Davidson, Dean R. Hoge, and Ruth A. Wallace. 1996. *Laity: American and Catholic: Transforming the Church.* Kansas City, MO: Sheed and Ward.

Dinges, William, Dean R. Hoge, Mary Johnson, and Juan L. Gonzales Jr. 1998. "A Faith Loosely Held: The Institutional Allegiance of Young Catholics." *Commonweal,* July 17, pp. 13–18.

Eberstadt, Mary. 2002. "The Elephant in the Sacristy." *Weekly Standard.* http://24.104.35.12/Content/Public/Articles/000/000/001/344fsdzu.asp, June 17.

Fox, Thomas C. 1995. *Sexuality and Catholicism.* New York: George Braziller.

Gallup, George, Jr., and Jim Costelli. 1987. *The American Catholic People: Their Beliefs, Practices, and Values.* Garden City, NY: Doubleday.

Greeley, Andrew M. 1989. *Religious Change in America.* Cambridge, MA: Harvard University Press.

———. 1990. *The Catholic Myth: The Behavior and Beliefs of American Catholics.* New York: Charles Scribner's Sons.

Hoge, Dean R., William D. Dinges, Mary Johnson, and Juan L. Gonzales. 2001. *Young Adult Catholics: Religion in the Culture of Choice.* Notre Dame, IN: University of Notre Dame Press.

Katzenstein, Mary Fainsod. 1998. *Faithful and Fearless: Moving Feminist Protest inside the Church and Military.* Princeton, NJ: Princeton University Press.

Kosnik, Anthony, William Carroll, Agnes Cunningham, Ronald Modras, and James Schulte. 1977. *Human Sexuality: New Directions in American Catholic Thought.* A study commissioned by the Catholic Theological Society of America. New York: Paulist Press.

Loseke, Donileen R., and James C. Cavendish. 2001. "Producing Institutional Selves: Rhetorically Constructing the Dignity of Sexually Marginalized Catholics." *Social Psychology Quarterly* 64, no. 4: 347–362.

Schoenherr, Richard A., and Lawrence A. Young. 1993. *Full Pews and Empty Altars: Demographics of the Priest Shortage in the United States Catholic Dioceses.* Madison: University of Wisconsin Press.

Wassmer, T. A. 1967. "Natural Law." Pp. 251–262 of the *New Catholic Encyclopedia.* Vol. 10. Washington, DC: Catholic University of America.

Wills, Garry. 2002. "Priests and Boys." *New York Review of Books,* June 13, pp. 10–13.

# Chapter 8

# Varieties of Interpretations
## Protestantism and Sexuality

*Amy DeRogatis*

*Adam, behind tree, is tempted by Eve with apples. Protestants have looked to the biblical creation stories to understand the meaning and purpose of sexuality, as well as the characteristics and responsibilities of men and women living in a "fallen state." (Library of Congress)*

Protestantism developed in sixteenth-century Europe as a reform movement within Christianity. Today it is a branch of worldwide Christianity. With its dual emphases on the Bible as the ultimate source of authority and on the individual believer's ability to read and interpret Scripture, Protestantism supports a range of beliefs and practices.

Historically, Protestants have resolved theological differences by dividing themselves into "denominations." This process has been accelerated in recent years. In the United States, for example, of the estimated 1,600 Protestant denominations, 800 have formed in the last twenty-five years. Although theological distinctions separate denominations, Protestants now generally categorize themselves as either mainline (liberal) or evangelical (conservative). Mainline Protestants generally hold a more interpretive view of Scripture and tend to focus on the social meaning of Protestantism, whereas evangelical Protestants generally adopt a more literal reading of scripture and emphasize the individual believer's conversion experience and personal morality.

As a group, Protestants hold a variety of views on sexuality. It is not the case, however, that liberal Protestants endorse human sexuality and conservative Protestants condemn it. For most Protestants, sex is a positive and crucial aspect of human life. Still, these two groups divide over the question of how sexuality relates to the family, reproduction, and social order, and scriptural interpretation lies at the core of this divergence.

Protestants have traditionally defined themselves against Catholic Christians, primarily because the movement began as a reform of the sixteenth-century Roman Catholic Church. Protestants sought to reform what they perceived to be unnecessary ritual practices and the corruption of clerical offices; both features of Catholicism that the Protestant reformers maintained separated believers from God. One of the principal areas of reform of the Catholic Church involved human sexuality—specifically, the practice of celibacy. Early and medieval Christians almost uniformly agreed that religious perfection came through celibacy. Celibate priests and nuns were "married" to Christ. Catholic Church fathers connected celibacy to clerical office, maleness, and spiritual maturity. Women, always connected to Eve's transgression and sexuality, could choose a celibate life, but they could not hold male-defined clerical roles (such as priest, bishop, or pope) outside the convent's walls. Despite the perceived difference between male and female spiritual maturity, celibacy, not marriage, remained the ideal for all believers.

In fact, it was not until the thirteenth century that the Catholic Church declared marriage a sacrament. Prior to that time, marriage was a civil union, viewed primarily as a family concern. At the same time that marriage became a sacrament, Catholic canon law codified "natural" and "unnatural" sexual behavior. "Sins against nature" (nonprocreative sex, including homosexuality) and sexual activity outside heterosexual marriage were deemed "unnatural" and criminal. Sexuality within marriage was legitimate as long as its primary function was procreation. The sixteenth-century reformers embraced the Catholic Church's position on "natural" and "unnatural" sexual activity but rejected celibacy as a prerequisite for clerical office. Protestants instead emphasized the divinely ordained role of procreative sex within heterosexual marriage. Thus, although Protestants and Catholics split over the connection between celibacy and spiritual maturity, they remained united around notions of "natural" sexual activity.

Protestants described spiritual union with Christ as a "marriage" between the soul as "bride" and Christ as "bridegroom," but this concept did not lesson their commitment to marriages in this world. The reformers held that the family was a microcosm of the larger relationship between Christ and the faithful. The family, therefore, became the primary arena for religious activity and instruction, with the father as its spiritual head. Although Protestants affirmed spiritual equality through the priesthood of all believers, the family was not necessarily conceived of as an egalitarian space. "Godly households" placed fathers as rulers, mothers as helpmates, and children as subjects of instruction and discipline. Sexuality within marriage led to the reproduction of such households, inscribing "God's design" on the world.

For scriptural guidance on the meaning and moral significance of human sexuality, Protestants looked to both the Hebrew Bible and the New Testament. Beginning with the creation stories of the first man and woman found in the book of Genesis, Jewish and Christian scriptures provided a divine blueprint for how Christian men and women should act in the world. There is a significant difference in the two biblical accounts of creation, a difference that holds theological as well as social ramifications for Protestantism. The first story (Gen. 1:1–2:4) tells of God's simultaneous creation of the first man and the first woman with the command to be fruitful and multiply. In the second, more elaborate creation account (Gen. 2:4–3), God creates the first woman, "Eve," from the body of the first man, "Adam." In this story, a snake tempts the woman and tricks the couple into disobeying God, and God responds by meting out severe punishments: the man and his descendents will forever toil, and the woman and her descendents must suffer pain in childbirth. The first humans, especially Eve, are responsible for humanity's fall from God's grace. Protestants throughout the ages have looked to these two creation stories to understand the meaning and purpose of sexuality, as well as the characteristics and responsibilities of men and women living in a "fallen" state.

The two prominent leaders of the Reformation, Martin Luther and John Calvin, both went back to the Genesis stories to understand human sexuality and the proper relationship between men and women. Martin Luther wrote commentaries on the book of Genesis arguing for Eve's equal position with Adam. According to Luther, women were created with equal mental faculties and an equal ability to obey God. Luther admitted that there were physical distinctions between Adam and Eve and that in the end Adam "excelled her in glory," but she was "in no respect inferior to Adam" (Luther 1958, 115). After the Fall, humans could no longer "naturally" obey God, so God instituted civil and family government. Luther believed that prior to the Fall, sex amounted to a passionless activity, but after the Fall it was marked by lust; thus marriage became a remedy for this passion. Luther viewed sex as natural and necessary and believed that marriage provided a proper arena for the natural tendency of humans to procreate.

Luther's positive view of marriage was expressed, not surprisingly, in opposition to the medieval Catholic Church's requirement that priests remain celibate. In his 1522 writings, *Against the So-Called Spiritual State,* Luther observed that a young woman "can do without a man as little as without food, drink, sleep, and other natural needs. And on the other hand: a man, too, cannot be without a woman. The reason is the following: begetting children is as deeply rooted in nature as eating and drinking. That is why God provided the body with limbs, arteries, ejaculation, and everything that goes along with them" (quoted in Oberman 1989, 275). God's power, he argued, was present in the sexual attraction between men and women, the most vital of human passions. Priestly celibacy, according to Luther, contradicted God's plan for nature. Luther, therefore, was as much concerned with denouncing celibacy as a means of receiving grace as he was with affirming sexuality.

Marriage became a proper locus of sexual activity because it served to regulate sexual behavior. Although Luther elevated women by claiming that Eve's original status was as "helpmeet" to Adam, after the Fall Eve became subordinate to Adam's governance. Women might find joy in motherhood, but they would not find equality in marriage; an imperfectable state instituted to provide a proper arena for sexuality after the Fall. Although in Luther's view we see the affirmation of sexuality as part of God's plan and the elevation of Eve as an important partner for Adam (not a depraved sexual temptress wholly responsible for the Fall of humanity), we also discover that sexual expression is limited to a patriarchal marriage.

John Calvin held a more elevated view of Eve, emphasizing the first creation story over the second. Calvin believed that Eve, also created in God's image, was not simply made to enable Adam to procreate but to bond them as husband and wife through physical and spiritual union. Like Luther, he also insisted that Adam was equally responsible for the Fall. Calvin stressed the partnership between Adam and Eve prior to the Fall but understood that Eve was always subject to Adam's rule. Before the Fall, Adam's superiority was his honor; after the Fall, Adam governed Eve in political and family matters. Calvin, like Luther, believed that women were *spiritually* equal to men; in marriage, however, women must submit to men.

Later Protestant men and women, following in the footsteps of Luther and Calvin, also drew on New Testament scriptures to understand their proper relationship to each other and the world. In 1

Corinthians 11:3–12, the Apostle Paul reminds Christians of the divinely sanctioned social order: "Christ is the head of every man, and the husband is the head of his wife, and God is the head of Christ." He continues his exhortation by stating that men should pray with their heads uncovered and women should pray with their heads covered. This is because of the order of creation: "he is the image and reflection of God; but woman is the reflection of man." Other Christian scriptures are more detailed about proper Christian sex roles. In 1 Timothy 2:8–15, the writer commands that in places where men pray, "women should dress themselves modestly and decently in suitable clothing, not with their hair braided, or with gold, pearls or expensive clothes, but with good works as is proper for women who profess reverence for God." In the next sentence, a verse that would codify Christian ecclesiastical roles and power for almost two millennia, the writer states, "Let a woman learn in silence with full submission. I permit no woman to teach or to have authority over a man; she is to keep silent. For Adam was formed first, then Eve; and Adam was not deceived, but the woman was deceived and became a transgressor. Yet she will be saved through childbearing." Protestant women, therefore, were instructed to dress modestly, keep quiet, cover their heads, submit to their husbands, and seek salvation through childbirth. They also learned that they were the original transgressors, that they were responsible for humanity's fall into sin, and that they were different from men, who reflected God's image. Over the course of time, they became closely connected to images of the naked body and sexuality.

## U.S. PROTESTANTS

The Puritans who came to the United States in the seventeenth century brought with them a set of beliefs about sexuality shaped by the Protestant Reformation. They combined Luther's belief that marriage channeled natural sexual lust and prevented sin with Calvin's assertion that sexuality within marriage not only expressed love but fulfilled the scriptural mandate to "be fruitful and multiply." Protestant attitudes toward sexuality preserved the family as a central unit of governance. Proper sexual expression occurred only within marriage to produce offspring. Sexual transgression happened outside marriage for purposes other than reproduction. Furthermore, Puritan sexuality was not a private matter but a community concern. The Puritans believed that civil and church government should enforce all public morality, including sexual offenses.

Although sexual union was a marital duty that Puritan husbands and wives owed each other and remained closely tied to procreation, it was also an acceptable means of pleasure for both men and women. Popular folk beliefs and midwife manuals carried over to New England held that female orgasm was crucial for women's health and ensured conception. Once married, Protestant women could expect to bear children until menopause, and Puritan women rejected forms of contraception and abortifacients as being opposed to the scriptural injunction to be fruitful and multiply.

Sexual relations within Puritan marriages were so important that male impotence was grounds for divorce. Puritans believed that sexual dissatisfaction would lead husbands and wives toward adultery and result in social disorder. Although sexual intimacy bound husband and wife in a spiritual and physical union, sexual excess in marriage was considered dangerous since its goal tended to satisfy the passions, with less regard for procreation. Puritan divorce cases are replete with complaints of adultery, sexual insatiability, and sexual indiscretion. There was no expectation that one should suffer sexual misconduct for the sake of saving a marriage.

In New England, sexual crimes were monitored and prosecuted by the churches as well as the courts. A "godly community," all members of Puritan society kept a watchful eye out for transgressive sexual behavior. Ministers preached the importance of corporate morality: the sexual misconduct of one person might bring the disfavor of God on all. Puritans settled in families from fairly homogeneous backgrounds and maintained a sex ratio of approximately three men to four women. Unlike in other colonies where men outnumbered women, the Puritan colonies were balanced and favorable to family stability and sexual regulation. Although sexual misconduct laws were rarely enforced to their fullest, sexual crimes such as adultery, sodomy, incest, and rape were capital offenses in the Massachusetts Bay Colony. Other forms of sexual misconduct such as masturbation, bestiality, and premarital sex were punishable by fines, public shamings, whippings, and sometimes banishment.

Young unmarried Puritan men were implored by clergy and parents to focus their energies on love of God rather than on sexual desire. Puritan writer Michael Wigglesworth, for example, sought to do just that. In his personal diary, he confessed that he suffered from "unresistable torments of carnal lusts" when he thought of his young male students at Harvard. He believed that such "filthiness" could only be overcome through prayer and marriage. Young Puritan women were instructed on the importance of chastity. They were told to dress modestly, speak politely, act piously, and refrain in general from enticing men into thoughts or acts of carnal pleasure.

Although Puritans believed that both men and women could be saints and sinners, the worst "sinners" were those who had signed a pact with the devil, and a disproportionate number of these "sinners" were women. Scholars debate the reasons that the fear of witchcraft escalated into the Salem witch trails of 1692, but all agree that the predominance of women as accusers and accused deserves special attention. That witchcraft was a singularly gendered religious threat is indisputable. Puritans, like generations of Christians before them, conceived of the soul as female and passive and the body as male and active. God and Satan, so the Puritans believed, were vying for their souls; but God spoke to their hearts, whereas Satan entered through their bodies to reach their souls. Because females were viewed as "weaker vessels," they were understood to be more vulnerable to Satan's attacks. Male souls, also thought of as feminine, were well protected by stronger male bodies and were therefore less likely to submit to the devil. Significantly, most of the "proof" of witchcraft was determined by marks on the bodies of the accused, which was seen as evidence of physical, often sexual contact with evil inscribed on the female body.

The accusation of witchcraft often implied the worst sort of sexual misconduct: intercourse with Satan. The connection of female bodies, sin, sexuality, and witchcraft did not originate with the Puritans but was articulated as early as 1496 in Jacobus Sprenger and Heinrich Kraemer's *Malleus Maleficarum* (the Hammer of Witchcraft), a document from the Inquisition in Europe. The text explains that Eve's carnal lust made women sexually insatiable and, therefore, more likely than men to accept Satan's sexual advances. Once in league with Satan, women would ravage men sexually (providing the explanation that male impotence was caused by a witch's spell) and overthrow society. Accusations of witchcraft reveal much about Puritan views of female sexuality but also suggest the contours of Puritan male sexuality. Puritan men, unlike Puritan women, were portrayed as physically strong, able to resist evil, and sexually controlled. Puritan women were understood to be physically weak and therefore prone to sexual insatiability.

Not all Protestant colonists, of course, were Puritans. Anglicans, Quakers, and other smaller Protestant groups populated the middle and southern colonies. Although the majority of the settlers in the southern and middle colonies shared Protestant sexual values with the Puritans, for demographic reasons they did not prosecute sexual crimes as vigorously as their New England neighbors. Unlike Puritan New England, settlers in the middle and southern colonies generally did not arrive in families; they did not "covenant" together around common religious and social goals. During the first years of settlement in the Chesapeake region, for example, men outnumbered women four to one, making it statistically less likely that sexual activity would be channeled through marriage. The distinct economic system that included indentured servants and, after 1670, slaves also influenced the extent to which civil authorities prosecuted sex offenders. Sexual crimes of adultery, sodomy, and rape were prosecuted by courts but less frequently than in New England.

In all the seventeenth-century Protestant colonies, sexual relations that took place outside marriage were criminal offenses. Typically, courts and churches operated together to prosecute offenders. Public humiliation through whippings, standing in stocks, or wearing marks on clothing to indicate the crime were standard forms of punishment in all the colonies. The main difference among the Puritan, Anglican, and Quaker responses to sex offenders was the frequency and extent to which they were punished. These responses clearly reflected their differing theological and social goals. The Quakers were the most rigorous in their prosecution of sex offenders but did so infrequently. The Puritans prosecuted both men and women frequently and severely. The Anglicans punished fewer sex crimes and were more severe with women than with men. In Anglican Virginia, for example, women were punished more severely than men for fornication (premarital sex) and adultery (sex outside marriage) because a wife's adultery was perceived to threaten the family bloodline through the birth of illegitimate children, whereas a husband's adulterous behavior did not. Polluting a family bloodline was directly related to the southern colonists' understanding of marriage as an eternal union; it also reflected a greater concern with keeping property in the family. In New England, marriage was a civil contract that could be broken if both parties did not fulfill their part. In the southern colonies, marriage was a sacred bond tied by Anglican clergy and cut only in rare cases.

Female indentured servants and slaves in the southern colonies were particularly vulnerable to sexual crimes. They were prosecuted for offenses against them if they bore "illegitimate" children. Interracial sex in the southern colonies—whether criminal or consensual—quickly came under public scrutiny with the first legal effort against it in Virginia in 1662. By the eighteenth century, the antimiscegenation laws would become stricter. White men were rarely convicted of sexual crimes against African American women, however. The sexual relationship that was most closely monitored was between white women and African American men. The most severe punishments (castration and lynching) were inflicted on African American men accused of raping white women. Although white Protestants up and down the eastern seaboard would loosen their prosecution of sexual crimes against each other, they tightened their enforcement of sexual crimes to maintain racial boundaries.

The Quakers who settled in Pennsylvania and Delaware promoted spiritual equality between men and women, which informed their views of sexuality. Quakers made a sharp distinction between the spiritual and the carnal, between love and lust. They affirmed that love must precede marriage, but that true love was spiritual love between two believers, not passionate love that aroused sexual desire. Many Quakers worried that too much sexual passion or activity between husband and wife would weaken the spiritual foundation of their marriage. In fact, some early Quaker settlers practiced celibacy within marriage. Most did not advocate lifelong celibacy within marriage, but many Quakers abstained from sexual activity for extended periods of time.

Quakers reported and judged sexual offenses in their "meetings of Friends." Although accusations of sexual crimes were rare, when they occurred, the judgments against offenders were severe. In Pennsylvania, the punishment for a first offense of adultery was a year's imprisonment; for the second offense, it was life imprisonment. Fornication before marriage could lead to disownment by the society. For single men, sodomy and bestiality carried the punishment of life imprisonment, with whippings every three months; married men were immediately divorced and then castrated. This punishment was later revoked for its unusual cruelty. Quakers, unlike Puritans, did not hang people for sexual offenses because they did not believe in capital punishment.

All the Protestants who settled in the colonies perceived immediately that the sexual customs of the native inhabitants differed from their own. For example, although Native American sexuality was informed by religious beliefs, it was not connected to sin. Puberty rituals and seclusion during menstruation, among other rituals, celebrated sexuality and in many cases allowed for sexual practices such as homosexuality and pre-marital intercourse; forms of sex that were forbidden by Protestants. Protestants viewed the sexual habits of Native Americans as "uncivilized" and "savage" and pointed to their "immoral" sexual acts as justification for conversion and conquest.

These general sexual trends continued after the Revolutionary War. There were, however, some notable changes in the way Protestants thought of male and female sexuality. Although Christianity had a long tradition of associating the female with the carnal and the male with the spiritual, by the nineteenth century, Protestant Americans had reversed that thinking. Women came to be described as "naturally" spiritual; men were "naturally" carnal. No longer the sexual temptress like their fore-mother Eve, Protestant white women in the United States came to be perceived as chaste and vulnerable to sexually aggressive men. Nonwhite, non-Protestant, and poor women did not enjoy the luxury of being considered chaste and vulnerable; they were nonetheless judged against this new sexual ideal. At the same time, male and female bodies came to be viewed as distinct entities. Up to this point, the scientific and theological standard viewed the human body on a "one-sex" model. The male and female body was exactly the same, simply inverted in male and female forms. Now male and female bodies were imagined to be com-pletely separate from each other, thus creating a "two-sex" model that is still with us today. Female bodies were still posited as weaker than male bodies and more prone to disease, but their moral backbone was stronger. Thus, through a cultural process that historian Barbara Welter (1974) termed the "feminization of Protestantism," nineteenth-century Protestant women became the religious leaders in the home, taking over the roles of spiritual instruction and moral guidance once held by men.

Many scholars have noted that this ideological shift occurred simulta-neously with social and economic changes in the United States. As the na-tion became increasingly industrialized, women's domestic role inside the household was elevated in direct relation to men's economic role outside the household. Masculine identity revolved around notions of economic com-petition, which was linked to sexual aggression, whereas feminine identity derived from an ideology of "true womanhood." Protestant women, accord-ing to this ideology, were portrayed as sexually restrained moral custodians for their families, the nation, and the world (Welter 1976).

Although most Protestants approved of sexuality in the "nuclear" fam-ily, by the mid–nineteenth century other options became available.

Communal and utopian movements within Protestantism that restructured sexual, economic, and family relationships drew men and women from their traditional homes and sexual practices. The people who joined these communities hoped to perfect themselves and advance society by creating "families" that either replicated their perception of the New Testament household families or reflected their understanding of families during the millennial reign of Christ. Restructuring the family required rethinking sexuality. The Shakers and the Oneida Perfectionists illustrate two radically different views of sexuality held by contemporary Protestant communal groups. Both the Shakers and the Oneida Perfectionists referred to New Testament passages in which Jesus states that in the afterlife there will be neither marrying nor giving in marriage, but they came to very different interpretations of what that passage meant for sexual relations. For the Shakers this text led to celibacy; for the Oneida Perfectionists, the text justified their practice of group marriage. In both cases, sexuality was a key component for the Protestant restructuring of the family in a new age.

Ann Lee (1736–1784), the founder and leader of the Shakers (the United Society of Believers in Christ's Second Appearing), promoted celibacy as the route to salvation. In a life-transforming revelation, she saw that the root of evil began with lust in the Garden of Eden. Thus understanding the cause of evil, she prescribed a cure: celibacy. She formed a religious community and with seven followers emigrated from England to western New York, where they lived in extended families characterized by "virgin purity," free from the entanglements of sexual desire. Having thus purged themselves of the cause of sin, Shakers could devote their energy to establishing God's kingdom on Earth. "Mother Ann," as she liked to be called, described herself as "mother to all living" and "lover of Christ," but testimonies written after her death by community members claimed that she *was* the second coming of Christ in female flesh. Shakers believed that God was both male and female and visited the earth first in a male body in Christ and then in a female body in Lee, thus completing the unity of God as both male and female. Although the communities prospered in the nineteenth-century United States, the Shakers were attacked routinely by outsiders, especially former Shaker apostates, who accused them of breaking up families, sexual licentiousness, and heresy. In the minds of many Protestant Americans, celibacy and female religious leadership threatened the new nation, a society they insisted be based on the maintenance of traditional families and traditional sex roles.

The Oneida Perfectionists, led by John Humphrey Noyes (1811–1886), moved as an extended "family" to Sherrill, New York, in 1848 to regenerate themselves and society by instituting "Bible Communism" there. Based on his reading of the Book of Acts, Noyes believed that his family, like the early Christians, must hold all things in common. Noyes's radical theology and the social vision that he and his "family" practiced for almost forty years included, among many other things, the assertion that a sinless existence was possible on earth and that he himself had achieved that state. The social and sexual implications of Noyes's theology of Bible Communism and "sinlessness" challenged sex norms in dramatic ways. In his "Bible Argument Defining the Relation between the Sexes" Noyes (1853) reasoned that the "restoration of true relations between the sexes" in God's kingdom could occur only by abolishing the unholy practice of marriage. In the kingdom of God on earth, which Noyes believed he was helping to inaugurate, there would be no marriage. Monogamous marriage, according to Noyes, was a sinful institution that "assigns the exclusive possession of one woman to one man." Noyes contended that monogamous marriages were a threat to society because they encouraged "special love" rather than social harmony. In its place, he set up a system of "Complex Marriage," in which each man and each woman in the community could enjoy, with the approval of Father Noyes, a sexual relationship with one another. To that end, the Oneida Perfectionists practiced "Male Continence," a surprisingly successful form of birth control to avoid unwanted pregnancies. They also found "spiritual" elevation in sexual encounters. During the final years of the community's existence, they practiced "Stirpiculture," a type of eugenics in which Noyes "mated" the most spiritually ascendant community members to produce the "best" offspring. The Oneida Perfectionists were harassed by Protestant neighbors and eventually forced to disband, but their radical restructuring of the family and sexuality, like that of the Shakers, provides an example of the range of ways that Protestants have addressed the issue of sexuality and its relation to family, reproduction, and social order.

## CURRENT ISSUES IN U.S. PROTESTANTISM

U.S. Protestants today still the face the same issues regarding sexuality, but new concerns have been added to the mix. Sexuality, reproduction, and the family have always been connected for Protestants, but now many Protestants are troubled by two pressing questions: What is a family? Is sexuality linked inextricably to reproduction? Although Protestants debate these two questions among themselves, they are also engaging in a larger cultural conversation about homosexuality, abortion, fertility technologies, sexually transmitted diseases, sexual experimentation, and abstinence. As Protestants consider the profound implications of a culture grappling with its sexual beliefs and practices, their responses range from active acceptance of to active resistance to changing sexual norms. In many ways, U.S. Protestants mirror the different sides of the contemporary cultural debates about sexuality. Conservative Protestant groups, such as the Moral Majority or the Christian Right, seek to defend "universal" sexual standards based on biblical teachings. Mainline Protestants tend to emphasize individual rights and sexual freedom, and their views are based on a more subjective interpretation of scripture informed by individual conscience.

Although procreation has traditionally been viewed as the goal of sexual activity for Protestants, technological advances and changes in cultural attitudes about sex present new challenges. Various forms of contraception are widely used among Protestant men and women. Abortions are legal in the United States, and many Protestants elect to terminate pregnancies. New medical technologies help Protestants to conceive children in ways that biblical writers and reformers like Martin Luther or John Calvin, of course, could never have imagined. Protestants today must ponder the meaning of sexual activity without procreation and procreation without the traditional conception of sexual activity.

### Pleasure and Procreation

As we have seen, Protestants have viewed the family as the union of a "believing" man and woman, the purpose of which is to have children and to raise them in the faith. Because reproduction has been the goal of Protestant marriages, sexual practices that do not lead to offspring within sanctioned marriages, until recently, were held in suspicion. This issue encompasses two large categories: sex within marriage for pleasure (but not offspring) and sex outside marriage.

The "sexual revolution" of the 1960s convinced many Americans that pleasure was an essential component of sexual activity, distinct from reproduction. The celebration of sexual pleasure became evident in the popularity of secular sex manuals such as Alex Comfort's *The Joy of Sex*

245

(1972). Liberal/mainline Protestants followed this cultural trend toward celebrating sexual pleasure and since the 1970s have tended to accommodate sexual relationships that do not produce offspring or that occur outside marriage. Although always affirming the importance of marriage, liberal Protestants are less likely to condemn sex outside marriage; some liberal Protestants reject scripture that prohibits nonprocreative sexual activity.

The emphasis on sexual pleasure that emerged from the 1960s was not limited to liberal Protestants. This trend can also be found among conservative Protestants, who made Marabel Morgan's *The Total Woman* (1973) a best-seller. Morgan's sex guidebook, like the scores of publications that would be modeled on her work, claimed that sexual ecstasy was a sign of a true Christian marriage. In fact, since the mid-1970s, evangelicals have created a booming industry in sex manuals. An early example, Tim and Beverly LaHaye's *The Act of Marriage: The Beauty of Sexual Love* (1978), combines scriptural injunctions with detailed anatomical diagrams as well as practical hints for sexual success. The primary audiences for these texts are newlywed evangelical couples, who hope to find spiritual and sexual fulfillment in their marriages. The contemporary evangelical sex guides are notable in their pro-sex stance and the creativity in which both marital partners may indulge to enjoy sexual fulfillment. Many of these guidebooks, for example, permit masturbation—often termed "self-pleasuring"—so long as the couple does not become dependent on it and forgo sexual intercourse altogether. All the evangelical sex manuals emphasize the importance of sexual satisfaction in forging a strong spiritual bond between husband and wife. Evangelical Protestants do place strict boundaries around acceptable sexual behavior, deeming only heterosexual marriage as the appropriate arena for sexual activity. Within that sacred arena, however, evangelical Protestants affirm the importance of frequent and mutually satisfying sexual encounters.

### Premarital Sex

Although most Protestants discourage premarital sex, in recent years conservative Protestants have taken the lead in promoting abstinence as a sign of faith. True Love Waits, a national abstinence group founded in 1993 by Southern Baptist youth leader Richard Ross, is the most prominent example. This Protestant group challenges youth to remain virgins until marriage as a testament to their commitment to Christ and their future spouses. What began with fifty-nine teenagers in Nashville,

Tennessee, signing chastity cards—"I make a commitment to God, myself, my family, my future mate, and my future children to be sexually abstinent from this day until the day I enter into a biblical marriage relationship"—evolved into a national movement that sponsors enormous abstinence rallies across the country.

The ultimate goal of True Love Waits is to guide teenagers to a "biblical marriage," but surprisingly, the chastity movement has spilled over into popular culture. Musicians, athletes, film stars, and television characters have joined the ranks of youth, proclaiming that "virginity is cool." Teens interested in joining the abstinence movement can sign pledges on the True Love Waits website, attend a rally, or read how-to-be-abstinent publications, such as Joshua Harris's *I Kissed Dating Goodbye* (1997). Unlike secular abstinence movements that aim to persuade youth to refrain from premarital sex by focusing on the transmission of sexual diseases such as acquired immunodeficiency syndrome (AIDS) and the risk of pregnancy, True Love Waits urges teens to avoid the inevitability of a "broken heart" given outside a Christian marriage. Abstinence promoters assure teenagers that sex within a Protestant marriage will be worth the wait.

## Abortion

The majority of Protestants, both clergy and laity, favor contraceptives and family planning within marriage, but they remain deeply divided over the permissibility of electing to terminate a pregnancy. Since *Roe v. Wade* (1973), when the Supreme Court ruled that women have a constitutional right to abortion, Protestants have mobilized both in protest and support of this decision. The underlying question that divides Protestants is whether morality is a public or private matter. In the case of abortion, should the matter be an individual decision or "choice," or should it be part of collective societal values? Like the majority of Americans, liberal Protestants affirm that abortions should be available in cases of rape and incest and when the mother's life is in jeopardy. Most liberal Protestants believe that abortion is an individual moral choice and appeal for the human rights and liberties of the mother as the proper moral agent to determine whether or not to end a pregnancy. Conservative Protestants, however, generally focus on the human rights and liberties of the fetus and view abortion as a moral evil that will bring danger to the well-being of the entire society. They point to scripture—"Thou shalt not kill"—as the final authority. Unlike liberal Protestants who contend that biblical scripture should be interpreted within changing historical circumstances, conservative Protestants contend that scripture mandates timeless, universal standards.

### Homosexuality

The emergence of the gay liberation movement in the 1970s has led Protestant gay men and lesbians to assert the compatibility of homosexuality and spirituality. Because of denominational diversity, a spectrum of Protestant opinions has emerged since the mid-1970s. They range from adamant rejection and exclusion of homosexuals to full acceptance and inclusion of gay men and lesbians in Protestant churches. Denominations have debated their stance on homosexuality, referring to scripture and science to support their positions. Not surprisingly, the most liberal Protestant groups have been the most accepting of including homosexuals in church life. Liberal Protestants have looked to scientific research on homosexual orientation to help them construct a theological response to homosexuality. In general, liberal Protestants are convinced that homosexuality is in part based on biology and is not voluntary. Following their belief that sin is voluntary, they cannot therefore consider homosexuality a sin. The United Church of Christ, for example, decided that because homosexuality is not a chosen orientation, it is not sinful, and any homosexual activity is subject to the same moral rules as heterosexual activity. Many Protestant churches, including the Presbyterian Church, USA, the Evangelical Lutheran Church, and the Unitarian Universalists have been politically active for decades in the fight to decriminalize same-sex acts. Some of these same Protestant groups, however, such as the Reformed Church and the Missouri Lutheran Synod, affirm the civil rights of gay men and lesbians even while opposing homosexuality on moral grounds. The Church of the Brethren, for example, continues to be morally opposed to homosexuality but issued a strong statement in 1983 that challenges hatred and fear of homosexuals and supports civil rights for gay and lesbian people.

A few Protestant groups openly endorse same-sex marriage. The Universal Fellowship of Metropolitan Community Churches (the oldest and largest independent gay and lesbian religious organization), the Unity Fellowship Church Movement founded by Bishop Carl Bean, the Unitarian Universalist Association, and the North Pacific Yearly Meeting affirm same-sex religious and civil marriages. Many other Protestant groups affirm the rights of homosexuals to have a civil union but do not authorize religious wedding ceremonies for gay men and lesbians. The United Methodist Church has maintained the rights of homosexuals to have same-sex civil unions, but—because it finds homosexuality incompatible with Christian teaching—the denomination is deeply divided over whether clergy may perform same-sex marriages.

Perhaps the most divisive issue for Protestant denominations is gay and lesbian ordination. Unitarian Universalists, the Unity Fellowship Church Movement, and the Metropolitan Community Churches ordain gay men and lesbians without requiring any restrictions on their sexual practices. Because most liberal Protestants believe that homosexuality is not a choice, they also believe that restricting ordination to heterosexuals would be unfair and unjust. These Protestant groups—Presbyterians, United Church of Christ, Society of Friends, United Methodists, and Episcopalians—focus instead on the question of whether clergy should be allowed to practice homosexuality after ordination.

Protestant denominations that are divided over homosexuality have placed many of the policy decisions at the local level. Individual congregations that affirm gay and lesbian clergy and laity define themselves as "welcoming." The Lambeth Conference and some of the bishops of the Episcopal Church in the United States have condemned same-sex marriage, but many members of the Episcopal Church affirm same-sex marriages, aligning themselves with the pro-gay Episcopal group Integrity. To reconcile this difference, U.S. bishops are now allowed to conduct same-sex marriages in their dioceses. Other examples of local dissent in favor of homosexual rights include Presbyterian More Light churches, Lutherans Concerned, the Association of Welcoming and Affirming Baptists, the Reconciling Congregations Program of the United Methodist Church, and the Open and Affirming congregations of the United Church of Christ.

Protestant denominations that oppose homosexuality, such as the Southern Baptist Conference, insist that homosexuality is a choice and is therefore subject to moral censure. In these cases, homosexuality is described as a "lifestyle" that can and should be altered. To this end, conservative Protestant groups seek to convert homosexual Protestants to their understanding of biblically based heterosexuality, citing scripture that prohibits homosexuality, such as Leviticus 18:22. They also support "ex-gay" ministries such as Exodus International and the publication and sales of "recovery" books, such as *Coming Out of Homosexuality* (1994) by Bob Davies and Lori Rentzel, that target an evangelical ex-gay audience.

249

## *Gender*

Besides the gay rights movement, U.S. politics and culture shifted after the Vietnam War and the civil rights movement and with the feminist movement. Labeled by many scholars as an era of "disenchantment," in the years following the Vietnam War many U.S. Protestants scrutinized basic components of modern life in the United States, including religion and gender. By the 1970s, it became apparent to many people that religion played an important part in sanctioning gender roles and reinforcing gender identity. Some Protestant theologians and activists advocated expanding gender roles or reinterpreting gender identity by reformulating or "uncovering" lost religious traditions. Feminist theologians, for example, argued that the concept of a male God needed to be discarded because it was a fictional symbol created by men to legitimate their social power (patriarchy) and oppress women. By imagining God as a father, they contended, maleness became deified, and femaleness became closely associated with evil. Protestant feminist theologians sought to reveal the gendered basis of Protestantism and to rectify what they perceived as their "secondary" status within the tradition. Scores of other feminist theologians (from other religious traditions) joined the conversation, some focusing on "inclusive language" in sacred texts, others seeking liturgical reform, and still others probing the past to find authentic female voices within their religious traditions. In general, this cross-tradition religious reform movement united around the belief that divine masculinity reinforced male domination and, reciprocally, that a patriarchal social order created a male divinity.

At the same time, many conservative Protestants saw the value in religiously defined gender roles and affirmed these religious and biological "truths" of masculine and feminine identity with renewed vigor. Both sides of the Protestant spectrum were responding to their perception of feminism and its influence—for better or for worse—on religion and U.S. culture. What came to be called the "pro-family" movement emerged as a conservative Protestant political answer to the social "problems" of abortion, homosexuality, the Equal Rights Amendment (ERA), and school board policies (such as prayer in school). As liberal Protestants sought to expand the role of women in religion, conservatives like James Dobson, in his weekly radio show and film series "Focus on the Family," explained the "true" equality between men and women in biblically defined roles. Dobson and many others inspired conservative Protestants to become politically active and also helped to articulate a response to feminism's challenge to religiously defined gender roles.

One such response came in 1987 from the Council on Biblical Manhood and Womanhood. "The Danvers Statement" (written in Danvers, Massachusetts) described the biblically based differences between men and women. This nondenominational conservative Protestant group proclaimed that masculine and feminine roles are ordained by God and that husbands must assume "loving, humble headship" of wives; wives, in turn, must practice "intelligent, willing submission." Simply put, men and women are equal before God but have specific roles of "headship" and "submission" within marriage.

Evangelical same-sex (not homosexual) support groups such as Women's Aglow Fellowship and the Promise Keepers helped men and women realize these goals. The Promise Keepers, an evangelical revival movement that encourages men to surrender to Christ and reclaim their "godly manhood," was founded by the former head football coach of the University of Colorado, Bill McCartney. Promise Keepers vary in age, ethnicity, and culture but unite around their belief that they are facing a spiritual crisis because they have lost control of their God-given authority in their families. Promise Keepers affirm that male and female spiritual makeup differs radically and that they require a "masculine context" to understand and express their spiritual longings. The Promise Keepers have attracted a lot of media attention since the early 1990s because of their insistence on the theological and biological underpinnings for male authority. In the conservative Protestant women's and men's groups, male and female gender identity is biblically defined: women are expected to willingly submit to their husbands in a marriage in which husband and wife are spiritually equal before God. Although liberal and conservative Protestants are deeply concerned with male and female gender identity, they come to radically different answers to the problems raised by feminism.

## CONCLUSION

Although it is impossible to provide a single description of Protestant views on sexuality, there are some common themes. Protestants generally view sexuality as positive and as part of God's plan for humanity. Protestants tend to look to Scripture to understand how sexuality relates to the family, reproduction, and social order, although their interpretations of Scripture often differ radically. Protestants participate in all the contemporary public debates about sexual orientation, sexual technologies, and sexual practices, and they voice a range of opinions from conservative to liberal. It seems unlikely that Protestants will ever present a unified view of sexuality, not simply because Protestants divide into liberal and conservative camps but more importantly because the tradition emphasizes the individual's interpretation of scripture. Protestantism will always accommodate new and competing interpretations of sexuality.

## REFERENCES

Comfort, Alex. 1972. *The Joy of Sex: A Gourmet Guide to Lovemaking.* New York: Crown.

Council on Biblical Manhood and Womanhood. 1991. "The Danvers Statement." In John Piper and Wayne Grudem, eds., *Recovering Biblical Manhood and Womanhood: A Response to Evangelical Feminism.* Wheaton, IL: Good News Publishers.

Davies, Bob, and Lori Rentzel. 1994. *Coming Out of Homosexuality: New Freedom for Men and Women.* Downers Grove, IL: Intervarsity Press.

Harris, Joshua. 1997. *I Kissed Dating Goodbye.* Sisters, OR: Multnomah Publishers.

LaHaye, Timothy, and Beverly LaHaye. [1978] 1998. *The Act of Marriage: The Beauty of Sexual Love.* Reprint. Grand Rapids, MI: Zondervan Press.

Luther, Martin. 1958. *Lectures on Genesis: Chapters 1–5.* Vol. 1 in George V. Schick, trans., and Jarsolav Pelikan, ed., *Luther's Works.* Saint Louis: Concordia Publishing House.

Morgan, Edmund S., ed. [1946] 1965. *The Diary of Michael Wigglesworth, 1653–1657: The Conscience of a Puritan.* New York: Harper and Row.

Morgan, Marabel. [1973] 1975. *The Total Woman.* New York: Pocket Books.

Noyes, John Humphrey. 1853. "Bible Argument Defining the Relations of the Sexes in the Kingdom of Heaven." In *Bible Communism: A Compilation of the Annual Reports and Other Publications of the Oneida Association and Its Branches.* Brooklyn, NY: Office of the *Circular.*

Oberman, Heiko A. 1989. *Luther: Man between God and the Devil.* Eileen Walliser-Schwarzbart, trans. New Haven: Yale University Press.

Sprenger, Jacobus, and Heinrich Kramer. [1496] 1968. *Malleus Maleficarum: The Hammer of Witchcraft.* Montague Summers, trans. Reprint. London: Folio Society.

True Love Waits website, http://www.lifeway.com.

Welter, Barbara. 1974. "The Feminization of American Religion: 1800–1860."
Pp. 137–157 in Mary Hartman and Lois W. Banner, eds., *Clio's Consciousness Raised: New Perspectives on the History of Women*. New York: Harper and Row.

———. 1976. *Dimity Convictions: The American Woman in the Nineteenth Century*. Athens: Ohio University Press.

Chapter 9

# Islamic Conceptions of Sexuality

Aysha Hidayatullah

*Muslims consider human sexuality an* ayah, *or a reminder of the many blessings of Allah. (*Heart and Soul IV *by Salma Arastu)*

$\mathcal{I}$slam, the last of the Abrahamic faiths, emerged in the Arabian Peninsula at the beginning of the seventh century C.E. God, referred to in the Arabic language as Allah, revealed the Qur'an in 610 C.E. to Muhammad, an illiterate tradesman belonging to the Quraysh tribe of Mecca. Chosen by Allah as the "seal" of the Judeo-Christian prophets beginning with Abraham, Muhammad is believed to be the last in the line of God's messengers. Muhammad received the oral revelation of the Qur'an, the Muslim holy book, over a period of twenty-three years. The verses of the Qur'an instructed his community to halt its practices of polytheistic worship and direct all worship to the one and only Allah. Over the course of its revelation, the Qur'an offered guidance on various spiritual, social, political, and legal issues that was immediately directed at the seventh-century members of the Meccan community but also held universal significance for human beings of all places and times. Those who heed the Qur'anic call are Muslims, literally meaning in Arabic "those who make peace with, or submit to God." Muslims testify their faith in the One God and His last prophet, and they maintain belief in His holy scriptures (including the Qur'an, the Gospels, and the Torah), His prophets, His angels, and the Day of Judgment (the time of one's invitation to heaven or dismissal to hell).

The Muslim calendar begins in 622 C.E. with the *hijra,* or migration, of Muhammad's community from the city of Mecca to nearby Medina. This first year of the *hijrae* calendar thus marks the beginning of Islam's subsequent spread outside Mecca, throughout the Arabian Peninsula, and later to other continents. With Muhammad's death in 632 C.E., the leadership of the Muslim community passed first into the hands of the Prophet's closest companions, known as the Rashiddun Caliphs (632–661 C.E.), and eventually to the caliphs of the Umayyad (661–750 C.E.) and 'Abbasid dynasties (750–1258 C.E.). These caliphate governments held jurisdiction in both religious and political matters. At the height of their political conquests, the empires of these successive caliphates extended from Spain and North Africa to the Middle East and Southeast Asia. After the 'Abbasid era, independent rulers of separate territories replaced the overarching government of what was known as the Islamic empire.

After the death of Muhammad, the teachings of Islam survived as oral traditions. They include the recitation of the Qur'an and the transmission of the Hadith—the oral accounts of the Prophet's Sunna (life practices) passed on by his relatives and close companions to succeeding generations. Not until the middle of the seventh century and after the Prophet's death did Muslim authorities begin preserving the Qur'an in writing. By the ninth and tenth centuries, Muslim 'ulema (Islamic scholars) codified a system of legal reasoning (*fiqh*) to regulate Islamic practice for successive generations of Muslims. Around the same time, Muslim authorities also began to compile and organize written records of the Hadith. Muslim jurists developed a body of law (*shari'a*) to standardize Muslim practice in their own changing societies by looking to the Qur'an and Hadith and relying upon the analogical reasoning and consensus rules of *fiqh*. Varied perspectives on *fiqh* later resulted in the emergence of four major schools of Islamic jurisprudence that differ only slightly in their legal rulings.

These four schools of Islamic jurisprudence represent the legal deductions of Sunni, or mainstream, Islam. However, members of the Shi'i and Sufi Muslim communities adhere to many of these rulings as well. The most notable differences between Sunni, Shi'i, and Sufi Muslims occur in matters of political history or ascetic practice. For Shi'is, the major contention with Sunni Islam lay in the determination of political authority over the Muslim community (*umma*). According to Shi'i Islam, leadership of the *umma* after the Prophet's death was passed on to imams who descended from the Prophet and were granted divine knowledge by Allah. The first of these imams was the Prophet's cousin and son-in-law, 'Ali (Muhammad was not survived by any sons). Shi'i Muslims look to these leaders as divine intercessors; in contrast, Sunni Islam strictly opposes any belief in divine intermediaries, and according to Sunni Muslims, the Prophet himself claimed no such divine authority. For Sufi Muslims, Sunni Islam is enhanced by ascetic worship of Allah. Under the guidance of a knowledgeable authority (shaikh), a Sufi Muslim seeks a path of worship and remembrance of God aimed at becoming completely united with Him. Generally speaking, all Muslims adhere to five core practices: (1) *shahadah*—testifying to their belief in Allah and that Muhammad is His Prophet, (2) *salah*—performing regular daily prayers, (3) *sawm*—fasting during the Islamic calendar month of *Ramadan,* (4) *zakah*—giving alms to the poor, and (5) *hajj*—making a pilgrimage to the city of Mecca.

Today, Islam claims over 1 billion followers worldwide.[1] Approximately 85 percent of all Muslims are Sunni; the remaining 15 percent are Shi'i or Sufi. Most notable has been the recent expansion of Islam in North America and Europe as a result of immigration following the Western colonization of Muslim countries. Although Islam finds its origins in the Arabian Peninsula, the overwhelming majority of Muslims are not Arab. The largest Muslim countries—including Indonesia, Bangladesh, and Pakistan—are not part of the Middle East, and Islam claims substantial followings in virtually every part of the world, including China, Russia, and the United States.

## RESISTING ESSENTIALIST VIEWS OF ISLAM

In any study of "sexuality in Islam," one inevitably risks the essentialization of a complex, multifaceted set of religious beliefs and practices. In short, *there is no one Islam,* just as there is no *one* understanding of sexuality. Universal claims of this sort are not only erroneous but also confess to the inequitable power differences that grant only certain persons the authority to make claims about what Islam *really* is. Ayesha Imam advocates a clear demarcation between the terms *Islamic* and *Muslim,* the former signifying a religion sent by Allah and the latter standing for fallible practitioners of a religion who understand Islam in diverse ways: "The recognition that *Islamic* and *Muslim* are not synonyms helps avoid essentializing not only Islam but the histories of Muslim communities, for it refuses to favor the dominant discourse—the formal expression of thought and behaviors—of any Muslim community over all others"

(Imam 2001, 15). Having raised this serious concern, I aim to qualify the simplified study that follows by reiterating that there are and have always been many "Islams" and many ways in which Muslims have chosen to practice their faith in different times and places. Likewise, Muslims have also approached their sexualities in countless different ways throughout history. Whether or not canonical Islam has endorsed or marginalized these perspectives is an entirely separate matter.

With this qualifier, I also remain self-conscious of scholarly structures that endorse authoritative Islam and repress the marginalized perspectives of Muslims who do not subscribe to authoritative, "establishment" Islam. As many contemporary scholars point out, *shari'a* rulings and Hadith accounts carry with them not only the authoritative voices of normative Islam but also the baggage of the cultural and personal prejudices of their composers, transmitters, and interpreters. According to Khaled Abou El Fadel (2001, 267–268), Hadith literature, which informs the *shari'a*,

> should . . . be seen as the product of an authorial enterprise . . . because of the widespread participation of so many individuals from a variety of sociohistorical contexts, with their own sense of values, levels of consciousness, and memories, who engage in the process of selecting, remembering, and transmitting the memory of the Prophet and the Companions.

The Hadith records and *shari'a* codes of the ninth and tenth centuries, along with their prejudices, continue to inform authoritative Islam at the expense of marginal Muslim perspectives. This is, of course, not to substantiate Orientalist characterizations of the moral stagnancy of Islam but rather to point to the power dynamic of an establishment Islam that relies on "early tenth century Muslim jurisprudence," which "formally recognized the body of already formulated legal opinion as final," rather than as temporal and subject to revision (Ahmed 1992, 90). Indeed, the aim of much contemporary scholarship on Islam involves the disentangling of 'Abbasid era cultural mores from the *shari'a* and the development of models for more fluid, temporal exegesis of legal sources. These scholarly processes, however, remain contested and inadequate to date. Although the study that follows attempts to uncover perspectives resistant to authoritative Islam, it is of course beyond its scope to undertake that task comprehensively. It is expected that subsequent works will elaborate on the revival of those marginal perspectives.

## SEXUAL PRESCRIPTIONS

Unlike many other traditions, Islam does not mark exclusive boundaries between the sexual and sacred spheres. Since it provides guidance to human beings with full acknowledgment of their social, physical, and psychological attributes, Islam not only tolerates the sexuality of human beings but expressly addresses it. In particular, the *shari'a,* Hadith, and Qur'an itself provide a wealth of guidance on topics, including creation, marriage, reproduction, and sexual etiquette.

### Ayahs of Creation

The notion of the *ayah* (sign) is central to understanding Islam's conception of sexuality. Humankind, according to Islam, is by nature forgetful of its own mortality and the omnipotence of Allah. Therefore, the Qur'an provides countless *ayahs* to remind human beings of God's greatness. In fact, the Qur'an itself is an *ayah* for humankind, a reminder of God. It calls upon human beings to reflect on the beauty of the earth and heavens, the wonders of the natural world, and the mysteries of humankind as reminders of the infinite, incomprehensible glory of Allah. A typical passage from Chapter 31 illustrates the Qur'anic use of such imagery: "He[2] [God] created the Heavens without any pillars that ye can see; He set on the earth mountains standing firm, lest it should shake with you; And he scattered through it beasts of all kinds. We[3] send down rain from the sky, and produce on the earth every kind of noble creature, in pairs" (31:10). As human beings marvel at the endurance and majesty of their natural surroundings, unable to grasp its workings fully, the Qur'an reminds them of Allah's magnificence. In pointing to the sustenance gained from a natural world that largely remains a mystery to them, the holy book demonstrates that Allah's blessings upon humankind are ever-present. Indeed, all of creation is unified under the *tawheedic* vision of Islam, or its vision of the unity of all things in the universe under God. All of nature testifies to Allah and worships Him alone; all creatures and natural forms remain united and originate from a single source.

Of special note in the verse above are the words "in pairs." Perhaps the most important detail of nature upon which the Qur'an asks its reader to reflect is the dual organization of natural life. From the simple to the most complex of creatures, the continuity of this dual scheme is another miracle pointing to the grace of Allah. The duality of the sexes in nature, then, is yet another marvel of the miracle of creation. The Qur'an expressly invokes the duality of the sexes as a warning to those who might forget their vulnerable human origins: "Does [the human being][4] think that [he or she] will be left uncontrolled, (without purpose)? Was [he or she] not a drop of sperm emitted (in lowly form)? Then did [he or she] become a clinging clot; then did (Allah) make and fashion [him or her] in due proportion. And of [him or her] He made two sexes, male and female" (75:36–39). For those who have faltered in their consciousness of God and his omnipresence, repeated remembrance of nature's miracles reorients human beings to their Creator (30:20–21):

> And among His signs is this, that He created you from dust; and then, behold, ye are [human beings] scattered (far and wide)! And among His signs is this, that He created for you mates from among yourselves, that ye may dwell in tranquility with them, and He has put love and mercy between your (hearts): Verily in that are Signs for those who reflect.

The dual organization of the sexes, therefore, is a focal point for Qur'anic meditation. This duality is regarded as a mercy and blessing upon human beings, who find comfort and love in their sexual partners. From such verses, Muslims learn that duality is the foundation of natural harmony. For, although the two sexes are distinct, the origin of both is the same,[5] and their creations are complementary. The Qur'an states: "O [humankind]! Reverence your Guardian Lord, Who created you from a single [self], created, of like nature, [its] mate, and from them twain scattered (like seeds) countless men and women" (4:1). Thus the Qur'an not only delineates the harmony of sexual pairs in nature as mere explanation of its origins but also stresses it as evidence for the presence of the sacred throughout nature. The topic of the sexes is not a matter of which to be ashamed, nor should it be taken lightly. Rather, it is part of the Muslim cognizance of Allah and His command in all facets of life. That is, the nature of the sexes is cause for religious reflection and prayer. The Qur'an addresses the sacred and the sexual as part of one another.

## Marriage

Islam considers marriage and procreation among the principal blessings of humankind. The miracles of love and childbirth bestowed upon human beings are gifts and signs pointing to Allah. The Qur'an (7:189) states:

It is He who created you from a single [self], and made [its] mate of like nature, in order that [he or she] might dwell with [him or her] (in love). When they are united, she bears a light burden and carries it about (unnoticed). When she grows heavy, they both pray to Allah their Lord (saying): If Thou givest us a goodly child, we vow we shall (ever) be grateful.

Such passages affirm the sacred quality of love between human beings, and its comfort is yet another sign of Allah's workings upon humankind. So great is the miracle of love between two partners that one of the results of their union is the conception of a child. The miracle of reproduction, then, is another occasion for reflecting upon Allah and praying for His blessings. According to the Qur'an, the proper vehicle for enjoying the union between sexual partners is marriage. In fact, it is the only acceptable framework for sexual relations between two human beings. The Qur'an insists upon this framework and repeatedly encourages all Muslims to marry: "Marry those among you who are single" (24:32). Marriage is a sacred act and the subject of serious consideration throughout the Qur'an. There is "more Qur'anic legislation on the subject of a proper ordering of the relationship of men and women than on any other subject" (Hassan n.d., 70).

The legal term for marriage in Islam is *nikah,* which involves a legal contract outlining the exclusive commitment of sexual duties to a partner. Sex outside *nikah* is *zina* (fornication). *Zina* is considered a flagrant crime against Islam and a disruption of Muslim social structure. In this sense, *zina* is a violation of the social contract upon which Muslim society is based. Therefore, marriage in Islam is not the concealment of sex nor its relegation to realms of the immoral or strictly corporal. Rather, the "aim of the ritual of marriage [is] precisely to surround the sexual relationship with the maximum publicity" (Bouhdiba 1985, 15). Muslim marriage is thus a public pronouncement of sexual license between two consenting,[6] acceptable[7] partners and the sanctification of their exclusive union.

As an acceptable vehicle for sex in Islam, *nikah* is a blessing from Allah and a protection for human beings against *zina*. Moreover, marriage increases a Muslim's *ihsan* (an Arabic word literally meaning "performance of good/beautiful deeds"), one's God-conscious behavior (Bouhdiba 1985, 15). One's spouse in Islam is a person who aids one in performing beautiful, God-conscious acts. The designation of the spouse as such demonstrates the sanctity of marriage and the honorable status granted to the marriage partner in Islam.

A source of much controversial debate among Sunni and Shi'i scholars is the issue of *muta'* (temporary marriage) in Shi'i Islam. This practice finds its origins in pre-Islamic culture and is now undertaken mainly by the Twelver Shi'is of Iran (Haeri 1989, 1). These Muslims may engage in marriage contracts with the deliberate intent to terminate marriage after a fixed, agreed-upon period of time. *Muta'* differs from *nikah* in that "the objective of *muta'* is sexual enjoyment, *istimta'*, while that of *nikah* is procreation" (Haeri 1989, 2). Through *muta'* marriage, Shi'is claim that they safeguard themselves against *zina* by allowing for the satiation of sexual desire within the conditions of publicly recognized marriage. Sunni scholars contend that marrying with the intention to divorce voids a marriage contract by trivializing the sacred commitment of marriage and that such practice sanctions promiscuity with multiple partners. Shi'is have continued the practice, although 'Umar, the second Rashiddun caliph, declared *muta'* illegal during the first century of Islam (Haeri 1989, 1).

To elucidate Islam's understanding of marriage, a look at the work of the medieval philosopher Abu Hamid al-Ghazali is especially helpful. Al-Ghazali is so famous for his prolific, eleventh-century works on a variety of Islamic topics that even today he remains a household name and is usually known only by his last name. Because he is among the few Islamic scholars ever to address sexuality extensively, al-Ghazali remains "an unquestioned authority on Muslim sexuality," and modern scholars still look to him for elaboration on topics of sexuality, among many others (Farah 1984, 6). For the purposes of this chapter, references to al-Ghazali are taken from his "Book on the Etiquette of Marriage," the twelfth section of his massive *Revival of the Religious Sciences.*

### Reproduction

Al-Ghazali organizes his initial discussion according to the general advantages and disadvantages of marriage. The advantages of marriage as outlined by al-Ghazali include procreation, satisfaction of sexual desire, and companionship. For him, the most important of these functions is procreation, the main purpose of sex and marriage.[8] According to al-Ghazali, procreation is "to conform to the love of God by seeking to produce [children] in order to perpetuate mankind" (al-Ghazali 1984, 53). The act of reproduction is thus a testimony to the wisdom of Allah in compliance with His command upon humankind to reproduce. Al-Ghazali (1984, 54) reasons the virtues of procreation by citing the extraordinary anatomical design and function of the human body:

> God Almighty has created the pair; He has created the male organ and the two ovaries . . . He has endowed both the male and the female with desire. These deeds and instruments bear eloquent testimony to the design of their creator and declare their purpose unto those imbued with wisdom.

Thus the remarkable structure of the human reproductive system is another indication of the beauty of God's creation and its sacred role in facilitating for humans the divinely ordained act of procreation. Since reproduction is the realization of God's intended purpose for human design, al-Ghazali argues that marriage—the legal precursor to procreation—is incumbent upon Muslims. According to him, "one who marries is seeking to complete what God has desired, and the one who abstains, wastes away what God detests to have wasted" (al-Ghazali 1984, 54–55). Failing to marry and reproduce amounts to failure to testify to God's intent for humankind to procreate.

### Divorce

Although many Hadith frown upon divorce, the Qur'an is very attentive to the disruption of marriage. According to Amina Wadud (1999, 74–78), the Qur'an expressly recognizes the case of discord in marriage (*nushuz*) and calls for a series of reconciliatory steps. Although encouraging patience and reconciliation, the Qur'an explicitly provides means for terminating the marriage contract publicly and equitably with the help of mediators. Both men and women are entitled to the rights of divorce and women to the return of the dower as a means for their financial sustenance.[9] The Qur'an expressly allows for just divorce proceedings and requires a waiting period before finalization, both to promote reconciliation and to confirm that there are no pregnancies resulting from the marriage.[10] In the case of children, the Qur'an suggests mutual counsel concerning the care of children and their financial support. Above all, the Qur'an recommends parting with kindness.

### Sexual Intercourse

The other major cause for marriage among Muslims lay in protection from the temptations of sex outside marriage. In al-Ghazali's words, marriage provides "fortification against the devil, curbing [of] lust, warding off of the excesses of desire, averting [of] the eye, and safeguarding relief" (1984, 59). By channeling natural sexual desires into a sanctified, publicly recognized, exclusive union, a Muslim protects himself or herself from committing fornication, a grave moral offense in Islam. By satisfying sexual urges within legally drawn boundaries, Muslims may avoid the dangers of extramarital sex. Thus protection of one's morality through marriage is another blessing from Allah. The Qur'an states, "The believers, men and women, are protectors, one of another" (9:71). Since marriage curbs sexual impropriety and promiscuity among Muslims, a marriage partner is a refuge from evil and a blessing from God.

Al-Ghazali is also concerned with the etiquettes of cleanliness and prayer surrounding sex. He outlines Islamic conduct before, during, and after marital intercourse.[11] Highlighting the *shari'a* guidelines for sex, al-Ghazali notes that intercourse is prohibited while one is keeping a fast (as in the month of Ramadan), while one is performing the hajj, and when a woman is menstruating. According to al-Ghazali, "intimate relations" between a married couple should begin by invoking and praising Allah (1984, 106). Next, as the Sunna recalls in the Prophet's example, the couple should engage in foreplay with "tender words and caresses" (1984, 106–107). Upon the male partner's ejaculation, one should again praise Allah, and al-Ghazali notes that some Hadith accounts advise against facing the direction of prayer (toward the *Ka'bah* in Mecca). Also, the male partner must ensure that a woman experiences orgasm in addition to his; sexual desire is not for men alone and should be shared by women as well. They should engage in intercourse to each other's satisfaction and desired frequency. The different schools of jurisprudence differ slightly on the permissible extent of nudity during intercourse and on the permissibility of oral sex; al-Ghazali recommends limitation in both matters.

Al-Ghazali also refers to the ritual ablutions before and after intercourse. Collectively, these recommendations demonstrate the reverential character of sex. Another Qur'anic verse addressed to husbands offers support for this observation: "Your wives are as a tilth unto you so approach your tilth when or how ye will; but do some good act for your souls beforehand; and fear Allah, and know that ye are to meet Him (in the Hereafter), and give (these) good tidings to those who believe" (2:223). As this verse indicates, acts of sex are not outside the realms of worship. Muslims strive to direct all of their actions toward remembrance of God, and sex is not an exception to these efforts. By expressly providing prescriptions for cleanliness and consciousness of God before, during, and after the act, Islamic *shari'a* supports the sacred quality of marital sex.

## Purity

Although intercourse is prohibited during certain times and necessitates ritual cleansing before the performance of subsequent acts of worship, it is important to note that the aim of such demarcation in "purity" (for lack of a better term) is not to indicate any impure or immoral sense of sex. Indeed, if it were the case, sexual ritual in Islam would involve neither ablutions nor remembrance of Allah. Instead, this demarcation, at least according to al-Ghazali, distributes one's attention to sex and worship in such a way as to facilitate satiation of sexual desire as well as maximum fulfillment in prayer. Prayer must be performed in full and undivided concentration. This distribution of attention does *not* serve to exclude sex from the realm of the sacred. The *shari'a's* concern with washing away the physical excretions of intercourse is a matter of hygiene. Ritual cleansing after sex does *not* imply that sex is spiritually "impure."

Menstruation provides an interesting case in point. Al-Ghazali strongly advises against intercourse with a menstruating woman, citing evidence for the prohibition of this act in the Qur'an, verse 2:222: "They ask thee [the Prophet] concerning women's courses. Say: They are a hurt and a pollution: So keep away from women in their courses, and do not approach them until they are clean." Al-Ghazali points out that a man can have contact with all parts of the female body with the exception of the vagina during this time. Intercourse with a menstruating woman, according to him, is harmful to the partners and to any child resulting from the union. The position among jurists has been that a woman's menses pollute her body, rendering it unclean for prayer. Scholarly opinions hold also that women should not touch or recite the Qur'an, fast, perform certain rites of the hajj, or enter a mosque while menstruating. The prohibition on sex with menstruating women suggests that contact with the menstrual blood renders *men* unclean as well. However, specific explanations regarding women's "impurity" during menstruation remain scarce and at times puzzling.

Some understanding may be found in Islamic rulings on the importance of general bodily cleanliness, which cover an astonishing variety of topics ranging from cleanliness in the toilet to bodily odor. It is important to understand, therefore, that impurity "has nothing to do with sin and it may derive . . . easily from lawful acts" (Bouhdiba 1985, 44). Under *shari'a* rules, bodily excretions of both men and women call for cleansing of the body. Sexual intercourse and the excretion of semen or menstrual blood are causes for major impurity of the body and require a major ritual cleansing (*ghusl*). The secretion of waste, flatulence, vaginal discharge, vomit, and blood from any part of the body constitute minor impurity and require the performance of *wudu'* ablutions (minor ritual cleansing of limbs, face, and head) before commencing worship. Therefore, physical cleanliness is a general virtue in Islam and is not concerned only with menstruation or sex-related emissions. That is, it is concerned with the body as a whole as well as the mind. As Abdelwahab Bouhdiba states, the "nature of the purificatory act is of a metaphysical order. It is the art of sublimating the body, of removing pollution and of placing it at the service of the soul and spirit" (1985, 43). Islam stresses the importance of physical cleanliness, but it does *not* claim that the body is sinful. This presents a fine distinction: ritual cleansing in Islam involves the mind and the body but does not imply that either sex or the body is inherently unclean.

### Contraception and Abortion

The Qur'an provides no explicit guidance regarding the use of contraception during sexual intercourse. Legal rulings on birth control have taken their basis from certain Hadith of the Prophet, most of which address the practice of coitus interruptus (*'azl*). In these sayings, the Prophet does not forbid the practice. Generally speaking, the schools of jurisprudence tend to agree that, based on the remarks of the Prophet, *'azl* is permissible with the permission of the woman partner (although some schools may differ on the specific conditions that permit *'azl* and the degree to which it is recommended or not). Looking to these rulings on *'azl,* the schools have reasoned by analogy that other known methods of contraception are also permitted, especially when a woman's life is endangered by pregnancy. The majority of scholars agree that abortion is allowable only in this latter case.

According to al-Ghazali, contraception is allowable since in the Prophet's words, "there is not a soul whose existence God has decreed but that will exist" (1984, 108). As the Qur'an confirms, nothing can stand in the way of God's willing of a child's life; Allah is the ultimate determinant in pregnancy, regardless of any human attempt at contraception.

Although scholars reason that infanticide—which the Qur'an adamantly forbids—and abortion in advanced stages of pregnancy both involve the killing of a developed human being, contraception does not involve such termination of life. According to al-Ghazali, "the initial stage of existence is the planting of the sperm in the uterus, not emission from the urethra; for the offspring is not produced by the sperm of the male alone but from the agglutination" with "a woman's fluid" (1984, 110). Therefore, preventing the sperm from entering the uterus does not interfere with an already existing life. Al-Ghazali does, however, discourage contraception for reasons he judges frivolous, in particular the personal preferences of women who dislike pregnancy and a couple's fear of giving birth to a girl. Acceptable reasons would generally include fear for the well-being of a new child or the well-being of a family as a whole if the means of sustenance available to them are seriously limited.

### Paradise

An interesting intersection between the sexual and sacred occurs in the Qur'anic promises of heavenly pleasure in the afterlife. In its description of the rewards of heaven and its eternal bliss, the Qur'an notes that human beings who enter the paradise will dwell in peace with their mates: "For the righteous are Gardens in nearness to their Lord with rivers flowing beneath; therein is their eternal home, with Companions pure (and holy) and the good pleasure of Allah" (3:15). In addition, traditional male interpreters of the Qur'an have been most interested in their reading of the promise of multiple sexual partners in paradise: "Moreover, We shall join them to Companions with beautiful, big, and lustrous eyes" (44:54). Based on such verses, traditional male commentators throughout the centuries have erected a vibrant mythology of the sexual pleasures that await men in heaven, provided by sensual women companions called *houris*. Revised readings of the Qur'an by women interpreters have yielded broader visions of heavenly pleasures for both men and women.[12] Whether the former reading reflects the sexual fantasies of frustrated male heterosexual readers is not, of course, important here. What is significant is that the Qur'an promises that one of the pleasures of paradise will be the enjoyment of companionship. Whether these companions are the same as those known in one's earthly marriage or of unknown heavenly origins, the notion of sexual companionship as a form of heavenly reward deserves special note. The human experience of sexual companionship is a reference point for human beings to imagine, metaphorically, the pleasures of paradise. The implication here is that companionship on earth is a blessing great enough to be compared to what is to come in heaven. Also, the Qur'an confirms that companionship and sexual union earn a presence among the eternal rewards beyond earth. Sex is worthy of a place in heaven, not simply forgotten in the afterlife.

## THE NOT-SO-PRIVATE LIFE OF THE PROPHET

The Hadith records of the Prophet's life, considered exemplary for Muslims, provide a rich account of his opinions and behaviors with regard to sex. Although traditions differ on numbers, the Prophet likely had fifteen wives during his lifetime. Thirteen of those marriages are said to have been consummated (the remaining resulted in divorce before consummation) (Khafaji 1987, 6). The women Muhammad married included widows, female prisoners of war, one virgin, and some women who themselves approached the Prophet for marriage (Stowasser 1994). Many of these marriages also established strategic alliances with other tribes.

The most famous of the Prophet's wives were Khadija and 'A'isha. At the age of twenty-five, the Prophet married Khadija, a wealthy, forty-year-old merchant. After Muhammad had worked for her as a trader, Khadija proposed to him, and he accepted. When Muhammad first began receiving revelations of the Qur'an with apprehension, she comforted him and became the first convert to Islam. Only after Khadija's death did the Prophet take other wives. Muhammad later married 'A'isha, the daughter of his friend Abu Bakr. At the time of the marriage contract, it is estimated that 'A'isha was most likely six years old (the only virgin Muhammad ever married), but consummation of the marriage occurred after she reached the age of either nine or ten. According to accounts of Muhammad's life, 'A'isha was the Prophet's favorite wife. Many Hadith recount the special love and friendship they shared; they recall, for example, the Prophet playing with her as a teen and later dying in her arms. The Hadith also recall that 'A'isha was outspoken and learned; she spoke her mind to the Prophet, and became a knowledgeable and powerful authority on Islam after his death, even fighting in battles alongside men.

One incident with 'A'isha in particular provoked intense debate over her chastity. While returning home from a campsite with the Prophet and other companions, 'A'isha became separated from the group while searching for her lost necklace. The next day she returned home escorted by a male stranger, which led members of the community as well as the Prophet himself to suspect that 'A'isha had committed adultery. Eventually, only revelations from the Qur'an supporting her innocence cleared 'A'isha of the charges. The Qur'an condemns slandering of people accused of sexual impropriety without proof. Accordingly, it requires four witnesses to adultery in order to protect the innocent from false accusations.[13]

The loss of large numbers of men in battle with opposing groups resulted in numerous widows and orphans, and the Qur'an permitted men to marry up to four women at one time, if they could provide for them adequately and justly. After his marriage to 'A'isha, the Prophet married a number of widows who had lost their husbands to war. However, the Prophet was allowed marriage privileges granted to no other male Muslim, since he had more than four wives at one time (Stowasser 1994, 102).[14] He divided his time among his wives by alternating nights spent with each one. The example of the Prophet and his wives is significant but also stands as an exception to the larger understanding of the historical role of sexuality in Islam.

Certain incidents in the Prophet's married life reveal fears that the women of the Prophet's family would become recognized as such and then harassed by nonbelievers as an insult to Muhammad and his religion (Ahmed 1992, 54). As the Prophet's house became a public venue for meetings and worship, the number of strangers that passed through it increased, as did the likelihood of inappropriate contact with Muhammad's wives (Ahmed 1992, 55). One of many noteworthy incidents in the Prophet's married life occurred when a male guest touched 'A'isha's hand, which reportedly annoyed the Prophet (Ahmed 1992, 54). In response, the Qur'an (33:53, 59) states:

> Oh ye who believe! Enter not the Prophet's houses – until leave is given you. . . . but when ye are invited, enter; and when ye have taken your meal, disperse, without seeking familiar talk. . . . And when ye ask (his ladies) for anything ye want ask them from before a screen: that makes for greater purity for your hearts and for theirs.

> O Prophet! Tell thy wives and daughters, and the believing women, that they should cast their outer garments over their persons (when abroad): That is most convenient, that they should be known (as such) and not molested.

During the Prophet's time, *only* the women of his family observed veiling and seclusion. Indeed, the Qur'an declared that the Prophet's wives were unlike other believing women, regarding them as the virtuous Mothers of the Believers. They were not allowed to remarry after his death; the Qur'an (33: 32–33) gave them their own sexual prescriptions:

> O consorts of the Prophet! Ye are not like any of the (other) women. If ye do fear (Allah), be not too complacent of speech, lest one in whose heart is a disease should be moved with desire. . . . And stay quietly in your houses, and make not a dazzling display, like that of the former times of Ignorance. . . . And Allah only wishes to remove all abomination from you, ye members of the Family, and to make you pure and spotless.

El Guindi's (1999, 154, 156) interpretation of these verses is helpful:

> The Sura (33:53) is ultimately about privacy of the Prophet's home and family and the special status of his wives in two ways—as Prophet's wives and as leaders with access to Islamic information and wisdom who are increasingly sought by community members.
>
> Prophet Muhammad instructed his wives . . . not to consider themselves to be like other women. . . . They were to protect their privacy, go out only when necessary not frivolously, and avoid exhibitionist dress.

These passages demarcate the boundaries between the sexual ethics of the Prophet's family and those of the rest of the Muslim community. They designate the sexual practices of the Prophet and his wives as extraordinary and unnecessary for ordinary Muslims. Their example also establishes the early women of Islam as the carriers and maintainers of culture and has made them subject to special scrutiny by (male) scholars since the first Islamic centuries. Furthermore, the accounts designate Muhammad as a sexual being; the Prophet was not beyond the desires and lures of sex. The ideal Muslim male, then, emerges as vigorously heterosexual. In short, the sexual practices of the Prophet and his wives point to the centrality of sex in the formative history of Islam. Although exceptional, these examples demonstrate that the ordering of the first Muslim society relied heavily upon the ordering of private sexual activity in the Prophet's own household. Express considerations of sex in the private sphere have been central to the public sphere of Islam since its beginnings. That is, sex has been a primary focus for the public ordering of Muslim society and the politics of Islam.

## SUFISM: GOD AS THE LOVER AND THE BELOVED

Sufism, generally referred to as Islamic mysticism, posits a love relationship between Allah and the worshipper. In the Sufi view of creation, God created the universe to make Himself known. Creation is therefore a reflection of Him, and the purpose of one's life is to fully realize the reflection of Allah in oneself. The believer earnestly seeks union with God and nothing else; the ultimate end of one's journey to unite with Allah is *fana*, self-annihilation and complete absorption into God.

Inspired by themes of the worshipper's desire for God, a rich tradition of Sufi poetry elaborates on the worshipper's quest for Allah. In these poems, the worshipper figures as a lover in search of Allah, the beloved. The verses narrate the pain of the lovers' separation and the joy of their union. Because God also desires to be "known," the roles of lover and beloved may alternate, designating God as a lover in turn.

It is interesting to note that al-Ghazali, the author of the most definitive treatise on love and sex in Islam, was a Sufi himself. Al-Ghazali was prolific on an astonishing number of topics, and he left his mark on Islamic philosophy in more than one way. Among his most important efforts was the demonstration of Sufism's reconcilability with orthodox Sunni Islam. He claimed that Sunni practices were in fact prerequisites to Sufi practice.

One of the most volatile subjects of eleventh-century debate on this topic concerned the matter of celibacy. Noted Sufi saints had advocated the celibacy of worshippers because of the distraction that sex, marriage, and other attachments to the world posed to faith and selfless devotion to Allah. However, al-Ghazali discouraged celibacy. He cited Islamic recommendations against sexual deprivation and asceticism in support of marriage, upholding the idea that marriage itself aids in satiating worldly desire that would interfere with complete union with Allah. Thus, a major impetus for Ghazali's work on the advantages and disadvantages of marriage was to aid Sufi readers in reevaluating the concept of marriage (Farah 1984, 30).

In general, the Sufi tendency to avoid marriage took on the poetic form of aversion to lust and its correlate (for men), women. Many Sufi poets left scathing verses on the hatefulness of women, whose impurity, religious inferiority, and temptations were regarded as obstructions in the path to God. On the contrary, some poets looked to women as authorities on the journey of the spirit; among the most praised of Sufi saints is Rabi'a al-'Adawiyya, famous for her spiritual outwitting of men and her extreme piety (Ahmed 1992, 96). Other poets consider the spiritual experience of human love as a metaphor or even a training ground for the transcendence of the material world and its illusions. This ambivalence regarding marriage and women also concerns Sufi meditations on the *nazar,* "the contemplation of a beautiful pubescent boy, who was considered a 'witness' (*shahid*) to the beauty of God and the glory of His creation" (Rowson 1991a, 62). The admiration of beardless youths is a motif in Sufi poetry that was inspired by the medieval Muslim awareness of men's desire for young, attractive boys. Writers and poets of the era have narrated the power of this desire to such an extent that a large portion of medieval Sufi literature by men praises a male beloved figure.

### Erotics of Literature

Although most of the Muslim world is not Middle Eastern, the textual and linguistic roots of Islam originate in this part of the world. Hence, a rich tradition of Arabic, Persian, and Turkish literature has been formative in the development of Muslim culture and its early responses to legalistic Islam (Rowson 1991a, 51). These categories of literature include medical essays, aphorisms, epics, fiction, a vast body of poetry, and literary and cultural criticism called *adab* literature (Rosenthal 1979, 15). In the rich tradition of "*mujun* literature, writing that used profligacy motifs or allusions to sexual deviations to flout social and religious norms," one finds some of the most interesting responses to normative Islam with regard to sex in medieval Arabic literature (Wright 1997, 2).

Before briefly discussing these works, it is necessary to observe that traditions of Western scholarship have used this literature for "characterization of these societies, or their dominant, religion, Islam, as sanctioning and even promoting self-indulgence, licentiousness, and sexual deviance" (Rowson 1991a, 50). Western comparativist scholars have also used such works to demonstrate the hypersexual character of Islam and Muhammad. As more recent critics of Arabic literature have pointed out, heteroerotic and "homoerotic allusions that create political and social satire . . . [have often been] mistaken as evidence of 'sexual culture of the Muslim societies' or as 'dimensions of gay religious history'" (Wright 1997, 2). Rather than indicating Islam's pathological obsession with sex, many of these works emerge as vehicles for political and religious dissent among Arab writers in medieval Islamic environments. Perhaps the most notable among *mujun* poets is Abu Nuwas (d. 814 C.E.), whose verse is replete with parody and satire designed to provoke the disapproval of the Islamic 'ulama. His work often conflates Islam's themes of spiritual submission with imagery of erotic submission during sex (Wright 1997, 9).

The famous *Thousand and One Arabian Nights* abounds with story after story containing surface and subtextual allusions to sex, both hetero- and homoerotic. A vast tradition of mystic Sufi poetry is also rich in heterosexual and same-sex metaphor. Among the most notable of medieval Sufi poets is the widely celebrated Rumi (d. 1273 C.E.), whose poems on the Sufi search for the beloved double as both love poetry and devotional poetry. The overt subject of these poems may be erotic desire for either a male or female figure; the most controversial implicate the Prophet in the trials of homoerotic desire.

From this Arabic literary tradition also emerges an abundance of classical and medieval works of erotology. These treatises on love and sex are often concerned with sexual methods and practices that might multiply the readers' erotic pleasures and solve problems of impotence or infertility. Since sexual pleasure is among God's blessings upon humankind, the purpose of these works was a matter of religious concern. In fact, these works take as their precedent the Hadith of the Prophet Muhammad, who recommended that foreplay, kisses, and romantic words precede the act of coitus in order to increase the pleasure of both partners. Among these erotological works is *The Perfumed Garden,* written by Shaikh Nafzawi (sixteenth century). The first lines of the book read, "Praise be given to God, who has placed man's greatest pleasure in the natural parts of woman, and has destined the natural parts of man to afford the greatest enjoyment to woman" (Nafzawi 1964, 7). Nafzawi goes on to prescribe the use of natural substances, various physical positions, arousal techniques, and suggestions for foreplay as advice to (male) seekers of increased pleasure. He also offers remedies for impotence in men and barrenness in women. Nafzawi praises the body and its enjoyment in graphic description while at the same time praising Allah.

## SEX AND DISORDER

Since the assumption of sexual roles in Islam is a testament to the bless-ings of Allah upon humankind and a vehicle for the remembrance of God, a breach in these roles constitutes a violation of codes that reach far beyond the bedroom. Abdelwahab Bouhdiba articulates it best in *Sexuality in Islam* (1985, 31):

> Islam remains violently hostile to all other ways of realizing sexual de-sire, which are regarded as unnatural purely and simply because they run counter to the antithetical harmony of the sexes; they violate the harmony of life. . . . As a result the divine curse embraces both the boy-ish woman and the effeminate man, male and female homophilia, auto-eroticism, zoophilia, etc. Indeed all these "deviations" involve the same refusal to accept the sexed body and to assume the female or male con-dition. Sexual deviation is a revolt against God.

As a result, Muslims have traditionally deemed sex outside the context of heterosexual marriage, with its rigidly defined gender roles, to be an abomination of nature and God's law. For the (male) authors of *shari'a,* a violation of sexual roles constitutes a threat to their vision of Islam and is *fitnah,* the disordering of Muslim society. Therefore the condemnation of "deviant" sexual acts occurs not necessarily because of their immoral character but namely for the disruption they cause to the social order of exclusive, heterosexual union.

In an attempt to prevent such "deviant" sexual acts, the *shari'a* pre-scribes strict rules regarding men's and women's *awra,* or private parts. Since *zina* of the eyes can occur not only between men and women but also among women and among men, rules of *awra* limit the amount of nudity one may display to members of the same sex. Some Hadith and *fiqh* even discourage looking at oneself nude and indulging in the sight of young boys to avoid auto- and homoerotic temptations.

As Bouhdiba suggests, Islamic dress codes call not only for modesty but also for clear distinctions between men and women. Both men and women must follow masculine and feminine codes of dress in order to an-nounce their sex clearly in public. To preserve the heterosexual order of Islamic societies, legal and political authorities in Islam have specifically condemned the inversion or overlapping of gender roles, along with same-sex sexuality. Although the Qur'an does not propose exclusive gender roles

for men and women (see Wadud 1999), the normative status given to heterosexuality—and not just in Muslim societies—has created anxiety
around the boundaries of masculinity and femininity. This anxiety has resulted in the absorption of cultural prescriptions of masculinity and femininity and strict differentiation of "masculine" and "feminine" attributes
in matters of behavior and dress. For example, men may not don gold jewelry or silk, and they are encouraged to wear beards. According to normative Islam, "masculine" women and "feminine" men (*mukhannithun*) are
deviants of society.[15] Muslims condemn transgenderism for its threat to
heterosexual harmony; some Hadith even allege that the Prophet scorns
"men who act like women and women who act like men" (Bellamy 1979,
36). Even more interesting are cases of individuals with genitalia of both
sexes. Historical and literary records reveal detailed classification systems
for assigning a hermaphrodite to one sex or the other: all people had to be
"either male or female; . . . they could not be both" (Sanders 1991, 77).
Some Hadith even allege that the Prophet expelled the hermaphrodite of
Medina for her or his sexual ambiguity (Bouhdiba 1985, 41).

Of course, these proscriptions constitute the practices and formula-
tions of Islam by Muslims within the context of sexist and homophobic
cultures. Although many contemporary scholars assert that sexual and
gender roles are the products of social construction rather than nature,
the traditional fear of *fitnah* remains dominant in Islamic legal rulings
today. Other scholar-activists contend that the rigidity of the *shari'a*
amounts to biological determinism in Islam and gives precedence to the
legal rulings of fallible human beings over the universal, divine precepts
of the Qur'an. In other words, traditional *shari'a* has developed through
the social mores created by human beings. These social mores are relative
to the time and place of the society in which they originate, as well as the
attitudes and prejudices of the scholars who pronounce such legal rulings.
Thus, the *shari'a* forces Muslim men and women to subscribe to socially
mandated sexual roles created by human beings, not Allah. Some contemporary scholars have sought to expose the flawed logic of the traditional *shari'a* that remains the unbending, authoritative voice of Islam
today. Since debates along these lines have yet to be fully articulated,
challenges to notions of sexual "deviance" in Islam remain to be seen.

### Same-Sex Sexuality

The Qur'an and classical Arabic have no equivalent for the English term
*homosexuality*. The term in English developed from a nineteenth-century

notion of the pathological condition of individuals engaging in any same-sex behavior at any time, a condition that only in the past 200 years has emerged as the totalizing measure of one's sexual identity in the West (Monroe 1997, 115). In contrast, Muslim societies have not developed a sense of homosexuality as a state of identity or being. For Muslims there is no "gay lifestyle," and therefore "the term 'homosexuality' . . . does not represent the practice of same-sex activity in these societies" (Jamal 2001, 9). There is among Muslims, however, an understanding of same-sex acts.

According to the *shari'a*, sodomy constitutes *zina* (sex outside marriage) and is punishable as such. Further, normative Islam considers sex outside the framework of heterosexual marriage to be a grave violation of the natural harmony of the sexes advocated by the Qur'an. Therefore all such behavior is strongly condemned as deviant and as a corruption of Islam, humanity, and God's order.

The Arabic term for sodomy is *liwat,* and a person who engages in sodomy is a *luti.* Both terms derive from Lut, the Arabic name for Lot, the prophet of God who appears both in the Qur'an and the Bible. The Qur'anic story of Lot as read by normative Islam in the tradition of the Bible condemns and prohibits the sexual behavior of the people of Sodom in multiple references. According to the story, the male members of Lot's community refuse to refrain from sex with other men. Among Qur'anic references to the story are 26:165–166: "Of all the creatures in the world, will ye approach males, and leave those whom Allah has created for you to be your mates? Nay, ye are a people transgressing (all limits)!" As a result, Allah destroys the village with a shower of stones but saves Lot and most of his family for their righteousness. Numerous sayings of Muhammad also regard male sodomy with disgust, deeming it an abomination that results in one's eternal damnation.

Both the Qur'an and Hadith focus their attention on acts of sodomy among men and generally ignore woman-woman acts, or *sahq.*[16] The *shari'a* assumes that *sahq* is also reprehensible by analogy since it constitutes adultery; however, punishment is less severe since lesbian sex does not involve penetration by the male organ. Similarly, Islam condemns all other types of "deviant" sexual behavior, such as heterosexual anal intercourse and autoerotic, bestial, or necrophiliac acts for their disruption to the Islamic order of the sexes.

The *shari'a* suggests punishments for sodomy that are similar to those for adultery: stoning to death for married people and 100 lashes for unmarried people.[17] Punishment may be more severe for the "active" participant in the act and less severe for the "passive" participant. Four males must witness the act of sodomy in progress, or the individuals in question must confess in order for punishment to ensue. As a consequence of these conditions, the punishment rarely occurs in actuality. A number of sociological studies have claimed that Islam's conditions for punishment suggest that the greatest threat of sodomy is its public display because it might inspire *fitnah* among Muslims and endanger the sexual order: "As with other offenses, the *shari'a* demands solid evidence and seems little concerned with what occurs in private. Like fornication, homosexuality has to assume the character of a public nuisance in order to become punishable" (Duran 1993, 183).

In fact, normative readings of the Qur'an and *shari'a* condemn acts of sodomy but have little to say on the matter of homosexuality itself, suggesting that only *acting upon* homosexual desire is grounds for punishment. "In practice it is only public transgression of Islamic morals that is condemned" (Schild 1990, 617). Nothing in Islamic theology clearly condemns homosexual desire that is not acted upon, a stark difference from conservative Christian interpretations, which tend to consider homosexuality "a pathological character defect and homosexuals to be abnormal, perverted individuals." By contrast, "Islamic jurisprudence adopts a more restrained attitude, according to which attraction toward members of one's own sex is viewed as entirely normal and natural" (Monroe 1997, 116–117). This conclusion, interestingly, is incongruous with Islam's more general posturing toward sexual desire, which acknowledges the sexual urges of human beings and, rather than favoring repression, expressly allows for their satiation. Thus the notion that Islam tolerates homosexual tendencies but not behaviors points to an inconsistency in Islamic allowances for the satiation of "natural" sexual desire.

## VEILS, HAREMS, AND THE SEXUAL REPRODUCTIONS OF ORIENTALISM

No discussion of sexuality in Islam can ignore the glaring Western fetishization of the harem and the veil. Nothing essential to Islamic theology endorses the harem, the veil, or the seclusion of women from public spaces. Rather, these sexual institutions are the contributions of cultures and social attitudes that have surrounded Islam since its beginnings. This distinction, however, does not aim to obscure Muslim practices of sexual seclusion. The apologist claim, for instance, that the harem has nothing to do with Islam is absurd. To the contrary, practices of sexual segregation have occurred in particular ways because of and alongside the development of Islam. In other words, neither the context of Islam nor the context of various cultures of the Muslim world can be separated from these issues.

The Muslim practice of sexual segregation emerged most conspicuously during the 'Abbasid era, with the rapid mass expansion of Muslim rule far beyond Arabia and into Persia and southwestern Asia. As Islam spread to other territories, Muslim communities tended to incorporate the cultural values of new lands in their practice of Islam, imbibing notions of gender and sexist prejudice among them. Scholars conclude that veiling was practiced "for millennia in the Mesopotamian/Mediterranean region (not Arabia)" long before the emergence of Islam (El Guindi 1999, 11). During these formative periods in Islamic history, Muslim theologians and jurists came to endorse the misogynist attitudes and practices of various cultures. The mandatory imposition of *hijab*—commonly translated in English as "veil"—for women, their confinement to domestic spaces, and men's practices of boundless polygamy became seamlessly incorporated into Muslim *shari'a*. Leila Ahmed's landmark book *Women and Gender in Islam* (1992, 87) recalls this rarely cited history:

> To the various prejudices against women and the mores degrading women that were part of one or other tradition indigenous to the area before Islam, Islamic institutions brought endorsement and license. In an urban Middle East with already well articulated misogynist attitudes and practices, by licensing polygamy, concubinage, and easy divorce for men, originally allowed under different circumstances in a different society, Islam lent itself to being interpreted as endorsing and giving religious sanction to a deeply negative and debased conception of women. As a result, a number of abusive uses of women became legally and religiously sanctioned Muslim practices.

Scholars such as Riffat Hassan have noted that nothing in the Qur'an or Sunna *explicitly* indicates that the wearing of *hijab* is required of Muslim women in general: "Certainly there are no statements in the Qur'an, which justify the extremely rigid restrictions regarding veiling and segregation which have been imposed on Muslim women by many Muslim societies" (Hassan, n.d., 72). Proponents of women's *hijab* most commonly cite verses 24:30–31 of the Qur'an:

Say to the believing men that they should lower their gaze and guard their modesty: That will make for greater purity for them. . . . And say to the believing women that they should lower their gaze and guard their modesty; that they should not display their beauty and ornaments except what (must ordinarily) appear thereof; that they should draw their veils [*khumur*] over their bosoms and not display their beauty except to their husbands, their fathers, their husbands' fathers, their sons, their husbands' sons, their brothers or their brothers' sons, or their sisters' sons, or their women, or the slaves whom their right hands possess, or male servants free of physical needs, or small children.

The most significant directive of these passages addresses the modesty of both men and women. The Qur'an instructs both men and women to refrain from gazing at members of the opposite sex excessively and with sexual desire. In addition, both men and women must "guard their modesty." The reasoning for these directives lies in many of the same principles upon which Islam bases its regulations for marriage. Modesty and regulation of the gaze are meant to limit a specific kind of *zina*—that of the eye—which in turn prevents the sexual transgression of literal *zina*.

In the above verses, the Qur'an is more specific on the matter of women's modestly than on men's. However, the word *hijab* does not appear in these verses. Instead, this and another passage from the Qur'an 33:59 refer to *khumur* (covering of the hair) and *jalabeeb* (loose covering of the body).[18] Of course, these and several related terms imply much the same sense as *hijab*, although in distinct ways. Debates continue over whether or not the Qur'an privileges a specific type of covering over others. The nuances of the various terms used to designate modest dress in the Qur'an and conflicting opinions regarding the degree to which these verses should be read literally or in the context of seventh-century Arabian mores are countless. Suffice it to say that the Qur'an expressly requires modesty of both men and women, regardless of how this injunction is interpreted and met by Muslims of different times and places.

It is important to note here that non-Muslims and Muslims alike are responsible for perceptions about sexual segregation in Islam. As a result of the history of Western aggression and colonization in Muslim countries, what is commonly referred to as the "harem" or the "veil" is as much the construct of non-Muslims as it is of Muslims. In general, much of sexuality in Islam is the reproduction of Orientalist notions of the Muslim Other. As Edward Said notes in his landmark study *Orientalism*

(1994), Western representations by European travelers, missionaries, and governments over the past several centuries have constructed Muslims as racially inferior, irrational, and uncivilized. European countries have historically used these representations to justify their brutal colonization and exploitation of Muslim countries. By depicting their presence in these parts of the world as generous attempts to civilize backward cultures, European imperialists sought to defend their colonial practices.

Citing the barbaric treatment of Muslim women as prime evidence for the necessity of civilizing Muslim countries, European reports of the misery of Muslim women—trapped in harems, bound in head-to-toe veils, and subjected to sexual slavery—have created a legacy of fascination with the "dark" sexual practices of Muslims. Representing Muslim women exclusively as victims of sexual repression and Muslim men as hypersexual fiends, Western traditions of literature and art have created a general portrait of Muslim sexuality as dark, repressive, and hopelessly Other, leaving an indelible mark upon both non-Muslims' and Muslims' perceptions of sexuality in Islam. By equating the veil and sexual segregation with oppression and European and American gender practices with liberation, Western traditions have continued to impose their arrogant gaze upon Muslim cultures. In response to such violence, even Muslim resistance to Western sexual prescriptions has remained mired in colonial frameworks. As Ahmed points out, the Muslim "resistance narrative thus reversed—but thereby also accepted—the terms set in the first place by the colonizers. And therefore, ironically, it is Western discourse that in the first place determined the new meanings of the veil and gave rise to its emergence as a symbol of resistance" (1992, 164).

Fadwa El Guindi's *Veil: Modesty, Privacy, Resistance* is perhaps the most sophisticated and carefully researched anthropological analysis of the history of the veil to date. El Guindi begins her examination by warning readers of the careless representations of the harem and veil in modern scholarship. Although I maintain the relevance of pursuing the historical origins of the harem and the veil as Ahmed has done, El Guindi warns that neither of these institutions is "monolithic, and cannot be reduced to a cultural artifact that passed in linear succession from . . . civilization to civilization" (1999, 28). Many Orientalists have been guilty of sloppy analyses along these lines, designating the harem "the ultimate locus of female oppression and subordination, thus reducing a complex sociopolitical structure purely to gender and sexuality" (25).

A vast body of literature narrates the experiences of women living in harems and living "behind" the veil. These popular descriptions range from the travel writings of Europeans visiting the Muslim world to Huda Shaarawi's *Harem Years* (1986). El Guindi declares the term *harem* highly problematic: "The English term *harem* . . . is a distortion of the Arabic word *harim*""a derivative of the same root . . . that yields the Arabic/Islamic notion of *haram* . . . , which means 'sacred'" (1999, 25). El Guindi locates the sacred connotations of the *harim* as it relates to women's spaces. She establishes that in Arab cultures, the term refers "to the women of a household and to women's quarters" (El Guindi 1999, 25). El Guindi stresses that women's quarters in the Arab world have traditionally taken on the sense of sanctuary and sacred family space (1999, 96).

El Guindi's study also takes up the notion of the *hijab* in a similar manner, clarifying the origins and influences of the term. She claims that the use of the word to describe veiling arose in reference to the specific injunctions for modesty among the wives of the Prophet (see Qur'anic verse 33:59, as discussed previously). The popular use of the term as we know it today arose only later in the context of modern colonial discourse, tossed around—perhaps less precisely—by politicians and feminist political activists (El Guindi 1999, 152–153). El Guindi concludes that the harem along with the "veil, veiling patterns and veiling behavior are therefore . . . about sacred privacy . . . , linking women as the guardians of family sanctuaries and the realm of the sacred in this world" (1999, 96).

However, this notion of gendered[19] sacred space is not to be confused with Christian or Jewish conceptions of gendered, private spaces: "There is a tradition of gender segregation and public seclusion of women in the Judaic and Christian traditions that is rooted in conceptions of the purity and impurity of women" (El Guindi 1999, 151). This crucial difference between the Judeo-Christian and Islamic traditions, however, has been obscured by Orientalist studies that have unduly attributed separation to pejorative rather than sacred understandings of gender: "The paradigm of public/private, and its corollary honor-shame, is the one most commonly imposed on Arab and Islamic cultural space to describe the division between the sexes" (El Guindi 1999, 79). El Guindi arrives at a stunning observation, substantiating the imposition of European mores onto Muslim sexuality:

> The European term "veil" (with its correlate "seclusion"), therefore, fails to capture these nuances, and oversimplifies a complex phenomenon . . .

Furthermore, "veil" as commonly used gives the illusion of having a single referent . . . Limiting its reference obscures historical developments, cultural differentiations of social context, class, or special rank, and sociopolitical articulations. In Western feminist discourse "veil" is politically charged with connotations of the inferior "other," implying and assuming a subordination and inferiority of the Muslim woman. (1999, 157)

As El Guindi points out, separation and privacy in Islam do not find their bases in the notions of shame or inferiority assumed by Western understandings of segregation. Contrary to popular belief, Muslim practices of privacy have no essential relationship to shame; nor are they predicated upon the absence of certain members of society. Rather, separate, gendered spaces facilitate the performance of tasks delegated to each gender, around which male and female agents build distinct same-sex communities. Ignoring this distinction, Western norms of the private as taboo continue to inform exotic fantasies of the harem, the veil, and the sexual slavery of women.

## OTHER HOT TOPICS: CIRCUMCISION AND HONOR KILLING

The Orientalist gaze has also penetrated issues of female circumcision and honor killing of women. Although male circumcision entails the removal of the foreskin from the penis, female genital mutilation (FGM) involves the cutting or removal of female genitalia (Toubia 1993, 9). FGM refers to the removal of the clitoris or to infibulation, the cutting of the labia in addition to the clitoris. The practice of FGM does not occur in any "predominantly Muslim countries" or any Middle Eastern countries except Yemen and southern Egypt (Toubia 1993, 26, 32). It has been most commonly documented in the countries of central Africa, India, and Malaysia and among immigrants from these countries living in North America and Europe (Toubia 1993, 22, 26). Among these populations, FGM occurs as a female rite of passage and is believed to enhance beauty, cleanliness, and fertility. Additionally, many cultures hold that the practice of circumcision is a moral safeguard against zina since it curbs the sexual desire of young girls.

FGM is a cultural, not religious practice; it is also pre-Islamic. However, many people associate Islam with FGM since African Muslim communities have traditionally claimed that Islam licenses the practice. The Qur'an does not call for the practice, although there are conflicting interpretations of Hadith that allegedly tolerate it. In the matter of male circumcision, only the Sunna recommends it as a matter of hygiene. Generally speaking, no clear theological grounds for female genital mutilation exist, but stereotypes about Islam and Eastern cultures have presented the matter as such, citing FGM as outstanding proof of the barbaric, inferior nature of those societies.

"Honor killings" of women in some South Asian and Arab countries have recently gained increased media attention throughout the world. This practice locates the honor of men in the sexual behavior of their female relatives. To preserve the honor of his family, a man may resort to burning or murdering a wife or female relative if she allegedly violates rigid *cultural* codes of sexual honor. This violation may occur if a woman has (or is rumored to have) sex outside marriage, is raped, desires a marriage partner of her own choice, or seeks to divorce her husband. Islam does *not* sanction the abuse or murder of women based on these alleged sexual transgressions; it secures women the right to divorce and the choice of a marriage partner, and it condemns rape and murder. Neither does it sanction the abuse of women at the hands of family members or punishment for *zina* without clear proof of the crime. In all these cases, crimes in the name of family honor are the symptoms of cultural views of women's sexuality and shame. Although many men may proclaim that honor crimes must be performed in the name of Islam, Islam does not tolerate such practices.

## PHANTOMS OF SECULAR FEMINISM

The secular feminist discourse that has ensued since the 1970s, particularly in response to works such as Fatima Mernissi's *Beyond the Veil: Male-Female Dynamics in Muslim Society* (1987) and Nawal El Saadawi's *The Hidden Face of Eve: Women in the Arab World* (1980)—both widely celebrated works in the West—has left an indelible mark, for better or for worse, upon feminist approaches to sex in Islam. A large audience of these works has deduced that Islam punishes women for being powerful sources of *fitnah* among men.

The argument reads something like this: women are such powerful temptresses that they cause men to lose their reason and engage in *zina,* forgetting their obligations to Islam. Because men are unable to resist sexual temptation, Islam must curb women's sexual power in order to preserve the order of Muslim society. To protect men from feminine evil, women must remain veiled and confined to their homes while men engage in the public practice of Islam, safe from temptation. Men also have the right in Islam to sexually satiate themselves by taking multiple wives and by repudiating one woman in order to enjoy a new sexual partner. In effect, Islam's treatment of women amounts to physical and intellectual slavery.

Uncritical readers have proclaimed that Islam has designated men the spiritual, physical, and intellectual superiors of women, whose most important Islamic virtue lies in submission and obedience to male authority. As such, Islam functions to repress the sexual desire of women and regulate the desire of Muslim men into the religiously sanctioned media of marriage, polygamy, and repudiation to satisfy sexual needs that might otherwise overpower their ability to worship. Therefore, women must open their eyes to their slavery in Islam and oppose the oppression of Allah.

The ultimate weakness of these secularist responses is their endorsement of Orientalist readings of Islam that characterize the religion as antiwoman. Secular feminists assume that Islam is inherently misogynistic, rather than perceiving that the misogyny in Islam—like that in other religions—is the product of misogynist interpreters. By taking the androcentric practices of Islam for granted and assuming they are inherent to the religion, they declare that women's sexual liberation and Islam are fundamentally contradictory and mutually exclusive. Thus they remain unable to reconcile the sexual and sacred for Muslim women, failing to imagine feminist visions for Islam's embrace of sexuality and stifling the potential development of such visions—a tremendous loss for the Muslim women they have sought to liberate.

## ISLAM AND SEX IN NON-MUSLIM SOCIETIES

Since the inception of Islam, there have always been Muslims living in non-Muslim societies—that is, societies in which the majority population is non-Muslim or Islam is not the state religion. From the first community of Muslims in Mecca to the West African Muslim slaves of antebellum America to the rapidly growing immigrant communities of

Muslims in the contemporary United States and Europe, Muslims have long practiced their religion in the absence of political systems that could be called Muslim. By relying on the traditions of the Qur'an, Sunna, and *shari'a,* they have practiced Islam as minorities, building their own communities and founding their own organizations. Local mosques have provided venues for worship, guidance, and learning. In the place of political enforcement, these minority communities have relied heavily on small mosques and informal community structures to regulate Islamic practice, including the implementation of sexual proscriptions. The consequences for moral and sexual improprieties not already addressed by the non-Muslim government usually occur in the form of public shame or renunciation by the Muslim community but may also occur less legitimately in the form of "private" punishment unsanctioned by the state (namely as domestic violence).

A nod must also be given to the idealization of "authentic" Islamic values among Muslims in both Muslim and non-Muslim societies, which partly finds its roots in the history of European colonization of Muslim countries. The legacy of colonialism and its assault upon Muslim cultures has in large part led to the emergence of so-called Islamic fundamentalist movements around the world. In an attempt to defend themselves against colonial powers that justified the exploitation of Muslims on the basis of their supposed racial and religious inferiority, Muslims have formed resistance movements that often look to a "romantic past" of Muslim identity. Much of this romantic vision has ignored the reality of lived Islam and has called upon a past of purity and congruence that never actually existed. Since colonial agendas targeted the treatment of women and sex in particular, much of the reconstructed Islamic past has concerned the return to precolonial visions of Muslim sexuality, with particular attention to the mobility of women. Thus, by using this notion of essential Muslim sexual identity, "Muslim patriarchs conspire with the salacious gaze of the West at the Other to present this as the single and typical discourse of sexuality in Muslim societies" (Imam 2001, 18). Any deviance from the prescriptions of this sexual ideal among Muslims, especially among women, has come to mean rejection of Islam itself and evidence of the "West-toxification" of Muslim societies. This phenomenon has had the effect of impeding contemporary revision of the sexual codes of Muslims.

Similarly, the discourse of sex among Muslims in non-Muslim countries largely overlaps with discourses of acculturation. Efforts to preserve religious practice and cultural tradition within immigrant Muslim communities in non-Muslim countries, particularly in the United States, have concentrated on the maintenance of sexual values from the home Muslim country. In this scheme, the "loss" of one's children "to America" amounts to sexual transgressions: premarital sex, immodesty in dress, promiscuity, and homosexuality. In this respect, the loss of Muslim identity has become equivalent to the adoption of non-Muslim sexual morals. Thus, sex figures at the center of the struggle to preserve Muslim identity in non-Muslim societies.

## NOTES

1.  Based on current statistics of the Council on American Islamic Relations (CAIR).
2.  In English translations of the Qur'an, God is designated by the masculine pronoun. This gendered sense of God, however, is not present in the original Arabic. The Arabic word *Allah* has no gender, and Muslims do not regard God as male or female since Allah transcends designation by sex. Because of linguistic limitations, however, translators resort to the use of the masculine pronoun to safeguard against the objectifying sense of the linguistic neuter. Theoretically, they may just as well use the feminine pronoun in their translations, but they uphold the use of the masculine by claiming that the so-called impersonal "he" is the standard expression of the nongendered. This selective gendering of pronouns, of course, is cause for debate among Muslims and non-Muslims alike.
3.  The Qur'an alternates between the third and first person when referring to God. God is one, but the Qur'an often employs the royal "we."
4.  A similar problem of masculine pronouns and nouns emerges in translating references to human beings in the Qur'an. I have used Abdullah Yusuf Ali's translation of the Qur'an but taken the liberty of replacing the word *man* or *mankind* with *humans* or *humankind* wherever the Qur'an *implies* both sexes. I have also included the feminine pronoun as an alternate translation in such cases. I have marked these changes clearly throughout the chapter by using brackets.
5.  Riffat Hassan asserts that the Qur'anic story of Adam and Eve's creation is an egalitarian one. The Qur'an does not claim that Eve tempted Adam or that woman was responsible for the Fall of man. Nor was Eve created for or from Adam: "The myth that Eve was created from the rib of Adam has no basis whatsoever in the Qur'an which never mentions Eve, and in the context of human creation speaks always in completely egalitarian terms. In

none of the thirty or so Qur'anic passages that describe the creation of humanity . . . is there any statement which asserts or suggests that man was created prior to woman or that woman was created from man" (93).

6. Islamic law condemns rape (*ightisab*) as a crime of physical violence (Rowson 1991a, 67).

7. (a) The Qur'an clearly defines incest. *Nikah* may not occur with a *mahram* ("forbidden") member of one's family: a parent, sibling, uncle, aunt, niece, nephew, foster-parent, foster-sibling, stepchild, stepparent, son-in-law, or daughter-in-law. (b) Interfaith marriage with a Jew or Christian is permissible but is permitted only for Muslim men by canonical Islamic law. (c) Marriage with up to four women at one time is also allowable to men by the Qur'an under certain strictly outlined conditions. For information on interfaith marriage and polygamy, subjects outside the scope of this chapter, consult the works of Azizah al-Hibri (see Suggestions for Further Reading).

8. It is important to note that al-Ghazali explicitly addresses a male audience in his eleventh-century works, directing his prescriptions specifically to heterosexual men.

9. It should be noted that there are different kinds of divorce under Islamic law, each varying slightly in rights and conditions. Such legalities are beyond the scope of this chapter.

10. In general, Islam insists upon the clear establishment of the paternity of children to the extent that it even discourages adoption. For this reason, textual sources adamantly condemn the bearing of "illegitimate" children. The benefit of establishing paternity for children (since maternity is obvious) is to ensure parental responsibility for their care. Male-centered interpretations, however, have cited these matters as evidence for Islam's alleged endorsement of patrilineality and patriarchy.

11. More precisely, al-Ghazali's recommendations for sex, like Islamic etiquette in any matter, are generally addressed according to "a scale of religious qualifications that included five categories: obligatory, recommended, neutral, reprehensible, and forbidden" (Sanders 1991, 80).

12. Amina Wadud's *Qur'an and Woman* is an excellent resource for more elaboration on the topic. Wadud contends that male heterosexual readings of heavenly pleasures such as that of the *houri* "limit the sensual descriptions of Paradise in the Qur'an to their narrowest literal meaning, rather than understand[ing] them as metaphorical indications of pleasure" (1999, 53). The "specific description here of the companions of Paradise demonstrates the Qur'an's familiarity with the dreams and desires of those Arabs," particularly the males of seventh-century Arabia who fantasized about sex with a certain kind of woman (1999, 55). As with the rest of the Qur'an, here "the terms are relative to the subconscious of a particular audience . . . yet, the notions are intended for the larger reading audience" (1999, 53).

13. Accusation of *zina* "without being able to prove that accusation true constitutes the most serious form of defamation known to the law" (Coulson 1979, 64).

14. Records indicate that the Prophet also took on at least one concubine, a Coptic woman named Mariya whom the Prophet had inherited after victory in a battle (Lings 1983, 233, 279). It is beyond the scope of this paper to explain the Prophet's practice of concubinage and its legality.

15. It is interesting to note that, as Everett Rowson points out, the effeminate male musicians of Medina in early Islam enjoyed a great deal of fame and status but once associated with homosexuality, experienced persecution (1991b, 671).

16. This term literally means "'pounding, rubbing, shaving'" (Rowson 1991a, 63).

17. Punishments for certain sins explicitly outlined by the Qur'an or Hadith (as in the case of murder, rape, and adultery) are called *hadd* punishments. Punishments determined by the discretion of scholars are called *ta'zir* punishments. However, punishments for sexual deviance have been debated as both *hadd* or *ta'zir;* the distinction remains unclear in these matters (Duran 1993, 183).

18. The Arabic root of the word *hijab* denotes "covering" or "separation," but this word, which has been used almost exclusively to describe the veiling of Muslim women, is the least precise of Arabic terms that refer to women's dress. The terms *khimar, abayya,* and *jalabiyya* are among the more specific Arabic terms that refer to Muslim and Arab women's different methods of covering in various contexts.

19. Arab men have been known to veil in some Muslim societies as well. In fact, "it has been reported that on a number of occasions Prophet Muhammad himself face-veiled, an image well-depicted in Turkish and Persian miniatures" (El Guindi 1999, 152).

# REFERENCES

Abou El Fadel, Khaled. 2001. *Speaking in God's Name: Islamic Law, Authority and Women.* Oxford: Oneworld.

Ahmed, Leila. 1992. *Women and Gender in Islam: Historical Roots of a Modern Debate.* New Haven: Yale University Press.

Ali, Abdullah Yusuf. 1989. *The Holy Qur'an: Text, Translation, and Commentary.* Brentwood: Amana Corporation.

Bellamy, James A. 1979. "Sex and Society in Islamic Popular Literature." Pp. 23–42 in Afaf Lufti al-Sayyid-Marsot, ed., *Society and the Sexes in Medieval Islam.* Malibu: Undena.

Bouhdiba, Abdelwahab. 1985. *Sexuality in Islam.* London: Routledge and Kegan Paul.

Coulson, Noel J. 1979. "Regulation of Sexual Behavior under Traditional Islamic Law." Pp. 63–68 in Afaf Lufti al-Sayyid-Marsot, ed., *Society and the Sexes in Medieval Islam.* Malibu: Undena.

Duran, Khalid. 1993. "Homosexuality and Islam." Pp. 181–197 in Arlene Swidler, ed., *Homosexuality and World Religions.* Valley Forge: Trinity Press International.

El Guindi, Fadwa. 1999. *Veil: Modesty, Privacy, and Resistance.* Oxford: Berg.

El Saadawi, Nawal. 1980. *The Hidden Face of Eve: Women in the Arab World.* Sherif Hetata, trans. London: Zed Books.

Farah, Madelain. 1984. "Introduction." In *Marriage and Sexuality in Islam: A Translation of al-Ghazali's Book on the Etiquette of Marriage from the Ihya.* Salt Lake City: University of Utah Press.

al-Ghazali, Abu Hamid. 1984. *Marriage and Sexuality in Islam: A Translation of al-Ghazali's Book on the Etiquette of Marriage from the Ihya.* Madelain Farah, trans. Salt Lake City: University of Utah Press.

Haeri, Shahla. 1989. "Introduction." In *Law of Desire: Temporary Marriage in Shi'i Iran.* Syracuse: Syracuse University Press.

Hassan, Riffat. N.d. *Women's Rights and Islam: From the I.C.P.D. to Beijing.* Self-published by the author.

Ilkkaracan, Pinar, ed. 2000. *Women and Sexuality in Muslim Societies.* Istanbul, Turkey: Women for Women's Human Rights (WWHR)/Kadinin Insan Haklari Projesi (KIHP).

Imam, Ayesha. 2001. "The Muslim Religious Right ('Fundamentalists') and Sexuality." Pp. 15–30 in Patricia Beattie Jung, Mary E. Hunt, and Radhika Balakrishnan, eds., *Good Sex: Feminist Perspectives from the World's Religions.* New Brunswick: Rutgers University Press.

Jamal, Amreen. 2001. "The Story of Lot and the Qur'an's Perception of the Morality of Same-Sex Sexuality." *Journal of Homosexuality* 41, no. 1: 1–88.

Khafaji, 'Abd al-Hakim. 1987. *Kawakib Hawl al-Rasul.* Alexandria: Dar al-Wafa'.

Lings, Martin. 1983. *Muhammad: His Life Based on the Earliest Sources.* Rochester: Inner Traditions International.

Mernissi, Fatima. 1987. *Beyond the Veil: Male-Female Dynamics in Modern Muslim Society.* Bloomington: Indiana University Press.

Monroe, James T. 1997. "The Striptease That Was Blamed on Abu Bakr's Naughty Son: Was Father Being Shamed, or Was the Poet Having Fun? (Ibn Quzman's *Zagal No. 133*)." Pp. 94–139 in J. W. Wright, Jr., and Everett K. Rowson, eds., *Homoeroticism in Classical Arabic Literature.* New York: Columbia University Press.

Nafzawi, Umar ibn Muhammad. 1964. *The Perfumed Garden of Shaykh Nafzawi.* Sir Richard F. Burton, trans. New York: Castle Books.

Rosenthal, Franz. 1979. "Fiction and Reality: Sources for the Role of Sex in Medieval Muslim Society." Pp. 3–22 in Afaf Lufti al-Sayyid-Marsot, ed., *Society and the Sexes in Medieval Islam.* Malibu: Undena.

Rowson, Everett K. 1991a. "The Categorization of Gender and Sexual Irregularity in Medieval Arabic Vice Lists." Pp. 50–79 in Julia Epstein and Kristina Straub, eds., *Body Guards: The Cultural Politics of Gender Ambiguity.* New York: Routledge.

———. 1991b. "The Effeminates of Early Medina." *Journal of the American Oriental Society* 111, no. 4: 671–693.

Said, Edward. 1994. *Orientalism.* New York: Vintage Books.

Sanders, Paula. 1991. "Gendering the Ungendered Body: Hermaphrodites." Pp. 74–95 in Nikkie R. Keddie and Beth Baron, eds., *Shifting Boundaries in Sex and Gender.* New Haven: Yale University Press.

Schild, Maarten. 1990. "Islam." Pp. 615–620 in Wayne R. Dynes, ed., *Encyclopedia of Homosexuality.* New York: Garland.

Shaarawi, Huda. 1986. *Harem Years: The Memoirs of an Egyptian Feminist.* Margot Badran, trans. New York: Feminist Press.

Spellberg, D. A. 1994. *Politics, Gender, and the Islamic Past: The Legacy of 'A'isha Bint Abi Bakr.* New York: Columbia University Press.

Stowasser, Barbara Freyer. 1994. *Women in the Qur'an: Traditions and Interpretation.* New York: Oxford University Press.

Toubia, Nahid. 1993. *Female Genital Mutilation: A Call for Global Action.* New York: Women, Ink.

Wadud, Amina. 1999. *Qur'an and Woman: Rereading the Sacred Text from a Woman's Perspective.* New York: Oxford University Press.

Wright, J. W., Jr. 1997. "Masculine Allusion and the Structure of Satire in Early 'Abbasid Poetry." Pp. 1–23 in J. W. Wright, Jr., and Everett K. Rowson, eds., *Homoeroticism in Classical Arabic Literature.* New York: Columbia University Press.

Part 2

# Religion, Gender, and Sexuality in the United States

# Chapter 10

# Casting Divinity in My Image

## Women, Men, and the Embodiment of Sacred Sexuality

*Nancy Ramsey Tosh and Tanya Keenan*

*Beltane rituals often involve celebrating sexuality and dancing around the phallic Maypole, a practice adopted from the fertility religions of ancient and pre-Christian Europe. Also during this celebration, in many Pagan groups, young single women jump over the belfire (a central ritual bonfire) in order to increase fertility. (The Scotsman/Corbis Sygma)*

*[Wicca] means the freedom to find my own path to the Divine, to worship as befits my needs. Most important aspect? Divinity cast in my image.*

—Female survey respondent

On April 2001, after a talk entitled "Mothers and Goddesses: Women in Search of the Feminine Divine," a man in the audience repeatedly asked the presenters why Witches place such emphasis on gender, sexuality, and the body—since, he claimed, humans are in reality purely spiritual beings. The importance of the body and embodiment sets Paganism apart from the dominant world religions. In fact, the sacralization of the human body seen in this family of new religious movements distinguishes them from the New Age movement, from most other new religious movements in the United States, and from other religions and philosophies that make up the occult undercurrent of U.S. society.

New religious movements in the United States that derive from Hinduism, such as the Ramakrishna Mission and the International Society for Krishna Consciousness (ISKCON, or the "Hare Krishnas"), and those deriving from Buddhism, such as American Zen Buddhism and Nichiren Shoshu, often favor the development of mind and spirit while paying little heed to the body. Even the more ritualistic new religious movements such as ISKCON balance the physical embodiment of their faiths with strong limitations on sexual expression. Among the new religious movements in the United States, only Paganism and some forms of feminist theology endeavor to redefine the human relationship to nature and thus to our bodies. Yet even radical forms of religions such as Christianity must balance traditional teachings with a heightened respect for human sexuality. Paganism, however, is in a position to redefine this relationship from scratch.

Paganism reflects a synthesis of ideas and practices available from within the occult counterculture of the United States. It encompasses many nature-based religions, including Wicca, goddess spirituality, and Native American spiritual traditions, although the inclusion of this last is still contested by many Native Americans. The term *neopagan* is used frequently by scholars but rarely by actual practitioners of this new religious movement. In this essay, we defer to the practitioners and use "Paganism" throughout.

Wicca, or Witchcraft, refers to a highly structured re-creation of what practitioners believe to be the pre-Christian religious practices of northern Europeans. Many forms of Wicca, including the Gardnerian and Alexandrian traditions, try to promote egalitarian ideals of gender by emphasizing a balance between Goddess and God, whereas other forms such as Dianic Wicca attempt to redress the imbalance of patriarchy by focusing on the worship of the Goddess.

Goddess spirituality, which is closely related to Dianic Wicca but is somewhat less structured, also addresses the patriarchal imbalance in dominant U.S. religions by focusing strictly on goddess worship. For inspiration, Dianic Wicca and goddess spirituality often look to a time before recorded history when some believe civilization was matriarchal.

Pagan practitioners generally possess a pantheistic worldview, believing that deity is everywhere and viewing deity as immanent and nontranscendent; that is to say, they see deity as universal (although expressions of it are culturally specific), available, accessible, and intimately connected with and located within our entire selves, body and mind. Concepts of deity include both a God and a Goddess, with primacy generally given to the Goddess, although this emphasis is changing. The Pagan worldview thus emphasizes immanence and the continuous cycle of birth, life, death, and rebirth. This cycle is represented by the trinity: the Goddess as Maiden, Mother, and Crone. Pagans embrace wholeheartedly the human reality as embodied creatures, male and female, sensual and alive. After all, a religion that can devote entire rituals to the pleasures of chocolate can hardly advocate the subjugation of the flesh![1]

Sexuality permeates Paganism in two main ways: first by redefining gender roles through promoting feminist ideals and sexual freedom and second by embodying these attitudes in lifestyle decisions that lie outside the social mainstream. The redefinition of gender roles is a crucial part of the Pagan view of sexuality. The struggle to break out of gender-based societal roles is intertwined with the struggle to break free of limiting and sometimes repressive sexual norms. Many Pagans feel that their religion offers a safe haven for the expression of their innate sexuality, which many majority religions censure and condemn.

That the theoretical underpinnings of the feminist movement have shaped and flavored goddess spirituality and Wicca in the United States to a large degree demonstrates the first way in which sexuality permeates Paganism. In contemporary U.S. society, men and women who embrace this movement engage the dominant culture in a struggle for legitimacy. Many feminists joined the goddess movement in search of a spiritual base for their politics. Likewise, many Pagans, male and female, find that the politics of their religion promote women's rights.

Defined over against what Pagans term the "death-affirming" patriarchal religions, ideas about the Goddess in this movement draw strength from Witchcraft's varied myths of origin, which describe a prehistoric matriarchal culture or an egalitarian matrilineal culture. The emergent character of Pagan thought and doctrine, however, allows for little uniformity or orthodoxy. Pagans often claim that their religion has no dogma or doctrine at all. In reality, adaptability and creativity rather than the complete absence of doctrine characterize most Pagan movements. Pagan traditions place great value on individualism and on the personal responsibility of individuals to seek out and develop truths suitable for them. Many Witches view this freedom as explicitly feminine, whereas they view hierarchy as a characteristic of the patriarchal peoples who destroyed the matriarchies of Pagan sacred history.

The embodiment of sexuality in the Pagan yearly ritual cycle demonstrates the second way in which sexuality permeates Paganism. Beltane (April 30 or May 1) is an especially important time in Paganism for the celebration of fertility. Beltane rituals often involve celebrating sexuality and dancing around the phallic Maypole, a practice adopted from the fertility religions of ancient and pre-Christian Europe. Also during this celebration, in many Pagan groups, young, single women jump over the belfire (a central ritual bonfire) to increase fertility. Some, however, stress nervously to the gods and goddesses that the fecundity they wish to bring into their lives has nothing to do with the actual bearing of children. Sexual jokes abound during these rituals, and couples of every gender combination leave the circle to experience sexual union as a form of worship in what is sometimes termed "greenwood marriages" (a term that indicates their temporary and ritual characteristics). This bawdy ritual, when Pagans "let their hair down," signifies the sensual and in many cases sexual abandon present in a religion where "all acts of love and pleasure are . . . rituals" of the Great Goddess (Farrar and Farrar 1991, 298).

The Pagan wheel of the year is a ritual cycle that is in itself a celebration of the earth as a body. During each of the eight major holy days (or Sabbats), Pagans celebrate cycles of the planet that relate to cycles of the body. For instance, Samhain, celebrated on October 31, is a time to prepare for the harshness of winter (because the Pagan calendar is based on northern European weather patterns). However, it is also a time to honor the body's barren times—fallow times in mind, body, and spirit that allow for rest and prepare for later growth.

Paganism has juggled contradictions and paradoxes since its inception in the 1950s.[2] On the fringes of society, its participants explore new frontiers of sexuality and push the boundaries of sexual mores. Fringe status comes naturally to new religions, but Pagans often seek further notoriety through unusual personal appearance and flaunted sexual behavior.

Pagans' perceived connections to the victims of earlier witch trials have their roots in the work of Gerald Gardner, who is considered to be the founder of modern Witchcraft. In his book, *Witchcraft Today* (1968), Gardner details the centuries of persecution, claiming that 9 million witches, mostly women, died during "the Burning Times," or the witch hunts of the Middle Ages. According to his biographer, Gardner possessed a strong desire to redress the wrongs done to generations of Witches (Bracelin 1960). Gardner went so far as to erect a memorial on the Isle of Man to the 9 million martyrs of the past persecutions. Other Pagan authors followed Gardner, providing horrific details of the tortures inflicted upon their spiritual ancestors as a standard part of their writing.

Although recent scholarship has suggested that the actual number of casualties in the witch trials was much lower than Gardner's estimate, this story is an important part of sacred history for many Pagans. The mythos of the Burning Times gives contemporary Pagans a sense of historical continuity, despite the recent origins of the religion. It also reinforces a sense of social cohesion by demonstrating that Witches, who were the healers and midwives of the Middle Ages rather than evil sorceresses, were persecuted for their gender as well as for the gender of one of their deities. This myth sets Pagans apart from and against society at large. Ironically, although feminists stress the liberating aspects of the religion, Gerald Gardner—considered the founder of contemporary Witchcraft, as already noted—stressed that only women fitting the traditional norm of (hetero)sexually attractive beauty are fit to be high priestesses and that the priestess should have the grace to step down when she can no longer adequately represent the "beauty" of the Goddess. Nonetheless, both the traditional Witchcraft that follows Gardner's teachings and the less structured, feminist goddess movement rely on a "herstory" that speaks of a great matriarchy predating recorded history. This reconstructed and feminized view of prehistory underlies the essentially feminist understandings of gender and sexuality in Paganism; it also suggests that an opposition has existed from time immemorial between a transcendent, all-powerful, sky-dwelling God and a Goddess who is closely connected to, if not fully identified with, the earth.

## CASTING THE CIRCLE

In an intricate dance of power, discipline, and mutual support, societies and their dominant religions mutually reinforce the status quo. The power of the state protects and promotes mainstream religion, while at the same time, the religion lends the status of universal truth to the implicit values underlying a given society. We have only to examine the religious rhetoric used in the 2000 campaign of U.S. president George Walker Bush to see evidence that the constitutional separation of church and state does not mean that religion has no effect on U.S. politics. Despite that constitutional separation, this country has hotly debated such topics as prayer in school, religious iconography in the workplace, and the appropriateness of religious expression that does not discriminate against other beliefs.

In western society, the status quo, both religious and secular, rests upon patriarchal foundations; that is to say, for centuries in western societies, men nearly always have been in charge of the institutions of religion, education, politics, and medicine. With few exceptions, men have been the rulers, heads of households, and captains of industry; the main forces behind health and medical technologies, and the prime movers of the public sphere. These foundations influence how men and women perceive themselves and their society and how they construct their religious beliefs and worldviews. The egalitarianism underlying Paganism challenges the social order supported by patriarchal religions, disrupting the dance of power that maintains the status quo. Almost since its beginning, Paganism has been defiantly nonpatriarchal, and this stance has enabled the religion to find nourishment in varying sources within the sexual revolution and the social unrest of the 1960s. Today, Paganism in the United States remains closely linked with the feminist movement and with an ecological and social consciousness that also grew out of the social reform movements of the 1960s.

Paganism's role in feminist ideas and politics in the United States springs from two related historical sources. Practitioners in the United States frequently mix the ideas of feminist Witch Starhawk with those of authors like Janet and Stewart Farrar, whose background lies in British Witchcraft and the legacy of Gerald Gardner. Both of these mainstays of modern Pagan tradition stand against the gender norms of most mainstream and conservative forms of Christianity, and both accomplish this feat in part through sexual license among consenting adults—giving women and men the power to make their own sexual decisions outside mainstream morality.

The development of Wicca in 1950s Britain came at a time when women were experiencing new freedom in terms of work and career in the wake of World War II, and this freedom led in part to a greater desire for freedom of sexual expression. The popularity of the birth control pill and the legalization of abortion gave women the freedom in the 1960s and 1970s to become equals to men in the realm of sexual politics. The surge of feminist consciousness in the 1960s grew alongside Paganism in Britain and the United States, and the postwar desire for freedom in both the sexual and the political arenas culminated in the turbulent 1960s. Although many dissidents later turned to middle-class values, comforts, and wealth, Pagans often continued their countercultural lifestyles, political activism, and social conscience, gaining political ground and adherents as a result. Today, many Pagans find the continuing struggles of the feminist movement to be similar to their own struggles for legitimacy and recognition.

Although Paganism drew from these broad social movements, it also carved out its own unique niche in U.S. culture. In a personal communication with one of the authors, a leader in a nationwide Pagan organization (the Church of All Worlds) explained one method by which this was accomplished:

> Benjamin Franklin was once asked what was his greatest invention. He replied, "Americans." Before Ben coined that term and began promoting it through his newspaper and almanac, European colonists in this country had no unifying name to encompass them all. There were Puritans and Quakers, Virginians and New Yorkers, Whigs and Tories, etc. But no one thought of themselves as being part of an all-encompassing whole. Ben changed that with his editorials, and the British found themselves in the Revolutionary War fighting no scattered factions, but a unified Nation. A nation of Americans. The word "Pagan" had the same impact. Where once there were scattered little occult and reconstructionist groups, each pursuing their own tradition, having little connection with each other, there has now become a Movement.[3]

Communities exist in the imagination as well as in the everyday world, providing strangers with a common identity. In a countercultural movement such as Paganism, the existence of the community in the minds of Pagans is as important as the physical community in which they may meet. Indeed, it gives disparate Pagan groups a shared goal, a common identity, and a ground upon which to meet as friends. Thus, even a solitary practitioner can be a part of the Pagan community because the community lives, in part, in the hearts and minds of its members.

Pagans rely in part on their sacred history to maintain their identities as members of a counterculture, connecting their religion with paganisms and persecutions of the past. The "actual" history of Paganism, which only dates to the 1950s, differs from the "imagined" history of Witchcraft, which goes back for centuries and even millennia. Thus, the meanings and history of the terms *Pagan*, *Witch*, and *Witchcraft* have remained a source of confusion and misunderstanding between Pagans and the dominant culture.

Just as autobiographers reconstruct their personal histories through their writing, communities add their own interpretations to their sacred histories. The primary issue confronting researchers does not necessarily lie in the ferreting out of the "truth"—as if such an entity existed—but in discerning the function of this recreated history in the life of the person or community. By exploring the function of the prehistoric Great Goddess religions and the Burning Times within Paganism, we can begin to understand how these sacred histories have helped to construct Pagan (and particularly female Pagan) identities.

The writings of J. J. Bachofen, Marija Gimbutas, Joseph Campbell, and Merlin Stone, all of whom researched ancient cultures and religions, weave a tale of an ancient prehistoric matriarchy that was eventually destroyed by warlike, patriarchal peoples. Although very little scholarly support exists for this theory, Paganism has adopted it as its own sacred myth of origin, likening the struggles of a goddess-worshipping prehistoric civilization against the influx of patriarchal religion to contemporary Pagans' struggles for acceptance and tolerance. Paganism's sacred myth of origin both elevates women (through their identification with the divine) and ties the contemporary movement to primal religions.

Pagans and their modern critics also connect the religion to medieval views of sorcery. The Christian view of the diabolical or devil-worshipping witch arose during the Middle Ages. Contemporary U.S. Witchcraft envisions itself as non-Christian or even anti-Christian and almost uniformly disavows any connection with evil, "black" magic, devil worship, or Satanism. However, Witches do connect themselves with the victims and survivors of the European witch craze, and some Christians build on this perceived connection in their condemnation of contemporary Paganism. Because the victims of the European witch hunts of the Middle Ages were mostly women, any attack against contemporary Pagans because of this association also has sexist implications.

The denigration of the Goddess by patriarchal religions, the fall of the ancient matriarchies, and the horrors of the Burning Times weave a backdrop of community and conflict through the narrative of Paganism. The sacred history of this movement pits Pagan against Christian, priest against priestess, and woman against man. Yet this overriding culture of victimhood lends strength and cohesiveness to an otherwise diffuse, loosely organized religion. The narrative elements of these stories and their origins and evolution throughout the history of contemporary Paganism provide glimpses into the heart of this movement's "imagined community." The kinship Pagans feel with the ancient inhabitants of a long-lost matriarchy and the victims of the Burning Times acts as a vital part of their religion and plays a central role in their interactions with U.S. society.

## GREETING THE GODDESS

The medieval European understanding of witches was mainly religious, in that they were considered to be the enemies of Christians and to worship the Christian Devil. Similarly, the term *Pagan* historically has denoted someone who is not Christian or Jewish, often including practitioners of many of the world's other dominant religions, such as Buddhism or Hinduism. Until relatively recently, both terms have been used to describe religious behavior that Christians see as being in opposition with their own. More recently, however, the terms *Witchcraft* and *Paganism* have begun to connote a different kind of opposition. In popular culture particularly, witches still are characterized almost exclusively as female, and although images of their consorting with the Christian Devil are less common today, their behavior is still considered to be antithetical to conventional U.S. values. They are thought to operate covertly, disguising themselves as benign and harmless members of society, while secretly destroying the very things upon which U.S. society is built. Although they may no longer be seen as overtly sexual, they do seem to be in the business of thwarting the pure emotional expression of chaste and sweet young women. They are usually seen as old women whose prime is past, and their desire to interfere with the emotional and sexual purity of young women carries a hint of jealousy. They are also usually seen as being carried away by and ultimately suffering from their passions.

Beginning in the 1960s, however, a new image of the witch emerged in popular culture that reflects some of the lesser known images from the European witch hunts. This newer image shows witches as young, nubile, sexually attractive, and sexually active women. The television series *Bewitched* and the film *Bell, Book, and Candle* show witches as young and attractive, and this trend has continued with the films *The Witches of Eastwick* and *Practical Magic,* along with the television shows *Charmed* and *Sabrina, the Teenage Witch,* which first appeared in the 1990s and have continued into the current decade. Although this new image is imperfect and implies that witches are supernatural beings—and therefore "Other"—they do represent a step toward a more positive image of witches.

Despite these conflicting images of the witch, contemporary Witches and Pagans willingly and often proudly own this label. By reclaiming and

redefining this terrible image of women, female Witches create a powerful countercultural religious and political expression. Contemporary
Witches refuse to leave the title of Witch behind, finding strength in this
marginalized and persecuted figure. Moreover, they have revealed the underlying misogyny of the image by using some of its elements to challenge the patriarchal status quo. Thus, in contemporary Paganism, the
sexual license that once was believed to be demonic now signifies a
woman's refusal to be held prisoner by a sexual code of conduct that was
designed by and for men. Similarly, Witches reconstruct the feared and
despised "old hag," redefining her as the wise crone to whom others turn
for wisdom and knowledge.

Indeed, even the sweet and chaste young women who once were seen
as the victims of witches now benefit from the same sexual liberties for
which contemporary female (and some male) Witches have been struggling. All too often in western cultures, women have been denied their
own sexuality because men supposedly could not contain theirs. But
today, women of all ages are finding the freedom to express their sexuality. Paganism and Witchcraft give some women the opportunity to do so
in a religious context.

Choosing Paganism as one's own religion carries with it threatened
and real persecution, yet it also provides political and personal power, especially to women. Some feminist Witches also base their religious identities on their experiences as women, allowing their feminist ideals to
serve as the center of their religion.

Most religions common in the United States conceive of deity primarily as transcendent and male, a patriarch above the visible, created
world. The primacy of a male God, with no reference to a female deity,
legitimates the secular patriarchalism of western society. This legitimation functions through a circular belief that since the (male) cosmic order
established the social order, the social order should in turn reflect the nature of the divine; in other words, since God is male, then men should be
in power, and since men are in power, God must be male. Pagans, along
with feminist Christians and Jews, criticize this cycle of legitimation,
which they perceive as promoting the religious and societal disenfran-
chisement of women.

The Pagan understanding of women's spirituality reverses the prevailing views of Western cultures. In their quest for a powerful female
identity, Pagan women turn from traditional and mainstream religious
expressions to embrace a spirituality that reflects their sexuality, their sen-

suality, and their divinity. The concept of divine immanence, or presence in and around us, that is prevalent in most forms of Paganism reverses the cycle of legitimation described earlier. Immanent thealogy[4] allows women to assert the existence of a Goddess since the divine lives within them and they are female. This thealogy enables women to experience themselves not only as free sexual beings but indeed as the Goddess incarnate. It makes available a wide variety of religious expressions that do not devalue the female body, and it provides a role model for female religious authority and leadership. Envisioning God as a woman changes a woman's relationships to her body, spouse or domestic partner, planet, children, spiritual community, and society.

The recognition of the divine Goddess within serves as a source of strength for women, as well as a way to affirm women's power and celebrate the female body. In a personal interview conducted by one of the authors, a forty-two-year-old Pagan from Missouri stated succinctly: "As a woman, I am the face of the Goddess on this earth." Indeed, this aspect of the religion serves as its main draw for many Pagans, particularly those women who come from a feminist background. A high priestess and crone in Florida spoke about her religious search and her ultimate decision more than ten years ago to become a Witch:

> I discovered that there were in fact religions still in the world today that honored the old goddesses. They just called it Witchcraft; they didn't call it religion. And, why do I stay there? It's woman friendly, earth friendly, life friendly, where I didn't find the other religions to be so. (personal interview)

Setting themselves against a discourse that they view as devaluing women and nature, Pagan women speak time and again of the importance of the Goddess, who provides both a feminine aspect to divinity and a divine aspect to women. The woman quoted above expanded in writing upon the importance of the Goddess: "Initially it was the concept of a *female* face to the Divine [that was most important to me]. As I grow older it is still the freedom to practice as fits *me* that is attractive, and my inability to believe in a religious system which has no justice for women imbedded in it" (Tosh 2000).

Writings by feminist theologians from a variety of religious backgrounds echo this insistence on the importance of the Goddess. The recognition of the female divine is an epiphany for many women in the

United States. Carol Christ writes: "It wasn't until I said Goddess that I realized how significant that remaining aura of masculinity was in my image of God. Not until I said Goddess did I realize that I had never felt fully included in the fullness of my being a woman in masculine or neuterized imagery for divinity" (1987, 67). Pagans believe that the presence of the Goddess and the integration of sacred and mundane in Pagan thought celebrates the equality of men and women.

The elevation of women through the imagery of the Goddess also appears in most Pagan literature. According to Starhawk, a popular writer whose thealogical works helped to shape Wicca in the United States, the exclusively male imagery of God in Judaism and Christianity authenticates men as the carriers of humanity while severely denigrating women. Focusing on the strength gained from the Goddess, many Pagans complain that Judaism and Christianity portray men as naturally superior while regarding women the "weaker sex" in bodily strength and ability, spirituality, morality, and intellect. According to Pagans, the dualism present in other religions excludes women from the realms of spirit, culture, and the sacred by identifying them with flesh, nature, and the profane and serves further to legitimate the persecution, subjugation, and devaluation of women.

The religious concepts of Paganism give women a role equal or superior to those offered to men. Witchcraft and concepts of matriarchy challenge women to envision themselves with power and to imagine what a society would be like in which women were truly free. A forty-five-year-old divorcee in Kentucky revels in this freedom:

> As an older Witch, and one who was a Witch when Witchcraft wasn't cool, I see myself as a role model for younger women coming up in the path, and I try to set an example of a strong, self-empowered, self-actualized woman. You don't have to spout the party line to be taken seriously—you can be different and still be respectable. I am not one of those sweet, nice, "shine the white light on 'em" Pagans. I hex and curse if the situation calls for it. I don't like to unleash anger on people but if they deserve it I don't have a problem with it. I give back what is given to me, good or bad. (personal interview)

For most women, this kind of freedom comes not as a given but as newfound liberation.

According to Carol Christ, the liberation that comes with a turn to the feminine divine also heals the Western rift between the material and the spiritual: "No longer do I stand in the shadow of male Gods who are defined in opposition to the powers of earth, nature, myself" (Christ 1987, 105). Pagans, who perceive Western society as battling both nature and the universe itself, focus on the balance and peace of Paganism:

> There is so much in our world and in our Western orientation that is inherently at war with who we are. Unfortunately, the Christian Church teaches us to suspect anything that is from our subconscious, it teaches us that it is our darker side, it has centuries of teaching us that women are inherently evil and the cause of many difficulties. I don't feel that's right. My inner sense tells me there's something wrong here. . . . There is a balance that we need to preserve, and Catholicism, or any form of Christianity, doesn't teach this part. What teaches this is [Paganism]. It helps us reaffirm our cycle of life, our affinity with the Earth, our interconnection with each other, and the necessity of always maintaining that balance, that balance of energies. That's what keeps me there. (personal interview)

By negating the traditional Christian opposition to "fallen" flesh, Paganism transfigures the mundane and the sexual, asserting the spiritual dimension of the material world and the flesh.

The Pagan view of sex as sacred grows out of the image of Goddess as immanent and feminine. Pagan ideas of womanhood stand in vibrant contrast to typical western images. In the mainstream culture of the United States, for example, women are often held to standards that are nearly impossible to maintain. According to feminist author Susan Griffin, women are frequently caught in a dichotomy between the stereo-typical roles of "virgin" and "whore" (Griffin 1981). "Proper" women—those in the first category—are supposed to be sexually pure, or at least not very experienced in the realm of sexual activity, until marriage. In re-turn for their sexual restraint, they are considered marriageable, deserv-ing of long-term commitment and devotion from a man. Many social in-stitutions, such as mainstream religious groups, schools, and even government agencies, promote abstinence and encourage respect for women who wait to engage in sexual activity.

However, women in the second category are desired for sexual pleas-ure but considered undeserving of marriage and commitment. Here again, U.S. culture sends mixed messages. Frequently, women on tele-vision and in feature films are shown engaging in sexual behavior with a man, often shortly after meeting him. These women are presented as glamorous, sexy, and intelligent; in short, desirable. Yet when real women emulate this behavior, they are usually censured. Often labeled "easy" or "loose," they are seen as having compromised their own safety and respectability. The next step in this kind of thinking is to expect that if a woman will share her sexuality willingly with some men, then she should share it with any man; her sexual expression becomes men's sexual license. This mode of thought leads to date rape, sexual harassment, and other forced sexual encounters. Yet, men who are the aggressors are not censured; indeed, they are often praised for their virility. Few women or men in our culture question the impossible ideal of women who can be both virginal and sexually adept.

Women in the Pagan community, by contrast, usually are not held up to this double standard. In this community, women may engage in sexual pleasure as freely and as openly as men do without their character coming under fire. The Pagan community encourages both women and men to engage in sexual activity safely and respectfully, as evidenced by the availability of free condoms at most Pagan festivals.

The thealogy of immanence is closely related to Pagans' sexual expression. If the God and Goddess live within us, they reason, then our sexual expression is also religious. In Pagan thought, every person is an embodiment of deity. Our every action, including sex, therefore, can be an act of worship. This view is incredibly empowering and leads to the conclusion that women's sexuality should not be demonized and men's sexuality (at least in theory) should no longer depend upon the conquest of "bad" girls and the search for a marriageable "good" girl.

In fact, Witches and Goddess worshippers often choose the "bad girls" of mythology as their personal heroines. Figures like Eve and Lilith (Adam's first wife, according to Jewish tradition, who refused to be dominated by Adam and thus was cast out of the Garden of Eden) provide powerful role models for Pagans. The juxtaposition of Mary with Eve illustrates the profound difference between the ideals of Paganism and those of mainstream Christianity. In traditional interpretations, Eve caused the Fall by asserting her will against that of God; Mary, however, began redemption with her submissive response to God's initiative: "Let it be done to me according to thy word" (Luke 1:38). In addition, Mary's virginal status at the time of Jesus' birth has been extended to include her whole life, so that the idea of Jesus having normally conceived brothers and sisters has become repugnant to many U.S. Christians, if it is even considered. Lilith, by contrast, is fully aware of and assertive about her sexuality. Presenting women as weak and in need of guidance, patriarchal constructs present the powerful Eve as "the most unnatural, untrustworthy and dangerous creation of God" (Parvey 1991, 51). Eve stands between Lilith and Mary, opening herself up to sensual fulfillment and then suffering punishment for it. It is Eve who is most closely related to women today, censured for her sensuality, considered a temptress and the downfall of men, yet also praised for being the mother of us all.

## GREETING THE GOD

Although female Pagans find strength in divine images of "bad girls," they are not the only ones to define their gender roles against those of the dominant society. For many Witches, respect for the Goddess and the God and the existence of both the male and female principles of deity set Paganism apart from the status quo. The divine male, consort and lover of the Great Goddess who is the divine creatrix of the cosmos, offers Pagan men an escape from strict gender norms that often promote behaviors the men in question find morally objectionable. Both the God and the Goddess speak to male Witches, giving them an escape from chauvinistic behaviors and providing them with positive ways in which to view their mothers, wives, lovers, and daughters, as well as other women in their lives.

Since the popular image of a witch—straight out of fairy tales and Disney movies—remains female, male Wiccans and other male Pagans must come to terms with being men in a religion in which the Goddess typically reigns supreme. In addition, as male Pagans welcome freedom from their own socially prescribed gender roles, they also sometimes struggle with their new understanding of women, contend with their own sense of self-loathing (which comes from being privileged in a male-dominated society), and field the often bitter recriminations of the feminist women in their religious circle. These issues spring from feminist origins, whether the person in question is male or female, gay or straight.

Socially prescribed gender roles often act as severe regulators of behavior and identity. In the West, patriarchal gender norms confine both men and women in rigid roles, seemingly providing nearly unlimited freedom to males while censuring the freedom of women. This method of control has long been recognized. Andrew Jackson Davis, a Spiritualist in nineteenth-century United States, wrote: "Woman has ever been the pet of man . . . regarded tenderly and protected as a weak, defenseless, necessary associate—regarded as a useful, beautiful, desirable creature. . . . As a dependent and relative being . . . woman is universally admired, worshipped, defended. But she is everywhere kept down by political injustice" (Isaacs 1983, 81–82).

The inevitable existence of dissident subcultures such as Paganism adds intricacy to the dance of power played out by the societal substructures of church and state. Many Pagans view their religion as a form of protest against the established, male-dominated social order. Feminist leanings and involvement in the politics surrounding women's rights issues draw many practitioners to Goddess worship. That women find these new ideas attractive startles no one; the fact that a large number of male Pagans also cite these ideas as vitally important to their religious identity may come as a pleasant surprise. A middle-aged lawyer in California explains that "the defining characteristics of my religion are recognition of the female aspects of Deity, combined with the recognition of natural forces and the ability (and willingness) to use those forces to effect change, and a strong belief in self-determination" (personal interview). Thus, male Pagans, like feminist women, often seek to change society into a fairer structure and to find like-minded individuals within the religion. For many practicing Pagans, the acknowledgment of the Goddess undercuts the theological foundation of the oppression of women and provides the means for rebelling against the status quo. This undercutting of mainstream theology also negates the separation of sexuality from spirituality by presenting sexuality instead as embodied spirituality. It thus makes male sexuality an act of reverence rather than violence, setting up a new paradigm for Pagan men.

The duality set up by many religious traditions—in U.S. society largely represented by Christianity—separates sex from spirituality, objectifying and alienating the body and viewing sexuality as a dangerous force to be crushed into submission. From this theological standpoint, sexuality and the women with whom it is associated are suspect and base, and men who associate physically with women become less spiritually pure. Pagans respond to this censure of sexuality by embracing the flesh, and many Pagan men embrace a view of sex as a celebration rather than a conquest of women, providing both sexes with a sexuality that no longer focuses on competition.

Sexual competition among men is especially hard on homosexual men. In mainstream society, they must juggle their own sense of masculinity with the deeply ingrained expectation of heterosexuality in U.S. culture. Paganism lessens this pressure by recognizing the multiple dimensions of human masculinity as multiple dimensions of Godhood. The Pagan acceptance of polytheism also offers respite from the singular image of God offered by monotheistic religions. Pagan men have the freedom to remake themselves in the image of a number of Gods or Goddesses—gay, straight, hermaphroditic, transgendered, or cross-dressing. Viewing the earth as Goddess also allows men to form bonds with her, reintroducing men to a long-dormant relationship with the environment. Shamanic undercurrents in Paganism encourage this relationship by urging men (and women) to view animals as companions and spiritual guides. Environmental ethics that celebrate life also serve as a new model for behavior, in opposition to the warlike and death-affirming models of mainstream Western masculinity. Even the warrior images present in many Pagan pantheons appear as lovers and protectors rather than destroyers, again changing the focus of male sexuality from conquest to communion. For Pagan men, this new view of their own sexuality can lead to a newfound relationship with the environment, approaching the planet itself as they would a lover.

Initially, the bulk of publications dealing with Pagan spirituality focused on women, women's spirituality, and the Goddess. In recent decades, several books have dealt with men's spirituality in a Pagan context, including *Goddess Power: An Interactive Book for Women . . . and Men* (1996) by Don H. Parker, *Earth God Rising: The Return of the Male Mysteries* by Alan Richardson (1992), and *The Way of Merlyn: The Male Path in Wicca* (1994) by Ly Warren-Clarke and Kathryn Matthews. A. J. Drew wrote two books dealing exclusively with male Wiccans: *Wicca Spellcraft for Men: A Spellbook for Male Pagans* (2001) and *Wicca for Men: A Handbook for Male Pagans Seeking a Spiritual Path* (1998).

Nicholas R. Mann's work *His Story: Masculinity in the Post-Patriarchal World* (1995) specifically addresses the concerns many men (and women) have about sex and gender issues in Paganism. In fact, Mann's book is meant to be read by any man who is influenced by feminism and who is struggling to define himself in light of feminist critiques of mainstream masculinity. Mann goes into great detail about the finer points of redirecting male sexuality in a way that is nonpatriarchal, insisting that "the new male sexuality . . . is a man becoming ecstatic, understanding that his whole body—not just the penis—is an organ for pleasuring his partner and himself" (Mann 1995, 186). For Mann, the new male sexuality is semen-retaining, recreative, and rejuvenating. It is about expressing care and devotion, about worshipful physical activity that need not be in the service of reproduction, and about the healing of the male psyche from the restrictions and trauma of patriarchal male sexuality. Yet redefining masculinity goes beyond sex and sexuality; Mann also addresses gender roles. *His Story* and the other books mentioned redefine male sex and gender roles, setting up new ideals in a spiritual context. Both gay and straight men find freedom in these images, a freedom played out in their relationships with men, women, and the deities. Paganism has long been a religion that primarily focused on single adults. Recently, however, as more and more Pagans "grow up" and begin families, issues of how to actualize new gender roles in a family context become more important. Male Pagans struggle to redefine fatherhood in a way that is strong, responsible, and loving, without reproducing what they view as unhealthy characteristics of fatherhood and masculinity associated with patriarchal paradigms. Raising daughters in Paganism has some evident advantages—the religion provides strong role models for women and girls, as well as an egalitarian atmosphere. Raising sons in the tradition may be a more difficult proposition, however, as Pagan parents have to balance feminist values with healthy masculine attributes. As Pagan men struggle to recreate themselves outside the bounds of the patriarchy, they also must find ways to act as effective role models for their sons. To raise a son in an atmosphere in which only women and female characteristics are valued is as harmful as raising a daughter in a culture in which only men and masculine traits are valued. It produces the same self-loathing and lack of self-confidence in boys that girls have experienced for millennia. Thus, in their zeal to raise children with feminist ideals, Pagan parents often find it challenging to raise confident boys who also can be critical of the broader culture in which they live.

New religions and new social movements exist at the cutting edge of social change. By providing creative space for critiquing and redefining the institutions and values that mainstream society takes for granted, Paganism and related religions have been particularly influential in critiquing and redefining sexual behavior, roles, and mores. This means one thing to a Pagan with no children, but it holds far more complex significance to a Pagan who is also a parent.

## THE GREAT RITE

Several years ago, the authors sat in the home of an older Pagan woman and discussed with several other women the role models accessible to Pagan women. All the women present recognized the validity and empowering nature of the triple Goddess image that is predominant in Paganism: the Maiden, Mother, and Crone. This triune image of deity honors the entire life cycle of women, from birth to death. Nevertheless, the image of Mother becomes problematic for women who are menstruating but have not borne children because of age, life circumstances, medical complications, or simply choice. Many participants in the discussion suggested that Witchcraft needed to devise a new role, such as that of Matron, in order to honor the fecundity of women's minds, hearts, and spirits on a level commensurate with the honor Paganism, as a group of primarily fertility religions, already pays to the fecundity of women's bodies. Although this discussion spoke to the concerns of childless Witches, there are also many female Witches bearing children who are concerned with redefining motherhood in nonpatriarchal terms.

Despite their religion's emphasis on the Goddess as Mother, Witches rarely mention motherhood as a means of identifying with the Goddess, seeking instead to distance themselves from ideals that consider motherhood the primary role of women. As one woman confided:

> I'm 29, recently married, and have no children; nor do I want any at this point. Neither does my husband, which makes it hard when it's a fertility ceremony and I want to have sex. Not that I'm trying to share too much info but he always worries that some fluke is going to happen and I'll go from maiden to mother. (personal interview)

The assumption underlying this concern is that a woman cannot go beyond the age of maidenhood without being a mother.

The mainstream feminine ideal in the West often equates womanhood with motherhood. Christian theology has often viewed motherhood as a woman's true vocation and sometimes even her salvation. Pagans' opposition to this single Christian tenet stands behind their embrace of the feminist claim that this stereotype of pious womanhood supports the denigration and powerlessness of women.

Despite this adamant opposition, adherence to the roles laid out for women by a male-dominated society remains the easiest course. Even

Pagan mothers find it difficult to mesh ideals of feminine power with the many roles they play in daily life and in turn pass on to their children. Like other feminists, Pagan women who bear children must balance the roles of motherhood with professional responsibilities and community obligations. In addition, Pagan women add the role of Goddess in the mix, trying to bring a sense of the sacred to their everyday activities. Today, as many Pagans begin having children and raising them in the Craft, both women and men find themselves rethinking their prior suppositions about gender. The ability of women to identify with the Goddess as Divine Mother adds new dimensions to Pagan spirituality and sexuality.

### Ritual Sexuality

Pagans have been vocal about their sexual license since the 1950s and have been adamant about viewing sex as a loving and pleasurable act of worship. This attitude toward sex is ritually embodied as the Great Rite in Wiccan circles. Whether performed literally (with respect and privacy) or symbolically (either by miming or by using a chalice and a dagger or wand to symbolize female and male genitalia in heterosexual rituals), the Great Rite is a celebration of the union of sexual energies.

Many Wiccan Great Rite rituals are distinctly heterosexual, perhaps in large part because the authors who first published books about Wiccan ritual were heterosexual, such as Gerald Gardner, Doreen Valiente, and Janet and Stewart Farrar. Nevertheless, the discussion of heterosexual Wiccan expression of the Great Rite bears some attention for its change in attitude from prior, more restrictive, attitudes toward heterosexual sex. "As the athame [dagger] is to male, so the cup is to the female; and conjoined, they become one in truth" (Farrar 1983, 46) is one invocation to consecrate the cakes and wine, the communion portion of every ritual. During the Great Rite, the high priestess is worshipped as the embodiment of the Goddess, and the high priest takes the part of the God. Thus, Pagans performing the Great Rite celebrate the ultimate creative act, whether that activity is used for procreation or re-creation. Symbolized in this Great Rite is the conception of suns and planets, as well as sons and daughters. Symbolized here also is the chemical union of elements to create compounds, the molecular union of compounds to create bodies. Here, heterosexual Pagans are free to celebrate their bodies, sexuality, fertility, and connection with the creative aspects of nature, their sensuality and longing for pleasure.

As empowering as this ritual can be for some, many who are not heterosexual find it restrictive and exclusive. Yet nonheterosexual Pagans abound, and their rites are creative and affirming of their own sexual expression. Many Pagans may take an established ritual, such as the Wiccan Great Rite mentioned above, as a template to be modified; others create a new Great Rite that is altogether different and that honors their own sexual practices. Z. Budapest envisioned a Dianic Great Rite that focused on sexual pleasure rather than procreation. However Pagans may celebrate them, ritual elements like the Great Rite purposefully muddy the distinction between sex and spirituality, insisting that these two elements of human experience are deeply intertwined and that a celebration of one is intimately involved with the celebration of the other.

The inherent violence in the imagery of the dagger used in the heterosexual Great Rite is also problematic, although not often recognized. Many feminists and pro-feminist men have already made the connection between unhealthy male heterosexuality and weaponry of all sorts (swords, firearms, bullets, and daggers all have been used to symbolize male genitalia, masculinity, and male orgasm). This unhealthy view of heterosexuality, particularly from the male perspective, culminates in rape, which is an assertion of power through sex. Some Pagans do recognize this connection, even on an unconscious level, and many use a wand to represent the male genitalia to try to alleviate the violent undertones of the dagger. Issues such as this symbolic representation highlight the efforts to rectify what heterosexual Pagans are now beginning to recognize as heterosexist and patriarchal images in Pagan practice. Although we are more familiar with the heterosexual Pagan community, we have suggested works beginning on p. 403 that go into more detail regarding the nonheterosexual practice of Paganism.

### The Liabilities of Sexual Freedom

This ardent vocalization of sexual freedom has a downside, however: it often attracts those who would exercise it irresponsibly. A forty-year-old graduate student complains that "Colorado Paganism evolved into a party-till-you-retch. High on the list: instant gratification, sex, justification of boorish behavior in the name of 'spirituality,' more weird sex, power games, etc." (personal interview). Such "party Pagans" are frustrating to those who take sexual responsibility seriously and who do not wish to be seen as a haven for the sex-crazed. In fact, this side effect of sexual freedom has polarized many Pagan communities when sexual license practiced without respect and responsibility has turned into sexual abuse.

Paganism exists within a dominant culture that values the virility of men and in women prizes the "virgin" while desiring the "whore." Most Pagans, particularly that majority that did not grow up in a Pagan household, carry this value system with them into the religion. Although some struggle to subvert it and reconstruct a healthier image of sexuality, many simply take advantage of the religion's tolerance of sexual diversity to embark upon their own string of conquests. Perhaps these conquests are aided by the fact that many who come to Paganism have experienced sexual abuse in their pre-Pagan past. They often see the creativity and healthy respect for sex in Paganism as an assurance that they are safe from further predation. Unfortunately, that is not the case. Many Pagan communities struggle to educate their newcomers that sexual predation still occurs in their religion while also attempting to locate and neutralize threats of predation from within their midst.

Power politics are inherent in any student-teacher relationship, and as in other religions, predators can take advantage by presenting themselves to newcomers as extremely knowledgeable and powerful teachers. Within the insulated environment of a small teaching coven, a sexual predator can cause a great deal of damage to a great many people. As one young woman relates:

> In high school I started reading a lot of books around historic Witchcraft and Paganism and thought that that seemed to be where it was going, so I started looking around for a teacher, had several bad experiences with teachers who weren't, they were using the cloak of being a witchy teacher, or whatever that might be, to attain sexual favors from young and innocent girls. (personal interview)

Yet "young and innocent girls" are not the only victims of this predation. The victims include men as well, many of whom were abused in one way or another during their childhood. Unfortunately, as in other religious communities, sexual assault is not always taken seriously, especially when the perpetrator is a respected or powerful member of the community.

Pagans struggle daily to balance the obvious benefits of viewing sex as healthy and pleasurable with the awareness that others may not have the same healthy respect for sexual choice and consent. Because Pagan religions are so new, they still experience growing pains with regard to the treatment of sexual predation and the victims thereof. For instance, Pagans seldom cover up incidents in which women are victims, but their occasional willingness to cover up the assault of a young man by another man indicates an underlying sexism. Despite the desire to change society that often leads Pagans into the religion, the goal of egalitarianism has found only partial realization in the dissident subculture. As stridently as Pagan communities strive to break out of restrictive sexual attitudes, they often are painfully reminded of their location within a larger, dysfunctional culture.

The freedom of sexual expression in Paganism also causes tension between parents and nonparents in the community. The Great Rite is an empowering ritual that could pave the way for a healthy, spiritually based sexuality, but there are questions as to the appropriateness of highly sexual versions of this ritual for younger Pagans. Many Pagan parents simply choose to express the sexuality of the Great Rite symbolically, using the consecration ritual described earlier.

The open and often bawdy atmosphere of many public rituals and Pagan festivals does not address the needs of Pagan parents or young children. However, many private covens, as well as several recent books, address such issues and discuss the complications of practicing a fertility-based religion in a way that takes into account the emotional needs and limitations of young children.

## OPENING THE CIRCLE

Despite and through these difficulties, Paganism continues to redefine sexual mores, behaviors, and roles, both within the Pagan community and within U.S. society at large. In an episode of the 1990s television show *Cybill,* Cybill Shepherd and her companions celebrate their womanhood and their embodiment of the Goddess by having a drum circle—and when Shepherd received an Emmy award for this series, she thanked the Goddess during her acceptance speech. Fifty years ago, both the episode and the acceptance speech would have been inconceivable. Since then, however, Paganism has left an indelible mark on U.S. society, giving women and men a way to redefine their spirituality while also offering a sacred space in which to celebrate their bodies, their sensuality, and their sexual desires.

The connection Pagans feel with an earlier age of peace and equality assures them that the status quo may once have been different. Their

319

foundational myth states with optimism that peace between peoples and peace and equality between the sexes are possible. The profound shift Paganism engenders in social constructs of the divine, the nature of women, and the nature of the cosmos challenges women and men to recreate themselves and society. For women, association with the Goddess and a thealogy of immanence bring both power and responsibility. Starhawk comments, "when I say Goddess I am not talking about a being somewhere outside of this world, nor am I proposing a new belief system. I am talking about an attitude: choosing to take this living world, the people and creatures on it, as the ultimate meaning and purpose of life, to see the world, the earth, and our lives as sacred" (Starhawk 1988, 11). Based on the inherent sanctity of the cosmos and grounded in equality, individual pride, and a sense of self-worth, Pagan ethics condemn patriarchalism, fear, blame, guilt, shame, and self-abasement. Many Pagans, especially those heavily influenced by Goddess spirituality and the feminist movement, strongly believe that working to reform existing institutions will prove inadequate. The Pagan worldview goes farther than this, establishing "a redefinition of reality, challenging the mechanistic views of science and religion as well as masculine politics" (Adler 1986, 181). In order to effect change, however, Pagans must speak this challenge openly.

The temptation to recreate patriarchal ideals in slightly altered packages remains a problem for both women and men in the Pagan movement. Some Pagan literature, for instance, suggests that any woman not interested in the conventional roles of wife and mother is a "psychic cripple . . . [and] an incomplete and inferior image of the Goddess" (Adler 1986, 212). According to Isaac Bonewits, one reason for this carryover of old ideas is that "it is easier to sound liberated than to go through the difficult psychological changes necessary to become liberated from sexual stereotypes" (Bonewits 1975, cited in Adler 1986, 213). The old maxim that "the more things change, the more they stay the same" reflects the power and longevity of social constructs. Western society has been patriarchal for a long time, and the influences of patriarchy are ingrained and insidious. The battle, therefore, remains an active one.

## NOTES

1.  There exists in Neo-Pagan practice a ritual known as the Chocolate Ritual, which celebrates sensual pleasure by honoring a food that brings delight to so many people.

2.  The 1951 repeal of the Witchcraft Act in England allowed Neo-Pagans freely and publicly to acknowledge the "Old Religion," which they believe predates recorded history.

3.  Many of the quotes in this paper come from individuals surveyed or interviewed by Nancy Ramsey Tosh. These data were gathered for her dissertation, "Fabulous Monsters: Identity Construction in Contemporary Paganism" (2000). Some of the quotes included here appeared in the dissertation, but by and large, quotes appearing here come from the bulk of the data gathered rather than from the dissertation text itself. Tosh asked a series of questions about the respondents' understanding of their religion and how it relates to their life and identity.

4.  "Thealogy" (as opposed to the grammatically masculine "theology") denotes the study of the Goddess and is an important term in feminist discursive politics.

## REFERENCES

Adler, Margot. [1979] 1986. *Drawing Down the Moon: Witches, Druids, Goddess-Worshippers, and Other Pagans in America Today.* Reprint. Boston, MA: Beacon Press.

Bracelin, J. L. 1960. *Gerald Gardner: Witch.* London: Octagon Press.

Christ, Carol P. 1987. *Laughter of Aphrodite.* San Francisco, CA: Harper and Row.

Drew, A. J. 1998. *Wicca for Men: A Handbook for Male Pagans Seeking a Spiritual Path.* Secaucus, NJ: Carol Publishing Group.

———. 2001. *Wicca Spellcraft for Men: A Spellbook for Male Pagans.* Franklin Lakes, NJ: New Page Books.

Farrar, Stewart. 1983. *What Witches Do: A Modern Coven Revealed.* Custer, WA: Phoenix Publishing.

Farrar, Stewart, and Janet Farrar. [1981] 1991. *A Witches Bible Compleat.* New York: Magickal Childe Publishing.

Gardner, Gerald B. [1954] 1968. *Witchcraft Today.* London: Jarrolds Publishers.

Griffin, Susan. 1981. *Pornography and Silence: Culture's Revenge against Nature.* New York: HarperCollins Books.

*The Holy Bible.* King James Version. Cleveland, OH: World Publishing.

Isaacs, Ernest. 1983. "The Fox Sisters and American Spiritualism." Pp. 79–110 in Howard Kerr and Charles L. Crow, eds., *The Occult in America: New Historical Perspectives.* Chicago: University of Illinois Press.

Mann, Nicholas R. 1995. *His Story: Masculinity in the Post-Patriarchal World.* St. Paul, MN: Llewellyn Publications.

Parker, Don H. 1996. *Goddess Power: An Interactive Book for Women . . . and Men.* Carmel, CA: Dynamic Publishing.

Parvey, Constance F. 1991. "A Christian Feminist's Struggle with the Bible as Authority." Pp. 52–64 in Leonard Grob, Riffat Hassan, and Haim Gordon, eds., *Women's and Men's Liberation: Testimonies of Spirit.* Westport, CT: Greenwood Press.

Richardson, Alan. 1992. *Earth God Rising: The Return of the Male Mysteries.* St. Paul, MN: Llewellyn Publications.

Scott, James C. 1990. *Domination and the Arts of Resistance: Hidden Transcripts.* New Haven: Yale University Press.

Starhawk. 1988. *Dreaming the Dark: Magic, Sex and Politics.* Boston, MA: Beacon Press.

Tosh, Nancy Ramsey. 2000. "Fabulous Monsters: Identity Construction in Contemporary Paganism." Ph.D. diss., University of California at Santa Barbara.

Warren-Clarke, Ly, and Kathryn Matthews. 1994. *The Way of Merlyn: The Male Path in Wicca.* Bellingham, WA: Prism Press.

## Chapter 11

# Innovation in Exile

## Religion and Spirituality in Lesbian, Gay, Bisexual, and Transgender Communities

*Melissa M. Wilcox*

*A lesbian couple exchanges wedding vows in Toronto on January 14, 2001. The women were one of two gay couples married in a ceremony at Metropolitan Community Church. Both couples were issued marriage licenses believed to be the first ever. (Reuters NewMedia, Inc./Corbis)*

Often in the contemporary United States, the term *sexuality* implies "sexual orientation" when used by itself. "Women's sexuality" refers to a broader range of issues, as does "men's sexuality" (though the two terms frequently evoke different issues), but phrases like "religion and sexuality," "sexuality in the workplace," and "sexuality and human rights" often either foreground or refer directly to sexual orientation. Moreover, it is not everyone's sexual orientation that is the focus here but rather what some call the "marked," nondominant categories: the sexual identities of gay men, lesbians, and bisexuals as opposed to the unmarked and often unnamed category of heterosexuality. All this implies that sexuality is somehow the special province of nonheterosexuals, and that misperception underlies the stereotypes of lesbians, gay men, and bisexuals as promiscuous and obsessed with sex. In reality, it is heterosexuals who are obsessed with *our* sex.[1]

This obsessive focus of heterosexuals on the sexuality (now meaning only sex *acts* rather than sexual identity) of lesbian, gay, and bisexual (LGB) people erases our identities as whole persons and reduces us to sexual bodies. It also has a second effect that is particularly destructive in the context of religion: in changing "LGB people" to "homosexuality" it narrows our sexual orientations from identities to acts. Thus religious organizations can more easily suggest that "homosexuality" is simply a behavior, something that one learned in the past and that one can unlearn in the future. Even organizations such as the Catholic Church, which holds that sexual orientation is innate, separate the orientation itself (unfortunate but not sinful, according to official doctrine) from *acting* on that orientation—again defining the "act" simply as sex or thoughts thereof.

The belief that homosexuality is just a behavior while heterosexuality is a normative, "normal" identity falsely suggests that all people are heterosexual by nature and that some have simply strayed or "deviated" from that truth. One result of this outlook is the so-called homosexuality debates that have raged in U.S. mainline Protestant churches since the 1970s. These debates, which will be covered in depth below, are heated battles between mostly heterosexual church members and clergy, along with some prominent LGB and transgender activists, over several key issues: the nature of homosexuality; God's opinion of homosexuality; the advisability of ordaining homosexuals, especially if they are sexually active (note that sexual activity is rarely relevant for heterosexual Protestants' ordinations); and the advisability of marrying same-sex couples. These debates turn on one critical presumption: that heterosexuals, as the socially dominant group, have the right to speak for, judge, and dictate rights for LGB people.

Where do transgender and transsexual people fit into these issues? As with LGB people, the answer to that question varies depending on the angle of vision. From the perspective of common stereotypes, transgender and transsexual people are often either invisible or fuzzily fused with the category of homosexuality. From the perspective of "trans" people themselves, the issues overlap: although they share many concerns with LGB people and some are themselves lesbian, gay, or bisexual, transgender and transsexual people also face unique challenges in both religion and society.[2]

Some of these negative effects of the stereotyping of lesbian, gay, bisexual, and transgender (LGBT) people are evident in early works on "homosexuality and religion." By defining the issue as homosexuality, these works introduce several problems. First, by discussing homosexuality instead of homosexuals, they imply a focus on sexual behavior rather than on people. Second, in limiting the discussion to homosexuality, they often erase the existence of bisexuals and of transgender and transsexual people (remember that since gender identity and sexual orientation are two different things, the latter two groups may or may not be homosexual). But there is often a third problem as well with such approaches: they focus on what is sometimes called "official religion."

Official religion refers to the religious beliefs and practices taught by sacred texts and religious leaders. It is the "official" teaching of a group—the religious party line, as it were. But focusing on official religion obscures the broad and diverse presence of what sociologist Meredith McGuire (1997) has called "nonofficial religion": the things everyday people believe and do. A focus on official religion and homosexuality, for example, might describe the formal position of the Catholic church on homosexuality and the differing opinions held by some Catholic leaders in various parts of the world. It would show how theological opinions of same-sex activity have shifted between disinterest, uneasy tolerance, disapproval, and violent persecution over the church's 2,000-year history. It also would explain what the Bible says about same-sex relations and how different Catholic theologians have interpreted those texts.

But such a study would not mention the many LGBT people who attend Mass around the world, aware of and often comfortable with their sexual orientation and/or gender identity despite the official stance of the church. It would not discuss the priests who are gay, bisexual, or transgender, nor would it comment on the heterosexual clerics and religious who serve the LGBT community as supporters and allies. Dignity, an international movement of LGBT Catholics that holds regular Masses in numerous cities, would remain invisible, as would the many liberal, heterosexual Catholics who believe the church's position on homosexuality to be wrong.

What has been missing from some older studies of religion and homosexuality, in other words, is the people—especially LGBT people and their allies. Also missing, frequently, are women. There are several reasons for the invisibility of women in earlier research. First, because women are often denied official religious leadership positions, a focus on official religion can exclude women's voices and experiences. Second, early anthropological studies of religion and homosexuality were conducted by male scholars; some of these men had fewer chances to learn about women's religiosity than they had to learn about men's religiosity, and others simply did not think about studying gender differences. Third, as several of the preceding chapters make clear, in many text-based religions, the written tradition addresses itself mostly or exclusively to male homosexuality, forcing those who write about such religions to make guesses about scriptural attitudes toward women's same-sex relations or to ignore them altogether.

Many contemporary texts challenge these tendencies toward the erasure of LGBT people in general, of transgender and transsexual people, and of women—some of them are listed in the suggested reading for this chapter. They include historical studies of same-sex attraction, theological works and autobiographies by LGBT people, and anthropological and sociological analyses of LGBT religious and spiritual experiences. This chapter is one such text and is intended in part to offer one more countervailing voice to the insistent cacophony of heterosexual voices that presume to speak for LGBT people.

The contemporary United States presents an unusual situation for studying LGBT religiosity and spirituality because of the presence of two seemingly unrelated factors: the rise of the gay liberation movement and, more recently, of "queer" politics and the simultaneous growth of religious individualism. These events, which are the focus of the first sections of this chapter, came together in a fortuitous way for LGBT people through the blossoming of a multitude of LGBT religious and spiritual groups. The fourth section of the chapter discusses these different organizational responses to organized religions' ambivalent or hostile attitudes toward LGBT people, and the fifth section takes up the question of individual LGBT people and the various strategies they find useful for dealing with the intersections of LGBT identity, religion, and spirituality. Finally, the chapter concludes with some thoughts on the future of LGBT religiosity in the United States.

## GAY LIBERATION, LESBIAN FEMINISM, AND QUEER POLITICS

Until the 1970s, the most well known and active groups supporting homosexual rights in the United States were the Mattachine Society and the Daughters of Bilitis. The Mattachine Society, founded as a semi-secret fraternal organization and named after an organization of unmarried men in medieval and Renaissance France, began in Los Angeles in 1948. As originally conceived, the group was intended to provide a central source of community for (primarily male) homosexuals and to foster public discussion of homosexuality. For this reason, founder Harry Hay included heterosexual professionals as well as homosexuals in the society. Included on the initial roster were a sociologist, a psychologist, and a

Unitarian minister, all ostensibly heterosexual but interested in promoting discussion of the issue of homosexuality.

In 1955, two San Francisco women who were inspired by the example of the Mattachine Society formed a women's organization, the Daughters of Bilitis. This group took its name from a fictional contemporary of the ancient Greek poet Sappho; it used the term *daughters* to make the group sound like other women's clubs in the United States, such as the Daughters of the American Revolution. The Daughters of Bilitis followed much the same path as the Mattachine Society, emphasizing community, education, and research; it, too, soon spread across the nation (like the Mattachine Society, its first East Coast outpost was in New York). In the 1960s, these two groups adopted the term *homophile*—originally coined in the 1950s as a synonym for "homosexual"—for the growing movement to promote homosexual rights.

During the first two thirds of the twentieth century, several major metropolitan areas included active "homophile" subcultures. But as anthropologist Toby Marotta (1981) argues, this was a time of reformist focus for such groups. The homophile movement, Marotta points out, was formed during the reign of McCarthyism in U.S. politics, when homosexuality often was believed to be connected to socialism or communism and was persecuted violently. Thus, as late as the 1960s, homophile leaders were careful to emphasize education rather than political activism, to work in concert with government groups, and to foster friendships among influential people. Moreover, except for the Mattachine Society's first few years, the central homophile message was a normalizing one: as Harry Hay described it in a 1974 interview, "that position—'we're exactly the same [as heterosexuals]'—characterized the whole Mattachine Society from 1953 to 1969" (Katz 1992, 417).

One event in 1969, however, sparked a change that had been building for several years: the Stonewall Riots. On June 27, police raided the Stonewall Inn on Christopher Street in New York's Greenwich Village, intending to close down the bar and to arrest employees, patrons without identification, and suspected cross-dressers. This was not an unusual occurrence in any city that housed gay or lesbian bars; the difference was that this time, for various reasons, the intended targets resisted. The resulting crowd threw bottles, rocks, and anything else they could find at the building; some threw a trashcan full of burning paper through a window. The uproar drew others, most notably homosexual members of New

Left organizations who had been planning and agitating for a homosexual revolution. These people saw the riot at the Stonewall Inn as their opportunity. Repeat riots at the same location followed for several successive nights, and the potential new leaders began printing flyers and looking for further chances to organize. They initially attempted to work together with the homophile organizations already in place in New York. Both the Mattachine Society and the Daughters of Bilitis had been under some internal pressure to radicalize their activities, but ultimately the radicals made little headway within the homophile movement. An alternative, more activist organization soon formed, known as the Gay Liberation Front; within a few years, many branches of the Mattachine Society and the Daughters of Bilitis had faded into the background or disappeared entirely.

Marotta sees the Gay Liberation Front, spearhead of the more commonly known gay liberation movement, as a combination of members he terms "cultural radicals" and those he calls "revolutionaries." Although the second group was concerned with taking radical, primarily political measures to change the place of homosexuals in society, the first, Marotta argues, took its cue from the Black Power movement and focused on creating a sense of identity and pride among homosexuals. It was out of this side of the movement that the now common gay pride celebrations stemmed; the earliest of these were held in June 1970 to commemorate the first anniversary of the Stonewall Riots.

During the late 1960s and early 1970s, the advent of second-wave feminism and the crossover of lesbians between feminist groups, homophile organizations, and the gay liberation movement indicated a testing and redefinition of gendered political boundaries. With the growing consciousness of feminism, lesbians became increasingly aware of sexism within the homophile and gay liberation movements; they also began to make the related observation that because of differences in the lesbian and gay male subcultures, many of the crucial issues for the gay population were of little concern to lesbians. The solution, however, was not simply to join the feminist movement, for although lesbians often experienced sexism in gay rights organizations, they encountered homophobia and heterosexism in feminist groups. Indeed, feminist leader Betty Friedan once referred to "out" lesbians within feminism as a "lavender menace" whose demands for rights as homosexuals could permanently damage feminist efforts to secure (heterosexual, and closeted lesbian and bisexual) women's rights (Marotta 1981, 263n).[3] Lesbian activists, influenced by both the feminist movement and the gay liberation movement but fully comfortable in neither, thus founded their own organizations, sparking a movement that became known as lesbian feminism.

Over the course of the 1980s, influenced in part by the resurgence of conservatives on the political and cultural scene, some branches of lesbian and gay activism gradually developed less radical tactics. Believing like some liberal feminists that the time had come to work for change within the system rather than trying to alter the system itself radically, these activists made their way into positions of political and social leadership. As lawmakers, lobbyists, and lawyers, they began working for lesbian and gay equality within governmental and legal structures. Those efforts have borne fruit in numerous ways, including the repeal of many sodomy laws, the cessation of police entrapment, the recognition of domestic partnerships, the growth of equal opportunity laws in employment and housing, and the slowly increasing attention paid to the severe oppression suffered by gays and lesbians in the military. Much more remains to be accomplished on these fronts, as those who continue to enter the political and legal arenas well know.

Many of these liberal political efforts, however, have been limited by their emphasis on only two facets of LGBT communities: lesbians and gay men. In the case of marriage rights and certain other battles, the field is narrowed further so that "gay and lesbian" includes only those already in or wishing to be in long-term partnerships. "We are just like you" is a powerful statement to make when working for equal rights. Not all LGBT people, however, *are* "just like you," if "you" means the dominant group in U.S. culture: white, adult, and upper middle class. LGBT communities encompass the same diversity as the United States itself, and many of those not represented in mainstream lesbian and gay politics have diverted their attention and their efforts to other movements—some focused on LGBT issues specifically, others on issues that affect LGBT and heterosexual people alike.

Queer activism is one major branch of radical LGBT activism today. With its roots in organizations such as Queer Nation and ACT-UP (AIDS Coalition to Unleash Power), this branch of activism revisits the radical politics and tactics of the late 1960s and early 1970s but often adds a creative, playful, or dramatic tactical twist borrowed from performance art. Like liberal activism, queer activism was sparked in part by the resurgence of social conservatism during the 1980s. In addition, however, its rise was affected by the perception that mainstream activism was making the same mistake as earlier political movements: it was excluding those it saw as less acceptable to mainstream society in order to meet its political goals. Just as some white feminists in the early twentieth century refused to advocate black voting rights and some heterosexual feminists in the 1970s cringed at the presence of lesbians in the movement, so some in the contemporary lesbian and gay rights movement exclude bisexuals, transgender and transsexual people, and those whose sexual practices (beyond being with a same-sex partner) deviate from what mainstream U.S. culture considers "normal."

Finally, and especially in the case of ACT-UP, the rise of queer activism was prompted by the Reagan administration's tragic neglect of the acquired immunodeficiency syndrome (AIDS) epidemic. Clearly, some concluded, the lesbian and gay rights movement had not made as much progress as it thought. Viewing lesbian and gay activism as having given in to a flawed system, queer activism returns to the literally radical goal of changing the system at its roots. Both lesbian and gay activism and queer activism continue to be widespread at the beginning of the twenty-first century. Moreover, LGBT communities also include old-school homophiles, nonactivists, lesbian feminists, activists who focus mainly on issues such as racism or economic injustice, and many others.

So where is religion in all of this? The answer to that question is complicated because of the many different political values discussed above. Additionally, many LGBT people become alienated from organized religion when they come out. Told by parents, friends, or religious leaders that they cannot "be" lesbian, gay, bisexual, or transgender and still fulfill their religious obligations properly (as though LGBT identity were something that easily could be stopped and started), many LGBT people developed a powerful animosity toward organized religion or toward religion in general. Moreover, all three major LGBT political movements were heavily influenced by Marxism. To Karl Marx, religion was "the opiate of the people": the drug that kept the working classes complacent by preventing them from feeling the pain of their oppression. Although later Marxist thinkers revised this opinion significantly, in the eyes of many LGBT activists, religion appears as the tool of an oppressive, heterosexist, and patriarchal system.

But religion has long been a concern of LGBT communities and has been addressed by activists since at least the latter days of the homophile movement.[4] There is evidence of LGBT concern with religion during the 1940s and 1950s, and in 1964 the Council on Religion and the

Homosexual was formed in San Francisco. The Metropolitan Community Church, a predominantly LGBT Christian denomination, held its first service in 1968, and numerous other LGBT religious groups formed shortly thereafter.

Even for the Marxists, there was an alternative to organized religion: spirituality. Harry Hay, the founder of the Mattachine Society, was the major driving force behind the formation of the Radical Faeries, an intentionally disorganized, nondoctrinal group that focuses on the playful expression of gay men's spirituality. And despite the strong influence of Marxist theory on feminism in the 1970s, lesbians had a wide range of resources available in the feminist spirituality developed by cultural feminists of the period.

Thus, since the beginning of the gay liberation movement, a number of religious and spiritual resources have been available to LGBT people. Before looking at them in depth and considering people's individual choices about how and whether to integrate religion and spirituality into their lives, we need to examine one other important factor affecting LGBT people's attitudes toward religion: the "homosexuality debates."

## ORGANIZED RELIGION RESPONDS TO LGBT PEOPLE

Along with race and gender, the sexuality of nonheterosexuals and women has been a central topic of debate for organized religions in the United States since at least the 1970s. As lesbians and gay men became increasingly visible and vocal in the political arena during that decade, some began to demand representation and rights in religion as well. In response, religious organizations began to issue official statements that outlined their policies on several issues: the reality or unreality of sexual orientation as an inborn, unchanging trait; the ordination of lesbians (in the few groups that ordained women at the time) and of gay men; special requirements regarding celibacy for ordained lesbian and gay men; civil rights *outside* religious organizations for lesbians and gay men; and the access of same-sex couples to the sacrament of marriage. Although these policies have shifted over time, usually in the direction of increasing acceptance and equality, they also have led to deep divides between (mostly heterosexual) liberals and conservatives in a number of religious groups. Hardest hit by these fissures, which some believe to be the most extreme since the debates among (mostly white) churches over slavery, are the mainline Protestant churches whose homosexuality debates are discussed in Chapter 8.

The increasing attention paid to lesbians and gay men (many of those involved in these debates overlook the presence of bisexual, transgender, and transsexual people in their churches) has produced a number of benefits, among them a blossoming of LGBT theological and religious writings within several traditions. However, it also has led to an increasing awareness among LGBT people of predominantly negative official religious stances on homosexuality and more intense policing of sexual orientation. Religious LGBT people who came of age since 1970 are far more likely than their elders to have heard official speeches, casual discussions, jokes, and the like that condemn same-sex attraction from a religious perspective. The rise of what is commonly known as the "ex-gay movement," comprising a number of religiously based (mostly Christian) organizations that claim to "heal homosexuality," has added another layer to the potential psychological damage faced by LGBT people—especially those newly exploring their sexual or transgender identities—in organized religions.

Of course, not all non-LGBT religious groups have proved unwelcoming of LGBT people. Every religious organization contains individuals and sometimes entire movements that are supportive of LGBT rights, and those movements have become one major source of religious expression for LGBT people. And despite official protests to the contrary, every group also contains LGBT people who are comfortable with their own identities no matter what the doctrinal position of their religion may be.

## RELIGIOUS INDIVIDUALISM

A third major factor affecting the rise and proliferation of religious options for LGBT people in the contemporary United States is the growth of religious individualism. Although the decline of traditional organized religions in the United States has been a topic of sociological concern for decades, it is only recently that the opposite side of this trend—the growth of religious individualism—has received serious attention. Two well-known sociological works on the topic are especially relevant here: Robert Wuthnow's *After Heaven* (1998) and Wade Clark Roof's *Spiritual Marketplace* (1999).

Wuthnow argues that during the second half of the twentieth century, religion in the United States has undergone a shift from a "spirituality of dwelling" to a "spirituality of seeking." The first, he explains, relies on the concept of a "spiritual home," usually a congregation and sometimes also a building or geographical location in which people experience spirituality and a sense of permanent "sacred space." In the second, however, people create their own religious identities rather than accepting the identities shaped for them by family, friends, society, religious leaders, and the like. Or as Wuthnow puts it: "Status is attained through negotiation. A person does not have an ascribed identity or attain an achieved identity but creates an identity by negotiating among a wide range of materials" (1998, 9–10).

In exploring the potential assets of a "spirituality of seeking," Wuthnow discusses two people whose life experiences have differed from the norm: one is a survivor of childhood sexual abuse, and the other had a father who was manic-depressive and alcoholic. These two and those like them, Wuthnow argues, "have been jarred out of socially acceptable ways of living and thus cannot create a self by playing the roles prescribed by social institutions. If their lives are to have coherence, it must be of their own making" (1998, 147). For LGBT people in the United States today, the experience of coming out is not always one that "jars" them "out of socially acceptable ways of living." However, it generally does raise questions, at least, regarding their social acceptability, and it certainly suggests to the heterosexual world a drastic change in *something*—judging, at least, from the frequent use by heterosexuals of the puzzling term *the gay lifestyle*. Certainly within the confines of Christianity, coming out still tends to call into question one's social acceptability. One lesbian pastor, for example, relates that when she came out to her parents, her mother's first words were: "I thought you believed in God!" (Wilcox 2000, 88). For this mother, there was apparently no way of being a lesbian *and* believing in God. For her daughter, of course, the two did go together—so well that she went to seminary and became a pastor. But in such cases of uncertainty about or direct challenge to one's place in the social order, the recent shift toward religious individualism may make it easier for LGBT people to bring together their religious and sexual or gender identities.

Wade Clark Roof offers another perspective on this shift toward the "spiritual." In *Spiritual Marketplace,* he argues that the relatively new term *lived religion* is helpful in understanding the current mixture of institutional and personal beliefs and practices in the United States (1999, 41). Roof suggests that there are three central aspects to lived religion: scripts, practices, and human agency. *Scripts,* which for LGBT people can be either negating, affirming, or neutral, come from the religious group in which a person was raised, the teachings of his parents, her partner's current beliefs, ideas embodied in the culture, and so on. Thus, Roof argues, spirituality is never entirely an individual issue because it is always shaped by surrounding institutions and influences.

*Practices,* too, are rooted in community, even if they are performed by the individual. They may link that individual, however loosely, to her community, but they also reinforce scripts, influencing beliefs through actions. But though these first two aspects seem to control the individual from outside, the third aspect of *human agency* complicates the other two. Roof explains: "People make choices, selectively engage scripts and practices, reflect upon themselves as meaning-making creatures. In this process biography and faith traditions interact" (1999, 43). In other words, "it becomes necessary to carry on a creative dialogue with tradition" (1999, 169). Echoing Wuthnow, Roof argues that those involved in such a dialogue "configure new spaces for making meaning and engage in a process of interiorizing and authenticating their own affirmations" (1999, 166).

The conflict between LGBT identity and traditional religious views of gender and sexuality often poses serious existential questions: Why me? What does my life mean? How am I to live? Yet Roof's and Wuthnow's works suggest an important strategy for solving such dilemmas: rather than being a rule book, religion has become a resource, to be brought in when it is useful and ignored or rewritten when it is not. As a bisexual Christian man once commented: "I take from the Bible what I can use, and I disregard a lot of what I can't use" (Wilcox 2000, 90).

This strategy also shows up outside of LGBT communities. Lynn Resnick Dufour, who uses the term *sifting* to describe such religious identity negotiation, has explored its presence among Jewish feminists. She explains:

> Sifting is a process by which many people construct cohesive, non-conflicted identities out of potentially conflicted ones. This process involves trying-on [*sic*] various practices and attitudes of a given reference group, evaluating them based on one's personal values, needs, or feel-

ings, and then either identifying with them or "screening them out" of one's identity. (Dufour 2000,104)

Like the feminists in Dufour's study, LGBT people often sift through the "practices and attitudes" of their religious backgrounds to assemble religious identities that can be integrated with their LGBT identities.

## ORGANIZED RESPONSES TO ORGANIZED RELIGION

These three factors—LGBT people's increasingly insistent demands for visibility and equality, the responses of LGBT and heterosexual people alike to the homosexuality debates, and religious individualism—have been the driving forces behind the development of numerous LGBT religious organizations. The Internet has been a critical resource as well because many religious people who are exploring their LGBT identities fear being seen while attending one of these groups. Surfing the web from a secluded computer, they can access both information and anonymous support. Many of the organizations discussed below maintain extensive web sites. Some of these groups are highly institutionalized, with formal organizational structures, strict doctrines, and carefully selected leaders. Others are loosely constructed movements, each local group resembling the others only through choice or consensus rather than at the direction of a central group or person. They can be divided, however, into five main types: internal groups, exit groups, safe space groups, alternative space groups, and indigenous and "blended" traditions.[5]

### Internal Groups

I have chosen the term *internal groups* to refer to those groups within pre-existing religious organizations that provide community for LGBT people and their heterosexual allies. The first such group to be formed was Integrity, an organization of LGBT Episcopalians. Begun in Georgia in 1974 by a gay man named Louie Crew, this group quickly took on a life of its own, expanding by 2001 to include over sixty chapters in the United States and others in Canada, Australia, and Africa. Although some Integrity chapters offer worship services (making them more like the "safe space" groups discussed below), many simply serve as a source of community or a base for activism within the Episcopalian and Anglican churches.

337

Integrity proved to be the first pebble in a near-landslide of internal groups within U.S. Christianity. American Baptists Concerned for Sexual Minorities traces its roots to events that took place in 1972, and the remainder of the 1970s saw the founding of many other LGBT groups, including those within evangelical Christianity (Evangelicals Concerned—1975), the Seventh-day Adventists (Kinship International—1976), the Anabaptist churches (Brethren/Mennonite Council for Lesbian and Gay Concerns—1976), and the Church of Jesus Christ of Latter-Day Saints (Affirmation—1977). Also active today, among others, are Emergence International (Christian Science); Friends for Lesbian and Gay Concerns (Quaker); Interweave (Unitarian Universalist); Lutherans Concerned; Gay, Lesbian, and Affirming Disciples Alliance (Disciples of Christ); Axios (Orthodox); and Honesty (Southern Baptist). Many of these groups have chapters outside the United States as well as inside it. Most offer education, community, and support for LGBT people and their allies but do not conduct services, leaving their members to continue worshipping in mainstream churches. However, many of these groups are also at the forefront of a spreading movement to create individual congregations that support LGBT members even when the denomination officially does not. Such congregations (within Christianity) are variously called Welcoming and Affirming; More Light; Welcoming; Open and Affirming; and so on. More recently, a similar movement has begun among synagogues in the Los Angeles area: "welcoming" congregations identify themselves by displaying the phrase "A Place to Belong" on their signs and on temple literature.

Because of differences in institutional organization, theology, need, and opportunity, LGBT groups in other religions have developed differently from those in Christianity. They are present and active, however, and many entered the limelight in the 1970s along with the blossoming Christian organizations.

Although there are LGBT branches or committees within local and national Jewish organizations, by far the most active and best-attended LGBT organizations within U.S. Judaism are the LGBT synagogues—a movement that began in the early 1970s. These fall under the designation of "safe space groups" and will be discussed below. Likewise, LGBT Buddhists, Hindus, and Muslims have tended to form broad support groups rather than dividing along lines of denomination or tradition. Few resources currently exist for LGBT Hindus and Muslims, although two recently formed groups known as Queer Jihad and Al-Fatiha have become relatively well-known. In part because of the strong draw Buddhism has held for liberal converts in the United States, there are also a number of LGBT Buddhist congregations and organizations in this country.

### Exit Groups

A second and much smaller type of LGBT religious or quasi-religious organization is the exit group, designed to provide support (but generally not worship services) for LGBT people who have left an anti-LGBT religious organization. A Common Bond is one of the better-known LGBT exit groups; although it welcomes active Jehovah's Witnesses, its chapters in the United States, Brazil, South Africa, Switzerland, the United Kingdom, and Canada are directed primarily at former Witnesses who are LGBT. Interestingly, some of these groups have found allies in the contemporary descendants of the 1970s anticult movement; A Common Bond's accusations against the Witnesses, for example, sometimes include not only anti-LGBT prejudice but also brainwashing, totalitarian rule, and the like.

### Safe Space Groups

A third type of LGBT religious organization, safe space groups, provide support, community, and religious services within a wholly or mostly LGBT congregation, and most importantly, they do so as independent organizations outside the control or influence of heterosexist religious hierarchies. Despite this independence, however, safe space groups also remain committed to a preexisting religious tradition. Thus, safe space organizations are those that offer fairly standard (though often progressive) religious services to predominantly LGBT congregations; are governed independently by mostly LGBT administrators; and serve LGBT Christians, Jews, Muslims, Buddhists, Hindus, or members of other world religions.

Safe space organizations took root at roughly the same time as did the internal groups discussed above; the first safe space organization, in fact, predates those groups and influenced their development. Interestingly, although the political wing of U.S. gay liberation began on the East Coast and moved west, the religious branch of the movement has most of its roots on the country's West Coast. For instance, the Metropolitan Community Church, which is the largest Christian safe space movement, began when defrocked Church of God minister Troy Perry placed an advertisement in the September 1968 issue of Los Angeles's fledgling gay magazine, the *Advocate*. Twelve people came to the first service; thirteen attended on the second Sunday, and fifteen on the third. Perry was discouraged by a drop to only nine on the fourth consecutive Sunday of services, but by the tenth week of services, the new church had outgrown Perry's house, and soon he had attracted a second pastor. Since that time, the church has continued to grow at an impressive rate, and in 2002 the denomination claimed approximately 300 churches and over 44,000 members in sixteen countries.

Because of its unusual status as an LGBT Christian denomination, MCC attracts Christians from a wide range of backgrounds: Catholic, Assemblies of God, metaphysical, and Lutheran, just to name a few. Some arrive at the church with staunchly conservative theologies and others with extremely liberal ones. Some are charismatic, some high church, some in favor of gender-inclusive language, others not—the MCC encompasses as much theological diversity among its members as some of the larger Protestant denominations, and far more diversity than many. This has had a number of effects on the organization, especially in the areas of ritual and doctrine.

Some MCC churches, in an effort to accommodate the needs of their members, offer different types of services at different times of the day: a formal, "high church" service in the early morning, for example, might be followed by a less formal, "mainline" service in the late morning, with a charismatic or gospel service that evening. Larger congregations often employ pastors from different church traditions to lead these varying services. Smaller congregations, restricted by size to a single service, may incorporate elements from different Christian traditions, perhaps combining the enthusiastic, casual singing style of a charismatic church with the theology of a metaphysical one and some of the ritual symbols of Catholicism. Theological diversity is also embraced (within limits) by MCC, which has far fewer official doctrines than many other denominations.

Because MCC's market for members is limited primarily to LGBT Christians, however, only large metropolitan areas tend to have more than one such congregation within a reasonable driving distance. As a result, MCC members moving from one city to another often find themselves in a church wholly different from the one in their former area. This situation leads some people who had not attended previously to join the denomination, but it also leads others to leave MCC in favor of other LGBT-friendly organizations.

MCC thus has its limits; it is not a one-shot solution for all Christians. One problem that has plagued the denomination throughout its history has been called by some the "revolving door syndrome." For many Christians who are coming out as LGBT and for many LGBT people who are rediscovering Christianity, MCC churches are a critically important resource: they provide role models and safe spaces in which both LGBT identities and Christian beliefs are solidly affirmed. Yet although some of these new attendees stay in MCC churches for years, others remain only until they have developed a strong fusion of LGBT and Christian identities. After a year or two, they leave MCC in favor of other religious groups they find more fulfilling.

Moreover, despite the good intentions of the denominational leadership, there are limits to MCC's inclusivity in terms of theology, gender, and race. For some people MCC is "too Christian," for others, "not Christian enough." Its churches tend to be in locations that serve predominantly white and frequently middle- or upper-middle-class congregations, although LGBT people of color and working-class LGBT people both belong to and pastor MCC churches across the country. In addition, questions of inclusive language and gender equity continue to surface in individual congregations during pastoral searches, liturgical planning, and so on.

Immediately on the heels of MCC came another LGBT Christian organization, this one intended specifically for Catholics: Dignity, founded in 1969 by a priest in San Diego. Although founder Patrick Nidorf was forced by the Los Angeles archbishop to resign from Dignity in 1971, the group continued as a lay movement and garnered support from numerous priests and nuns, some of whom attend or run its services regularly. Although it has had a tumultuous relationship with Rome and with many influential Catholic leaders in the United States and it remains officially unrecognized by the church hierarchy, Dignity has chapters across the country and a sister organization in Canada. It continues to be active and vocal in the movements for LGBT rights and women's ordination, among other causes.

A third national movement, the Unity Fellowship Church Movement (UFCM), was founded in 1985 by gospel singer Carl Bean. Beginning as a small Bible study group in the Crenshaw district of Los Angeles, the movement attracted a rapidly growing number of LGBT

African Americans who felt rejected by their own churches and marginalized in other LGBT Christian groups. Within three years, the movement's "mother church" had moved into a permanent location; by 1991 there were Unity Fellowship churches in Detroit and New York City, and by 2002 the movement claimed fourteen churches across the United States. In addition to its churches, the movement also runs the Minority AIDS Project (MAP) in Los Angeles, which Bean founded simultaneously with the church itself.

For LGBT Christians whose needs are not met by MCC, Dignity, or the Unity Fellowship Church Movement, there are a number of other safe space groups, existing mostly at the local level rather than as national organizations. These include charismatic and evangelical groups, feminist groups, African American LGBT churches, and small "house churches" aimed at LGBT members of a specific Christian denomination. The black LGBT churches are perhaps the most actively growing group at this point, spurred in part by the efforts of James S. Tinney in Washington, D.C.

Another widespread safe space movement consisting of locally organized congregations comprises the impressive number of LGBT synagogues that have been founded since the early 1970s. The LGBT synagogue movement began in Los Angeles in 1972, with the founding of a group inspired largely by MCC. Calling themselves the Metropolitan Community Temple, the fledgling organization first met in the basement of MCC–Los Angeles in 1972. A year later, it was renamed Beth Chayim Chadashim (BCC), and in 1974 it was accepted into the Union of American Hebrew Congregations (a Reform organization), making it the first LGBT synagogue to achieve official recognition outside LGBT circles. BCC still exists today and is no longer the only LGBT synagogue in the greater Los Angeles area. In addition, the efforts of BCC members to create a safe space for themselves inspired the creation of other synagogues across the country. The second to be formed was Congregation Beth Simchat Torah (CBST) in New York, which began in 1973. With more than 800 members in 2001, it claims to be the world's largest LGBT synagogue.

Like MCC, the LGBT synagogues often include members from a wide range of Jewish backgrounds. In response to this internal diversity, many offer a variety of services and small groups tailored to meet the needs of different constituents. In 2001, for example, CBST offered the following on at least a monthly basis, in addition to its main Friday night service: a lesbian text study group, a liberal service using a Reconstructionist prayer book, a community Shabbat dinner, a children's service, a *Havdalah* (end of Shabbat) service, traditional Friday evening and Saturday morning services using a Conservative prayer book, and a feminist service using Marcia Falk's *Book of Blessings*. CBST literature also emphasizes the fact that its rabbi, Sharon Kleinbaum, has extensive experience with all four major Jewish traditions.

Buddhism is the third world religion to be well represented among LGBT safe space organizations. The Hartford Street Zen Center in San Francisco's heavily LGBT Castro District is perhaps one of the best-known LGBT Buddhist congregations because Issan Tommy Dorsey, one of its founders and its first resident teacher, was the subject of David Schneider's *Street Zen* (1993). A student of Sōtō Zen master Shunryu Suzuki, Dorsey came to Zen through the San Francisco Beat community. He was ordained by Suzuki's successor Richard Baker in 1975 and worked for many years at the San Francisco Zen Center and the Tassajara Zen Mountain Center, a monastery south of San Francisco, before becoming the first teacher-in-residence at Hartford Street in the mid-1980s. Today, the center offers daily meditation sessions, lectures, and classes. In addition, it hosts a women's meditation group and offers special meditation sessions for those with human immunodeficiency virus (HIV).

Care for those with HIV/AIDS was a central topic of concern for Dorsey, in part because of the importance of compassion in Buddhist teachings and in part because he himself was diagnosed with the disease in the late 1980s (he died of AIDS complications in 1990). Working in the middle of San Francisco's Castro District during this period, Dorsey saw the disease at its worst. Members of UFMCC–San Francisco remember conducting several funerals each week during this time, and although the HIV virus and the method of infection had been identified by the mid-1980s, few medications were available. Dorsey began housing late-stage AIDS patients in the Hartford Street center, and soon thereafter founded the Maitri Hospice. Maitri moved from its original location in the late 1990s, but it still thrives as a Buddhist hospice.

Though they differ across religious traditions, these safe space organizations also share a number of traits. Because there are generally fewer LGBT congregations than non-LGBT congregations in any given area, these groups often serve members from a variety of religious backgrounds, and their services and classes reflect this diversity. Like the

Hartford Street center and the Maitri Hospice, most LGBT congregations also offer special services and counseling for their HIV-positive members and grief counseling for members bereaved by the disease. Awareness and celebration of LGBT identities are another typical characteristic: many of these groups display the rainbow colors of LGBT pride on their literature, their sacred spaces, their web sites, and even the clothing and jewelry of their members and leaders. In a world in which being both LGBT and religious is often seen as odd by heterosexuals in the religion and by nonreligious members of LGBT communities, these congregations provide safe havens in which religious LGBT people can celebrate both aspects of their identities without challenge.

Many LGBT people, however, are uncomfortable with any sort of traditional, organized religion. There are several reasons for this discomfort. First, many who once were religious have experienced varying degrees of rejection from organized religious communities. Moreover, rejection often comes in the name of a sacred figure: people may be told, for example, that God does not wish them to be LGBT or that they have displeased God by expressing their LGBT identity. Faced with such accusations, many LGBT people understandably reject organized religion in turn. Although some eventually return to it in the form of safe space congregations, many others seek their religiosity, or "spirituality," as they often prefer to call it, elsewhere. One important source of such spirituality is the fourth type of LGBT religious organization: alternative space.

### Alternative Space Groups

Alternative space groups are those that offer LGBT people an innovative form of religion. Although some alternative groups claim a long history or ancient forerunners, they are not part of the larger world religions, and many define themselves explicitly as *not* religious but spiritual. These groups are numerous, widespread, and highly diverse in the United States; often they are local phenomena and are unconnected to any broader organization. A few of them, however, have blossomed into loosely connected national or international movements.

As Nancy Ramsey Tosh and Tanya Keenan mention in Chapter 10, Dianic Wicca, or Dianic Witchcraft, is one such movement. Although it is not and never has been intended solely for lesbian and bisexual women, the movement was founded by a lesbian and continues to attract a number of lesbians and bisexuals to its circles. Like many safe space groups,

Dianic Wicca evinces strong feminist sympathies and offers women-only rituals. Unlike those groups, however, it is completely separatist: although Dianic Witches may interact with men on a daily basis, their rituals and most of their teachings are reserved solely for women.

As with many of the movements already discussed, Dianic Wicca began in the 1970s. First and foremost, it was inspired not by the gay liberation movement but by radical feminism. Its founder, Zsuzsanna Budapest, was a feminist activist in the Los Angeles area who decided that the women's movement needed a religion that valued and celebrated women's experiences, women's life cycles, and women's divinity. Drawing together the folk magic of her Hungarian foremothers with the ritual and myth structure of a (nonfeminist) new religious movement known as Wicca, Budapest created a new religion named after the goddess Diana.[6]

Tosh and Keenan describe Wicca in depth in Chapter 10, so only a brief overview is necessary here. Like most Wiccans, Dianics follow a ritual calendar that focuses on a goddess and a god. Mother and son at the beginning of the year (the winter solstice), lovers during the summer months, these two deities are understood to be evident in divine images from around the world. But Dianic Wicca diverges from other forms of witchcraft in that it keeps the goddess far in the forefront throughout the year. She receives more attention than the god during most rituals (indeed, often the god is not even represented), and although many Dianics wear jewelry in the shape of goddess images, very few wear symbols representing the god.

In keeping with Budapest's vision for the movement, Dianic rituals (held, like other Wiccan rituals, on eight agricultural holidays and often on the full moon) typically focus on themes that empower women through developing a sense of women's own divinity and celebrating women's bodies. Because they are safe, women-only, lesbian and bisexual–positive, and feminist spaces, Dianic circles have been and continue to be attractive to some lesbian and bisexual women. However, like much of the neopagan movement and also like separatist feminism in general, the movement appeals mostly to women of European descent. This occurs for a number of reasons, including the movement's focus on European and ancient Mediterranean goddesses (although appropriation of Native American sacred figures also is not uncommon), its focus on the needs and political goals of middle-class white women and its general lack of attention to the ways in which other women's needs and goals differ from theirs, and its gender separatism in general. It also is an unwelcoming environment for transgender women; with their roots in a feminist movement that believed in the innateness of male and female characteristics, Dianic circles usually refuse to admit women who were not born in female bodies.

Just as safe space movements may include men-only groups as well as women-only ones in their calendar of events (though men's groups are generally less common than women's groups), so there is a men-only counterpart to Dianic Wicca among the alternative movements. The Radical Faeries were officially founded in the late 1970s by a group of gay men who met in Arizona to explore their spirituality; the late Harry Hay, founder of the Mattachine Society, is generally thought to have been the driving force of this group. Like Dianic Wicca, the Faeries can be considered a part of the broader neopagan movement. However, they are even more loosely structured than most neopagan groups: they have no central organization, no set doctrine or ritual, no formal initiation, and no specific sacred texts. If anything, their practices are set by type rather than by details. In other words, certain types of ritual holidays and practices (such as celebrating agricultural holidays and wearing drag—or nothing—during rituals) are more to be expected at a Faerie gathering than others (such as celebrating the resurrection of Christ or listening to sermons). What is most characteristic of Faerie gatherings is their anything-goes eclecticism—some Faeries say, in fact, that the resulting "chaos" is itself sacred.

Like Dianics, Faeries tend to be politically active and often link their spiritual beliefs and practices to politics. Because they are a movement (some say a "dis-organization") specifically for gay men, much of their activism focuses on gay rights. But as a neopagan movement, they are also concerned with the earth, and they take part in ecological activism as well. Ultimately, though, the greatest similarity between the Radical Faeries and Dianic Wicca is the focus in both groups on celebrating and strengthening their participants—as (sometimes lesbian or bisexual) women in the case of Dianics and as gay men in the case of the Faeries.

The same is true of many smaller alternative movements. Some of them are regional, whereas others have affiliated groups scattered across the country; many others are single groups and sometimes are quite short-lived. They arise in response to needs that go unfulfilled in more traditional settings and even in safe space groups. For some, the need to avoid organized, traditional religions combines with a need for religious expression of some sort to make alternative groups a necessity. For others, the need centers around avoiding both homophobia and sexism or finding a spiritual outlet that is not racist or ethnocentric. In each case, these alternative movements rely on the ingenuity of their founders and their participants for their ritual practices. They tend in general to be doctrinally lenient and to focus on ritual that fulfills and affirms the entire person—including especially body and sexuality.

One example of these smaller groups was described by Irene Monroe in a 1993 article. The Aché Sisters took their name from a Yoruba word for power. Founded by Monroe and five other women, the group described its members as "Zamis," rejecting the term "lesbian" as too loaded with Euro-American overtones (the term *Zami* comes from Audre Lorde's book of the same title). They were Christians and "post-Christians," some still members of a church, others having left out of frustration with the sexism and homophobia of their congregations. Their loosely structured rituals addressed the needs of both groups, including Christian elements but also avoiding specific references to Christianity when necessary.

Like other alternative LGBT religious movements, the Aché Sisters consciously designed their rituals around themes of empowerment—empowering themselves as women, as African Americans, and as Zamis. Monroe describes place settings at the ritual table that included quotations from African American women and a ritual space hung with the pictures of "African diaspora women of history" (Monroe 1993, 132). When Monroe wrote her article, the rituals included elements of African tradition, womanist music and theology, and celebrations of their identity as Zamis. And importantly, like other alternative religions, the Aché Sisters celebrated women's bodies and the inner power that womanist author Audre Lorde called "the power of the erotic" (Lorde 1982).

Also like other alternative movements, the Aché Sisters were activists. Their rituals and their community lent each member the strength to fight homophobia, racism, and sexism in the world around them—whether in traditional African American churches, in LGBT churches, or in nonreligious areas of U.S. society. As Monroe put it, "we indict the black church for spiritually abusing its own people in the face of its God. . . . We want to be allowed our full spiritual development. We want to articulate truth as we know it in worship undefiled by sexist and heterosexist interpretations" (1993, 129).

### Indigenous and Blended Traditions

The example of the Aché Sisters demonstrates the importance of non-Christian, indigenous traditions for some LGBT people of color. For the Aché Sisters that tradition was African; for others it is Native (North or South) American or one of the Caribbean and South American religions that blends Catholicism with African traditions. The importance of tradition in the lives of Native American LGBT and two-spirit people is covered in depth in Chapter 2 and will not be revisited here. The blended religions, however, have only been mentioned in passing in Chapter 1 and deserve further attention.

When the Atlantic slave trade brought Africans to the Americas to serve as the labor machine of a plantation economy, the varied religious traditions of West African nations met the colonizing forces of Catholic and Protestant Christianity. In such areas as Cuba, Puerto Rico, Haiti, and Brazil, where the slave population was high relative to that of the European overseers, indigenous African traditions combined with Catholicism to produce a unique family of religions. In the United States today, the most well known members of this family are those practiced by sizable populations: Vodou in Louisiana and among Haitian immigrants in many areas and Santería among those of Puerto Rican and Cuban descent. Both religions have also become somewhat popular among African Americans, Caribbean Americans, and Latinos in general.

Because of their strong roots in African practices, these religions share many of the general characteristics described by Randy P. Conner in Chapter 1. The cultural disruption of slavery and the imposition of Catholicism, however, introduced several significant changes. First, because most groups of slaves included people from several, if not many, different cultures, their religious practices underwent a certain standardization: although the blended traditions of the Americas closely resemble several African traditions, they are not identical to the African religions but rather incorporate their common elements. Additionally, because a certain level of Catholic practice was frequently forced upon the slaves as their own traditions were outlawed, they soon found overlaps between their traditional practices and Catholic ones. As a result, blended religions such as Vodou and Santería include a pantheon of spirits (deities) who are referred to by both African names and the names of Catholic saints. Their rituals retain many African practices, including most notably the "mounting" or possession of a devotee by a visiting spirit, but they also include Catholic elements.

Very little has been published to date on the status of LGBT people within these religions, but the work that is available suggests that at least some communities are cautiously accepting of their LGBT members. Salvador Vidal-Ortiz (forthcoming) argues that this attitude may be due to the powerful importance of community in these religions; enforcing a certain sexual norm may be less important than keeping the community whole. However, Vidal-Ortiz also suggests that transgender people may have greater difficulty in the religion, especially if they have begun to alter their bodies physically through hormones or surgery. He reports one anecdote in which a transgender person undergoing such a transition was "mounted" and then rejected by a spirit, who complained that she no longer recognized her "child's" body.

A countervailing story from my own research on the West Coast of the United States shows the complexity of these issues. Corinne, a Pueblo Indian who was raised as a Latina in East Los Angeles (her grandmother changed the family's ethnic identity out of shame at being Native American), is female by biology and male by gender. Born female, Corinne has long identified with the male gender and recalls being puzzled as a child when clothed in dresses. Yet, Corinne relates, one day a small boy appeared on the other side of the backyard fence, wearing a red-and-white checked dress. When grilled by Corinne's brother, the boy responded that he was wearing a dress because he liked to wear dresses—and in so doing, he allayed Corinne's concerns. Years later, Corinne became involved in Santería and was initiated as a child of Changó—a deity identified as both male and female in African traditions who is also identified with the Catholic Saint Barbara. The seemingly perfect match for a transgender person, Changó also favors the colors red and white, leading Corinne to believe that it was he who appeared that day in the checkered dress.

## INDIVIDUAL RESPONSES

LGBT and welcoming religious organizations are only a few of the many paths available to LGBT people. The growth of religious individualism in the United States has been extremely advantageous—in some cases, literally lifesaving—for this group. In the face of blatantly anti-LGBT policies, religious leaders who threaten eternal spiritual consequences for coming out, and insidious debates in which LGBT people are either ignored or forced to defend their very right to exist, individualism is a valuable development indeed.

Moreover, LGBT identity is not intrinsically related to religious identity—in other words, LGBT people come from all religions and all branches within any given religion. There is no single religion, religious group, or even set of beliefs that can fill the needs of all LGBT people; instead, each person makes individual choices about what to believe, what to practice, where and with whom to practice, and even whether to believe at all. This section of the chapter reviews some of the religious choices made by LGBT people.

### Staying In

Every religion and denomination has self-identified LGBT people in its midst. Depending on the group's attitude toward these people, they may be more or less visible and more or less content with that identity—but they are there. Many people, upon coming out, choose to stay in the religion in which they were raised or the religion to which they converted before coming out. Some belong to religions that are openly supportive of LGBT people; others whose religions are officially intolerant may belong to a congregation that is supportive, such as certain Catholic or even Southern Baptist churches. In some congregations (Conservative and Orthodox Judaism are often examples), lesbian or gay identity may be quietly accepted as long as one is discreet. Some people find this requirement of discretion to be oppressive, but others feel it is an acceptable price to pay to remain in their congregations. And in many other cases, people who choose to stay within their chosen religious groups must be "closeted," knowing that any revelation of their LGBT identity would lead to immediate expulsion from the group and the accompanying loss of friends, family, and possibly employment. Although such a sacrifice is difficult and disheartening for any LGBT person, it is especially challenging for transgender people, who often feel they are living in "drag" when they are forced to express their socially assigned gender rather than the one with which they identify.

Why stay with a religion whose official doctrine denigrates your very identity, even if your own congregation does not? Why stay with one that forces you to be "discreet" or completely closeted? Why endure, on at least a weekly basis, religious teachings that condemn your very existence, ignorant questions about your (heterosexual) marital status, or enforced silence about your spouse? For many people, religion is simply too important to give up, and the LGBT organizations are often insufficient—at least by themselves—because of theological or ritual differences. Frequently, however, those in such situations continue attending traditional services but supplement them with membership in an LGBT-supportive internal group or even attendance at meetings of a safe space or alternative organization. Additionally, precisely *because* of the importance of religion in their lives, some people remain in these religions in order to change them—they fight from within for LGBT acceptance and celebration. It is a long and difficult struggle, but those engaged in it firmly believe that the true way of their religion is to celebrate LGBT identities equally with heterosexual and orthodox-gendered ones.

### Switching

Some people compromise to remain in the religion of their choice yet also to be supported as LGBT people. Generally this compromise involves switching denominations or congregations within the religion. A Conservative Jew might begin attending a Reform synagogue, for example, or a Southern Baptist might switch to an accepting American Baptist church. This strategy is effective only in the case of religions that are large enough to have several congregations in a given area and that are diverse enough in that area to include religious leaders who are supportive of LGBT people. The strategy is less likely to work (although it is still far from impossible) for a Mormon or a Muslim, for example, simply because of the smaller size and general social conservatism of these two religions. Another option is more likely to be useful for those in smaller, conservative religions but is also common among those who are switching denominations: given the opportunity, numerous LGBT people stay within their religions but switch to an LGBT congregation.

### Converting

Less common but still possible is conversion to another religion. LGBT people, of course, convert for as many different reasons as do heterosexuals and the orthodox-gendered—and these reasons may have nothing to do with sexual or gender identity. In addition, though, some people leave their religion because of its intolerance or insufficient support of LGBT

351

identities. Often this intolerance is the proverbial "last straw": the person may already have become unhappy with the religion's position on other social issues, its theology, its ritual, or other aspects.

LGBT converts generally switch from a less supportive religion to a more supportive one—as was the case in denominational or congregational switching but on a larger scale. In some tragic cases, however, LGBT people switch or convert to *less* accepting congregations, denominations, or religions in an effort to change their sexual or gender identities. Circumstantial evidence strongly suggests that this tactic does not work, and in fact many of the groups that claim to "heal" LGBT identities (ignoring the fact that it is the pain of intolerance and oppression that truly needs to be healed) admit that they cannot change participants' sexual orientation or gender. Instead, they claim only to train people to live against their innate identities. For some people, this appears to be the sole viable solution to an otherwise insoluble conflict between LGBT identity and an LGBT-condemning religion; unfortunately, this heavily oppressive system will remain in place until homophobia, biphobia, and transphobia are eradicated from the religious sphere.

### Seeking

Although many LGBT people use Dufour's "sifting" strategy, as described above, to stay within their chosen religions, another option for those who leave those religions is what Wuthnow called a "spirituality of seeking." Some "seekers" consider themselves agnostics—people who believe there may be a "truth" out there but do not believe it is possible to have certain knowledge of that truth. Others identify with a particular religion or at least a religious culture—Christian, Jewish, Buddhist, and so on—but seek multiple ways of expressing or experiencing that identity. People who are seekers sometimes also define themselves as "spiritual" rather than "religious." They find spiritual fulfillment in texts, teachers, and practices from a variety of religions, both new and old. For instance, a seeker might consider her spiritual practice to consist of a yoga class on Tuesdays, a meditation group on Fridays, and a women's drumming circle every full moon. Like religious individualism in general, "seekerism" is an extremely important development for LGBT people in the United States because it allows them to select only those groups, teachings, and practices that are both spiritually fulfilling and supportive of LGBT identities.

## Atheism

Atheism also appears to be quite common in LGBT communities, although because of the varying importance of religion among different cultures in the United States, the prevalence of atheism seems to vary depending on ethnicity and religious background. Additionally, many who call themselves atheists may in fact fit better into the category I have termed "seeking," for even as they deny the existence of any deity, they still consider themselves spiritual. Others, though, actively separate themselves from anything religious *or* spiritual. Some of these people have never been interested in things religious; they may have been raised as atheists or may have become dissatisfied with religion and spirituality at an early age. Others rejected religion as forcefully as it rejected them: given the choice between religious belonging and LGBT identity, they chose LGBT identity and pushed religion as far away as possible. In 2003, religion is still a touchy subject in LGBT communities, although many people seem to be more accepting of and interested in spirituality. LGBT Christians, for example, sometimes report facing greater rejection when they come out as Christians in their LGBT communities than they did when coming out as LGBT in their Christian communities.

## Effects of Gender

Along with ethnicity and religious background, gender is also a significant factor in individual decisions regarding religion and spirituality. Many lesbian, bisexual, and transgender (LBT) women—and some gay, bisexual, and transgender (GBT) men—are proponents of feminism and thus may have two reasons to reject traditional, organized religions. Not only are such groups frequently insufficient in their support of LGBT identities, but many of them also are embroiled in debates over the inclusion of women. Faced with male images of the divine, male religious leaders, and misogynist or at least subtly sexist religious texts and teachings—in addition to the homophobic or heterosexist aspects of the religion—many feminists decide to leave such religions. As a result, even LGBT congregations, if they subscribe to a traditional religion, often have more male than female members. That is certainly not always true; for instance, the use of inclusive language and the presence of a female religious leader tend to attract more women to the congregation, and some LGBT congregations are in fact composed mainly of women. Overall, however, it appears that LBT women have a greater tendency than GBT men to avoid organized religion in favor of alternative religious groups and spiritual seeking (see Shokeid 2001).

## CONCLUSIONS: THE FUTURE OF LGBT RELIGIOSITY IN THE UNITED STATES

Where is LGBT religiosity heading in the twenty-first century? It has seen phenomenal changes just in the last three decades of the twentieth century, and there is no reason to believe that those changes will not continue. As LGBT people continue to be vocal and visible within their religions and within U.S. cultures themselves, it does not seem unreasonable to expect that an increasing number of heterosexual-dominated religious organizations will come to support them. It will not be true of all groups, of course: just as some religions today still condemn all nonprocreative heterosexual sex, it is likely that there will always be some religions that condemn homosexual sex. But it is also possible that as the twentieth-century panic about homosexuality dies down, same-sex sexuality will be treated as casually as nonprocreative heterosexual encounters are frequently treated today.

Religious individualism does not seem to be fading; if anything, indications are that the trend is growing stronger within the United States. If so, then LGBT people will continue to have a variety of religious options available to them, and those who are willing to shift or alter their religious loyalties will be able to find a supportive space within which to develop their religiosity or their spirituality. Indeed, despite the strongly antireligious attitude prevalent among LGBT people in the United States today, there seems to be a great deal of interest in spirituality—in other words, in religious individualism. The diversity of religious expression in the LGBT community is unlikely to lessen; in fact, it will probably grow along with (or perhaps even faster than) the religious diversity of the United States in general.

Moreover, as LGBT people in organized religions increasingly reclaim their traditions as their own and stake out a space for themselves within those traditions, heterosexual religious leaders and their followers will be under increasing pressure to acknowledge those claims. LGBT people, like the members of other subcultures in the United States, may choose to remain in LGBT congregations for the sake of community and to celebrate their own unique cultures, but it does not seem too far-fetched to hope that those congregations will increasingly be a choice rather than a necessity.

## NOTES

1. Portions of this chapter have been published in "Of Markets and Missions: The Early History of the Universal Fellowship of Metropolitan Community Churches," *Religion and American Culture* 11, no. 1 (2001): 83–108.

2. *Transgender* is the term commonly used by people whose gender identity does not match the biological sex with which they were born: biological males who identify themselves as women and biological females who identify themselves as men. In addition, younger members of these communities sometimes use the term to identify themselves as *transcending* gender. Some self-identified transgender people do not alter their bodies to match their gender identity, either because they do not wish to or because they cannot afford to (health insurance companies consider this often critical operation to be "cosmetic surgery"). Others shift their bodies closer to their gender identities through the use of hormones or surgery. Some transgender people who have undergone sex-change operations consider themselves "transsexual," others continue to use the term "transgender," and still others identify as "formerly transgender." In all cases, transgender identity is different from sexual orientation, as transgender people—like orthodox-gendered people—may be homosexual, bisexual, or heterosexual. But because of long-term confusion in the dominant U.S. culture between transgender identity and homosexuality (falsely identifying "sexually active" lesbians as women who want to be men and "sexually passive" gay men as men who want to be women), transgender communities often overlap with lesbian, gay, and bisexual communities.

3. LGBT people of color encountered similar problems within both the gay liberation movement and the feminist movement, resulting in a double or even triple bind: their sexuality was not accepted within their own cultures, and their ethnicity was not affirmed within the LGBT community. Lesbians of color, furthermore, encountered sexism in addition to racism and homophobia in their communities.

4. There are two possible explanations for religion's absence as a central issue for the earlier homophile movement. First of all, the movement was founded by communists, who would have had little patience for organized religion. Second, because LGBT people were far less visible and vocal before the 1960s than they became after that decade, organized religion had less to say about them. Not until the late 1960s did religious groups begin

making regular policy statements on the religious value (or lack thereof) of LGBT people.

5. Edward Gray and Scott Thumma (forthcoming) suggest an alternative grouping: denominational heritage groups, subaltern/sectarian groups, and popular religiosity.

6. The naming of Dianic Wicca is an interesting and somewhat convoluted story. Diana, of course, was a Roman goddess, the counterpart of the ancient Greek goddess Artemis. A goddess of animals, children, and the woods and protector of the wood nymphs who were her companions, she is an excellent candidate for the patron of a women-only, feminist religion. Interestingly, although Budapest herself does not mention any outside sources, the major influence on her choice of names may be not Roman mythology but a little-known text called *Aradia, or the Gospel of the Witches* published by anthropologist Charles Leland in 1899. The myths included in this book, ostensibly collected in rural Italy, name Diana as high goddess, consort, and mother of the god Lucifer, and mother of the goddess Aradia. In this text, Aradia appears as a savior figure, bringing magical arts that allow the poor and disenfranchised to fight back against wealthy landowners and corrupt priests. This understanding of witchcraft as a tool for fighting oppression would have appealed to Budapest, whose early books consistently tie Dianic Wicca to political activism.

## REFERENCES

Dufour, Lynn Resnick. 2000. "Sifting through Tradition: The Creation of Jewish Feminist Identities." *Journal for the Scientific Study of Religion* 39, no. 1: 90–106.

Gray, Edward, and Scott Thumma. Forthcoming. *Gay Religion: Innovation and Tradition in Spiritual Practice.* Walnut Creek, CA: Alta Mira.

Katz, Jonathan Ned. 1992. *Gay American History: Lesbians and Gay Men in the USA.* Rev. ed. New York: Meridian.

Lorde, Audre. 1982. *Zami: A New Spelling of My Name.* Watertown, MA: Persephone Press.

Marotta, Toby. 1981. *The Politics of Homosexuality.* Boston: Houghton Mifflin.

McGuire, Meredith. 1997. *Religion: The Social Context.* 4th ed. Belmont, CA: Wadsworth.

Monroe, Irene. 1993. "The Aché Sisters: Discovering the Power of the Erotic in Ritual." Pp. 127–135 in Marjorie Procter-Smith and Janet R. Walton, eds., *Women at Worship: Interpretations of North American Diversity.* Louisville, KY: Westminster John Knox.

Roof, Wade Clark. 1999. *Spiritual Marketplace: Baby Boomers and the Remaking of American Religion.* Princeton, NJ: Princeton University Press.

Schneider, David. 1993. *Street Zen: The Life and Work of Issan Dorsey.* Boston: Shambhala.

Shokeid, Moshe. 2001. "The Women are Coming: The Transformation of Gender Relationships in a Gay Synagogue." *Ethnos* 66, no. 1: 5–26.

Vidal-Ortiz, Salvador. Forthcoming. "Sexuality, Gender, and Race: LGBTs at the Crossroads of Santería Religious Practices and Beliefs." In Edward Gray and Scott Thumma, eds., *Gay Religion: Innovation and Tradition in Spiritual Practice.* Walnut Creek, CA: Alta Mira.

Wilcox, Melissa M. 2000. *Two Roads Converged: Religion and Identity among Lesbian, Gay, Bisexual, and Transgender Christians.* Ph.D. diss., University of California at Santa Barbara.

Wuthnow, Robert. 1998. *After Heaven: Spirituality in America since the 1950s.* Berkeley: University of California Press.

Chapter 12

# Religion and Sexual Liberty

### Personal versus Civic Morality in the United States

*David W. Machacek*

*Protesters express opposing viewpoints at the State House in Trenton, New Jersey, June 11, 1979. (Bettmann/Corbis)*

*J*s the United States a Christian nation? The answer is yes and no. It is undeniably true that the vast majority of U.S. citizens identify with one of several Christian denominations and sects. Yet that fact makes no difference whatsoever when it comes to public policy, at least when the role of the state in governing U.S. public life is properly understood. Indeed, as will be demonstrated below, the proper role of the state is to prevent such facts from influencing public policy, not as a means of *restricting* the role of religion in U.S. public life, but rather for the purpose of *protecting* it. Although that answer may be unsatisfying to many, it is an important part of an informed understanding of contemporary debates over sexual morality in the United States, the proper role of the state in regulating sexual behavior, and the authority of religion in deciding these matters.

## AMERICA'S SACRED GROUND

It is often argued that many of the Founders of the United States, in composing the First Amendment to the Constitution, intended to protect religion from the state, not to protect the state from religion. Others, pointing to the historical fact that the Founders were rationalists and freethinkers, argue that a secular state was intended that had no interest in matters of religious truth or morality but only in instrumental concerns of social life. In fact, both arguments overstate the case. One mistake is in thinking that the Constitution privileges the authority of traditional religion in U.S. society. Another lies in thinking that the rationalists and freethinkers who designed the U.S. system of government were secular humanists who wanted to sequester religion from public life, making religion and morality matters of private and not public concern.

Barbara McGraw (2003) makes a compelling case that what the Founders intended in composing the First Amendment was to create a sacred ground, a hallowed public space for religion beyond the reach of legislative power. They did so mainly because they believed religion had a unique, indispensable role to play in sustaining a society that is both free and good.

In fact, they had good reason to fear the consequences of freedom uninformed by religion. During the colonial period, only about 17 percent of the population was involved in organized religion (Finke and Stark 1992). Contrary to the image of colonial life portrayed in school textbooks, irreligiousness, not piety, was the order of the day. This was particularly true of the frontiers, which attracted people seeking freedom from the constraints of social life and sometimes avoiding punishment or shame for misdeeds. All forms of licentious behavior were common, including drunkenness, gambling, prostitution, theft, and violence. The Founders wanted to form a free society, but freedom without the moral guidance of religion did not look very appealing; it certainly was not conducive to social order.

At the same time, they had reason to distrust religious establishments modeled after those of Europe. It is often suggested that religious disestablishment—the separation of church and state, or a system in which religion exists without state sponsorship and control—was merely a practical response to the fact that, already in 1791 when the Bill of Rights was ratified, the United States was a religiously plural society. Thus, it would have been impossible to get the various states to ratify a constitution that established one national religion. In fact, however, the Founders cited quite different reasons for prohibiting religious establishments; they had seen for themselves the destructive potential of such an arrangement. Indeed, many of the colonists in America had come to escape religious persecution by such establishments. Already at the time of the nation's founding, therefore, religious dissent was emerging as the dominant theme in U.S. religion, and it was the right of dissent that the Founders sought to protect. Religious bodies that were allied with the government, furthermore, were inherently unstable. They could be replaced with each change in the political regime. When religion was allowed to use the coercive powers of the state to enforce its orthodoxy, those powers could establish "false" as well as "true" religion. And the risk of such a system was great: to force people to profess a false religion, saving their lives at the expense of their souls.

Wishing, on the one hand, to avoid repeating the mistakes of the political regimes of Europe from which they had recently established independence and wanting, on the other hand, to preserve the role of religion in maintaining moral order, the Founders constructed a social system that bypassed these problems. It was a system built on two fundamental beliefs: (1) the existence of a *higher law* (2) that can be known through *revelation and reason.*

### Higher Law

When, in May 2001, President George W. Bush invoked James Madison as his guide in the selection and appointment of federal judges who would "enforce the rule of law," he revealed a misunderstanding of the role of the judiciary in Madison's thinking. President Bush had in mind the enforcement of civil laws—that is, legislation that requires or prohibits certain behavior, such as laws prohibiting the use of narcotics.

As he himself had revealed during the presidential debates, Bush is a "constitutional constructionist," as are, presumably, his judicial appointees. The philosophy of constitutional constructionism holds that moral behavior is defined by obedience to the laws as they are written by the powers governing society. In other words, to take an extreme example, in this perspective murder is wrong because it is forbidden; it is not forbidden because it is wrong.

To understand how fundamental is this misunderstanding of the intentions of the Founding Fathers, we have only to observe that under such a principle, the Revolutionary War was clearly immoral. The "laws of the land" at the time were those defined by the English monarchy and Parliament, which required that British citizens in the colonies pay taxes and recognize the authority of the Crown. The problem with a constructionist understanding of the law becomes immediately evident: it leaves no apparent basis on which to question the legitimacy of the laws and thus no means of challenging unjust laws short of political revolution. The potential for tyranny and political instability is apparent. Clearly, the Founders did not intend to create a society in which citizens could be held accountable to unjust laws or to construct a political system in which revolution would be required to correct injustices. Indeed, they took great pains to prevent these outcomes.

They did so, first, by affirming their belief in the existence of a universal moral order—a higher law, the "laws of Nature and of Nature's God" to which the Declaration of Independence makes its appeal. They held this higher law to be both universal and unchanging and, therefore, beyond the reach of human legislation. Hence, the Declaration of Independence, which makes little sense from a constructionist viewpoint, becomes meaningful:

> We hold these truths to be self-evident, that all men are created equal, that they are endowed by their Creator with certain unalienable Rights, that among these are Life, Liberty, and the pursuit of Happiness. That to secure these rights Governments are instituted among Men.

The Declaration makes its appeal, not to any human law—nor, notably, to biblical law or rational, secular logic—but to a higher law that cannot be changed by legislation. Indeed, both civil law and governments themselves can be held accountable to this higher law.

The accountability of governments to higher law offers a clearer understanding of both the language of the Bill of Rights and the proper role of the judiciary in the Founders' thought. At first glance, the language of the first ten amendments to the Constitution—the Bill of Rights—seems puzzling. As written, the Bill of Rights does not grant any positive rights to the citizens of the United States—a right *to* free speech or a right *to* trial by jury. Rather, it prohibits the government from passing legislation abridging these rights that are conferred on citizens not by the government but by higher law. The rights protected by the Constitution are understood to be prior to any government, and thus no government—whether in the form of a monarchy or a democracy—can legitimately take them away. They are *unalienable*. It is not within the power of any government to grant or suspend these rights; it is, rather, the proper role of the government to protect and preserve them. To hold the state accountable for this responsibility, the Founders established a judiciary independent of the legislative and executive branches of government, which is empowered to overturn legislation that violates the principles set forth in the Constitution.

In fact, at the time in which these amendments were written, the very subject of a Bill of Rights was highly controversial (Hutson 1991). Some feared that such an enumeration of rights could be misunderstood as having been granted by the state. If civil rights could be granted by the state, they also could be taken away. The Founders clearly dreaded such a possibility, and in a letter to a Jewish congregation in Newport, President George Washington specifically condemned this opinion: "It is now no more that *toleration* is spoken of, as if it was by the indulgence of one class of people, that another enjoyed the exercise of their inherent national rights" (Washington 1996, 6:284).

Others argued that if a list of civil rights were composed, it could be misinterpreted as an exclusive list—that is, that those rights named in the Constitution might be construed as the *only* rights enjoyed by the nation's citizens. Certainly, even a careful enumeration of specific rights would miss something, and to add new rights to the list would require a long process of deliberation and ratification (the difficulty of which is evidenced by the fact that, since 1791, only sixteen new amendments to the Constitution have been passed). This concern was so great that it led to the addition of the all-important but seldom cited Ninth Amendment, which attempted to prevent such a misunderstanding by prohibiting it:

> Amendment IX: The enumeration in the Constitution, of certain rights, shall not be construed to deny or disparage others retained by the people.

This amendment makes no sense whatsoever without reference to a higher law. In essence, it says that U.S. citizens enjoy other rights than those specifically enumerated in the Constitution. And implicitly, it is the responsibility of civil government to protect these unspecified rights as well. To what rights could the amendment be referring, if the only rights enjoyed by citizens were those conferred by the law of the land? Obviously, the Ninth Amendment intends to protect those rights that are not listed but are nonetheless inalienable under higher law. But how are we to know what these rights are?

### Religious Conscience

The solution to the puzzle posed by the Ninth Amendment lies in the First:

> Amendment I: Congress shall make no law respecting an establishment of religion, or prohibiting the free exercise thereof; or abridging the

freedom of speech, or of the press; or the right of the people peaceably to assemble, and to petition the government for a redress of grievances.

Although there is considerable debate over what the Founders intended to protect by prohibiting religious establishments and guaranteeing the freedom to practice the religion of one's choosing, the historical evidence points to one conclusion: religious *conscience* (Hammond 1998; McGraw 2003). And the reason they protected conscience forms the second element of America's sacred ground. The Founders believed that the unwritten, higher law—the laws of Nature and Nature's God—could be known through revelation and reason.

As the guardians of revealed truth, churches, synagogues, mosques, and temples enjoy a privileged position in U.S. civil society. However, given the variety of religions, all claiming to represent the truth, one must ask who should be responsible for choosing between them. If the state were empowered to decide which religion or church represented true religion, clearly the secular powers would select those groups most likely to support their own political agenda. Under such a system, religion could become the instrument of a tyrannical government rather than a source of protection against tyranny.

Furthermore, an establishment system in which religion could use the coercive powers of the state to force its beliefs and practices on the people posed the risk of religious tyranny, and there was no guarantee that false religions would not gain access to coercive power to enforce false beliefs and false morality. In the words of Thomas Jefferson, "Impious . . . legislators and rulers, civil as well as ecclesiastical . . . have established and maintained false religions over the greater part of the world and through all time" (Smith 1993, 198).

The solution was to forbid the government from using its powers to influence matters of religious conscience. Hence, the disestablishment clause does protect religion from state interference, but it necessarily does so by denying religion access to the coercive powers of the state. Thus, the free exercise and disestablishment clauses of the First Amendment, which are often seen as contradictory, can be seen as complementary: religious free exercise is made possible by prohibiting religious establishment.

Consequently, persuasion rather than coercion was to be the primary means by which religion would exercise influence over public morality. Indeed, the Founders thought it the surest way to encourage truth and morality over falsehood and immorality and the only way the former could come to dominate in a free society. Following the logic of John Locke, the Founders held that Truth did not need the assistance of secular powers but was more likely to be impeded by them:

> Truth certainly would do well enough if she were once left to shift for herself. She seldom has received, and I fear never will receive, much assistance from the power of great men, to whom she is but rarely known, and more rarely welcome. She is not taught by laws, nor has she any need of force to procure her entrance into the minds of men. Errors indeed prevail by the assistance of foreign and borrowed succours. (Locke 1983, 79).

The individual, guided by reason and conscience, was held to be the best judge of religious truth and morality because it was through reason and conscience that God spoke to the hearts and minds of humans. Out of concern for the state of his or her own soul, Locke believed, the individual is more likely to make a correct assessment of God's will on the basis of conscience than is some legislative or judicial body. The Founders, therefore, envisioned a system in which religions would be free to exercise their influence over the minds of individual citizens, attempting to persuade them of the truth of their beliefs by appealing to reason and conscience. Individuals would be free to accept or reject those convictions on the basis of conscience. This freedom was even extended to heretical, unpopular, and subversive opinions, for only by protecting such opinions could the Founders guarantee protection from political and religious tyranny.

A free conscience is meaningless, of course, if it cannot be freely expressed and acted upon. Indeed, the whole system of promoting public morality by persuasion rests upon the freedom to publicly express religious and moral convictions, as well as the freedom to express dissent. Even erroneous opinions were protected because the Founders believed that error could only be corrected through exposure. Thus, in the words of Thomas Jefferson, "errors cease to be dangerous when it is permitted freely to contradict them" (Smith 1993, 198–199). Truth has only to fear when it is deprived of its natural weapons: debate and free argument.

The freedom of religious conscience, although held to be of intrinsic value, was also the best protection for those natural rights not specifically listed in the Constitution but protected under the Ninth Amendment. A free conscience, freely expressed, would no doubt sound an alarm in the presence of injustice.

Hence, the meaning and significance of the remaining clauses of the First Amendment come into full view. The amendment not only ensures the freedom of conscience but also provides that citizens will have the right to freely express their convictions both in speech (freedom of speech, freedom of the press) and in action—by forming associations to publicize their convictions (freedom of peaceful assembly), as well as by taking their case before the judiciary (the right to petition for redress of grievances).

The above discussion provides two general principles that must inform any discussion involving religion, morality, and the law:

1. Under the U.S. Constitution, the state does not have the power to grant or deny natural, civil rights. These rights are held to derive from a law higher than the laws of the land; they are inalienable. The state is responsible for protecting those rights derived from higher law and can itself be held accountable to the higher law by its citizens.

2. The higher law and thus the natural rights enjoyed by citizens are believed to be known through conscience, and the U.S. Constitution provides specific protection for the freedom of conscience in the First Amendment. It does so first by prohibiting the state from lending assistance to any particular conscientious position and second by preserving the right of individuals to make conscientious judgments, to express and promote them without fear of political reprisal, and to bring a conscience-based case before an impartial court, even when the defendant is the state.

If this higher law is more likely to be known to the conscience of individual citizens than to the state, and if the citizens can hold the state accountable to that law, under what circumstances is the state justified in restricting the behavior of citizens at all? The answer is surprisingly simple. The state can legitimately pass laws designed to protect the rights of citizens from harm by other citizens; from harm by local, state, or federal government bodies; and from harm by foreign powers. The social contract, in other words, specifies that citizens shall be free to pursue their interests and desires and to act upon their idea of the good according to the dictates of conscience, but that freedom extends *only to the point at which one's freedom to act on his or her convictions infringes upon the freedom of others.* At this point, as the protector of the rights of its citizens, the state is empowered to intervene. Apart from this situation, however, the state's interests are best served by allowing the individual to decide on the morality of his or her own actions.

## RELIGION AND SEXUAL LIBERTY

Two conclusions follow from the above discussion. First, not all actions motivated by religious conviction are legally protected under the First Amendment. If my conscience tells me, for instance, that sexually explicit films promote temptation to sin, I still am not justified in burning down theaters that show them. Why? Simply because my right to express my conscientiously held belief in this way infringes upon the theater owner's right to express her conviction that nothing is wrong with such films, to say nothing of her right to be secure in her person and property. I retain the right to express my moral outrage, but I am bound to express that outrage in a way that does not infringe upon the rights of others.

Second, when the courts are asked to decide cases involving claims of conscience, it is not the job of the court to determine the truth of the opinions represented. In other words, to continue the example above, if the court ruled that the act of burning a theater was unjustifiable as an expression of conscience, it would not be saying that the theater owner is right in her belief that sexually explicit films are morally neutral or good and that the person who burned the theater is wrong in believing that sexually explicit films are evil. The person who objects to such films remains free to condemn them as morally objectionable and even to act on those convictions by forming a neighborhood alliance to protest.

However, if a community group makes a compelling case that the operation of such a theater harms their rights in some way, then laws may be passed restricting the freedom of the theater owner. For instance, communities commonly pass zoning ordinances that prohibit adult theaters and bookstores from doing business within a certain distance of schools. The logic of such a prohibition is not that children should not be exposed to morally objectionable material but rather that the presence of such a theater might put children at risk of unwanted sexual advances or expose them to behavior that could be harmful in other ways.

369

In short, cases involving morally loaded issues do have a rightful place in U.S. courts, and religious opinions can inspire public policy. They certainly have a place in public discourse. However, the court is not empowered to decide the morality of behavior; it is only empowered to decide whether one person's moral autonomy comes at the expense of another's. And the purpose of public policies cannot be to privilege one conscientiously held religious conviction at the expense of another; it must be to serve some secular purpose on which all parties, in principle, can agree (Hammond 2000). Furthermore, even though the system promotes discourse and debate over issues of moral concern, representatives of the various positions on such issues must rely on persuasion, not coercion, to promote their viewpoints.

This is not to say, however, that constitutional principles promote a philosophy of moral relativism. It is true for several reasons. First, the constitutional principles described here provide a clear basis for evaluating the *civic morality* of behaviors and laws because they define legitimate and illegitimate reasons for restricting freedom. Second, they allow for the existence of absolute moral laws but hold that moral truth is best revealed through free debate and argument rather than by government dictate. Third, they allow both religious and nonreligious ideologies the freedom to attempt to persuade the public of the rightness of their moral convictions. Finally, it might be argued that such a system actually promotes *personal morality* by promoting in individual citizens the habit of exercising moral judgment. Moral behavior, under such a system, is shaped less by compliance and more by inward moral conviction.

Indeed, it could be said that, historically, movements of moral reform have been most effective when they appealed directly to the conscience of the individual rather than relying on the state to impose a moral position on its citizens. The temperance movement, for example, was very successful; Prohibition decidedly was not.

Churches, synagogues, mosques, and other religious institutions therefore play an important role in a free society, but not because they represent moral authorities to which the public must bow. Rather, such organizations serve the dual function of supporting those people who subscribe to a particular religious and moral viewpoint and promoting that viewpoint among others. Such organizations, however, cannot enlist the assistance of the state for these purposes—that is the cost of freedom from state interference in their activities. They succeed or fail on the basis of their own merits—the extent to which they are able to sustain the commitment and conviction of existing members and to inspire conviction in others.

In general, then, to whatever extent premarital sex, unplanned pregnancy, homosexuality, the consumption of erotic entertainment, and so on do represent moral decline in the United States, it must be attributed to a failure on the part of those individuals and religions who find such behaviors morally objectionable to persuade others to share their point of view. It is not a failure by the state to sustain public morality because promoting morality is not the constitutional role of the state, but rather that of individuals and religious groups. The state's role is to protect the freedom of citizens to make moral judgments on the basis of conscience and to organize to promote their moral convictions. Indeed, the history of sexual liberty under U.S. law is one in which the state increasingly has divorced itself from making moral assessments.

In sum, it can be said that, on the one hand, religion plays an indispensable role in U.S. society by training individuals in the habit of exercising moral judgment. We can rightly say, therefore, with Alexis de Tocqueville, that religion "should . . . be considered as the first of [Americans'] political institutions, for although it did not give them the taste for liberty, it singularly facilitates their use thereof" (1969, 292). On the other hand, it also must be said that this system relies upon religious freedom. Groups that succeed in enlisting the coercive powers of the state to enforce a particular conception of personal morality actually undermine the very civic morality that secures their own right to exist.

## HOMOSEXUALITY AND ABORTION

Two issues have dominated both public and academic discourse about sexual morality since the 1970s: homosexuality and abortion. Beyond the matter of moral autonomy, there are several good reasons for treating these two together as instances of a single underlying problem. First, both issues grew out of the feminist movement's challenges to conventional beliefs about gender. The rallying cry of the women's movement— "Biology is not destiny"—finds further expression in the claim that women should have the right to choose whether to carry a pregnancy to term and in the claim of gays, lesbians, and bisexuals to the freedom to express their sexual desires. More importantly, both represent significant challenges to traditional sexual mores and assumptions about family life in the United States and therefore have been opposed by defendants of "traditional family values." The result appears on the surface to be what James Davidson Hunter calls a "culture war" (1991) between competing value systems: one embracing and even actively promoting value changes and the other defending the values of the late nineteenth and early twentieth centuries.

In this battle of opposing wills, positions of political power and judicial authority have come to be seen as the ultimate prize. By electing politicians who will represent these priorities in government and by appointing judges who are likely to rule in favor of one or the other position, Americans on both sides of the issue have attempted to tip the battle in their favor. However, it should be clear from the preceding discussion that although Hunter accurately represents the tenor of sexual morality politics in recent years, both sides in the culture war have attempted a constitutionally improper use of the powers of the state.

## *Homosexuality*

In December 1997, a New Jersey court allowed a young gay couple to adopt a boy they had been raising as foster parents since the child's birth (*Holden and Galluccio v. New Jersey Department of Human Services,* Bergen County Superior Court, 1997). The child, who was placed in foster care because of his mother's drug abuse problems, was born with a cocaine addiction and infected with human immunodeficiency virus (HIV). Since there were no other potential adoptive parents willing to take the child, the court decided that the interests of the child were best served by allowing adoption by the gay couple, who already as foster parents had demonstrated their sincere intentions to provide a good home for the boy.

Needless to say, this decision sounded an alarm among religious conservatives. Their position on the issue of adoption by same-sex couples was voiced by Reverend Jerry Falwell during an appearance on *Larry King Live,* on which the new parents were also guests. The course of the debate that ensued between King and Falwell is instructive and worth recounting at some length.

Falwell's initial objection to the adoption was based on his deeply held conviction that homosexuality is immoral. His understanding of Christianity compelled him to object to the possibility that the child would be raised in a home where such "unchristian" behavior was modeled as normal and even desirable. His conviction is no doubt shared by many Americans, even some who would otherwise encourage tolerance of homosexuals. Indeed, Falwell himself has encouraged such toleration, although he continues to oppose same-sex marriage and parenting by same-sex couples.

However, such religious convictions have no weight before the law, and King quickly pointed out why. If adoption rights could be denied to this couple on the basis that they would not raise the child in a good "Christian" home, then the right to adopt also could be denied to Muslims, Hindus, Buddhists, and even other Christians whose moral convictions differ significantly from those of Reverend Falwell. Indeed, the pastor of the Episcopal Church to which the gay couple belonged phoned in to the show to express her support and the support of their congregation for the adoption.

Falwell next reframed his argument, raising concerns about the well being of the child. Might not a child with two fathers be subject to teasing and harassment at school?

Indeed, he or she might. King and the other guests acknowledged this point. However, children find all manner of things to tease each other about—clothing and hairstyle, food preferences, and so on—but the possibility that a child might be subject to unkind treatment by peers has never been used to prevent anyone from raising children. Moreover, given the prevalence of racism in schools, this argument could be expanded to prevent minority ethnic groups in any neighborhood from raising children.

Finally, Falwell appealed to the authority of social science, basing his objection on the assertion that "studies show" that children fare best when they are raised in a home with both a mother and a father. He claimed that such children perform better academically, are better adjusted socially, and are less likely to suffer psychological problems.

Here was a potentially compelling argument. If, indeed, it could be demonstrated empirically, without recourse to prejudice or to purely subjective beliefs about the morality of homosexuality, that being raised by two parents of the same sex results in serious social or psychological harm, then there would be a sound legal reason to restrict adoption to heterosexual couples: to protect the rights of the child. Such a decision could be agreed upon by everyone, regardless of opinions about the morality of homosexuality.

However, when asked to name the studies to which he was referring, Falwell was unable to do so. Without proof that gay parenting had harmful consequences for children, the argument reverted to one based on personal opinions and prejudice, which have no merit under the law.[1]

In fact, pressed further on this point, Falwell ultimately admitted that the studies to which he was referring were based on comparisons of children raised in single-parent homes with children raised in heterosexual two-parent homes. However, again pressed on the point by King, Falwell added that he did not intend to argue that single parents should not be allowed to raise children. Indeed, by the end of the interview, Falwell professed a certain admiration for the sincerity of the new parents' desire to provide a good home for the boy. He even admitted that, were it not for their "unchristian" lifestyle, they would probably make good parents.

Even though he was wrong about the implications of social scientific research for gay parenting, in shifting from an argument based on subjective moral convictions to one based on objective, instrumental values, Falwell implicitly acknowledged the boundary between the role of religion and the role of the state in issues of sexual morality. In the realm of public discourse, individuals and groups are free to voice their objections to behaviors that they find morally objectionable, and they are free to try to persuade others of the truth of their convictions. However, it is not the concern of the state to decide the truth of these various opinions. Thus, it becomes apparent that some behaviors may be unobjectionable in terms of *civic* morality that are objectionable in terms of some people's *religious* morality. The state may intervene in the former case, but its intervention is forbidden in the latter.

Unless it can be demonstrated that being raised by gay parents is intrinsically harmful to the child, to restrict adoption rights solely on the basis of a general dislike for homosexuals would be clearly unconstitutional, and apparently the New Jersey court agrees. Ironically, in spite of the social scientific evidence that the security of a two-parent household is beneficial to children, in most states it is easier for gay would-be parents to adopt children as single parents than it is for them to adopt jointly with their same-sex spouses. This is because with the exception of Vermont, where civil unions have recently been recognized as the functional equivalent of marriage, neither the states nor the federal government recognizes same-sex marriages.

The case for same-sex marriage has been tried, unsuccessfully, on the grounds that denying marriage to same-sex couples violates the due process and equal protection clauses of the Fourteenth Amendment, which guarantee equal treatment under the law for all citizens. In his review of the relevant court decisions, William Eskridge (1996) argues that current state policies unconstitutionally discriminate when they pick and choose, rather arbitrarily, which citizens should enjoy a right that the courts have determined to be fundamentally linked to political citizenship:

> Wisconsin's marriage statute codifies the understanding of marriage that recurs in the case law: "Marriage is the institution that is the foundation of family and society. Its stability is basic to morality and civilization, and of vital interest to society and the state." Consistent with this philosophy, the states are not discriminating about who can partake of this institution. It is open to any consenting nonrelated couple—except lesbian or gay couples. . . . no state refuses to issue a marriage license to a couple on the ground that society disapproves of their erotic practices or their sexual orientation—unless they are homosexual. The state will issue a marriage license to sadists, masochists, transvestites, and fetishists, so long as they are heterosexual sadists, masochists, transvestites, and fetishists. . . . the pedophile (someone who is sexually attracted to minors) can also get a marriage license, so long as he or she is a heterosexual pedophile and is willing to go to some trouble. (Eskridge 1996, 63–64)

The implication of the pattern drawn by Eskridge is clear: the right of marriage is so fundamental that it is protected by the courts for murderers, pedophiles, and rapists. Only homosexuals must "sit at the back of the bus" (1996, 65).

If marriage is so fundamental, both as a civil right and as a preservative of social morality, that the right is extended even to criminals, then certainly there must be some truly compelling purpose served by prohibiting it in the case of homosexuals. In fact, however, no legitimate secular purpose has been identified so far. On the contrary, the court decisions that have upheld the gay marriage ban have been based entirely on symbolic (and therefore illegitimate) grounds.

In 1980, for instance, a federal court in California refused to recognize same-sex marriage on the grounds of biblical tradition (*Adams v. Howerton*). A Kentucky court in 1973 upheld Kentucky's denial of marriage rights to same-sex couples on the grounds that marriage cannot include same-sex couples as a matter of definition (*Jones v. Hallahan*). Both arguments, curiously, had been rejected earlier by the Supreme Court as legitimate reasons for antimiscegenation laws (laws that prohibited interracial marriages; *Loving v. Virginia*, 1967).

The symbolic nature of the decisions regarding same-sex marriage is further highlighted by two cases involving transsexuals. A New Jersey appellate court in 1976 ruled that a male-to-female transsexual could marry a man since the transsexual counted as a woman (*M. T. v. J. T.*), and in a similar Ohio case, a probate court ruled against such a marriage because it would amount to a prohibited same-sex marriage (*In re Ladrach,* 1987). The outcome of these two cases was entirely arbitrary and rested on determining whether the transsexual was male or female—a consideration prohibited by federal laws against discrimination on the basis of gender.

The lack of instrumental reasons led state courts in Hawaii and Vermont to rule in the 1990s that bans on same-sex marriage are illegal under those states' constitutions. In *Baehr v. Lewin* (1993), the Hawaii Supreme Court ruled that denying marriage licenses to same-sex couples is discriminatory and that unless the state could demonstrate a compelling interest to refuse such marriages, same-sex marriages must be allowed. Failing to discover any such interest, the court ordered the state to permit same-sex couples to marry. That decision was reversed, however, as a result of Hawaiians' 1998 passage of an amendment to the state constitution reserving marriage to opposite-sex couples. In December 1999 the Hawaii Supreme Court finally dismissed *Baehr v. Lewin* as moot under the amended constitution, although it left open the question of whether the state's refusal to recognize same-sex marriage violates the equal protection clause of the state constitution.

In the case of *Baker v. State* in Vermont (1998), the state supreme court ruled in favor of the plaintiffs on the basis of the common benefits clause of the state constitution.[2] The court rejected the State's claim that preserving marriage as a heterosexual union "reasonably served the State's interest in promoting the 'link between procreation and child rearing'" because the number of childless opposite-sex couples and the growing number of same-sex couples with children essentially nullified the point. Thus compelled by the court, the Vermont legislature passed a law recognizing "civil unions" between same-sex couples, which took effect in June 2000.

In cases involving the restriction of civil rights, the burden of proof always rests on the state. Quite a number of legal scholars and a small number of state courts concur that either the due process or the equal protection claim should be sufficient grounds for nullifying prohibitions on same-sex marriage, unless the state can demonstrate some compelling interest. So far, the states have failed to do so, resting their defense of anti-gay marriage policies on entirely symbolic grounds, which are clearly insufficient.

However, the symbolic nature of the arguments against same-sex marriage suggests a First Amendment challenge—one that might, in fact, be more persuasive to erstwhile opponents of same-sex marriage. That is the argument for moral autonomy and freedom of conscience.

Although it has not yet been tried in court, the argument for gay rights on the basis of protecting moral autonomy has been presented forcefully by David A. J. Richards. The denial of marriage and other rights solely on the basis of sexual orientation amounts to what Richards calls "moral slavery," which is characterized by two features: "First, abridgment of basic human rights to a group of persons; and second, the unjust rationalization of such abridgement on the inadequate grounds of dehumanizing stereotypes" (1999, 53). The unconstitutional logic of legal discrimination against homosexuals, in Richards's view, goes something like this: Homosexuality involves a moral choice. Because homosexuals make what some people perceive to be the wrong choice, they are deemed incapable of exercising moral judgment. Since homosexuals are seen as incapable of exercising moral judgment, the state considers itself justified in restricting their freedom to make moral judgments.

At stake is not only the right to marry, to be free from discrimination in employment and housing, and so on but also, and more importantly, the right to the free exercise of conscience. To make some behavior illegal solely on the grounds that a powerful group in society finds it morally objectionable is to deprive dissenters of the freedom to exercise moral judgment. The evil of such institutionalized prejudice is, again in Richards's words, "its unjust abridgment of the inalienable right to conscience, the free exercise of the moral powers of rationality and reasonableness in terms of which persons define personal and ethical meaning in living" (1999, 86). It is, in other words, an unjust abridgment of the very rights protected by the First Amendment.

A preliminary view of the power of such an argument to secure gay and lesbian rights may be found in a case that overturned Colorado's Amendment Two (*Romer v. Evans,* 1996). The amendment attempted to ban all laws that recognized antidiscrimination claims by gays and lesbians. According to Richards, "Its aim was decisively that advocates of gay and lesbian identity should be compelled to abandon their claims to personal and moral legitimacy and either convert to the true view or return to the silence of their traditional unspeakability" (1999, 92). Both sides could agree that the expression of gay or lesbian identity is a moral choice. However, "the opposition (on sectarian religious grounds) interprets the choice as a moral heresy, [while] its advocates construe the choice as an exercise of legitimate moral freedom" (92). The underlying issue, as decided by the courts, is not whether the gay and lesbian claim to moral legitimacy is right or wrong, but rather whether or not the law restricts the freedom of individual citizens to make the moral choice. The court agreed.

Unless it can be demonstrated that the right of homosexuals to raise children, marry, and expect fair treatment under the law in some way harms the rights of others to do the same, then the current restrictions on their rights levy an unconstitutional burden on their inalienable right to freedom of conscience. To deny human rights—of equal protection and due process and of privacy in one's intimate life—to those who dare to act on their belief that homosexuality is morally neutral or good is to punish them unconstitutionally for conscientious dissent. Whether homosexuality is moral or immoral in an absolute sense is not a matter for the state or the courts to decide. Instead, the mandate of the courts is to protect the right of the individual to make moral assessments, even if the conclusions reached by the individual are wrong; in matters of conscience, the First Amendment protects the right to err. Indeed, from the perspective developed here, the freedom only to make the "correct" assessment of religious and moral matters would be no freedom at all. So far, without any apparent reason apart from popular prejudice, the courts have failed to protect the First Amendment rights of homosexuals, and in so doing they undermine the very foundation of religious liberty.

### Abortion

Although similar in many respects to the question of gay and lesbian rights, at least where the Constitution is concerned, the issue of abortion rights differs in one significant way that must be addressed at the outset. There is no question that homosexuals are persons and therefore are entitled to the protections guaranteed to all persons by the U.S. Constitution. The personhood of a fetus, however, is *the question* where abortion rights are concerned. If human fetuses are persons, then they are entitled to protection by the state and abortion can be made illegal. If fetuses are not yet persons, then the rights of the mother—who is unquestionably a person entitled to protection—outweigh other concerns, and the interests of the state are best served by leaving to the mother the decision of whether to carry a pregnancy to term.

At what point does a fetus become a person? Herein lies the rub. We do not know, and we have no way of knowing apart from subjective, conscientious judgments. To make this point, Peter Wenz (1992) likens the question of the personhood of a fetus to arguments about the existence of God. He recounts a story told by philosopher John Wisdom:

> Two people return to their long neglected garden and find among the weeds a few of the old plants surprisingly vigorous. One says to the other, "It must be that a gardener has been coming and doing something about these plants." Upon inquiry, they find that no neighbor has ever seen anyone at work in their garden. The first man says to the other, "He must have worked at night while people slept." The other says, "No, someone would have heard him and besides, anybody who cared about the plants would have kept down these weeds." The first man says, "Look at the way these are arranged. There is purpose and feeling for beauty here. I believe that someone comes, someone invisible to mortal eyes." (Quoted in Wenz 1992, 168)

Based on identical evidence, the two people reach different conclusions about the existence of the invisible gardener. The empirical evidence is inconclusive. That is, the evidence does not establish that there *is* an invisible gardener; neither does it establish that there *is not* an invisible gardener. The personhood of a fetus is similarly invisible and thus is beyond the reach of the available empirical evidence. Like the case of the invisible gardener, the personhood of the fetus is thus a matter of subjective judgment and belief. In Wenz's view, therefore, to make abortion illegal on the basis that a fetus is a person entitled to the state's protection amounts to an unconstitutional establishment of religion. It is tantamount to enacting legislation premised on the existence of God.

The logic of the First Amendment, as developed above, suggests a correction to Wenz's conclusion, although it is a change in emphasis rather than substance. As described above, the First Amendment preserves religious freedom by prohibiting the state from lending assistance to any particular religion or preferring religion to irreligion. Establishment claims, therefore, necessarily involve claims of free exercise as well (Hammond 1998). In this case, antiabortion legislation lends state assistance to the religious claim that fetuses are persons and, on that unconstitutional basis, abridges women's rights to exercise their religious conscience.

The need for the correction becomes clearer when we consider an antiabortion argument built on the very same premises developed by Wenz. Kent Greenawalt (1989) argues that because the status of the fetus cannot be settled by ordinary, secular reasoning, the issue must be settled by appeal to convictions: "If this is inevitable, the religious believer has a powerful argument that he should be able to rely on his religiously informed bases for judgment if others are relying on other bases of reasoning that reach beyond common premises and forms of reasoning" (quoted in Wenz 1992, 184). In other words, people may make their judgments about whether or not abortion should be legal on a variety of bases, both religious and secular. In this case, religious votes do not count any more than secular votes and should not, he argues, count any less. The outcome of a vote indicating the will of the majority with regard to abortion, then, does not constitute an establishment of religion in the usual sense.

Here, Greenawalt perverts a principle that Wenz entirely misses. Both are correct in observing that the personhood of fetuses is beyond the reach of secular, empirical assessment. Consequently, the question of the status of the fetus is one that can be decided only on the basis of subjective, conscientious judgments. As described above, the free exercise clause of the First Amendment reserves to the individual the right to make such conscientious judgments. Consequently, legislation restricting the ability of women to terminate a pregnancy places an unconstitutional burden on their right to the free exercise of conscience. Greenawalt is therefore correct in asserting that individuals should be allowed to make an assessment about the morality of abortion on the basis of religious convictions. Indeed, he and Wenz concur that they *must* make that assessment on the basis of religious convictions, given the uncertainty about the status of the fetus. Greenawalt errs, however, in asserting that the moral assessment of the majority in such a case can be enacted into law. Because the status of the fetus is a matter of religious conscience, it is beyond the reach of the law.

Of course, it must be noted that the argument for abortion rights as a First Amendment right of conscience does not reflect the reasoning of the courts. In its well-known decision on *Roe v. Wade* (1973), the Supreme Court ruled that legislation restricting access to abortions violated women's right to privacy, a right implied (but not explicitly stated) in the First, Third, Fourth, and Fifth Amendments. Despite the interpretation of the Bill of Rights given above, which suggests that new rights could be discovered over time (not by the Supreme Court but by the people on the basis of conscience), Wenz is probably correct in asserting that a ruling on the basis of an implied but not explicitly protected right leaves the question of the legitimacy of antiabortion legislation very much up in the air.

The First Amendment argument for abortion rights as a matter of free exercise of religious conscience is a much stronger foundation. However, like the case for gay rights described above, it is one that has not yet been tried in court. As was the case in the argument for gay and lesbian rights, however, there is some precedent for the argument.

The preview of the free exercise argument for abortion rights comes from a dissent by Justice John Paul Stevens to the Supreme Court's ruling in *Webster v. Reproductive Health Services* (1989). At issue in the case was a Missouri bill requiring that no public funds, employees, or facilities be used in performing abortions and that a viability test be performed on the fetus if the woman seeking an abortion is twenty or more weeks pregnant. The Court upheld the bill, but Justice Stevens dissented on the basis that the preamble to the bill, which declared that the life of "each human being begins at CONCEPTION," violated the First Amendment:

> I am persuaded that the absence of any secular purpose for the legislative declarations that life begins at conception and that conception occurs at fertilization makes the relevant portion of the preamble invalid under the Establishment Clause.... This conclusion does not, and could not, rest on the fact that the statement happens to coincide with the tenets of certain religions ... or on the fact that the legislators who voted to enact it may have been motivated by religious considerations.... Rather, it rests on the fact that the preamble, an unequivocal endorsement of a religious tenet of some but by no means all Christian faiths, serves no identifiable secular purpose. That fact alone compels a conclusion that the statute violates the Establishment Clause. (quoted in Hammond 1998, 69)

And, one might add, because the bill restricts the moral autonomy of citizens by establishing a religious tenet as law, it also violates the free exercise clause.

## CONCLUSION

The issues of homosexual rights and abortion are but two instances in which the boundary between civic morality (public interest) and personal morality (private conscience) must be clarified if the state is to avoid overstepping the boundaries of America's sacred ground. Other issues not addressed here remain in the public mind: divorce, the use of contraceptives, premarital and extramarital sex, pornography, and so on. They are important and appropriate issues for debate in U.S. public discourse, and religion both can and should be a voice in the debate. After all, the First Amendment protections of religious freedom were designed to ensure that on such matters religion *would* have a voice.

Religious liberty—the freedom of the individual to exercise moral judgment and the freedom of religions to attempt to shape the individual's moral judgment—makes possible a free society that will not decay into social chaos or totalitarianism. Indeed, the Founders' vision of a good society, as laid out in the Constitution and the Bill of Rights, was one that achieved a balance between the value of individual freedom and the demands of social order: the state would restrict freedom only as much as was necessary to preserve it. In the words of Peter Wenz:

> The value of democracy rests . . . on the value of peace and of equal respect for people and for their powers of self-determination. In principle, democracy gives each an equal chance to determine for herself the rules that will govern everyone's behavior. . . . [Democratic action] is required only in situations where people depend on others with whom they cannot realistically negotiate a private accord. Where people are independent of one another, or can protect their interests through private negotiations without jeopardizing the interests of others, the value of self-determination is best served by allowing adults to act as they choose. (Wenz 1992, 25)

We should add, "according to the dictates of conscience," in order to recognize the indispensable role of religion in making that balance possible. When the system is working properly, Americans are self-governing. Restrictive legislation is not required because religious freedom trains Americans in the use of conscience to guide their own actions.

382

Recognizing and clarifying the boundary between the proper realm of state jurisdiction and America's sacred ground becomes increasingly important as the diversity of religious opinion becomes more apparent. Indeed, as noted by Phillip Hammond in *With Liberty for All* (1998), it was only in the twentieth century, in response to the growing numbers of Catholics, Jews, and later Buddhists, Hindus, Muslims, and others in the U.S. population, that church-state cases began to come before the Supreme Court with any regularity. Although it is probably true that the primary concern of the Founders of the nation was to prevent conflict between the various sects of Christianity, it is no small testament to the quality of their work that the nation has been able to accommodate, with minimal conflict and maximum liberty, such a rich variety of religions as now exists in the United States.

## NOTES

1. It must be noted here that both pro–gay rights and anti–gay rights reviews of the existing research on the children of gay parents concur that the existing data are too sparse to draw any firm conclusions. The difference in conclusions about the implications of the existing research comes down to a matter of personal bias and rhetorical strategy: pro–gay rights authors conclude that there is no evidence to suggest that gay parenting is harmful; anti–gay rights authors conclude that there is no evidence to suggest that gay parenting is *not* harmful (see Cameron 1999; Fitzgerald 1999; Allen and Burrell 1996; Belcastro et al. 1993).

2. It is notable that the court was careful to clarify that its decision was based on the Common benefits clause of the state constitution and not the equal protection clause of the Fourteenth Amendment to the U.S. Constitution. In so doing, the state court protected its jurisdiction over the case and averted the possibility of an appeal to the U.S. Supreme Court.

## REFERENCES

Allen, Mike, and Nancy Burrell. 1996. "Comparing the Impact of Homosexual and Heterosexual Parents on Children: Meta-analysis of Existing Research." *Journal of Homosexuality* 32, no. 2: 19–36.

Belcastro, Philip A., Theresa Gramlich, Thomas Nicholson, Jimmie Price, and Richard Wilson. 1993. "A Review of Data Based Studies Addressing the

Affects of Homosexual Parenting on Children's Sexual and Social Functioning." *Journal of Divorce and Remarriage* 20, no.1–2: 105–123.

Cameron, Paul. 1999. "Homosexual Parents: Testing 'Common Sense'—A Literature Review Emphasizing the Golombok and Tasker Longitudinal Study of Lesbians' Children." *Psychological Reports* 85, no. 1: 282–323.

Eskridge, William N., Jr. 1996. *The Case for Same-Sex Marriage: From Sexual Liberty to Civilized Commitment.* New York: Free Press.

Finke, Roger, and Rodney Stark. 1992. *The Churching of America 1776–1990: Winners and Losers in Our Religious Economy.* New Brunswick, NJ: Rutgers University Press.

Fitzgerald, Bridget. 1999. "Children of Lesbian and Gay Parents: A Review of the Literature." *Marriage and Family Review* 29, no. 1: 57–76.

Greenawalt, Kent. 1989. *Religious Convictions and Political Choice.* New York: Oxford University Press.

Hammond, Phillip. 1998. *With Liberty for All: Freedom of Religion in the United States.* Louisville, KY: Westminster John Knox Press.

———. 2000. "Can Religion be Religious in Public?" Pp. 172–183 in *The Dynamics of Religious Organizations: The Extravasation of the Sacred and Other Essays.* By Phillip E. Hammond. Oxford: Oxford University Press.

Hunter, James Davison. 1991. *Culture Wars: The Struggle to Define America.* New York: Basic Books.

Hutson, James H. 1991. "What Are the Rights of the People?" *Wilson Quarterly* 15, no. 1: 56–70.

Locke, John. 1983. "A Letter Concerning Toleration." Reprinted in M. Montouri, *John Locke: On Toleration and the Unity of God.* Amsterdam: J. C. Gieben.

McGraw, Barbara. 2003. *Rediscovering America's Sacred Ground.* Albany: State University of New York Press.

Richards, David A. J. 1999. *Identity and the Case for Gay Rights: Race, Gender, Religion as Analogies.* Chicago: University of Chicago Press.

Schwartz, Bernard, ed. 1971. *The Bill of Rights: A Documentary History.* 2 vols. New York: Chelsea House Publishers.

Smith, Craig R. 1993. *To Form a More Perfect Union: The Ratification of the Constitution and the Bill of Rights, 1787–1791.* New York: Center for First Amendment Studies, California State University at Long Beach.

Tocqueville, Alexis de. 1969. *Democracy in America.* George Lawrence, trans. Garden City, NY: Anchor Books.

Washington, George. 1996. *The Papers of George Washington.* D. Twohig et al., eds. Presidential Series. 7 vols. Charlottesville: University Press of Virginia.

Wenz, Peter S. 1992. *Abortion Rights as Religious Freedom.* Philadelphia: Temple University Press.

# Suggestions for Further Reading

## GENERAL

Douglas, Mary. 2002. *Purity and Danger: An Analysis of the Concepts of Pollution and Taboo.* 2d ed. London: Routledge.

Dynes, Wayne R., and Stephen Donaldson, ed. 1992. *Homosexuality and Religion and Philosophy.* New York: Garland.

Foucault, Michel. 1988–1990. *The History of Sexuality.* Robert Hurley, trans. New York: Vintage Books.

Halperin, David. 1990. *One Hundred Years of Homosexuality and Other Essays on Greek Love.* New York: Routledge.

Kvam, Kristen E., Linda S. Schearing, and Valerie H. Ziegler, eds. 1999. *Eve and Adam: Jewish, Christian, and Muslim Readings on Genesis and Gender.* Bloomington: Indiana University Press.

Laqueur, Thomas. 1990. *Making Sex: Body and Gender from the Greeks to Freud.* Cambridge: Harvard University Press.

Runzo, Joseph, and Nancy M. Martin, eds. 2000. *Love, Sex, and Gender in the World Religions.* Oxford: Oneworld.

Sharma, Arvind, ed. 1987. *Women in World Religions.* Albany: State University of New York Press.

Swidler, Arlene, ed. 1993. *Homosexuality and World Religions.* Valley Forge: Trinity Press International.

## AFRICAN TRADITIONS

Abimbola, Wande. 1997. *Ifa Will Mend Our Broken World: Thoughts on Yoruba Religion and Culture in Africa and the Diaspora.* Roxbury, MA: Aim Books.

Amadiume, Ifi. 1987. *Male Daughters, Female Husbands: Gender and Sex in an African Society.* London: Zed Books.

Beckwith, Carol, and Angela Fisher. 1999. *African Ceremonies.* New York: Harry N. Abrams.

Beier, Ulli, ed. 1970. *Yoruba Poetry: An Anthology of Traditional Poems.* Cambridge, MA: Cambridge University Press.

Cameron, Elisabeth L. 1996. *Isn't S/he a Doll? Play and Ritual in African Sculpture.* Los Angeles: UCLA Fowler Museum of Cultural History.

Christoph, Henning, Klaus E. Müller, and Ute Ritz-Müller. 1999. *Soul of Africa: Magical Rites and Traditions.* Cologne: Könemann.

Conner, Randy P., David H. Sparks, and Mariya Sparks. 1996. *Cassell's Encyclopedia of Queer Myth, Symbol, and Spirit.* London: Cassell.

Coulson, David, and Alec Campbell. 2001. *African Rock Art.* New York: Abrams.

Epega, Afolabi A., and Philip John Neimark. 1995. *The Sacred Ifa Oracle.* San Francisco: HarperSan Francisco.

Estermann, Carlos. 1976. *The Ethnography of Southwestern Angola.* New York: Africana Publishing.

Ford, Clyde W. 1999. *The Hero with an African Face: Mythic Wisdom of Traditional Africa.* New York: Bantam Books.

Gleason, Judith. 1994. *Leaf and Bone: African Praise-Poems.* 2nd ed. New York: Penguin Books.

Griaule, Marcel. 1975. *Conversations with Ogotemmêli: An Introduction to Dogon Religious Ideas.* Ralph Butler and others, trans. New York: Oxford University Press.

Heald, Suzette. 1999. *Manhood and Morality: Sex, Violence and Ritual in Gisu Society.* New York: Routledge.

Jacobson-Widding, Anita, ed. 1991. *Body and Space: Symbolic Models of Unity and Division in African Cosmology and Experience.* Acta Universitatis Upsaliensis, Uppsala Studies in Cultural Anthropology 16. Stockholm: Almqvist and Wiksell International.

Jacobson-Widding, Anita, and Walter van Beek, eds. 1990. *The Creative Communion: Folk Models of Fertility and the Regeneration of Life.* Acta Universitatis Upsaliensis, Uppsala Studies in Cultural Anthropology 15. Stockholm: Almqvist and Wiksell International.

Matory, J. Lorand. 1994. *Sex and the Empire That Is No More: Gender and the Politics of Metaphor in Oyo Yoruba Religion.* Minneapolis: University of Minnesota Press.

Nnaemeka, Obioma, ed. 1998. *Sisterhood, Feminisms, and Power: From Africa to the Diaspora.* Trenton, NJ: Africa World Press.

Olupona, Jacob K., ed. 2000. *African Spirituality: Forms, Meanings, and Expressions.* New York: Crossroad Publishing.

Somé, Sobonfu. 1997. *The Spirit of Intimacy.* Berkeley, CA: Berkeley Hills Books.


## NATIVE AMERICAN WORLDVIEWS

Arviso Alvord, Lori, and Elizabeth Cohen Van Pelt. 2000. *The Scalpel and the Silver Bear: The First Navajo Woman Surgeon Combines Western Medicine and Traditional Healing.* New York: Bantam.

Bean, John Lowell, and Katherine Siva Saubel. 1972. *Temalpakh: Cahuilla Indian Knowledge and Usage of Plants.* Banning, CA: Malki Museum Press.

Beauvoir, Simone de. [1961] 1973. *The Second Sex.* H. M. Parshley, trans. and ed. New York: Bantam Books.

Blackburn, Thomas C., ed. 1975. *December's Child: A Book of Chumash Oral Narratives.* Berkeley: University of California Press.

Brant, Beth. 1984. *A Gathering of Spirit: A Collection by North American Indian Women.* New York: Firebrand Books.

Brown, Lester B., ed. 1997. *Two-Spirit People: American Indian Lesbian Women and Gay Men.* New York: Haworth Press.

Cajete, Gregory. 2000. *Native Science: Natural Laws of Interdependence.* Santa Fe, NM: Clear Light Publishers.

Dynes, Wayne R., and Stephen Donaldson, ed. 1992. *Ethnographic Studies of Homosexuality.* New York: Garland Publishing.

Feinberg, Leslie. 1996. *Transgender Warriors: Making History from Joan of Arc to Dennis Rodman.* Boston: Beacon Press.

Fife, Connie, ed. 1994. *The Colour of Resistance: A Contemporary Collection of Writing by Aboriginal Women.* Boston: South End Press.

Gay American Indians, with Will Roscoe (coordinating editor). 1988. *Living the Spirit: A Gay American Indian Anthology.* New York: St. Martin's Press.

Grounds, Richard A. 2001. "Tallahassee, Osceola, and the Hermeneutics of American Place Names." *Journal of the American Academy of Religion* 55: 287–322.

Hallowell, A. Irving. 1975. "Ojibwa Ontology, Behavior, and World View." In Dennis Tedlock and Barbara Tedlock, eds., *Teachings from the American Earth: Indian Religion and Philosophy.* New York: Liverwright.

Harjo, Joy, and Gloria Bird, eds. 1997. *Reinventing the Enemy's Language: Contemporary Native Women's Writing of North America.* New York: W. W. Norton.

Hill Witt, Shirley. 1976. "The Brave-Hearted Women: The Struggle at Wounded Knee." *Akwesasne Notes* 8, no. 2: 14–25.

Hudson, Travis, and Ernest Underhay. 1978. *Crystals in the Sky: An Intellectual Odyssey Involving Chumash Astronomy, Cosmology, and Rock Art.* Santa Barbara, CA: Ballena Press/Santa Barbara Museum of Natural History.

Hurtado, Albert L. 1988. *Indian Survival on the California Frontier.* New Haven: Yale University Press.

Jacobs, Sue-Ellen, Wesley Thomas, and Sabine Lang, ed. 1997. *Two-Spirit People: Native American Gender Identity, Sexuality, and Spirituality.* Urbana: University of Illinois Press.

Jaimes, M. Annette, and Theresa Halsey. 1992. "American Indian Women: At the Center of Indigenous Resistance in Contemporary North America." In M. Annette Jaimes, ed., *The State of Native America: Genocide, Colonization, and Resistance.* Boston: South End Press.

Klein, Laura F., and Lillian A. Ackerman, ed. 1995. *Women and Power in Native North America.* Norman: University of Oklahoma Press.

Kroeber, Alfred L. [1925] 1953. *Handbook of the Indians of California.* Reprint Berkeley: California Book Company.

Lang, Sabine. 1998. *Men as Women, Women as Men: Changing Gender in Native American Cultures.* Austin: University of Texas Press.

———. 1999. "Lesbians, Men-Women, and Two-Spirits: Homosexuality and Gender in Native American Cultures." In Evelyn Blackwood and Saskia E. Wieringa, eds., *Female Desires: Same-Sex Relations and Transgender Practices across Cultures.* New York: Columbia University Press.

Margolin, Malcolm, ed. 1981. *The Way We Lived: California Indian Songs, Stories, and Reminiscences.* Berkeley: Heyday Books.

Margolin, Malcolm, and Yolanda Montijo, eds. 1995. *Native Ways: California Indian Stories and Memories.* Berkeley: Heyday Books.

Miller, Christine, and Patricia Chuchryk, eds. 1996. *Women of the First Nations: Power, Wisdom, and Strength.* Winnipeg: University of Manitoba Press.

Ortiz, Beverly. 1991. *It Will Live Forever: Traditional Yosemite Indian Acorn Preparation.* Berkeley: Heyday Press.

Perrone, Bobette, H. Henrietta Stockel, and Victoria Krueger. 1989. *Medicine Women, Curanderas, and Women Doctors.* Norman: University of Oklahoma Press.

Roscoe, Will. 1991. *The Zuni Man-Woman.* Albuquerque: University of New Mexico Press.

———. 1998. *Changing Ones: Third and Fourth Genders in Native North America.* New York: St. Martin's Press.

Rose, Wendy. 1992. "The Great Pretenders: Further Reflections on Whiteshamanism." In M. Annette Jaimes, ed., *The State of Native America: Genocide, Colonization, and Resistance.* Boston: South End Press.

Sarris, Greg. 1994. *Mabel McKay: Weaving the Dream.* Berkeley: University of California Press.

Shipek, Florence Connelly. 1991. *Defina Cuero: Her Autobiography, an Account of Her Last Years, and Her Ethnobotanic Contributions.* Menlo Park, CA: Ballena Press.

Silko, Leslie Marmon. 1981. *Storyteller.* New York: Arcade Publishing.

Stannard, David T. 1992. *American Holocaust: The Conquest of the New World.* New York: Oxford University Press.

Swanton, John R. [1931] 1995. *The Source Material for the Social and Ceremonial Life of the Choctaw Indians.* Reprint. Philadelphia, MS: Choctaw Museum of the Southern Indian.

Tiger, Lisa. 1995. "Woman Who Clears the Way." In Barbara Findlen, ed., *Listen Up: Voices from the Next Feminist Generation.* Seattle: Seal Press.

Van Kirk, Sylvia. 1980. *Many Tender Ties: Women in Fur-Trade Society, 1670–1870.* Norman: University of Oklahoma Press.

Wallace, Anthony F. C. 1947. "Women, Land, and Society: Three Aspects of Aboriginal Delaware Life." *Pennsylvania Archaeologist* 17: 1–35.

Wallis, Velma. 1993. *Two Old Women: An Alaska Legend of Betrayal, Courage, and Survival.* New York: HarperPerennial.

———. 1996. *Bird Girl and the Man Who Followed the Sun: An Athabaskan Legend from Alaska.* New York: HarperPerennial.

Weslager, C. S. 1947. "The Delaware Indians as Women." *Journal of the Washington Academy of Science* 37 (September 15): 298–304.

Williams, Water L. 1992. *The Spirit and the Flesh: Sexual Diversity in American Indian Cultures.* Boston: Beacon Press.

# DAOISM

Beurdeley, Michel, Kristofer Schipper, Chang Fu-Jui, and Jacques Pimpaneau. 1969. *The Clouds and the Rain: The Art of Love in China.* Diana Imber, trans. London: Hammond.

Blofeld, John. 1973. *The Secret and the Sublime: Taoist Mysteries and Magic.* London: George Allen and Unwin.

Cary F. Baynes, trans. 1950. *The I Ching or Book of Changes: The Richard Wilhelm Translation Rendered into English.* New York: Pantheon Books.

Chang, Jolan. 1977. *The Tao of Love and Sex: The Ancient Chinese Way to Ecstasy.* London: Wildwood House.

Chia, Mantak. 1984. *Taoist Secrets of Love: Cultivating Male Sexual Energy.* New York: Aurora Press.

Chia, Mantak, and Maneewan Chia. 1986. *Healing Love through the Tao: Cultivating Female Sexual Energy.* Huntington, NY: Healing Tao Books.

Ching, Julia. 1993. *Chinese Religions.* Maryknoll, NY: Orbis Books.

Clarke, J. J. 2000. *The Tao of the West: Western Transformation of Taoist Thought.* London: Routledge.

Creel, Herrlee G. 1970. *What Is Taoism? And Other Studies in Chinese Cultural History.* Chicago: University of Chicago Press.

Harper, Donald. 1987. "The Sexual Arts of Ancient China as Described in a Manuscript of the Second Century BC." *Harvard Journal of Asiatic Studies* 47, no. 2: 539–593.

Huang, Hui. 1990. *Lun Heng Jiaoshi.* Beijing: Zhonghua Shuju.

Kleinjans, Everett. 1990. "The Tao of Women and Men: Chinese Philosophy and the Women's Movement." *Journal of Chinese Philosophy* 17: 99–127.

Kohn, Livia, ed. 1993. *The Taoist Experience: An Anthology.* Albany: State University of New York Press.

Kronhausen, Phyllis, and Eberhard Kronhausen. 1961. *Erotic Arts.* New York: Grove Press.

Lao Tzu. 1979. *Tao Te Ching.* D. C. Lau, trans. Baltimore: Penguin Books.

Maspero, Henri. 1981. *Taoism and Chinese Religion.* F. Kierman, trans. Amherst: University of Massachusetts Press.

Mou Zhonghian and Zhang, Jian. 2000. *Zhongguo zongjiao tongshi (A general history of Chinese religions).* Vol. 2. Beijing: Shehui Kexue Wenxian Chubanshe.

Needham, Joseph. 1956, 1967. *Science and Civilisation in China.* Vols. 2, 5 (part 3). Cambridge: Cambridge University Press.

Robinet, Isabelle. 1993. *Taoist Meditation: The Mao-shan Tradition of Great Purity.* Julian F. Pas and Norman J. Girardot, trans. New York: State University of New York Press.

———. 1997. *Taoism: Growth of a Religion.* Phyllis Brooks, trans. Stanford, CA: Stanford University Press.

Saso, Michael R. 1990. *Taoism and the Rite of Cosmic Renewal.* 2nd ed. Pullman: Washington State University Press.

Schipper, Kristofer. 1993. *The Taoist Body.* Karen Duval, trans. Berkeley: University of California Press.

van Gulik, Robert Hans. 1961. *Sexual Life in Ancient China.* Leiden: E. J. Brill.

Veith, Ilza, trans. 1966. *The Yellow Emperor's Classic of Internal Medicine.* Berkeley: University of California Press.

Waley, Arthur. 1977. *The Way and Its Power: The Tao Te Ching and Its Place in Chinese Thought.* London: George Allen and Unwin.

Wang Ming. 1985. *Baopuzi Neipian Jiaoshi.* Beijing: Zhonghua Shuju.

Welch, Holmes. 1957. *The Parting of the Way.* Boston, MA: Beacon Press.

Wile, Douglas, ed. and trans. 1992. *Art of the Bedchamber: The Chinese Sexual Yoga Classics, Including Women's Solo Meditation Texts.* New York: State University of New York Press.

Wong, Eva. 1997. *The Shambhala Guide to Taoism.* Boston: Shambhala.

Zhuangzi. 1996. *The Book of Chuang Tzu.* M. Palmer et al., trans. London: Arkana.

**Internet Sources**

http://www.taorestore.org
http://www.thetemple.com
http://www.alchemicaltaoism.com
http://www.healingtaousa.com
http://www.tao.org

# HINDUISM

Allen, Michael, ed. 1990. *Women in India and Nepal.* New Delhi: Sterling Publishers.

Altekar, Anant Sadashiv. 1978. *The Position of Women in Hindu Civilization.* Delhi: Motilal Banarsidass.

Basu, Amrita, ed. 1995. *The Challenge of Local Feminisms: Women's Movements in Global Perspective.* Boulder, CO: Westview Press.

Bhaskaran, Suparna. 2002. "The Politics of Penetration: Section 377 of the Indian Penal Code." Pp. 15–29 in R. Vanita, ed., *Queering India: Same-Sex Love and Eroticism in Indian Culture and Society.* New York: Routledge.

Butler, Judith. 1990. *Gender Trouble: Feminism and the Subversion of Identity.* London: Routledge.

Cabezon, José Ignacio, ed. 1985. *Buddhism, Sexuality, and Gender.* Albany: State University of New York Press.

Caldwell, Sarah. 1999. *Oh Terrifying Mother: Sexuality, Violence, and Worship of the Goddess K_li.* New Delhi: Oxford University Press.

Daniélou, Alain. 2001. *The Hindu Temple: Deification of Eroticism.* Ken Hurry, trans. Rochester, VT: Inner Traditions.

De, Sushil Kumar. 1961. *Early History of the Vaisnava Faith and Movement in Bengal.* Calcutta: Firma K. L. Mukopadhyay.

Devi, Shakuntala. 1977. *The World of Homosexuals.* New Delhi: Vikas Publishing House.

Dimmitt, Cornelia, and J. A. van Buitenen. 1978. *Classical Hindu Mythology: A Reader in the Sanskrit Puranas.* Philadelphia: Temple University Press.

Dimock, Edward, Jr. 1966. *The Place of the Hidden Moon: Erotic Mysticism in the Vaisnava Sahajiya Cult of Bengal.* Chicago: University of Chicago Press.

Doniger, Wendy. 1973. *Asceticism and Eroticism in the Mythology of Siva.* New York: Oxford University Press.

Eliade, Mircea. 1990. *Yoga: Immortality and Freedom.* New York: Bollinger Foundation.

Flood, Gavin. 1993. *Body and Cosmology in Kashmir Saivism.* San Francisco: Mellen Research University Press.

Fruzzetti, Lina M. 1982. *The Gift of a Virgin: Women, Marriage, and Ritual in a Bengali Society.* Delhi: Oxford University Press.

Halan, Lindsay, and Paul B. Courtright, ed. 1995. *From the Margins of Hindu Marriage: Essays on Gender, Religion, and Culture.* New York: Oxford University Press.

Heyward, Carter. 1989. *Touching Our Strength: The Erotic as Power and the Love of God.* San Francisco: HarperSan Francisco.

Jamison, Stephanie W. 1991. *The Ravenous Hyenas and the Wounded Sun: Myth and Ritual in Ancient India.* Ithaca: Cornell University Press.

———. 1996. *Sacrificed Wife, Sacrificer's Wife: Women, Ritual, and Hospitality in Ancient India.* New York: Oxford University Press.

Kaelber, Walter O. 1989. *Tapta Mārga: Asceticism and Initiation in Vedic India.* Albany: State University of New York Press.

Kakar, Sudhir. 1989. *Intimate Relations: Exploring Indian Sexuality.* Chicago: University of Chicago Press.

Kakar, Sudhir, and John Munder Ross. 1986. *Tales of Love, Sex, and Danger.* Oxford: Oxford University Press.

Kelly, John D. 1991. *A Politics of Virtue: Hinduism, Sexuality, and Countercolonial Discourse in Fiji.* Chicago: University of Chicago Press.

Kripal, Jeffrey J. 1995. *Kālī's Child: The Mystical and the Erotic in the Life and Teaching of Ramakrishna.* 2nd ed. Chicago: University of Chicago Press.

Kumar, Nita. 1994. *Women as Subjects: South Asian Histories.* Charlottesville: University Press of Virginia.

Larson, Gerald James. 1976. "The Aesthetic (Rasāsvāda) and the Religious (Brahāmsvāda) in Abhinavajupta's Kashmir Shaivism." *Philosophy East and West: A Quarterly of Asian Comparative Thought* 26, no. 4: 371–388.

Leslie, Julia I. 1989. *The Perfect Wife: The Orthodox Woman According to the Strīdharmapaddati of Tryambakam.* Delhi: Oxford University Press.

Leslie, Julia, and Mary McGee. 2000. *Invented Identities: The Interplay of Gender, Religion, and Politics in India.* SOAS Studies on South Asia: Understandings and Perspectives. New Delhi: Oxford University Press.

Lidke, Jeffrey S. 2000. *The Goddess beyond Yet Within the Three Cities: Śākta Tantra and the Paradox of Power in Nepāla-Maṇḍala.* Ph.D. diss., University of California at Santa Barbara.

Manu. 1991. *The Laws of Manu.* Wendy Doniger, with Brian K. Smith, trans. London: Penguin Books.

Marglin, Frédérique Apffel. 1985. *Wives of the God-King: The Rituals of the Devadasis of Puri.* Delhi: Oxford University Press.

Meyer, Johann Jakob. 1930. *Sexual Life in Ancient India: A Study in the Comparative History of Indian Cultures.* 2 vols. New York: E. P. Dutton.

Muktananda, Swami. 1976. *Satsang with Baba: Questions and Answers with Swami Muktananda.* Vol. 2. Oakland, CA: SYDA Foundation.

———. 1978. *Play of Consciousness.* San Francisco: Harper and Row.

Nanda, Serena. 1990. *Neither Man nor Woman: The Hijras of India.* Belmont, CA: Wadsworth Publishing.

Nandy, Ashis. 1998. *Exiled at Home: Comprising, At the Edge of Psychology, The Intimate Enemy, Creating a Nationality.* Oxford: Oxford University Press.

Nelson, James B., and Sandra P. Longfellow. 1994. *Sexuality and the Sacred: Sources for Theological Reflection.* Louisville, KY: Westminster John Knox Press.

O'Flaherty, Wendy Doniger. 1980. *Women, Androgynes, and Other Mythical Beasts.* Chicago: University of Chicago Press.

———. 1985. *Tales of Sex and Violence: Folklore, Sacrifice, and Danger in the* Jaiminīya Brāhmana. Chicago: University of Chicago Press.

Randall, Richard S. 1989. *Freedom and Taboo: Pornography and the Politics of a Self Divided.* Berkeley: University of California Press.

Ranchhoddas, Ratanlal, and Dhirajlal Keshavlal Thakoree. 1992. *The Indian Penal Code.* 27th ed. Nagpur: Wadhwa.

Sinclair-Brull, Wendy. 1997. *Female Ascetics: Hierarchy and Purity in an Indian Religious Movement.* Religion and Society in South Asia Series. Richmond: Curzon Press.

Sweet, Michael J., and Leonard Zwilling. 1993. "The First Medicalization: The Taxonomy and Etiology of Queerness in Classical Indian Medicine." *Journal of the History of Sexuality* 3, no. 4: 590–607.

Sweet, Michael J., and Leonard Zwilling. 1996. "'Like a City Ablaze'": The Third Sex and the Creation of Sexuality in Jain Religious Literature." *Journal of the History of Sexuality* 6, no. 3: 359–384.

Tannahill, Reay. 1982. *Sex in History.* New York: Stein and Day.

Thapan, Meenakshi, ed. 1997. *Embodiment: Essays on Gender and Identity.* Delhi: Oxford University Press.

Vanita, Ruth, ed. 2002. *Queering India: Same Sex Love and Eroticism in Indian Culture and Society.* New York: Routledge.

Vanita, Ruth, and Saleem Kidwai. 2000. *Same-Sex Love in India: Readings from Literature and History.* New York: St. Martin's Press.

Vātsyāyana. 1994. *Kāma sūtra.* Translated by Alain Daniélou as *The Complete Kāma Sūtra: The First Unabridged Modern Translation of the Classic Indian Text by Vātsyāyana, Including the* Jayamangalā *Commentary from the Sanskrit by Yashodhara and Extracts from the Hindi Commentary by Devadatta Shāstrā.* Rochester, VT: Park Street Press.

White, David Gordon. 1996. *The Alchemical Body: Siddha Traditions in Medieval India.* Chicago: University of Chicago Press.

# BUDDHISM

Allen, Michael. 1973. "Buddhism without Monks: The Vajrayana Religion of the Newars of the Kathmandu Valley." *South Asia* 3: 1–14.

Allen, Michael, ed. 1990. *Women in India and Nepal.* New Delhi: Sterling Publishers.

Altekar, Anant Sadashiv. [1938] 1978. *The Position of Women in Hindu Civilization.* Reprint, Delhi: Motilal Banarsidass.

Anderson, Dines, and Helmer Smith, eds. 1913. *Sutta Nipāta.* London: Pali Text Society.

Bartholomeusz, Tessa. 1994. *Women under the Bo Tree.* New York: Cambridge University Press.

Batchelor, Martine. 1996. *Walking on Lotus Flowers: Buddhist Women Living, Loving, and Meditating.* Gill Farrer-Halls, eds. London: Thorsons.

Burlingame, Eugene Watson, trans. 1990. *Dhammapadātthakathā: Buddhist Legends.* London: Pali Text Society.

Butler, Katie. 1990. "Encountering the Shadow in Buddhist America." *Common Boundary* (May–June): 14–22.

Cabezon, José Ignacio, ed. 1985. *Buddhism, Sexuality, and Gender.* Albany: State University of New York Press.

Chalmers, Lord, ed. 1932. *Sutta-Nipāta, or Discourse Collection.* Cambridge, MA: Harvard University Press.

Childs, Margaret. 1980. "Chigo Monogatari: Love Stories or Buddhist Sermons?" *Monumenta Nipponica* 35, no. 2 (Summer): 127–151.

Conner, Randy, and Stephen Donaldson. 1990. "Buddhism." Pp. 168–171 in *Encyclopedia of Homosexuality.* Vol. 1. New York: Garland Press.

Davids, Caroline A. F. Rhys. 1948. *Psalms of the Early Buddhists 1: Psalms of the Sisters.* London: Pali Text Society.

Falk, Nancy Auer. 1989. "The Case of the Vanishing Nuns: The Fruits of Ambivalence in Ancient Indian Buddhism." Pp. 190–222 in Nancy Auer Falk and Rita M. Gross, eds., *Unspoken Worlds: Women's Religious Lives.* Belmont, CA: Wadsworth.

Faure, Bernard. 1998. *The Red Thread: Buddhist Approaches to Sexuality.* Princeton, NJ: Princeton University Press.

Findly, Ellison Banks, ed. 2000. *Women's Buddhism, Buddhism's Women: Tradition, Revision, Renewal.* Boston: Wisdom Publications.

Friedman, Lenore, and Susan Moon, eds. 1997. *Being Bodies: Buddhist Women on the Paradox of Embodiment.* Boston: Shambhala.

Goldstein, Melvyn C. 1964. "A Study of the Ldab Ldob." *Central Asiatic Journal* 9: 123–141.

Gombrich, Richard. 1988. *Theravada Buddhism: A Social History from Ancient Benares to Modern Columbo.* London: Routledge and Kegan Paul.

Gross, Rita M. 1993. *Buddhism after Patriarchy: A Feminist History, Analysis, and Reconstruction of Buddhism.* Albany: State University of New York Press.

Hardacre, Helen. 1997. *Marketing the Menacing Fetus in Japan.* Berkeley: University of California Press.

Hare, E. M., trans. [1933–1936] 1973–1979. *The Book of Gradual Sayings (Anguttara Nikāya).* 5 vols. Reprint. Oxford: Pali Text Society.

Hinsch, Bret. 1990. *Passions of the Cut Sleeve: The Male Homosexual Tradition in China.* Berkeley: University of California Press.

Horner, I. B. 1930. *Women under Primitive Buddhism: Lay Women and Alms Women.* New York: E. P. Dutton.

Jackson, Peter A. 1995. *Dear Uncle Go: Male Homosexuality in Thailand.* Bangkok: Bua Luang Books.

Jones, John Garrett. 1979. *Tales and Teachings of the Buddha: The Jātaka Stories in Relation to the Pali Canon.* London: George Allen and Unwin.

Kabilsingh, Chatsumarn. 1996. *Women in Buddhism.* Manila, Philippines: Isis International.

Karma Lekshe Tsomo, ed. 1999. *Buddhist Women across Cultures: Realizations.* Albany: State University of New York Press.

———. 2000. *Innovative Buddhist Women: Swimming against the Stream.* Richmond, VA: Curzon.

Kornfield, Jack. 1985. "Sex Lives of the Gurus." *Yoga Journal:* 26–66.

LaFleur, William. 1992. *Liquid Life: Abortion and Buddhism in Japan.* Princeton, NJ: Princeton University Press.

Law, Bimala Churn. 1927. *Women in Buddhist Literature.* Varanasi, India: Indological Book House.

Levering, Miriam. 1982. "The Dragon-Girl and the Abbess of Mo-Shan: Gender and Status in the Ch'an Buddhist Tradition." *Journal of the International Association of Buddhist Studies* 5, no. 1: 19–30.

Leyland, Winston, ed. 1998. *Queer Dharma: Voices of Gay Buddhists.* Vol. 1. San Francisco: Gay Sunshine Press.

Morris, R., and E. Hardy, ed. [1885–1900] 1961–1979. *Anguttara Nikāya.* 5 vols. Reprint, London: Pali Text Society.

Müller, E. ed. 1893. *Paramatthadīpanī: Dhammapāla's Commentary on the Therīgāthā.* Vol. 30. London: Pali Text Society.

Patchen, Ani, and Adelaide Donnely. 2000. *Sorrow Mountain: The Journey of a Tibetan Warrior Nun.* New York: Kodansha America.

Paul, Diana. 1979. *Women in Buddhism: Images of the Feminine in Mahayana Tradition.* Berkeley: Asian Humanities Press.

Piyadassi (Thera). 1980. *The Virgin's Eye: Women in Buddhist Literature.* Colombo: Buddhist Publication Society.

Ray, Reginald. 1994. *Buddhist Saints in India: A Study in Buddhist Values and Orientations.* New York: Oxford University Press.

Schalow, Paul Gordon, trans. 1990. *The Great Mirror of Male Love.* Stanford: University of California Press.

Schelling, Andrew, and Anne Waldman, trans. 1996. *Songs of the Sons and Daughters of Buddha.* Boston: Shambala Publications.

Schneider, David. 2000. *Street Zen: The Life and Work of Issan Dorsey.* New York: Marlowe.

Shaw, Miranda. 1994. *Passionate Enlightenment: Women in Tantric Buddhism.* Princeton, NJ: Princeton University Press.

Sidor, Ellen S., ed. 1987. *A Gathering of Spirit: Women Teaching in American Buddhism.* Cumberland, RI: Primary Point Press.

Snellgrove, David. 1987. *Indo-Tibetan Buddhism.* 2 vols. Boston: Shambala.

Spiro, Melford. 1970. *Buddhism and Society: A Great Tradition and Its Burmese Vicissitudes.* New York: Harper and Row.

Talim, Meena. 1972. *Woman in Early Buddhist Literature.* Bombay: University of Bombay.

Thurman, Robert, trans. 1976. *The Holy Teachings of Vimalakīrti.* University Park: Pennsylvania State University Press.

Tompkins, Jane. 1992. *West of Everything: The Inner Life of Westerns.* New York: Oxford University Press.

Vidyabhusan, S. C. A., trans. 1898. "The Story of Mahākaśyapa." *Journal of the Buddhist Text and Anthropological Society* 6: 18–19.

Watanabe, Tsuneo, and Jun'ichi Iwata. 1989. *The Love of Samurai: A Thousand Years of Japanese Homosexuality.* D. R. Roberts, trans. London: GMP Publishers.

Williams, Paul. 1989. *Mahayana Buddhism: The Doctrinal Foundations.* New York: Routledge.

Wilson, Liz. 1996. *Charming Cadavers: Horrific Figurations of the Feminine in Indian Buddhist Hagiographic Literature.* Chicago: University of Chicago Press.

Young, Katherine. 1987. "Hinduism." Pp. 59–103 in Arvind Sharma, ed., *Women in World Religions.* Albany: State University of New York Press.

Zwilling, Leonard. 1992. "Homosexuality as Seen in Indian Buddhist Texts." In José Ignacio Cabezón, ed., *Buddhism, Sexuality, and Gender.* Albany: State University of New York Press.

# JUDAISM

Adler, Rachel, 1998. *Engendering Judaism: An Inclusive Theology and Ethics.* Philadelphia: Jewish Publication Society.

Alpert, Rebecca. 1997. *Like Bread on the Seder Plate: Jewish Lesbians and the Transformation of Tradition.* New York: Columbia University Press.

Alpert, Rebecca, et al., eds. 2001. *Lesbian Rabbis: The First Generation.* New Brunswick, NJ: Rutgers University Press.

Balka, Christie, and Andy Rose. 1989. *Twice Blessed: On Being Lesbian or Gay and Jewish.* Boston: Beacon Press.

Beck, Evelyn Torton, ed. 1982. *Nice Jewish Girls: A Lesbian Anthology.* Watertown, MA: Persephone Press.

Biale, David. 1992. *Eros and the Jews: From Biblical Israel to Contemporary America.* New York: Basic Books.

Biale, Rachel. 1984. *Women and Jewish Law.* New York: Schocken Books.

Borowitz, Eugene. 1969. *Choosing a Sex Ethic: A Jewish Inquiry.* New York: Schocken Books for B'nai B'rith Hillel Foundations.

Boyarin, Daniel. 1993. *Carnal Israel: Reading Sex in Talmudic Culture.* Berkeley: University of California Press.

———. 1997. *Unheroic Conduct: The Rise of Heterosexuality and the Jewish Man.* Los Angeles: University of California Press.

Brod, Harry, ed. 1988. *A Mensch among Men: Explorations in Jewish Masculinity.* Freedom, CA: Crossing Press.

Dorff, Elliot. 1998. *Matters of Life and Death: A Jewish Approach to Modern Medical Ethics.* Philadelphia, PA: Jewish Publication Society.

Eilberg-Schwartz, Howard. 1994. *God's Phallus and Other Problems for Men and Monotheism.* Boston: Beacon Press.

Eilberg-Schwartz, Howard, ed. 1992. *People of the Body: Jews and Judaism from an Embodied Perspective.* Albany: State University of New York Press.

Fonrobert, Charlotte Elisheva. 2000. *Menstrual Purity: Rabbinic and Christian Reconstructions of Biblical Gender.* Stanford, CA: Stanford University Press.

Gordis, Robert. 1967. *Sex and the Family in Judaism.* New York: Burning Book.

Graetz, Naomi. 1998. *Silence Is Deadly: Judaism Confronts Wifebeating.* New Jersey: Jason Aronson Press.

Hauptman, Judith. 1998. *Rereading the Rabbis: A Woman's Voice.* Boulder, CO: Westview Press.

Jung, Patricia B., et al., eds. 2001. *Good Sex: Feminist Perspectives from the World's Religions.* New Brunswick, NJ: Rutgers University Press.

Kaye-Kantrowitz, Melanie, and Irena Klepfisz, eds. 1986. *Tribe of Dina: A Jewish Women's Anthology.* Montpelier, VT: Sinister Wisdom.

Moore, Tracy, ed. 1995. *Lesbiot: Israeli Lesbians Talk about Sexuality, Feminism, Judaism, and Their Lives.* London: Cassell.

Olyan, Saul. 1994. "'And with a Male You Shall Not Lie the Lying Down of a Woman': On the Meaning and Significance of Leviticus 18:22 and 20:13." *Journal of the History of Sexuality* 5, no. 2: 179–206.

Peskowitz, Miriam. 1997. *Spinning Fantasies: Rabbis, Gender and History.* Berkeley: University of California Press.

Plaskow, Judith. 1990. *Standing Again at Sinai: Judaism from a Feminist Perspective.* San Francisco: Harper and Row.

Prell, Riv-Ellen. 1999. *Fighting to Become Americans: Jews, Gender, and the Anxiety of Assimilation.* Boston, MA: Beacon Press.

Satlow, Michael. 1995. *Tasting the Dish: Rabbinic Rhetorics of Sexuality.* Providence, RI: Brown Judaica Series.

Shneer, David, and Caryn Aviv, ed. 2002. *Queer Jews.* New York: Routledge Press.

Solomon, Lewis D. 2002. *The Jewish Tradition, Sexuality, and Procreation.* Lanham, MD: University Press of America.

Walzer, Lee. 2000. *Between Sodom and Eden: A Gay Journey through Today's Changing Israel.* New York: Columbia University Press.

Waskow, Arthur. 1997. *Down to Earth Judaism: Food, Money, Sex and the Rest of Life.* New York: William Morrow.

Wegner, Judith Romney. 1988. *Chattel or Person? The Status of Women in the Mishnah.* New York: Oxford University Press.

Wolfson, Elliot. 1994. *Through a Speculum that Shines: Vision and Imagination in Medieval Jewish Mysticism.* Princeton, NJ: Princeton University Press.

## CATHOLICISM

Boswell, John. 1980. *Christianity, Social Tolerance, and Homosexuality: Gay People in Western Europe from the Beginning of the Christian Era to the Fourteenth Century.* Chicago: University of Chicago Press.

———. 1994. *Same-Sex Unions in Premodern Europe.* New York: Villard Books.

Callahan, Daniel. 1970. *Abortion: Law, Choice, and Morality.* New York: Macmillan.

Curran, Charles E. 1985. *Directions in Fundamental Moral Theology.* Notre Dame, IN: University of Notre Dame Press.

D'Antonio, William V., James D. Davidson, Dean R. Hoge, and Katherine Meyer. 2001. *American Catholics: Gender, Generation, and Commitment.* Walnut Creek, CA: Altamira Press.

D'Antonio, William V., James D. Davidson, Dean R. Hoge, and Ruth A. Wallace. 1996. *Laity: American and Catholic: Transforming the Church.* Kansas City, MO: Sheed and Ward.

Davidson, James D., Andrea S. Williams, Richard A. Lamanna, Jan Stenftenagel, Kathleen Maas Weigert, William J. Whalen, and Patricia Wittberg, S.C. 1997. *The Search for Common Ground: What Unites and Divides Catholic Americans.* Huntington, IN: Our Sunday Visitor Publishing Division.

Fox, Thomas C. 1995. *Sexuality and Catholicism.* New York: George Braziller.

Gallup, George, Jr., and Jim Costelli. 1987. *The American Catholic People: Their Beliefs, Practices, and Values.* Garden City, NY: Doubleday.

Greeley, Andrew M. 1989. *Religious Change in America.* Cambridge, MA: Harvard University Press.

———. 1990. *The Catholic Myth: The Behavior and Beliefs of American Catholics.* New York: Charles Scribner's Sons.

Hoge, Dean R., William D. Dinges, Mary Johnson, and Juan L. Gonzales. 2001. *Young Adult Catholics: Religion in the Culture of Choice.* Notre Dame, IN: University of Notre Dame Press.

Jenkins, Philip. 1996. *Pedophiles and Priests: Anatomy of a Contemporary Crisis.* New York: Oxford University Press.

Jordan, Mark D. 2000. *The Silence of Sodom: Homosexuality in Modern Catholicism.* Chicago: University of Chicago Press.

Katzenstein, Mary Fainsod. 1998. *Faithful and Fearless: Moving Feminist Protest inside the Church and Military.* Princeton, NJ: Princeton University Press.

Kosnik, Anthony, William Carroll, Agnes Cunningham, Ronald Modras, and James Schulte. 1977. *Human Sexuality: New Directions in American Catholic Thought.* A study commissioned by the Catholic Theological Society of America. New York: Paulist Press.

Leaper, Campbell, and Dena Valin. 1996. "Predictors of Mexican American Mothers' and Fathers' Attitudes toward Gender Equality." *Hispanic Journal of Behavioral Sciences* 18: 343–355.

Loseke, Donileen R., and James C. Cavendish. 2001. "Producing Institutional Selves: Rhetorically Constructing the Dignity of Sexually Marginalized Catholics." *Social Psychology Quarterly* 64, no. 4: 347–362.

McNeill, John J. 1993. *The Church and the Homosexual.* 14th ed. Boston: Beacon Press.

Schoenherr, Richard A., and Lawrence A. Young. 1993. *Full Pews and Empty Altars: Demographics of the Priest Shortage in the United States Catholic Dioceses.* Madison: University of Wisconsin Press.

Wassmer, T. A. 1967. "Natural Law." Pp. 251–262 of the *New Catholic Encyclopedia.* Vol. 10. Washington, DC: Catholic University of America.

## PROTESTANTISM

Bartowski, John. 2000. "Breaking Walls, Raising Fences: Masculinity, Intimacy and Accountability among the Promise Keepers." *Sociology of Religion* 61 (Spring): 33–53.

Bendroth, Margaret Lamberts. 1999. "Fundamentalism and the Family: Gender, Culture, and the American Pro-Family Movement." *Journal of Women's History* 10, no. 4: 35–54.

Brekus, Catherine A. 1998. *Strangers and Pilgrims: Female Preaching in America, 1740–1845.* Chapel Hill: University of North Carolina Press.

Butler, Judith. 1990. *Gender Trouble: Feminism and the Subversion of Identity.* New York: Routledge Press.

Comstock, Gary D. 1996. *Unrepentant, Self-Affirming, Practicing: Lesbian/ Bisexual/Gay People within Organized Religion.* New York: Continuum.

D'Emilio, John, and Estelle B. Friedman. 1988. *Intimate Matters: A History of Sexuality in America.* New York: Harper and Row.

Deberg, Betty A. 1990. *Ungodly Women: Gender and the First Wave of American Fundamentalism.* Minneapolis, MN: Fortress Press.

Ellison, Marvin M. 1993. "Homosexuality and Protestantism." Pp. 149–179 in Arlene Swidler, ed., *Homosexuality and World Religions.* Valley Forge: Trinity Press International.

Fessenden, Tracy, Nicholas F. Radel, and Magdalena J. Zaborowska, eds. 2001. *The Puritan Origins of American Sex: Religion, Sexuality, and National Identity in American Literature.* New York: Routledge Press.

Fischer, David Hackett. 1989. *Albion's Seed: Four British Folkways in America.* New York: Oxford University Press.

Foster, Lawrence. 1984. *Religion and Sexuality: The Shakers, the Mormons, and the Oneida Community.* Urbana: University of Illinois Press.

Godbeer, Richard. 2002. *Sexual Revolution in Early America.* Baltimore: Johns Hopkins University Press.

Kvam, Kristen E., Linda S. Schearing, and Valerie H. Ziegler, eds. 1999. *Eve and Adam: Jewish, Christian, and Muslim Readings on Genesis and Gender.* Bloomington: Indiana University Press.

Luther, Martin. 1958. *Lectures on Genesis: Chapters 1–5.* Vol. 1 in George V. Schick, trans., and Jarsolav Pelikan, ed., *Luther's Works.* Saint Louis: Concordia Publishing House.

Morgan, Edmund S., ed. [1946] 1965. *The Diary of Michael Wigglesworth, 1653–1657: The Conscience of a Puritan.* Reprint. New York: Harper & Row.

Noyes, John Humphrey. 1853. "Bible Argument Defining the Relations of the Sexes in the Kingdom of Heaven." In *Bible Communism: A Compilation of the Annual Reports and Other Publications of the Oneida Association and Its Branches.* Brooklyn, NY: Office of the *Circular.*

Oberman, Heiko A. 1989. *Luther: Man between God and the Devil.* Eileen Walliser-Schwarzbart, trans. New Haven: Yale University Press.

Reis, Elizabeth. 1997. *Damned Women: Sinners and Witches in Puritan New England.* Ithaca, NY: Cornell University Press.

Sands, Kathleen M., ed. 2000. *God Forbid: Religion and Sex in American Public Life.* New York: Oxford University Press.

Smith, Merril D., ed. 1998. *Sex and Sexuality in Early America.* New York: New York University Press.

Sprenger, Jacobus, and Heinrich Kramer. [1496] 1968. *Malleus Maleficarum: The Hammer of Witchcraft.* Montague Summers, trans. Reprint, London: Folio Society.

Taves, Ann. 1997. "Sexuality in American Religious History." Pp. 27–56 in Thomas A. Tweed, ed., *Retelling U.S. Religious History.* Berkeley: University of California Press.

Thompson, Roger. 1986. *Sex in Middlesex: Popular Mores in a Massachusetts County, 1649–1699.* Amherst: University of Massachusetts Press.

Welter, Barbara. 1974. "The Feminization of American Religion: 1800–1860." Pp. 137–157 in Mary Hartman and Lois W. Banner, eds., *Clio's Consciousness Raised: New Perspectives on the History of Women.* New York: Harper and Row.

———. 1976. *Dimity Convictions: The American Woman in the Nineteenth Century.* Athens: Ohio University Press.

Wuthnow, Robert. 1988. *The Restructuring of American Religion.* Princeton: Princeton University Press.

## ISLAM

Abou El Fadel, Khaled. 2001. *Speaking in God's Name: Islamic Law, Authority, and Women.* Oxford: Oneworld.

Ahmed, Leila. 1992. *Women and Gender in Islam: Historical Roots of a Modern Debate.* New Haven: Yale University Press.

Ali, Abdullah Yusuf. 1989. *The Holy Qur'an: Text, Translation, and Commentary.* Brentwood: Amana Corporation.

Alloula, Malek. 1986. *The Colonial Harem.* Myrna Godzich and Wlad Godzich, trans. Minneapolis: University of Minnesota Press.

Barlas, Asma, ed. 2002. *Believing Women in Islam: Unreading Patriarchal Interpretations of the Quran.* Austin: University Press of Texas.

Bouhdiba, Abdelwahab. 1985. *Sexuality in Islam.* London: Routledge and Kegan Paul.

Duran, Khalid. 1993. "Homosexuality and Islam." Pp. 181–197 in Arlene Swidler, ed., *Homosexuality and World Religions.* Valley Forge: Trinity Press International.

El Guindi, Fadwa. 1999. *Veil: Modesty, Privacy, and Resistance.* Oxford: Berg.

El Saadawi, Nawal. 1980. *The Hidden Face of Eve: Women in the Arab World.* Sherif Hetata. London: Zed Books.

Farah, Madelain. 1984. *Marriage and Sexuality in Islam: A Translation of al-Ghazali's Book on the Etiquette of Marriage from the Ihya.* Salt Lake City: University of Utah Press.

al-Ghazali, Abu Hamid. 1984. *Marriage and Sexuality in Islam: A Translation of al-Ghazali's Book on the Etiquette of Marriage from the Ihya.* Madelain Farah, trans. Salt Lake City: University of Utah Press.

Haeri, Shahla. 1989. *Law of Desire: Temporary Marriage in Shi'i Iran.* Syracuse: Syracuse University Press.

Hasan, Asma Gull. 2000. *American Muslims: The New Generation.* New York: Continuum.

Hassan, Riffat. N.d. *Women's Rights and Islam: From the I.C.P.D. to Beijing.* Self-published by the author.

al-Hibri, Azizah. 1995. "Marriage and Divorce: Legal Foundations." Pp. 48–50 in *The Oxford Encyclopedia of the Modern Islamic World,* vol. 3. John L. Esposito, ed. New York: Oxford University Press.

———. 2000. "An Introduction to Muslim Women's Rights." Pp. 51–71 in *Windows of Faith: Muslim Women Scholar-Activists in North America.* Gisela Webb, ed. Syracuse: Syracuse University Press.

Ibn Hazm. 1953. *The Ring of the Dove: A Treatise in the Art and Practice of Arab Love.* A. J. Arberry, trans. London: Luzac.

Imam, Ayesha. 2001. "The Muslim Religious Right ('Fundamentalists') and Sexuality." Pp. 15–30 in Patricia Beattie Jung, Mary E. Hunt, and Radhika Balakrishnan, eds., *Good Sex: Feminist Perspectives from the World's Religions.* New Brunswick: Rutgers University Press.

Jamal, Amreen. 2001. "The Story of Lot and the Qur'an's Perception of the Morality of Same-Sex Sexuality." *Journal of Homosexuality* 41, no. 1: 1–88.

Khafaji, 'Abd al-Hakim. 1987. *Kawakib Hawl al-Rasul.* Alexandria: Dar al-Wafa.

Khan, Badruddin. 1997. *Sex, Love, and Not Belonging: A Gay Muslim's Quest for Love and Meaning.* Oakland, CA: Floating Lotus.

Lings, Martin. 1983. *Muhammad: His Life Based on the Earliest Sources.* Rochester: Inner Traditions International.

Mernissi, Fatima. 1987. *Beyond the Veil: Male-Female Dynamics in Modern Muslim Society.* Bloomington: Indiana University Press.

Murata, Schiko. 1992. *The Tao of Islam: A Sourcebook on Gender Relationships in Islamic Thought.* Albany: State University of New York Press.

Murray, Stephen O., and Will Roscoe, eds. 1997. *Islamic Homosexualities: Culture, History, and Literature.* New York: New York University Press.

Musallam, B. F. 1983. *Sex and Society in Islam: Birth Control before the Nineteenth Century.* Cambridge: Cambridge University Press.

Nafzawi, Umar ibn Muhammad. 1964. *The Perfumed Garden of Shaykh Nafzawi.* Sir Richard F. Burton, trans. New York: Castle Books.

Omran, Abdel Rahim. 1992. *Family Planning in the Legacy of Islam.* London: Routledge.

Rowson, Everett K. 1991a. "The Categorization of Gender and Sexual Irregularity in Medieval Arabic Vice Lists." In Julia Epstein and Kristina Straub, eds., *Body Guards: The Cultural Politics of Gender Ambiguity.* New York: Routledge.

———. 1991b. "The Effeminates of Early Medina." *Journal of the American Oriental Society* 111, no. 4: 671–693.

Said, Edward. 1994. *Orientalism.* New York: Vintage Books.

Sanders, Paula. 1991. "Gendering the Ungendered Body: Hermaphrodites." Pp. 74–95 in Nikkie R. Keddie and Beth Baron, eds., *Shifting Boundaries in Sex and Gender.* New Haven: Yale University Press.

al-Sayyid-Marsot, Afaf Lufti, ed. 1979. *Society and the Sexes in Medieval Islam.* Malibu: Undena.

Schild, Maarten. 1990. "Islam." Pp. 615–620 in Wayne R. Dynes, ed., *Encyclopedia of Homosexuality.* New York: Garland.

Schmitt, Arno. 1995. *Bio-bibliography of Male-Male Sexuality and Eroticism in Muslim Societies.* Berlin: Verlag rosa Winkel.

Schmitt, Arno, and Jehoeda Sofer, eds. 1992. *Sexuality and Eroticism among Males in Moslem Societies.* New York: Haworth.

Shaarawi, Huda. 1986. *Harem Years: The Memoirs of an Egyptian Feminist.* Margot Badran, trans. New York: Feminist Press.

Spellberg, D. A. 1994. *Politics, Gender, and the Islamic Past: The Legacy of 'Aisha Bint Abi Bakr.* New York: Columbia University Press.

Stowasser, Barbara Freyer. 1994. *Women in the Qur'an: Traditions, and Interpretation.* New York: Oxford University Press.

Toubia, Nahid. 1993. *Female Genital Mutilation: A Call for Global Action.* New York: Women, Ink.

Wadud, Amina. 1999. *Qur'an and Woman: Rereading the Sacred Text from a Woman's Perspective.* New York: Oxford University Press.

Webb, Gisela, ed. 2002. *Windows of Faith: Muslim Women Scholar Activists in North America.* Syracuse: Syracuse University Press.

Wright, J. W., Jr., and Everett K. Rowson, eds. 1997. *Homoeroticism in Classical Arabic Literature.* New York: Columbia University Press.

Yegenoglu, Meyda. 1998. *Colonial Fantasies: Towards a Feminist Reading of Orientalism.* New York: Cambridge University Press.

## PAGANISM

Adler, Margot. [1979] 1986. *Drawing Down the Moon: Witches, Druids, Goddess-Worshippers, and Other Pagans in America Today.* Reprint. Boston, MA: Beacon Press.

Bracelin, J. L. 1960. *Gerald Gardner: Witch.* London: Octagon Press.

Campbell, Joseph. [1949] 1973. *The Hero with a Thousand Faces.* Reprint. Princeton, NJ: Princeton University Press.

Christ, Carol P. 1987. *Laughter of Aphrodite.* San Francisco: Harper and Row.

Drew, A. J. 1998. *Wicca for Men: A Handbook for Male Pagans Seeking a Spiritual Path.* Secaucus, NJ: Carol Publishing Group.

———. 2001. *Wicca Spellcraft for Men: A Spellbook for Male Pagans.* Franklin Lakes, NJ: New Page Books.

Farrar, Stewart, and Janet Farrar. [1981] 1991. *A Witches Bible Compleat.* Reprint. New York: Magickal Childe Publishing.

Gardner, Gerald B. *Witchcraft Today.* [1954] 1968. Reprint, London: Jarrolds Publishers.

Gimbutas, Marija. 1991. *The Civilization of the Goddess: The World of Old Europe.* San Francisco: HarperCollins Publishers.

Griffin, Susan. 1981. *Pornography and Silence: Culture's Revenge against Nature.* New York: HarperCollins Books.

Grob, Leonard, Riffat Hassan, and Haim Gordon, eds. 1991. *Women's and Men's Liberation: Testimonies of Spirit.* Westport, CT: Greenwood Press.

Isaacs, Ernest. 1983. "The Fox Sisters and American Spiritualism." Pp. 79–110 in Howard Kerr and Charles L. Crow, eds., *The Occult in America: New Historical Perspectives.* Chicago: University of Illinois Press.

Keen, Sam. 1992. *Fire in the Belly: On Being a Man.* New York: Bantam Books.

Mann, Nicholas R. 1995. *His Story: Masculinity in the Post-Patriarchal World.* St. Paul, MN: Llewellyn Publications.

Parker, Don H. 1996. *Goddess Power: An Interactive Book for Women . . . and Men.* Carmel, CA: Dynamic Publishing.

Richardson, Alan. 1992. *Earth God Rising: The Return of the Male Mysteries.* St. Paul, MN: Llewellyn Publications.

Scott, James C. 1990. *Domination and the Arts of Resistance: Hidden Transcripts.* New Haven: Yale University Press.

Starhawk. 1988. *Dreaming the Dark: Magic, Sex, and Politics.* Boston, MA: Beacon Press.

Stone, Merlin. 1976. *When God Was a Woman.* New York: Dial Press.

Tosh, Nancy Ramsey. 2000. *Fabulous Monsters: Identity Construction in Contemporary Paganism.* Ph.D. diss., University of California at Santa Barbara.

Warren-Clarke, Ly, and Kathryn Matthews. 1994. *The Way of Merlyn: The Male Path in Wicca.* Bellingham, WA: Prism Press.

# LGBT COMMUNITIES

Alpert, Rebecca T. 1997. *Like Bread on the Seder Plate: Jewish Lesbians and the Transformation of Tradition.* New York: Columbia University Press.

Balka, Christie, and Andy Rose, eds. 1989. *Twice Blessed: On Being Lesbian, Gay, and Jewish.* Boston: Beacon Press.

Booher, Gary, and Paul Mortensen, eds. 1985. *Affirmations: A Select Anthology of Writings for Gay and Lesbian Mormons.* Los Angeles: Affirmation/Gay and Lesbian Mormons.

Bouldrey, Brian, ed. 1995. *Wrestling with the Angel: Faith and Religion in the Lives of Gay Men.* New York: Riverhead Books.

Boykin, Keith. 1999. *Respecting the Soul: Daily Reflections for Black Lesbians and Gays.* New York: Avon Books.

Brown, Lester B., ed. 1997. *Two Spirit People: American Indian Lesbian Women and Gay Men.* New York: Haworth Press.

Carey, John Jesse, ed. 1995. *The Sexuality Debate in North American Churches, 1988–1995: Controversies, Unresolved Issues, Future Prospects.* Lewiston, NY: Edwin Mellen.

Comstock, Gary David. 1996. *Unrepentant, Self-Affirming, Practicing: Lesbian/Gay/Bisexual People within Organized Religion.* New York: Continuum.

———. 2001. *A Whosoever Church: Welcoming Lesbians and Gay Men into African American Congregations.* Louisville, KY: Westminster John Knox Press.

Conner, Randy P. 1993. *Blossom of Bone: Reclaiming the Connections between Homoeroticism and the Sacred.* San Francisco: HarperSan Francisco.

Cooper, Aaron. 1989. "No Longer Invisible: Gay and Lesbian Jews Build a Movement." *Journal of Homosexuality* 18, nos. 3–4: 83–94.

Dynes, Wayne R., and Stephen Donaldson, eds. 1992. *Homosexuality and Religion and Philosophy.* New York: Garland.

Dufour, Lynn Resnick. 2000. "Sifting through Tradition: The Creation of Jewish Feminist Identities." *Journal for the Scientific Study of Religion* 39, no. 1: 90–106.

Gill, Sean, ed. 1998. *The Lesbian and Gay Christian Movement: Campaigning for Justice, Truth, and Love.* London: Cassell.

Gray, Edward R., and Scott L. Thumma. Forthcoming. *Gay Religion: Innovation and Tradition in Spiritual Practice.* Walnut Creek, CA: Alta Mira.

Gray, Edward R., and Scott L. Thumma. 1997. "The Gospel Hour: Liminality, Identity, and Religion in a Gay Bar." In Penny Edgell Becker and Nancy L. Eiesland, eds., *Contemporary American Religion: An Ethnographic Reader.* Walnut Creek, CA: Alta Mira.

Hartman, Keith. 1996. *Congregations in Conflict: The Battle over Homosexuality.* New Brunswick, NJ: Rutgers University Press.

Jordan, Mark D. 2000. *The Silence of Sodom: Homosexuality in Modern Catholicism.* Chicago: University of Chicago Press.

Katz, Jonathan Ned. 1992. *Gay American History: Lesbians and Gay Men in the USA.* Rev. ed. New York: Meridian.

Leyland, Winston, ed. 1998. *Queer Dharma: Voices of Gay Buddhists.* San Francisco: Gay Sunshine Press.

Lorde, Audre. 1982. *Zami: A New Spelling of My Name.* Watertown, MA: Persephone Press.

Mahaffy, Kimberly A. 1996. "Cognitive Dissonance and Its Resolution: A Study of Lesbian Christians." *Journal for the Scientific Study of Religion* 35, no. 4: 392–402.

Manodori, Chiara. 1998. "This Powerful Opening of the Heart: How Ritual Affirms Lesbian Identity." *Journal of Homosexuality* 36, no. 2: 41–58.

Marotta, Toby. 1981. *The Politics of Homosexuality.* Boston: Houghton Mifflin.

Monroe, Irene. 1993. "The Aché Sisters: Discovering the Power of the Erotic in Ritual." Pp. 127–135 in Marjorie Procter-Smith and Janet R. Walton, eds., *Women at Worship: Interpretations of North American Diversity.* Louisville, KY: Westminster John Knox Press.

Murray, Stephen O., and Will Roscoe, eds. 1997. *Islamic Homosexualities: Culture, History, and Literature.* New York: New York University Press.

Oppenheimer, Mark. 1996. "Inherent Worth and Dignity: Gay Unitarians and the Birth of Sexual Tolerance in Liberal Religion." *Journal of the History of Sexuality* 7, no. 1: 73–101.

Perry, Troy D., with Thomas L. P. Swicegood. 1990. *Don't Be Afraid Anymore: The Story of Reverend Troy Perry and the Metropolitan Community Churches.* New York: St. Martin's.

Primiano, Leonard Norman. 1993. "'I Would Rather Be Fixated on the Lord': Women's Religion, Men's Power, and the 'Dignity' Problem." *New York Folklore* 19, nos. 1–2: 89–99.

Procter-Smith, Marjorie, and Janet R. Walton, eds. 1993. *Women at Worship: Interpretations of North American Diversity.* Louisville, KY: Westminster John Knox Press.

Rakesh, Ratti, ed. 1993. *A Lotus of Another Color: An Unfolding of the South Asian Gay and Lesbian Experience.* Boston: Alyson Publications.

Schneider, David. 1993. *Street Zen: The Life and Work of Issan Dorsey.* Boston: Shambhala.

Shallenberger, David. 1998. *Reclaiming the Spirit: Gay Men and Lesbians Come to Terms with Religion.* New Brunswick, NJ: Rutgers University Press.

Shneer, David, and Caryn Aviv, eds. 2002. *Queer Jews.* New York: Routledge.

Shokeid, Moshe. 1995. *A Gay Synagogue in New York.* New York: Columbia University Press.

———. 2001. "The Women are Coming: The Transformation of Gender Relationships in a Gay Synagogue." *Ethnos* 66, no. 1: 5–26.

Thumma, Scott. 1991. "Negotiating a Religious Identity: The Case of the Gay Evangelical." *Sociological Analysis* 52, no. 4: 333–347.

Tinney, James S. 1986. "Why a Black Gay Church?" In Joseph Beam, ed., *In the Life: A Black Gay Anthology.* Boston: Alyson.

Wagner, Glenn, James Serafini, Judith Rabkin, Robert Remien, and Janet Williams. 1994. "Integration of One's Religion and Homosexuality: A Weapon against Internalized Homophobia?" *Journal of Homosexuality* 26, no. 4: 91–110.

Wilcox, Melissa M. 2003. *Coming Out in Christianity: Religion, Identity, and Community.* Bloomington: Indiana University Press.

Wilson, Nancy. 1995. *Our Tribe: Queer Folks, God, Jesus, and the Bible.* San Francisco: Harper.

*Witness Aloud: Lesbian, Gay, and Bisexual Asian/Pacific American Writing.* 1993. New York: Asian American Writers' Workshop.

## SEXUAL LIBERTY

Craig, Barbara Hinkson, and David M. O'Brien. 1993. *Abortion and American Politics.* Chatham, NJ: Chatham House.

Dworkin, Ronald. 1993. *Life's Dominion: An Argument about Abortion, Euthanasia, and Individual Freedom.* New York: Alfred A. Knopf.

———. 1996. *Freedom's Law: The Moral Reading of the American Constitution.* Cambridge, MA: Harvard University Press.

———. 2000. *Sovereign Virtue: The Theory and Practice of Equality.* Cambridge, MA: Harvard University Press.

Eskridge, William N., Jr. 1996. *The Case for Same-Sex Marriage: From Sexual Liberty to Civilized Commitment.* New York: Free Press.

———. 1997. *Sexuality, Gender, and the Law.* Westbury, NY: Foundation Press.

———. 2002. *Equality Practice: Civil Unions and the Future of Gay Rights.* New York: Routledge.

Flowers, Ronald B. 1994. *That Godless Court?* Louisville, KY: Westminster John Knox Press.

Greenawalt, Kent. 1989. *Religious Convictions and Political Choice.* New York: Oxford University Press.

Hammond, Phillip. 1998. *With Liberty for All: Freedom of Religion in the United States.* Louisville, KY: Westminster John Knox Press.

Himmelfarb, Gertrude. 1999. *One Nation, Two Cultures.* New York: Vintage Books.

Hunter, James Davison. 1991. *Culture Wars: The Struggle to Define America.* New York: Basic Books.

McGraw, Barbara. 2002. *Rediscovering America's Sacred Ground.* Albany, NY: State University of New York Press.

Nava, Michael, and Robert Dawidoff. 1994. *Created Equal: Why Gay Rights Matter to America.* New York: St. Martin's Press.

Richards, David A. J. 1986. *Toleration and the Constitution.* New York: Oxford University Press.

———. 1993. *Conscience and the Constitution: History, Theory, and Law of the Reconstruction Amendments.* Princeton, NJ: Princeton University Press.

———. 1998a. *Free Speech and the Politics of Identity.* New York: Oxford University Press.

———. 1998b. *Women, Gays, and the Constitution: The Grounds for Feminism and Gay Rights in Culture and Law.* Chicago: University of Chicago Press.

———. 1999. *Identity and the Case for Gay Rights: Race, Gender, Religion as Analogies.* Chicago: University of Chicago Press.

Smith, Craig R. 1993. *To Form a More Perfect Union: The Ratification of the Constitution and the Bill of Rights, 1787–1791.* New York: Center for First Amendment Studies, California State University at Long Beach.

Sullivan, Andrew. 1995. *Virtually Normal: An Argument about Homosexuality.* New York: Alfred A. Knopf.

Wenz, Peter S. 1992. *Abortion Rights as Religious Freedom.* Philadelphia: Temple University Press.

# Index

Abhinavagupta and Tantric sexuality, 118–119
Abimbola, Wande, 21
Ablutions ritual (Islam), 266–267
Abortion, 247, 378–381
    in African spiritual traditions, 22
    and Catholic Church, 224–225
    as conservative-liberal Protestant issue, 245, 247–248
    legislation against, 380–381
    as means of family planning (Japan), 169
    as orthodox-liberal Jewish issue, 195–197, 200
    when woman's life is endangered, 268
Abou El Fadel, Khaled, 260
Abstinence, 59, 189
    in Judaism, 182, 192
    within marriage (Quakers), 241
    movements, 246, 247
    from premarital sex, 246–247
    from sexual contact or relations, 15, 84, 85, 222
    as virtue (Catholic), 212
    See also Celibacy
Abuse of women, 24, 285
Aché Sisters, 347
Ackerman, Lillian A., 48
Acquired immunodeficiency syndrome. See AIDS
The Act of Marriage (LaHaye and LaHaye), 246
Act-centered morality, 217, 221, 227
Adolescent homosexuality, 162
Adoption
    by homosexual parents, 372–374
    Jewish, 197

Adultery, 180, 197
    in African spiritual traditions, 17, 23
    as capital offense (Puritan), 238
    as harmful (Buddhist), 138, 161
    resulting from dissatisfaction, 238
    witnesses required to prove (Islam), 271
    women punished for, 182, 240
Advocate, 340
Aesthetic and religious experience merged, 120
Affirmation, 338
African Americans, 241, 342, 347
African religions, 5, 348. See also African spiritual traditions
African spiritual traditions, 5–6
    androgynous practices, 19
    fertility symbols, 9
    magical practices of, 24
    masculinity and femininity, 7, 8, 18
After Heaven (Wuthnow), 334
Afterlife. See Paradise (Islam)
Against the So-Called Spiritual State (Luther), 236
Agnostics, as LGBT seekers, 352
Ahmed, Leila, 280, 282
AIDS (acquired immunodeficiency syndrome), 247, 332, 343
    Buddhist hospice, 168
    and Native American gay men, 59–61
AIDS Coalition to Unleash Power, 331
'A'isha, wife of Muhammad, 270–271
Al-'Adawiyya, Rabi'a, 274
Alchemy, 84, 89, 105
Alexandrian rule of procreative sex, 213
Alexandrian tradition (Wicca), 298
Al-Fatiha group, 338

Algeria, 14

Allah, 262, 266, 268–269

Altekar, Anant Sadashiv, 145

Alternative space groups for LGBT people, 344–347, 351

American Baptists Concerned for Sexual Minorities, 338

American Zen Buddhism, 297

Amma (Dogon), 18

Amritananda Mayi Ma, 111

Anabaptist churches, 338

Androgyny
    in African religions, 6, 18, 19
    of souls reincarnated (Hindu), 125
    spiritual, 125
    *See also* Bi-gender

Anglican Church
    contraceptives permitted, 215
    in early United States, 240
    internal LGBT groups, 337

Anguksuar, 58, 61

*Anguttara Nikāya,* 142

Animals
    as companions, spiritual guides, 313
    deities, 14
    as elder species, 39

Anticult movement, 339

Antimiscegenation laws, 241, 375

Anti-Semitism, 185, 200

Antiviolence groups, 194

Architecture
    and mandala-logic, 122
    and religious concepts of sexuality, 11

Aristotle, 211

Army acceptance of Israeli gay men and lesbians, 190

Arts of bedchamber (Daoism), 87
    compared to paired cultivation, 90
    opposed by Confucians, 87, 88

Aryal, Mukunda Raj, 129

Asceticism, 111
    Jewish, 180, 200
    for sexual control (Hindu), 103, 115, 116

Atheism, 353

*Ātiswin* (Chumash), 40

Augustine, Saint, 213, 224

Autonomy
    moral, 377, 381
    religious, 141
    of women (Buddhist), 145, 146, 148

Avalokiteshvara, bodhisattva of (Buddhist), 152, 153

Axios, 338

Azande (Africa)
    male-male intimacy, 21
    menstruation beliefs, 10
    traditional medicine practiced by men, 25

Bachofen, J. J., 304

*Baehr v. Lewin* (1993), 376

Baker, Richard, 343

*Baker v. State* (1998), 376

Barrenness caused by witchcraft, 24–25

Bartholomeusz, Tessa, 159

Baule otherworldly partners (Côte d'Ivoire), 26

Bean, Carl, 248, 341

Beards (Islam), 277

Beauvoir, Simone de, 35

Beltane rituals (Pagan), 299–300

Beng (Côte d'Ivoire), 15

Bennett, Ramona, 44

*Berdache* (Native American), 50

Beth Chayim Chadashim, 342

*Beyond the Veil* (Mernissi), 285

Bharati, Uma, 111

Bible
    and Catholic morality of sexuality, 211
    Hebrew. *See* Hebrew Bible
    on same-sex relations, 327
    as source of authority, 233

Bible Communism (Oneida Perfectionists), 244

Bi-gender, 106, 122, 124–125. *See also* Androgyny

Bill of Rights of U.S. Constitution, 364, 365

*Binukedine* androgynous spiritual leader (Africa), 20

Birth control, 268
    availability, 217
    for frivolous reasons (Islam), 269
    Jewish views of, 194, 195, 200
    prohibition rejected by laity, 218

Bisexuality
    and Dianic Wicca, 344
    and Judaism, 187, 189

Blackfeet (Native American), 46

Blofeld, John, 69

*Blolo* (Côte d'Ivoire), 26–27

Body, 75, 76, 297
Bonewits, Isaac, 320
*Book of Blessings* (Falk), 343
*Book of the Former Han Dynasty,* 88
Boston Archdiocese (Catholic), 221, 223
Boswell, John, 218, 219
*Boté* two-spirit person (Native American),
   52, 53, 54
Botswana, fertility rite, 14
Bouhdiba, Abdelwahab, 268, 276
Brahmins, 107, 148
   couples as models for Hindu sexuality,
     115, 116
Brazil, 29
Brethren/Mennonite Council for Lesbian
   and Gay Concerns, 338
Bride seclusion, 16
Bride-price, 15
Budapest, Zsuzsanna, 345
Buddha, 139–140
   against gender-atypical people, 163
   as social reformer, 144
   as spiritual father, 150
   women followers of, 146
Buddhism, 135
   criticism of Daoism, 86, 89
   Eternal Mother, 80
   and individualism, 140
   laity, 140, 142, 148, 157
   and LGBT people, 338–339, 343
   mind-spirit development, 297
   monasticism, 84, 86, 138, 148, 158,
     169
   and problem of suffering, 136
Buissi lesbian relationships (Democratic
   Republic of Congo), 21
Bureau of Indian Affairs (BIA), 53
Burkina Faso, 8
Burning Times, 300, 301, 304
Bush, George Walker, 301, 363
*Buyazi* gender ambiguous spiritual leader
   (Africa), 20

Cabrillo, Juan, 43
Cain and Abel Bible story, 196
Caldwell, Sarah, 113
Calvin, John, 235, 236, 245
   on sexuality within marriage, 237
Campbell, Joseph, 304
Capital punishment for sexual offenses,
   238, 241

Castes
   acquired by moral virtue (Buddhist), 144
   boundaries for sexuality, 123
   Hindu, 107
*Casti Connubii* (Pope Pius XI), 215
Catholic Church
   and abortion issue, 224–225
   blended with African religions,
     348–349
   celibacy issues, 222–224
   complementarity of men and women,
     225
   divergence with laity, 205–206, 216–217,
     226–227
   homosexuality positions, 219, 325, 327
   LGBT movement, 221, 341
   morality of sexuality, 211–216
   natural law, 210
Catholicism. *See* Catholic Church
Celestial Master Daoism sexuality, 70, 84,
   90
Celibacy
   and boys' rituals (Hindu), 109
   of clergy, 138, 169, 140, 222, 223
   Daoist, 84, 85, 86, 96
   denounced by Luther, 236
   ecclesiastical stances toward, 170, 213
   in marriage, 142–143, 241
   for ordained lesbians and gay men, 333
   to reach religious autonomy (Buddhist),
     141
   reformed by Protestantism, 234
   requirement abolished (Japanese
     Buddhist), 169
   as route to salvation (Shakers), 243
   of Sufism, 273–274
   and Tantra sexuality, 119
   valued above marriage (Catholic), 212
Champagne, Duane, 57
Chang, Jolan, 96
Changó, 349
Chastity
   importance of (Puritan), 239
   as virtue (Catholic), 212
   for youth, 246–247
Chia, Mantak, 96
Chidvilasananda, Gurumayi, 111
Chiefs (Native American), 43–44
*Chigo monogatari* (Japanese Buddhist), 166
Childbearing (African spiritual traditions),
   21–22, 23, 25

Children
  in cases of divorce (Islam), 265
  illegitimacy threatening family
    bloodline, 240
  inappropriate fertility rites, 319
  raised as Pagans, 314
  raised by same-sex couples, 373–374
  sexual abuse by Catholic priests, 220,
    223
Childs, Margaret, 166
China, 165
Ching, Julia, 71
Choctaw (Native American), 44, 47
Christ. *See* Jesus Christ
Christ, Carol, 308
Christian Right, 245
Christian Science, 338
Christianity, 298, 373. *See also* Catholic
  Church; Protestantism
  fused with Greek philosophy, 213
  influence on African spiritual traditions,
    28
  for LGBT people, 338–344
  and Native American culture/religion,
    36, 47, 56
  opposed by Paganism, 302, 305
  Protestant Reformation, 233
*Christianity, Social Tolerance, and*
  *Homosexuality* (Boswell), 218
Chumash (Native American), 40, 43–44, 47
Church of Jesus Christ of Latter-Day
  Saints, 338
Church of the Brethren, 248
Church-state issue, 362, 383
Circumcision, 285
  African spiritual traditions, 11, 12, 13
Civic morality, 370, 371, 382
  state intervention in, 374
Civil contract of marriage (Protestant), 240
Civil law accountable to higher law, 364
Civil rights, 333, 365, 368, 376
Civil unions, 234, 376
Clairvoyance, 25
Clan matriarchs (Native American), 44
*The Classic of Su Nü,* 78, 83, 93
Cleanliness (Islam), 267, 268
Clitoridectomy, 284. *See also* Female genital
  mutilation (FGM)
  human rights efforts against, 12–13
  mythological background of, 12
Coitus interruptus, 214, 268

Columbus, Christopher, 37
Comfort, Alex, 245
A Common Bond, 339
Communal movement (U.S. Protestant), 242
Compassion (Buddhist), 343
Competition among men, 313
Complementarity of men and women
  (Catholic), 225–226
Complex Marriage (Oneida Perfectionists),
  244
Conception, 224, 245, 381
Concubines, 197, 198
Confucians
  opposed to Daoist sexuality, 86, 87, 89
  social-political gender differentiation, 79
  views of women, 81
Congregation Beth Simchat Torah,
  342–343
Connor, Randy, 161, 164, 165, 348
Conscience, 370. *See also* Religious
  conscience
  free exercise of, 377, 380
Conscientious dissent, 378
Conservative Christianity, 372, 373
Conservative Protestants, 245, 246–247
  compared to Mainline Protestants, 233,
    245
  emphasizing pleasure within marriage,
    246
  as pro-family, 250
Constitution of United States, 370
  and church-state issues, 362
Constitutional constructionism, 363
Continence, Male (Oneida Perfectionists),
  244
Contraception
  Catholic Church's position, 214, 217,
    218
  Islamic issues, 268–269
  Protestant position, 245
  rejected by Puritan women, 238
Convents (Buddhist), 148
Cosmology (Daoism)
  and understanding of sexuality, 76, 77,
    78, 91, 95
  yin-yang, 74
Costelli, Jim, 206
Council on Biblical Manhood and
  Womanhood, 251
Council on Religion and the Homosexual,
  332

Counterculture
    occult, 298
    of Paganism, 303
    witchcraft, 306
Courtesans supporting Buddha, 149
Courts (United States). *See also* Supreme
        Court (United States)
    not empowered to decide moral
        behavior, 370
    protecting individuals' rights to moral
        choices, 378
    recognizing antidiscrimination claims, 377
    religious conscience issues, 369
    and rights of homosexuals, 376, 378
Courtship role in Africa, 15
Craving (Buddhist)
    binding to suffering, 137
    eliminating, 161
    leading to rebirth, 136
    as nirvana, 153
Creation stories
    Adam and Eve, 236
    Islamic, 261
    Sufi Islam, 273
    with two-spirit people (Native
        American), 58
    to understand purpose of sexuality
        (Protestant), 235
Cremation (Hindu), 109
Crew, Louie, 337
Crimes
    in name of family honor (Islam), 285
    and prostitution (Israel), 193
Crocodile as deity, 14
Cross-dressing, 188
Crow (Native American), 54
Cuba, 29
Culture war, 372
Culture-brokers, 149
*Cybill,* 319

Dagara (West Africa), 16, 21
Dahomey (Benin), 14, 15
Dakota (Native American), 61
Dalai Lama, 167
D'Antonio, William V., 206, 217
Dao, 85
    manifested as *qi,* 74
    as origin of universe, 71
*Daode jing (The Way and Its Power),* 68, 70,
    71, 90

Daoism, 68, 69
    celibacy practices, 84, 85, 86
    gender equality, 79
    philosophical, 68, 69–70
    religious, 68, 70, 80
    sexuality issues, 67, 86–90, 91
    view of women compared to Confucians,
        81
    as way of life, harmony, 71, 76
    yin-yang polarity, 73
*Daojia* (philosophical Daoism), 69–70
*Daojiao* (religious Daoism), 69–70
Daughters of Bilitis, 329, 330
David and Jonathan, 188
Davies, Bob, 249
Davis, Andrew Jackson, 312
Death, 75, 144
Declaration of Independence (United
        States), 364
Deities
    bi-gendered (Hindu), 122
    bipolar, 117
    embodiment of, 310
    female, 80, 312
    homoerotic, 125
    immanent and nontranscendent, 298
    male and female principles, 311
    same-sex (African), 6
    unions with mortals, 26, 27, 28
    as universal, 298
Devadāsīs initiates of Tantra, 122–123
Devil, 305
Dharma, 109, 142, 155
Dianic Wicca, 298, 317, 344–346
Diasporic religions, 27
Dignity/USA, 221, 341
Diné (Navajo), 44
Disciples of Christ, 338
Discretion requirement, 350
Discrimination against homosexuals, 377
Dissatisfaction (Buddhist), 136, 137, 140
Divination, 22
Divorce, 382
    under Judaism, 186–187, 191, 193
    men and women entitled (Islam), 265,
        285
Dobson, James, 250
Doctors (Native American), 41
Dogon (West Africa), 8, 18
    and circumcision, 11
    menstruation beliefs, 10

pregnancy beliefs, 22
transgender or genderless spiritual
    leaders, 20
Dogon Door, 11
Dolls (Africa), 25
Domestic partnerships, 331
Domestic violence, 193
Domesticity, renouncing, 141, 145, 158
Donaldson, Stephen, 161, 164, 165
Dorsey, Issan Tommy, 168, 343
Double standard, 310
Dower returned (Islam), 265
Dreams, 26–27
Dress (Islam), 276, 277, 281
Drew, A. J., 313
Dualism
    of body-soul philosophy, 211
    of natural life (Islam), 261–262
    in religions, 308, 312
    worldview, 35
Dufour, Lynn Resnick, 336, 337, 352
*Dukkha* state of dissatisfaction (Buddhist),
    136, 140
*Dybbuk, Yentl the Yeshiva Boy,* 185

Earth as Goddess, 313
*Earth God Rising: The Return of the Male
    Mysteries* (Richardson), 313
Ecological activism, 346
Ecosystems, 42
Education, religious, denied to women
    (Buddhist), 146
Egalitarianism, 302, 319
Egypt, 284
El Guindi, Fadwa, 282
El Saadawi, Nawal, 285
Elderly people, 213
Embryo transplants, 198
Emergence International 338
Emptiness doctrine (Buddhist), 152, 154
Episcopal Church in United States, 249,
    337
Equal opportunity laws, 331
Equal Rights Amendment, 250
Erotic art, 82
Erotic literature, 274–275
Eroticism
    directed toward divine consciousness,
        120
    for Hindu women, 111
    literary (Islam), 274–275

mystico-erotic, 122
    poetry, 183, 275
Eskridge, William, 375
Establishment clause of First Amendment,
    365–366, 380, 381
Esù (Yoruba), 7, 10, 14
Ethics, 210–211
    environmental, 313
    sexual, 216, 219, 272
Ethiopia, 10
Eunuchs, 162
Evangelical Lutheran Church, 248
Evangelicals Concerned, 338
Eve, 239, 310, 311
Ex-gay movement, 334
Exit groups for LGBT people, 339
Exodus International, 249
External Alchemy (Daoism), 89
Extramarital sex, 382
    criminal offense (Protestant), 240
    sinful (Catholic), 213
    transgression (Puritan), 237
    violation of social contract (Islam), 263
Ezra, Moses Ibn, 183

Falk, Marcia, 343
Falwell, Jerry, 372–374
Family
    arena for religious activity and
        instruction, 234
    central unit of governance, 237
    criticism of, 140
    family-honor crimes, 285
    and Paganism, 314
    restructured, 243, 244
    traditional values, 372
    union of believing man and woman,
        245
Family purity (Judaism), 182, 184, 187
Fang (Africa), 20–21
*Fang shi* medicine practitioners (Daoism),
    68
Fanti (Ghana), 20
Farrar, Janet and Stewart, 302, 316
Father, 150, 234
Faure, Bernard, 135, 167
Feinberg, Leslie, 53
Female(s),
    ascetics (Hindu), 111
    associated with evil, 250
    bodhisattvas (Buddhism), 156

circumcision. *See* Clitoridectomy;
  Female genital mutilation (FGM)
  as closest to Dao, 72, 80
  deities' loss of spiritual authority, 8–9
  genitalia symbols, 10
  image of Mary (Catholic), 208
  indentured servants and slaves, 240–241
  interrelated to male (Daoism), 84
  orgasm for health, 238
  renunciants (Buddhist), 144–149
  vulnerable to Satan's attacks (Puritan),
    239
  and yin and yang *qi*, 73, 95
Female-female
  marriages (Judaism), 187
  premarital intimacy (Africa), 21
Female genital mutilation (FGM), 284. *See
  also* Clitoridectomy
Female-to-male transgender, 19, 127
Femininity
  cosmic conception (Daoism), 80
  in deities (Yoruban), 7, 8
  equated to water (Hindu), 105
  Islamic prescriptions for, 277
  sexually restrained, 242
  in two-spirit people (Native American),
    50, 53
  Western ideal, 315
  yin qualities, 74
Feminism
  and Buddhist sex-change narratives, 155
  Catholic, 226
  challenge to religiously defined gender
    roles, 250–251
  of Dianic Wicca, 345
  dimension of Daoism, 95
  influence on divorce, 191
  Jewish, 185, 190–194, 198
  of Paganism, 302, 313
  as reason to reject organized religion,
    353
  second wave, 330
  secular, 285–286
  sexual ethos of, 191
Feminist goddess movement, 298, 301, 320
Feminist movement, 299, 320, 371
Feminist spirituality, 333
Feminist theology, 250, 298, 307
Fertility
  rites, 14, 23, 299–300, 319
  symbols, 9

Fetus, 197
  formed and unformed distinction, 224
  personhood of, 378–380
  as potential life (Jewish), 195–196
FGM. *See* Female genital mutilation
  (FGM)
*Fiddler on the Roof,* 185
Films featuring witches, 305
*Fire,* 127
Fire (Hindu), 107, 108, 128
  characterized as masculine, 105–106
  of cremation, 109
  leading to spiritual liberation, 116
Fire/fluid metaphor for sexuality/spirituality
  (Hindu), 104, 110, 117, 125
First Amendment (U.S. Constitution), 362,
  378
  Establishment clause, 365–366
  Free Exercise clause, 380
  and institutionalized prejudice against
    homosexuality, 377
  preserving religious freedom, 380
  protecting freedom of conscience, 368
  and religious conscience issues, 369
First Nations people, 38. *See also* Native
  American
Focus on the Family, 250
Foreplay, 266
Fornication (Islam), 263, 266
Foucault, Michel, 160
Founders (of United States)
  and church-state issues, 361
  and higher law principle, 363–365, 366
  prohibiting religious establishments,
    362
Four Noble Truths of Buddha, 136
Fourteenth Amendment, 374
Fox, Thomas C., 220
Frank, Jacob, 183
Free Exercise clause of First Amendment,
  366, 380
  and abortion issue, 381
  of conscience, 377
Freud, Sigmund, 185
Friedan, Betty, 330
Friends for Lesbian and Gay Concerns, 338
Friendship, 164
Fundamentalism (Islam), 287
Funeral rites (Hindu), 109–110

Gabirol, Solomon Ibn, 183

Gallup, George, Jr., 206
Ganges River, 103, 130
  and death rites, 109
  and Hindu sexuality, 104
  as Śiva's power, 104
Gardner, Gerald, 300, 301, 302, 316
Gardnerian tradition (Wicca), 298
Gargi, 111
Gatherers of food and medicine (Native
  American), 42
Gay American Indians group, 52, 61
Gay, Lesbian, and Affirming Disciples
  Alliance, 338
Gay Liberation Front, 330
Gay liberation movement, 188, 198, 248,
  328, 339
Gay men
  American Indians, 61
  Catholic, 220, 221
  civil rights, 248
  Jewish, 188, 190
  ordination, 249, 333
  parenting, 372, 374
  pride celebrations, 330
  priest scandal, 221–222
  Protestant, 248
  Radical Faeries, 346
  sexual cultures (Hindu), 127
  *See also* Homosexuality
Gaze regulation (Islam), 281
Ge Hong, 86, 88
Gelede masquerade, 9, 17
Gender, 37, 51, 52
  ambiguity (African spiritual traditions),
    19
  change, 154, 187, 352
  crossing, 276
  discrimination, 376
  equality (Daoist), 79, 81, 82
  related to religion and spirituality, 6,
    124–125, 155, 250, 353
  of God, 155, 180, 206
  as insignificant for bisexuals, 189
  in interpersonal relationships (Native
    American), 34
  issues in Paganism, 311, 313, 345, 346
  and LGBT identity, 336, 341
  morality (Daoism), 80
  in mythology (Hindu), 125–127
  transcended, 18, 124
  and yin-yang balance, 74

Gender roles
  crossed, 37, 51, 54
  defined, 37, 250, 276
  expectations (Buddhist), 162
  in India prior to Buddhism, 145
  as means to power, 39, 40
  of Native American women, 39, 43, 44,
    50
  in New Testament, 236–237
  ordained by God, 251
  patriarchal, 311
  redefined (Paganism), 299, 314
Gender status, 37
  as choice, 51, 52, 57
  nontraditional, 50
Gimbutas, Marija, 304
Giriama (Kenya), 11
God, 236, 379
  balanced with Goddess, 298
  as both male and female (Shakers), 243
  as male, 250, 308
  Mary as feminine image (Catholic), 208
  without biological sex, 180, 206
*Goddess Power: An Interactive Book for
  Women . . . and Men* (Parker), 313
Goddesses
  African spiritual traditions, 13–14, 22
  Buddhist, 145, 156
  of Dianic Wicca, 345
  Hindu, 112–113
  Pagan, 298, 301, 307, 309, 313, 315, 319
Goldstein, Melvyn, 167
*Goodbye, Columbus* (Roth), 200
Great Goddess (Paganism), 300, 304, 311
Great Rite (Wiccan), 316, 317
Greek philosophers, 211
Greeley, Andrew, 208, 218, 227
Grief counseling, 344
Griffin, Susan, 309
Gross, Rita, 155, 156–157
Gynandry, 19

Ha Levi, Judah, 183
Hadith records (Islam), 258, 260, 268, 270,
  275
Haiti, 29
Halperin, David, 160
Hammond, Phillip, 383
*Handbook of Indians of California* (Kroeber),
  45
Hao Tzu, 68

Hare Krishnas, 297
Harems, 281, 282
Harijan, 113
Harlan, John, 382
Harmony (Daoism), 76, 82, 87
Harris, Joshua, 247
Harrison, Melvin, 60
Hartford Street Zen Center, 343
Hasidism, 184, 186
Hassan, Riffat, 280
Hawaii, 376
Hay, Harry, 328, 329, 333, 346
*He yin-yang (Uniting Yin and Yang),* 78
Healers, 41, 55, 301
Health, 85
    through sexual practices, 87, 92, 238
Hebrew Bible, 196, 211, 235
    complex views of sexuality, 180
    procreation commandment, 194
    Torah, 179, 181
Herdt, Gilbert, 52
Hermaphroditism, 18, 124, 277
Heterosexuality, 181, 183, 246, 316, 374
    of African deities, 6
    as dimension of divine, 183, 234
    normative, 124, 326
    order of society (Islam), 276
*The Hidden Face of Eve: Women in the Arab
    World* (El Saadawi), 285
Hierophay, 166
Higher law, 364, 365
    civil rights derived from, 368
    known through (religious) conscience,
    366, 368
    universal moral order, 364
Himba (Namibia), 13, 16
Hinduism, 103, 105, 108–109
    allowing sexual pleasure, 129
    castes' sexuality, 113–114, 123
    LGBT people, 338
    life-cycle rituals, 108–110
    mind-spirit development, 297
    mythology's alternative sexuality,
    125–127
    reincarnation of bi-gendered souls, 125
    Tantric texts, 156
    women's place/fulfillment, 110–113,
    145
*His Story: Masculinity in the Post-Patriarchal
    World* (Mann), 313
HIV. *See* Human immunodeficiency virus

*Hogon* transgender spiritual leader (Africa),
    20
Holocaust, 195
Homelessness of Buddhist renunciants, 140,
    141, 146, 147
Homicide, 224–225
Homoeroticism, 161, 188
    acceptable for monastics (Buddhism),
    165
    age-based clerical, 166
    classical Sanskritic sources, 123
    in Hinduism, 128
    in Judaism, 188
    literary (Islam), 274
    of Sufi poetry, 275
Homophile movement, 329, 332
Homophobia, 56, 58, 60
    fight against, 347
    in Hindu India, 127
    in religious spheres, 352
Homosexuality, 279
    acceptance/tolerance during Middle
    Ages, 218–219
    age-based clerical, 165–167
    Catholic laity views, 221
    as choice (Southern Baptist
    Conference), 249
    compatible with spirituality, 248
    and competition among men, 313
    cultural context of Buddhism, 160–161
    Daoist perceptions, 96
    distinct from pedophilia, 221–222
    as issue dividing Protestants, 249
    Jewish views, 187, 200
    Mattachine Society, 329
    not freely chosen, 218, 220, 248
    perceived as behavior, 325, 326
    perceived as immoral, 372
    transitory and definitive distinction, 219
Homosexuals
    marriage prohibited, 375
    right to same-sex civil unions, 249
    spiritual leaders (Africa), 19
Homosocial bonding in India, 164
Honesty, 338
Honor killings of women, 285
Hopkins, Jeffrey, 167
Hospice (Buddhist), 343
*Houris* sexual companions in paradise
    (Islam), 269
Households, godly, 235

*Huangdi Neijing Suwen (Yellow Emperor's Classic of Internal Medicine)*, 92
Human agency of lived religion, 336
Human immunodeficiency virus, 343, 372
Human rights, 13, 247
*Humanae Vitae* encyclical, 217–218
Hunter, James Davidson, 372
Hupa (Native American), 45
Hygiene (Islam), 267, 285
Hypersexuality, 198, 274

*I Kissed Dating Goodbye* (Harris), 247
Idemili (Igbo), 8
Ifá oracle (Yoruba), 21, 22
Igbo (Nigeria), 8
    fertility symbols, 9
    prohibitions of eroticism, 15
    and prostitution, 17
    spirit houses, 15
    transgender intimacy, 20
    wedding ceremonies, 16
Imam, Ayesha, 259
Immanent thealogy (Paganism), 307, 309, 310, 320
Immortality
    and Daoism, 68, 74, 84, 85
    goal of Daojiao, 70
    through sexuality, 90
Impotence
    in African spiritual traditions, 22
    caused by witchcraft, 239
    as grounds for divorce, 238
Impurity
    of bodily excretions (Islam), 268
    of women, 274, 267
In vitro fertilization, 198
Incest, 17, 197, 238, 247
Indians, 37, 38. *See also* Native Americans
Indigenous people, 38
    cultural beliefs, mixed with western religions, 33–34
    holistic inclusion of all genders, 34
    women doctors, 41
    *See also* Native Americans
Indio, 37, 38. *See also* Native Americans
Individualism, 299
    religious. *See* Religious individualism
Indus Valley, 105
Infant mortality, 143–144, 159
Infanticide, 269
Infertility, 22, 24–25, 194, 197–198

Infibulation, 284. *See also* Female genital mutilation (FGM)
Initiation rites, 11, 12
    gift of Vedic fire, 108–109, 110
    into religions or cults, 27
    Tantra, 117–118
Inner Alchemy Daoism, 89
Insemination, donor, 197
Integrity chapters (LGBT), 337, 338
Intentionality in sexual morality, 214
Intercourse
    as means of access to mind state, 167
    among novices and priests (Buddhist), 164, 165
Internal groups (LGBT), 337–339, 351
International Society for Krishna Consciousness, 297
Interracial sex, 241
Intersexed people, 50, 58
Interweave, 338
Islam, 257–259
    created under *tawheedic* vision, 261
    dress codes, 276, 277
    marriage's sacred quality, 263–264 (Islam)
    mysticism (Sufi), 273
    sexual prescriptions/issues, 261–262, 266
    Western perceptions of, 282
    worldwide expansion, 259
Islamic compared to Muslim, 259
Israel, 190, 193

Jainism, 148
Japan, 165, 166, 169
Jefferson, Thomas, 366, 367
Jehovah's Witnesses, 339
Jesus Christ
    as bridegroom to the church, 206, 225
    indifferent to issues of sexuality, 211
Jewish American Princess stereotype, 198–200
Jewish mother stereotype, 200
Joan of Arc, 52
John Paul II, 220
*The Joy of Sex* (Comfort), 245
Judaism, 179
    complex sexuality, 180, 201
    feminist, 190–194
    liberal, 186, 190, 193
    marriages with Christians, 187

Orthodox, 186
sexuality incorporated into belief system,
    183
in United States, 185
women as source of temptation, 182

Kabbalists, 183
*Kali's Child* (Kripal), 128
*Kāma Sūtra (Verse on Erotic Love)*
    (Vatsyayana), 111, 123
Kaśyapa and Bhadrā, 142–143
Keenan, Tanya, 344, 345
Khadija, 270
Kidwai, Saleem, 123, 124
Kings (Hindu), 120–121, 122
Kinship International, 338
Klah, Hastíín, 55
Klamath (Native American), 54
Kleinbaum, Sharon, 343
Koma (Africa), 10
Kosnik, Anthony, 212
Kou Qianzhi, 90
Kraemer, Heinrich, 239
Kripal, Jeffrey, 128
Kroeber, Alfred, 45, 49
Kutenai (Native American), 55

Laguna Puebloans, 24
LaHaye, Tim and Beverly, 246
Laity, 142
    divergence with Catholic Church,
        216–217, 218, 220, 225, 226–227
    and doctrine of emptiness (Buddhist),
        154
    support of monastics, 147, 148, 157
    Theravādin, 161, 163
Lakota (Native American), 55, 58, 59
Lalleśvarí, 111
Lambeth Conference, 249
Land (Native American), 41, 42
Lang, Sabine, 37, 52, 53
Laozi, 69, 70, 84, 90
*Larry King Live,* 372
Larson, Gerald, 120
Law, Bimala Churn, 158
*The Laws of Manu,* 146
Lay nuns of Sri Lanka (Buddhist), 160
Laywomen, 149–151, 226
*L'cha Dodi,* 183
Ldab Ldob monastic bodyguards,
    167–168

Leaders
    female religious (Daoism), 80
    same-sex and transgender, 19
    women (Native American), 43–44
Lee, Ann, 243
Leo IX, 222
Leo XIII, 214
Lesbian, gay, bisexual, and transgender
    people. *See* LGBT
Lesbian, gay, bisexual, transgender,
    intersexed, queer people. *See*
    LGBTIQ
Lesbians, 127, 278
    Catholic movement, 221
    civil rights, 248
    crossing over between groups, 330
    in Daoist texts, 96
    and Dianic Wicca, 344–346
    feminism, 330–331, 333
    Jewish, 188, 189, 190
    ordination, 249, 333
    permitted to marry priests, 188
    premarital relationships (Africa), 21
    Protestant, 248
    raising children, 198
    witches (Azande), 19
Levering, Miriam, 154
LGBT (lesbian, gay, bisexual, and
    transgender people)
    African American churches, 342
    alternative space groups, 344–347
    antireligious attitude, 354
    as atheists, 353
    blended religions, 348–349
    Christian organizations, 339–344
    diverse congregations, 343
    identities, 344, 350, 353
    internal groups within Christianity,
        338–339
    MCC Christians, 333, 340
    negative stereotypes, 326
    and official/organized religion, 327,
        332
    religiosity, 334, 337–349, 354
    religious converts, 351–352
    seeking spirituality, 352
    stereotypes, 326
    switching congregations, 351
    synagogues, 189, 190, 338, 342–343
    and traditional religious views of gender,
        336

LGBTIQ (lesbian, gay, bisexual,
   transgender, intersexed, queer
   people), 33, 37
   and homophobia, 60
   identities in Native Americans, 51, 55,
      59–61
   pressures to conform, 61
   rights, 50
Li Dongxuan, 91
Liberation. *See* Spiritual liberation
Libya, 14
Life passages aided by deities, 6
Life-cycle rituals (Hindu), 108–110
Lilith, 183–184, 310, 311
Little Thunder, Beverly, 59, 60–61
Lived religion, 335–336
Lizard symbol, 12, 18
Locke, John, 367
Longevity (Daoism), 88, 89, 92
Lorde, Audre, 347
Lot, Qur'anic story of, 278
Love
   exclusive and inclusive (Hindu), 120
   sacred quality of (Islam), 263
   Song of Songs as metaphor, 183
Lu Xiujing, 84, 89
Luhui, Chumash woman chief, 43–44
Lust, 235, 237
Luther, Martin, 237, 245
   equality of men and women, 235
   positive view of marriage, 236
Lutherans Concerned, 338

Madison, James, 363
Madonna image, 208
Mahāprajāatī, 147
Mainline Protestants, 245
   celebrating sexual pleasure, 246
   distinct from evangelical Protestants,
      233, 245
   homosexuality issue, 248, 326
Maitri Hospice, 343–344
Male
   aggression, 310
   attraction to boys (Sufism), 274
   authority over women, 146, 251
   biblically based differences with females,
      251
   circumcision (Sunna Islam), 285
   continence (Oneida Perfectionists), 244
   deities, 8

genitalia symbols (Africa), 10
   interrelated to female (Daoism), 84
   as manifestation of yang (Daoism), 73
   Pagans, 312, 313
   reciprocating female roles, 34
   sexual pleasure in paradise (Islam), 269
   sexualized images/stereotypes (Judaism),
      185, 199
   witches, 311
Male-male relations, 21, 278
Male-to-female transgender, 19, 376
Mali, 8
*Malleus Maleficarum (Hammer of Witchcraft)*
   (Sprenger and Kraemer), 239
Mami Wata cult (West Africa), 27
*Maṇḍala*-logic, 121
*Maṇḍalas*, 120, 122
   sexual symbolism, 121
Mandja, (Central African Republic), 15
Manifest Destiny, 36
Mann, Nicholas R., 313, 314
Man-woman role (Native American), 54
Marotta, Toby, 329, 330
Marriage, 142, 236, 263, 266, 375
   arranged, 15, 146, 186
   celibate, 142–143, 241
   civil union, 234
   companionate, 185
   contract, 15
   distraction from cultivating Dao, 85
   feminist influence on (Jewish), 191
   group (Oneida Perfectionists), 242
   with intention to divorce, 264
   legal precursor to procreation, 265
   patriarchal, 158
   polygamous, 86, 159
   as religious metaphors, 180, 206, 225,
      234
   rituals (African), 16
   sacrament, 234, 240
   same-sex, 248, 333, 374–378
   sexual ecstasy within, 246
   source of dissatisfaction/bondage, 140,
      143
   spiritual foundation (Quakers), 241
   temporary (Islam), 264
   unholy practice of, 244
Marxism, 332, 333
Mary, 208, 310
   and Nomkhubulwana, 14
Masai (Africa), 8, 13, 25

Masculinity
    characterized by fire (Hindu),
        105–106
    critiques of, 313
    deified, 7, 8, 250
    Islamic prescriptions for, 277
    Jewish, 198–199
    lacking, 162, 163
    linked to sexual aggression, 242
    Native American, 50
    redefining (Paganism), 308, 314
    yang qualities, 74
Masked rites, 9, 13
    of gender and sexuality, 19
Maspero, Henri, 95
Masturbation, 164, 182, 197
Matchmaker, 185
Matriarchy, 44, 304
Mattachine Society, 328, 330, 346
Matthews, Kathryn, 313
Mahāyāna Buddhism, 165, 169
    gender-neutral narratives, 152, 156
    ideal of bodhisattva, 153
MCC. *See* Metropolitan Community
    Churches
McCarthyism and homosexuality, 329
McCartney, Bill, 251
McCloud, Janet, 44
McGraw, Barbara, 362
McGuire, Meredith, 327
McKay, Mabel, 41
Medicine (Africa), 25
Medicine specialists (Native American),
    53
Meditation as Daoist sexual art, 92–93
Men. *See* Male
Mende (Sierra Leone), 9, 13, 15
Menopause, 194
Menstruation, 22
    blood as magical substance, 10
    as powerful force (Native American),
        45–48
    prohibitions (Islam), 267–268
    rabbinic laws governing, 182
    restrictions (Hindu), 123
Mental health, 187
Men-women (Native American), 52, 54
    as healers, 55
Mermaid image, 16
Mernissi, Fatima, 285
Mestiza, 38. *See also* Native Americans

Metropolitan Community Churches
    (MCC), 249, 333, 339–341
    inclusivity of, 341
    theological diversity, 340
Metropolitan Community Temple, 342
Mewok (Native American), 41
Midwives, 301
*Mikveh* ritual bath (Judaism), 192
Military, gays and lesbians in, 331
Minority AIDS Project, 342
Mirabai, 111
Miscarriages, 22, 23
Mishnah (Judaism), 196
Misogyny
    cultural (Islam), 280, 286
    in organized religion, 353
    witch image, 306
Missionization for two-spirit people, 56
Missouri Lutheran Synod, 248
Modesty of dress (Islam), 281
Modjadji V (Zulu), 9
Mojave (Native American), 52
Monastic law (Buddhist), 138
    against ordination of gender-atypical
        people, 163
Monasticism
    acceptance of homosexual activity, 166
    as alternative society, 144–145
    Buddhist, 84, 86, 138, 148, 158, 169
    Daoist, 96
    freedom from domesticity, 169
    heterosexual acts as grounds for
        expulsion, 164
    as release from samsara cycle, 145
    Zen Buddhist, 343
Monks (Buddhist),
    avoiding suffering of domestic life,
        143–144
    forbidden intentional sexuality, 164
    homelessness, 141
    homoerotic activity, 165
    Ldab Ldob (Tibetan), 167–168
    total celibacy, 138, 140
Monogamy
    for gay men and lesbians, 190
    Hindu, 123
    opposed by bisexuals, 189
    serial (Judaism), 187
    as unholy practice, 244
Monotheism, 180
Monroe, Irene, 347

Moon lodges, 49
Moral authority of Catholic Church, 220
Moral autonomy, 377, 381
Moral choices for individuals, 378
Moral judgments, 371
Moral laws and constitutional principles, 370
Moral Majority, 245
Moral order (universal), 364
Morality
    and adoption by same-sex couples issue, 374
    and antidiscrimination claims, 377
    of behavior, 370
    civic, 370, 371, 374, 382
    decided by individuals, not state, 368, 369
    personal, by exercising moral judgment, 370
    protected through marriage (Islam), 266
    as public or private matter (Protestant), 247
    and religious truth, 367
Morality of sexuality, 210, 211–216, 371
    corporate (Puritan), 238
    not act-centered but person-centered, 217, 227
    opposition to homosexuality, 248
    procreation emphasized (Catholic), 211, 214, 215–216
More Light congregations, 338
Morgan, Marabel, 246
Mormons, 350
Mossi (Burkina Faso), 17
Mother(s)
    Goddess, 315
    honor of, 22
    Pagans as, 315, 316
    sanctified by Brahmanical authorities, 145
Muhammad and sexuality, 270–273
Murder, 285
Muslim compared to Islamic, 259
Muslims, 257–259, 350
    identity, 288
    intolerance of gender diversity, 28
    LGBT, 338
    as minorities, 287
    practicing FGM (Africa), 284–285
*Muta'* temporary marriage (Shi'i Islamic), 264

Mysterious Female as Dao, 71, 91
Mythology
    bad girls, 310
    Hindu alternative sexuality, 125–127
    Mary (Catholic), 208
    of origin (Paganism), 299, 304
    *sati*, 112–113
    sexual pleasure in paradise for men, 269

*Nádleehí* (Navaho), 58
Nafzawi, Shaikh, 275
Native American Church (Peyote Church), 48
Native Americans, 38, 59, 298
    chiefs, 43–44
    effects of European economic expansion, 36
    focus on gender over sexuality, 51
    nonnormative gender identities, 56
    religious worldview, 35
    sexuality informed by religious beliefs, 241
    two-spirit people, 34, 50–59, 60, 61
    Westernization, 56
    women 34, 39, 43–44
Natural law (Catholic), 209, 210
    ethics, 210–211, 227
    sexual morality of, 214
Nature, 6, 39, 41–42
Nazism, 185
Ndebele (Africa), 16
Needham, Joseph, 96
New Testament, Bible, 211
    on male-female relationships, 235, 236–237
    on marriage, 243
*Nice Jewish Girls* (Beck), 189
Nichiren Shoshu, 297
*Niddah* seclusion (Judaism), 182, 192, 194
Nidorf, Patrick, 341
*Nikah* legal marriage contract (Islam), 263
Ninth Amendment, 367
    and higher law principle, 365
Nirvana (Buddhist), 137
    through celibate monastic life, 154
    and doctrine of emptiness, 153
Noble Eightfold Path to Nirvana (Buddhist), 137
*Nomdede* women's ritual (Zulu), 13–14
Nomkhubulwana goddess (Zulu), 13–14, 22
Noyes, John Humphrey, 244

Nudity, 266
Nummo hermaphroditic twins, 18
Nuns
    Buddhist, 144–149
    forbidden intentional sexuality, 164
    free from domesticity, 158
    gender-atypical women denied
        ordination, 163
    lacking support, 157
    lay, 160
    as refuge from patriarchal marriage, 158
    second-class status, 148
    supporting LGBT Dignity organization,
        341
    total celibacy, 138, 140
Nuwas, Abu, 275

Obàtálá deity (Yoruban), 7, 11, 18
Ògún deity (Yoruban), 7, 9, 12, 13, 22
*Omasenge* gender ambiguous spiritual leader
    (Africa), 19
*Onah* obligation to pleasure wife (Judaism),
    182
Oneida Perfectionists, 243–244
Ordination, 226
    of Catholic married men, 223
    of homosexuals, 249, 333
    *paṇḍakas* denied, 163
    women's (Catholic), 224, 226
Organized religion
    animosity toward LGBT, 332
    and feminism, 353
    negativity toward homosexuality, 334
    rejected by LGBT people, 344
    in U.S. colonial period, 362
Orgasm, 238, 266
*Orientalism* (Said), 281
Orisa Oko (Yoruba), 10, 15
Ortiz, Beverly, 43
Osh-Tisch, 53, 54
Òsun deity (Yoruba), 7, 17, 23
Oya deity (Yoruba), 7
Oyěwùmí, Oyèrónké, 7

Paganism, 298, 305, 320
    community of, 303
    heterosexuality of, 316
    linked to feminist movement, 302
    against male-dominated social order,
        312
    males, 311, 314

neopaganism, 298, 346
nonheterosexual participation, 317
sexuality, 299–301, 306
spirituality of material world and flesh,
    309
Paired cultivation of yin-yang (Daoism), 87,
    88, 89
Pāli monastic code of conduct (Buddhist),
    136, 147, 162
*Paṇḍakas* (Buddhist), 162, 163
Pantheism, 5, 298
Paradise (Islam), 269
Parents, same-sex, 372–374
Parker, Don H., 313
Parker, Julia, 41
Paternal lineage, 145, 146
Patriarchal, 320
    control over women's sexuality
        (Buddhist), 158
    creating male divinity, 250
    foundations of society, 301
    paradigms, 314
    religious imbalance, 298
    status quo, 306
Patterson, Victoria D., 48
Paul, Saint/Apostle, 211
    celibacy valued above marriage, 212
    Protestant teachings, 237
Paul VI, Pope, 216, 217
Pedophilia, 220–222, 223
*The Perfumed Garden* (Nafzawi), 275
Perry, Troy, 340
Personal morality, 370
Persuasion to influence public morality, 366,
    370
Petzoldt, William A., 54
Phallic deities, 10
Pius IX, 224
Pius XI, 215
Plants, 40
Plateau tribes (Native American), 48
Plato, 211
Pleasure, 246
    as blessing (Islam), 275
    dimension of marriage, 181, 194,
        245–246
    linked to original sin, 213
    and procreation (Protestant), 245–246
    sexuality for, 198, 317
    and Tantric culture, 123
    vehicle for liberation (Hindu), 129

Politics
    conservative Protestants, 250–251
    for gay/lesbian equality, 331, 346
    and sexual morality, 372
Polyandry, 17
Polygamy, 286
    in Buddhism, 159
    in Judaism, 186
    Muslim, 270, 271, 280
Polygyny, 17, 23
Polytheism, 313
Pomo (Native American), 41, 48
Pornography, 382
*Portnoy's Complaint* (Roth), 200
Power
    of courtesans (Buddhist), 149
    of eroticism, 347
    for Native Americans, 40
    of state to enforce religious beliefs, 363, 366
    of women's sexuality, 286, 317, 345
Prayer, 21, 22, 191, 250
Predators presenting themselves as teachers, 318–319
Pregnancy, 22, 268
Premarital sex, 288, 382
    abstinence from, 246–248
    acceptable (Judaism), 186
    female-female (Africa), 21
    Native American, 242
    punishable, 238, 240
Presbyterian Church, USA, 248
Priest pedophilia scandals, 220–222, 223
Priesthood
    of all believers (Protestant), 234
    married, 223, 224
    women excluded from (Catholic), 207–208
Priests
    androgynous, 6
    required to be male, 208, 225
    supporting LGBT Dignity organization, 341
    transgender or genderless, 20
Privacy practices (Islam), 282, 284
Procreation, 181, 211, 215–216
    distinct from sexuality, 169, 185, 197, 245
    as God's blessing, 211, 262
    most important function of marriage, 264–265
    as primary sexual function, 194, 214, 234

Prohibitions (Native American), 48
Promiscuity curbed by marriage (Islam), 266
Promise Keepers, 251
Proper action, 138
Prostitution
    African spiritual traditions disapproval, 17, 23
    legal in Israel, 193
    male (Hindu), 124
Protestant Reformation, 35, 237
Protestantism, 237
    abortion issue, 247–248
    communal movements, 243
    conservative. *See* Conservative Protestants
    defined against Catholics, 234
    diverse views on homosexuality, 248–249
    in early United States, 240
    feminization of, 242
    ideological shift, 242
    liberal. *See* Mainline Protestants
    mainline and evangelical distinctions, 233, 245. *See also* Mainline Protestants; Conservative Protestants
    as reform movement, 233
Puberty rituals (Native American), 241
Public morality, 366, 371
Purdah, 158
Puritans' beliefs about sexuality, 237–239
Purity as metaphysical order (Islam), 268
Puruṣa
    as bi-gendered Cosmic Person (Hindu), 106
    compared to sacrificer and wife, 115
    and feminine self Virāj, 107, 109
    Hindu boys' celibacy, 109

*Qi,* 79, 92
    defined as manifestation of Dao, 74
    genders of, 75
Quakers, 240, 338
    promoting male/female spiritual equality, 241
*Quanzhen* (Perfect Truth Daoism), 70
Queer activism, 331–332
Queer Jihad, 338
Queer Nation, 331
Ququnak patke (Native American), 55

Qur'an, 257
. discord in marriage, 265
marriage, 263
menstruation prohibitions (Islam), 267
modesty, 281
promises of pleasure in afterlife, 269
revelations of Prophet, 270
veiling and seclusion of women, 272

Rabbinical laws, 191, 193
Race as sexual misconduct issue, 241
Radical Faeries, 333, 346
Ramakrishna Mission, 297
Rape, 164, 317
and abortion issue (Protestant), 247
African spiritual traditions, 17
condemned as harmful 138, 161, 285
severe punishment for 238, 241
Rationalists, 361, 362
Rebirth, 124, 136
Reciprocity principle (Native American), 41–42
Red Earth, Michael, 61
*The Red Thread: Buddhist Approaches to Sexuality* (Faure), 135
Reformation. *See* Protestant Reformation
Reformed Church, 248
Reincarnation, 124–125, 129
Religion
as antiwoman (Islam), 286
beyond legislative power, 362
blended, 47, 348–349
complications of Daoism, 68
dissent protected, 362
freedom of, 366, 382
gender roles sanctioned, 250
LGBT responses to, 337–349, 353
merged with aesthetic experience, 120
nature-based, 298
official, 327
organized. *See* Organized religion
reinforcing status quo, 301
state-sponsorship prohibited, 362
unconstitutional establishment of, 366, 380
Religious conscience
to determine morality, 367
and gay parenting issue, 374
and personhood of fetus issue, 380
protected freedom of, 366, 367

Religious individualism, 328, 334, 349, 352
as growing trend, 354
ideal (Buddhist), 140
and LGBT people's place in social order, 335
Renouncers/renunciants (Buddhist), 141, 144–149, 180
lay nuns of Sri Lanka, 160
Rentzel, Lori, 249
Renunciation and internal fire (Hindu), 109–110
Reproduction, 211, 245, 264. *See also* Procreation
*Revival of the Religious Sciences* (al-Ghazali), 264
Richards, David A. J., 377
Ritual sexuality (Pagan), 299, 316, 317
*Roe v. Wade* (1973), 224, 247, 380–381
Roman Catholic Church. *See* Catholic Church
Roof, Wade Clark, 334, 335, 336
Roscoe, Will, 52, 53
Rosh Hodesh feminist celebration, 192
Ross, Richard, 246
Roth, Philip, 200
Rowell, Ron, 59, 60
*Rudrayāmala-Tantra,* 104
Rumi, Sufi poet, 275
Ruth and Boaz, 181
Ruth and Naomi, 188
Rwanda, 15

Sabbath, 183, 191
Sacrifice, 112–113
in African spiritual traditions, 23, 24, 25
in Hinduism, 106–107, 108, 109
to Vedic gods and goddesses (Buddhist), 145
Safe sex, 187
Safe space groups for LGBT people, 339–344, 351
Said, Edward, 281
*Śakti,* 104, 112, 121
Salvation, 117–118, 153, 243
Same-sex civil unions, 249
Same-sex marriage, 374–378
endorsed, 248
Jewish, 189
prohibitions on, 376
rights denied, 375
symbolic nature of arguments, 377

Same-sex sexuality, 52, 54, 123, 124, 127, 183, 276. *See also* Homosexuality
Samsara (Buddhist), 137, 143, 152
    dissatisfying cycle, 145, 147
    as nirvana, 153
Sande secret society (Sierra Leone), 9
Sàngó deity (Yoruba), 7, 27
Sanskritic Hinduism, 114
Santería, 29, 348, 349
Satan, 239
*Satī* widows' funeral pyre self-sacrifice, 112–113
Schalow, Paul Gordon, 165
Schipper, Kristofer, 69, 82
Schneider, David, 168, 343
Schoenherr, Richard A., 223
Scorpion symbol, 12, 18
Scripts of lived religion, 336
Se-buh-ta, Gordon, 46
Seclusion of women, 187, 241, 272
Secular humanism, 362
Segregation (Islam), 280, 283
Semen, 10
    retention, 88, 93, 314
Senufo (Côte d'Ivoire), 9
Seventh-Day Adventists, 338
Sexual abuse, 167
    of minors, 220, 223
    resulting from sexual license, 318
    systematic, 168
Sexual desire purged, 243, 284
Sexual expression, 298, 302
Sexual freedom, 317–318, 319
    and religion, 369–371
Sexual insatiability of women (Puritan), 239
Sexual license, 302, 306, 318
Sexual manuals
    Arabic literary, 275
    Daoist, 81, 82, 83, 93
    of evangelical Protestants, 246
    secular, 245
Sexual misconduct
    and accusation of witchcraft (Puritan), 239
    by Catholic priests, 220–222
    prosecuted (Protestant), 240
    suffered for sake of marriage (Puritan), 238
Sexual morality. *See* Morality of sexuality
Sexual orientation, 325
    efforts to change, 352

    as inborn trait, 333
    in metaphysical terms (Hindu), 124
Sexual practices (Daoism), 90, 92
Sexual relationships (Judaism)
    expanded and acceptable, 186
    forbidden, 181, 186–190
Sexual revolution, 217, 245
Sexual union
    form of worship, 300
    heavenly reward (Islam), 270
    marital duty, 238
    ritualized (Buddhist), 157
Sexuality, 91, 122, 287, 325
    community concern (Puritan), 237–238
    Daoist, 76, 77, 78, 79, 80, 87–90
    as focus rather than gender, 56
    forbidden, 164, 181
    for health, 92, 238
    independent of reproduction, 169, 185, 197, 245
    for longevity, 90
    as natural (Martin Luther), 235
    negative dimensions (Hindu), 111
    of Paganism, 298, 299–301, 312, 314
    as positive (Protestant), 251
    power, 121, 317, 347
    procreative function, 194, 213
    restructuring (Oneida Perfectionists), 244
    sacred quality/act of worship, 88, 103, 104, 115, 117–118, 129, 169, 190, 266–267, 316
    satisfaction needed for husband/wife spiritual bond, 246
    as source of sin (Catholic), 212
*Sexuality in Islam* (Bouhdiba), 276
Sexually transmitted diseases, 194
Shakers, 243
*Shari'a,* 260, 276, 277
Shaw, Miranda, 157
Shekinah feminist celebration, 192
Shepherd, Cybill, 319
*Shi wen (Ten Questions),* 77
Shi'i Islam, 258–259, 264
Shingon Buddhism, 166
Siddhartha, Gotama, 139–140
Sifting as religious identity negotiation, 336, 352
Sins
    homosexual activity, 219
    monogamous marriage (Oneida Perfectionists), 244

against nature, 234
original, 213
sexuality as source, 212
violating procreative intent, 214
Sirimā, 149–150
Śiva, 104
alternative sexuality with Agni, 125
erotic ascetic (Hindu), 117
as fire, 105
union with Śakti, 121
Social acceptability, 335
Social order maintained through religion, 362, 363
Socioreligious worldviews, 36
Sodom in Genesis, 187, 278
Sodomy, 238, 278, 331
Song of Songs in Bible/Hebrew Bible, 181, 183, 191
Sorcery, 304
South Africa, 9
Southern Baptist Church, 338
Southern Baptist Conference, 249
Sowo (Mende), 13, 15
Spirit houses (West African), 9, 15
Spiritual liberation (Hindu), 110, 116
sexual practices for, 114
through Tantra sexuality, 117–118
for women, 111, 112–113
*Spiritual Marketplace* (Roof), 334, 335
Spiritual quest for two-spirit status (Native American), 57
Spirituality
connected to sexuality, 190–194, 262, 306, 317
male-female differences, 251, 313
and LGBT people, 353
of seeking, 335, 352
women equal to men, 234, 236, 241, 251
women viewed as lacking, 146, 274
Sponberg, Alan, 147
Sprenger, Jacobus, 239
Sri Lanka monastics, 159–160, 165
State, 368
accountable to higher law, 364
boundary with religion, 380, 383
enforcing all public morality (Puritan), 238
Status quo, 301, 306
Stereotypes, 198–200, 326
Stevens, John Paul, 381
Stick game (Native American), 46

Stirpiculture, 244
Stoics, 211
Stone, Merlin, 304
Stonewall Riots, 329–330
*Street Zen* (Schneider), 343
Study as men's antidote to desire, 183, 198
Su Nü (Plain Girl), 78, 83
Sudan, 10
Suffering, 136, 143, 159
Daoist relief of, 68
and doctrine of emptiness (Buddhist), 153
Sufi Islam. *See* Sufism
Sufism, 258–259, 273
aversion to women, 274
mysticism, 273, 275
Suku (Democratic Republic of Congo), 10
Sumedhā laywoman (Buddhism), 151
*Summa theologiae* and natural law, 210
Sun Simao, 93
Sundance (Native American), 48
Sunna Islam, 285
Sunni Islam, 258–259
related to Sufism, 273
Supreme Court (United States)
and abortion rights, 380, 381
church-state cases, 383
rejection of antimiscegenation laws, 375
Surma (Ethiopia), 13
Surrogate mothers, 198
Suzuki, Shunryu, 343
Sweet, Michael, 164
Switching denominations within a religion, 350
Synagogues, LGBT, 189, 190, 338, 342–343

Tabwa (Democratic Republic of Congo), 10
Talmud, 179, 196
birth control, 195
homoeroticism (Judaism), 188
sexual activity, 181, 186
unnecessary contact with women, 182
Taneka (Benin), 12
*Tanhā* craving (Buddhism), 136
Tantra, 114, 117
Buddhist tradition, 157
left-hand path of, 118–119
sexuality/eroticism, 119, 120, 123
Tantric Buddhism, 156. *See also* Tantra
Tasks, feminine/masculine, 39, 53, 54
Tattoos, 13

Teachers
female, 111, 157
teacher-student abuse, 318–319
Teena, Brandon, 52
Temples (Japanese Buddhist), 166
Temptation (Judaism), 183–184, 191
Ten Commandments, 209
Theology
feminist, 250, 298, 307
inclusive at MCC, 340, 341
Theravādin monastic code of conduct, 164
Third nature (Hindu), 123
Thomas Aquinas, Saint, 210, 214, 224
*Thousand and One Arabian Nights,* 275
Tibet, 168
Tiger, Lisa, 59, 60
Tinney, James S., 342
Tobacco as offering (Native American), 42
Tocqueville, Alexis de, 371
Torah. *See* Hebrew Bible, Torah
Tosh, Nancy Ramsey, 344, 345
*The Total Woman* (Morgan), 246
Traditional belief systems, 33–34
Transgender people, 326, 346
in blended religions, 349
condemned (Islam), 277
elements in Hindu mythology,
125–127
priests and priestesses, 6, 20
rights, 190
*See also* LGBT (lesbian, gay, bisexual,
and transgender people)
*Transgender Warriors* (Feinberg), 52
Transgressions, 237, 288
committed for sake of awakening, 154
public (Islam), 278
Transsexual people, 326, 376. *See also*
LGBT (lesbian, gay, bisexual, and
transgender people)
Transvestite beauty pageant, 13, 26
*Tricycle,* 168
*Trikona,* 127
True Love Waits, 246, 247
Twins myths, 18, 58
Two-spirit people (Native American), 50,
55
in creation myths, 58
described, 34, 51
genders as chosen, 51
historical roles, 58–59
and homophobia, 60

ontology, 52
status found through spiritual quest, 57
*Two-Spirit People: American Indian Lesbian
Women and Gay Men* (Champagne),
57

Union of American Hebrew Congregations,
342
Unitarian Universalists, 248, 249, 338
United Methodist Church, 249
United States
African spiritual traditions, 29
contemporary Judaism issues, 185
domestic violence, 193
Jewish assimilation, 200
masculine image, 199
with patriarchal religions, 306
Protestantism, 237–244
United States government. *See* State
Unitive purpose of sexuality, 215
Unity Fellowship Church Movement, 248,
249, 341–342
Universal Fellowship of Metropolitan
Community Churches, 248
Unnatural sexual behavior, 214, 234
Upaniṣads (Hindu), 116–117, 124
Utopian movement, 243

Vagina, 10
Vajrayāna Buddhism, 169
sexuality as means to awakening, 167
women, 156, 157
Valiente, Doreen, 316
Van Gulik, Robert Hans, 94, 95
Vanita, Ruth, 123, 124, 125
Vatsyāyana, 111
Vedas (Hindu), 106, 108
ritual practices, 114
sacrificer and wife model, 115, 116
Vedic hymns, 145
*Veil: Modesty, Privacy, Resistance* (El
Guindi), 282
Veiling (Islam), 280, 286
and sacred privacy, 282
Vermont, 376
Vespucci, Amerigo, 38
Vices against nature, 219
Vidal-Ortiz, Salvador, 349
Vimalakīrti (Buddhist), 154
*Vinaya* monastic rule (Buddhist), 138
Virgin Mary. *See* Mary

Virginity, 188
  as Catholic value, 212, 213
  until marriage, 246–247
Vodou, 27, 29, 348

Wadud, Amina, 265
Wang Chong, 75
Warren-Clarke, Ly, 313
Warriors
  images (Pagan), 313
  women (Native American), 54
Water, 108
  equated to feminine (Hindu), 105
*The Way of Merlyn: The Male Path in Wicca*
  (Warren-Clarke and Matthews),
  313
*Webster v. Reproductive Health Services*
  (1989), 381
Wedding ceremonies, 16
Wei Huacun (Daoism), 80
Welcoming and Affirming congregations,
  338
Welter, Barbara, 242
Wenz, Peter S., 379
Western cultures, 39, 40
White, David, 105
Wicca, 316
  defined, 298, 302
*Wicca for Men: A Handbook for Male Pagans
  Seeking a Spiritual Path* (Drew), 313
*Wicca Spellcraft for Men: A Spellbook for Male
  Pagans* (Drew), 313
Widows, 112–113, 271
Wigglesworth, Michael, 238
Wile, Douglas, 92, 96
Williams, Walter, 56
*Winkte* women-men healers (Native
  American), 55, 58, 61
Wintun (Native American), 46
Wisdom, John, 379
Witch Starhawk, 302, 308, 320
Witch trials, 300
Witchcraft, 304, 315
  and barrenness, 24–25
  defined, 298, 305
  evil in African spiritual traditions, 24
  history, 303
  linked to adultery, 23
  means of control, 8
  practiced by men, 25–26
  religious context for sexuality, 306

single-gender religious threat (Puritan),
  239
  traditional and modern, 300, 301
*Witchcraft Today,* 300
Witches
  African spiritual traditions, 24
  antithetical to conventional U.S. values,
  305
  description, 297
  as healers and midwives, 301
  male, 311, 313
  TV and films featuring, 304, 305
Witch-hunts of Middle Ages, 300, 304
*With Liberty for All* (Hammond), 383
Wodaabe transvestite beauty pageant, 13,
  26
Women
  abuse of, 24, 285
  committing *sati* (Hindu), 112–113
  and Dianic Wicca, 344–345
  disenfranchised as religious actors, 28,
  145, 182
  and Goddess imagery, 308, 316
  Hindu, 110–113
  invisibility of, 327
  in LGBT congregations, 353
  Jewish stereotypes, 200
  misogyny toward, 49, 274
  naturalists, 40, 41, 42
  ordination issue (Catholic), 224, 226
  powerful and respected (Native
  American), 34, 35, 39, 41, 44, 56
  protected from premarital sex
  expectations, 186
  religious leaders in home, 242
  sexuality issues, 80, 111, 182, 242, 310,
  312
  spirituality, 112–113, 235, 236–237, 306
  in submission to men, 146, 237
  temptresses, 183–184, 191
  Vajrayāna Buddhists, 156, 157
  veiling and seclusion (Islam), 272, 280,
  282, 286
*Women and Gender in Islam* (Ahmed), 280
*Women under the Bo Tree* (Bartholomeusz),
  159
Women-men (Native American), 52
  celibacy, 53
  as healers, 55
Women's Aglow Fellowship, 251
Women's movement, 371

Women's rights, 299, 312
  and Buddhism, 144, 145
  and lavender menace, 330
Worldviews
  connected to sexuality (Native
    American), 35, 57, 61
  defined, 36
  European, 39
Woyo (Democratic Republic of Congo), 16
Wuthnow, Robert, 334, 336, 352

Yaka (Democratic Republic of Congo), 8,
  10, 13, 18
Yang (Daoism), associated with male
  qualities, 73, 75
Yellow Emperor, 69, 78, 83, 85
Yemen, 284
Yin (Daoism), associated with female
  features, 73, 75
Yin-yang (Daoism)
  complementary/interdependent, 73, 78,
    93
  as means to harmony, 86, 91
  paired cultivation, 87–90
  polarity, 72–73
  for superior offspring, 86
  union through sexuality, 77–78, 81, 86, 88

*Yoginīs,* as teachers of sexual yoga, 157
Yoruba (Nigeria), 10, 21, 26
  adultery, 17
  clitoridectomy and circumcision, 12
  deities' genders, 7
  oracles and divination rites, 9, 23
  pantheism, 5
  and prostitution, 17
  ritual eroticism, 14, 15
  same-sex intimacy, 21
  tattoos as erotic attraction, 13
  weddings, 16
  witches, 24
Young, Katherine, 145
Young, Lawrence A., 223
Yurok (Native American), 41

Zambia, 10
Zamis, 347
Zhang Daoling, 84, 91
Zhang Lu, 84, 91
Zhuangzi (Daoism), 69, 70, 84, 90
*Zina* fornication (Islam), 263, 281, 285
Zionism, 185, 199
Zulu (South Africa), 9, 13–14, 22
Zvi, Sabbati, 183
Zwilling, Leonard, 161, 162

CPSIA information can be obtained
at www.ICGtesting.com
Printed in the USA
BVHW061418140722
641978BV00001B/2

9 781576 073599